D1085167

IDEAS IN CONTEXT

THE ENLIGHTENMENT'S FABLE
Bernard Mandeville and the Discovery of Society

IDEAS IN CONTEXT

Edited by QUENTIN SKINNER *General Editor*
Series editors
LORRAINE DASTON, WOLF LEPENIES, RICHARD RORTY AND
J.B. SCHNEEWIND

The books in this series will discuss the emergence of intellectual traditions
and of related new disciplines. The procedures, aims and vocabularies that
were generated will be set in the context of the alternatives available within
the contemporary frameworks of ideas and institutions. Through detailed
studies of the evolution of such traditions, and their modification by different
audiences, it is hoped that a new picture will form of the development of ideas
in their concrete contexts. By this means, artificial distinctions between the
history of philosophy, of the various sciences, of society and politics, and of
literature may be seen to dissolve.

The series is published with the support of the Exxon Foundation

A list of books in the series will be found at the end of the volume.

THE ENLIGHTENMENT'S FABLE

Bernard Mandeville and the
Discovery of Society

E.G. HUNDERT

Associate Professor of History
The University of British Columbia

CAMBRIDGE
UNIVERSITY PRESS

Published by the Press Syndicate of the University of Cambridge
The Pitt Building, Trumpington Street, Cambridge CB2 1RP
40 West 20th Street, New York, NY 10011-4211, USA
10 Stamford Road, Oakleigh, Victoria 3166, Australia

© Cambridge University Press 1994

First published 1994

Printed in Great Britain at the University Press, Cambridge

A catalogue record for this book is available from the British Library

Library of Congress cataloguing in publication data

Hundert, E.J.
The enlightenment's 'fable': Bernard Mandeville and the discovery
of society/E.J. Hundert.
p. cm. – (Ideas in context)
Includes bibliographical references.
ISBN 0 521 46082 4
1. Mandeville, Bernard, 1670–1733–Contributions in sociology.
2. Mandeville, Bernard, 1670–1733–Contributions in economics.
3. Mandeville, Bernard, 1670–1733. Fable of the bees. 4. Self-interest.
5. Economic man. 6. Enlightenment. 1. Title.
II. Series.
HM22.G8M334 1994 93-36440
301'.092–dc20 CIP

ISBN 0 521 46082 4 hardback

for Martha

Whenever anyone speaks, without bitterness . . . of man as a belly with two needs and a head with one; when ever anyone sees, seeks and *wants* to see only hunger, sexual desire, and vanity, as though these were the actual and sole motives of human actions; in brief, whenever anyone speaks "badly" of man – but does not speak ill of him – the lover of knowledge should listen carefully and with diligence.

Nietzsche, Beyond Good and Evil

Though words be the signs we have of another's opinions and intentions; yet, because of the equivocation of them is so frequent according to the diversity of contexture, and the company wherewith they go (which the presence of him that speaketh, our sight of his actions and conjecture of his intentions, must help to discharge us of): It must be extremely hard to find out the opinions and meanings of those men that are gone from us long ago, and have left us no other signification thereof but their books; which cannot possibly be understood without history enough to discover those aforementioned circumstances, and also without great prudence to observe them.

Hobbes, Human Nature

Contents

Acknowledgements

This book would still be unfinished were it not for the generous support of my research by the Social Sciences and Humanities Research Council of Canada. Particularly important was a Release Time Stipend granted by the Council which permitted me the luxury of devoting an entire academic year to this project. I worked for a period at the Library of Cambridge University where John Dunn, ever a gracious and astute friend, arranged my stay at King's College and was a forbearing host during a most difficult time. While at Cambridge, conversations with Istvan Hont helped me to clarify a number of my ideas.

Hayden White and Perez Zagorin have offered consistent encouragement to me over many years and, most importantly, have long served as exemplars of intellectually invigorating scholarship. Dario Castiglione, M.M. Goldsmith, Charles Griswald, Jr., Irwin Primer, John P. Wright and Donald Winch kindly sent off-prints or typescripts of their work. Robert Anchor and David Wooton made useful suggestions about the book's organization. Christa Canitz and Wayne Thorpe took time from their own work to offer assistance with a text in German and Dutch, repectively. The staff of the Interlibrary Loan Department of the Library at the University of British Columbia cheerfully and efficiently dealt with my many requests. Mark Glouberman, Harvey Mitchell, Roger Seamon and Kay Stockholder discussed all phases of the project with me, listened thoughtfully to my concerns, and read drafts of the entire manuscript. I am most grateful for the critical intelligence each brought to bear upon my writing. Most of all, I am indebted to my wife, Carol Gibson, for her encouragement, support, toleration of a near obsession and, above all, for the companionship without which this book would seem no more than a trifle.

The last section of Chapter 2 has appeared in abbreviated form as

"The Thread of Language and the Web of Dominion: Mandeville to Rousseau and Back," *Eighteenth-Century Studies* 21, 2 (1987/8), pp. 169–191, as has the fourth section of Chapter 3, as "Performing the Enlightenment Self: Henry Fielding and the History of Identity," in Bonnelyn Kunze and Dwight Braughtigan (eds.), *Court, Country and Culture: Festschrift for Perez Zagorin* (University of Rochester Press, 1992), pp. 223–244.

A note on the text

All references placed parenthetically in the text refer to the volume and page number as they appear in the great edition of F.B. Kaye, *The Fable of the Bees: Or, Private Vices, Publick Benefits. By Bernard Mandeville. With a Commentary Critical, Historical, and Explanatory by F.B. Kaye*, 2 volumes (Oxford: Clarendon Press, 1924). Whenever possible, I have used modern standard editions or reprints of eighteenth-century works, including Mandeville's other writings. When these were unavailable to me or nonexistent, I used the most generally accessible editions. In either case, I refer the reader to the part, section, chapter and, where useful, to paragraph or page number.

I have adopted the eighteenth-century custom of referring to persons as "he," and of treating "he," "his," etc. as standing for "he or she," "his or hers," when appropriate. This is more than a simple convenience, since part of the burden of my argument, especially in Chapter 4, "*Homo economica* and her double," is to examine the importance of the gendered character of eighteenth-century economic and moral discourse. Unless otherwise noted, translations are my own.

Introduction and agenda

In the spring of 1723, a London physician nearing his fifty-third birthday anonymously published an enlarged version of a barely noticed satire which he had written nine years earlier. The work aroused little immediate reaction. Then, during the following July, *The Fable of the Bees: Or, Private Vices, Publick Benefits* was twice presented by the Grand Jury of Middlesex to the Court of the King's Bench as a public nuisance, with a recommendation that its publisher be prosecuted. While the book was never censored, its author, Bernard Mandeville, "Snatched from Oblivion's Grave by Infamy,"[1] at once became associated with wickedness. *The Fable of the Bees* was immediately reviled by a chorus of clergymen, journalists and philosophers.[2] Astonished and delighted, Mandeville found himself a national celebrity.

Writing in his third or, more probably, his fourth language (after Dutch, French and academic Latin), Mandeville devoted much of the remaining ten years of his life to the elaboration, refinement and defense of his now notorious thesis: contemporary society is an aggregation of self-interested individuals necessarily bound to one another neither by their shared civic commitments nor their moral rectitude, but, paradoxically, by the tenuous bonds of envy, competition and exploitation. In the midst of a decade of virtually unrelieved criticism and polemic, and while continuing to support his family by treating the nervous diseases of his patients, he published *A Modest Defence of Publick Stews* (1724), a provocative plan for the establishment of public houses of prostitution; *An Enquiry into the*

---

[1] John Brown, *Honour, a Poem* (London, 1743).
[2] For summaries of this literature see F.B. Kaye, "Criticisms of the Fable," in *Fable*, II, pp. 401–417, and Paul Sackmann, *Bernard de Mandeville und die Bienenfabel-Controverse* (Leipzig: Mohr, 1897).

Causes of the Frequent Executions at Tyburn (1725), an attack upon the ceremonies of public execution with recommendations for greater severity in the treatment of criminals; a second volume of *The Fable* in 1728; and then in 1732, *An Enquiry into the Origins of Honour, and the Usefulness of Christianity in War*, which amounted to a third. Later in the same year, Mandeville produced his last work, *A Letter to Dion.* This was a polemical reply to *Alciphron: Or, The Minute Philosopher* (1732), in which Bishop Berkeley attacked various freethinkers and cast Mandeville as Lysicles, a lawless libertine and atheist. Mandeville exposed in detail Berkeley's wholesale misrepresentation of *The Fable.* He also forcefully reasserted his thesis that a strict interpretation of Christian conduct, which requires self-denial and the sacrifice of impulse, fatally compromises Christians like Berkeley, who hypocritically pretend to charity and benevolence while reaping the benefits of modern forms of affluence and exchange.

Mandeville did his most creative work and produced a masterpiece during what until recently was considered the onset of old age – an accomplishment surpassed in the eighteenth century only by Kant, one of *The Fable*'s great admirers. For his immediate audience, however, and then for the two succeeding generations of European intellectuals, "Mandeville" was less the person who wrote an infamous book, than an ideologically charged symbol constituted by the eighteenth century's intense and prolonged dispute about how to understand and evaluate the liberation of acquisitive instincts engendered in modern polities by the infusion of commercial relations into the centers of public life.

Bernard de Mandeville was born in or near Rotterdam in 1670, the son of Judith (Verhaar) and Michael de Mandeville, a doctor, as was Michael's own grandfather, also named Michael, who had served as municipal physician and rector of the Latin school in Nijmegen. No portrait of Mandeville is known to exist, and little can be gleaned about the details of his life from the few surviving relevant documents in the British Library and Somerset House. Save for an off-hand remark by Benjamin Franklin to the effect that Mandeville was "a most facetious, entertaining companion,"[3] we know almost nothing of his character. Indeed, more is known about *The Fable*'s minor critics than of its author, despite his rise to prominence, and immeasurably

---

[3] Benjamin Franklin, *Autobiography*, in *Works*, ed. J. Bigelow (New York: Putnam, 1904), I, p. 92.

less of Mandeville than about virtually all of his philosophically significant adversaries, particularly Hume, Rousseau and Adam Smith, so much of whose seminal work was shaped in confrontations with *The Fable of the Bees*.[4] While his family name suggests French ancestry, the de Mandevilles were not recent immigrants to Holland but had lived in Leeuwarden in Friesland from at least the late sixteenth century, later establishing themselves in Nijmegen. After attending the Erasmian school in Rotterdam, to which Michael had moved when young, Bernard followed his father and great-grandfather in the study of medicine, matriculating at the University of Leiden in 1685 after submitting a medical subject for his obligatory inaugural address, *De oratorio scholastica*.

During his years of study at this major European medical faculty riven by disputes between Cartesians and their critics, Mandeville published a required dissertation entitled *Disputatio philosophica de brutorum operationibus* (1689), in which he argued the Cartesian case for animal automatism. Before receiving his medical degree in 1691 after a largely ceremonial public examination of his thesis on digestive disorders,[5] Mandeville may well have made his literary debut during the so-called 1690 Costerman tax riots in Rotterdam – in which both he and his father participated – by anonymously publishing a satirical lampoon about the town Bailiff, Jacob Van Zuilen van Nievelt, a "sanctimonious atheist" whose harsh prosecution of the tax farmer Costerman on a charge of smuggling precipitated the disturbances. The riots led to direct military intervention by the government of the States of Holland, public vindication of the Bailiff, and the subsequent removal by banishment of Michael de Mandeville from Rotterdam.[6] Perhaps in response to this sudden decline of his family's fortunes, Bernard, shortly after being granted the MD, travelled in France, Italy and then to England, "to learn the Language; in which

---

[4] F.B. Kaye first brought together most of the existing documentary materials relating to Mandeville's life into biographical order and produced the publication history of his work upon which everyone still must rely. See *Fable*, I, pp. xvii–xxxvii. In addition, see P.A. Christiaans, "De Mandeville," in *Jaarboek Centraal Bureau voor Genealogie* 33 (1979), pp. 118–125; Richard I. Cook, *Bernard Mandeville* (New York: Twayne Publishers, 1974), pp. 11–20, and Irwin Primer, "Bernard Mandeville," in *The Dictionary of Literary Biography* (Detroit: Gale Research Company, 1991), CI.

[5] *Disputatio medica inauguralis de chylosi vitiata . . . Publico examini subjicit Bernardus de Mandeville* (Leiden: Apud Abrahamum Elzevier, Academiae Typograph, 1691).

[6] Rudolf Dekker, "'Private Vices, Public Virtues' [*sic*] Revisited: The Dutch Background of Bernard Mandeville," *History of European Ideas* 14, 4 (1992), pp. 481–498.

[I] happen'd to take great delight,"[7] returning to Holland in 1694. A short time later Mandeville immigrated to England and settled in London, where he married Ruth Elizabeth Laurence in 1699, fathered at least two children, and remained until his death from influenza in 1733.

Until late in life, when fame assured him access to an audience, the fulfillment of Mandeville's literary ambitions depended upon the rapidly changing opportunities for writers provided by the dramatic enlargement of the English reading public in the early eighteenth century. Most importantly, a writer's success hinged upon the ability of the bookseller–publishers who organized the London Grub Street presses to offer to an easily bored metropolitan audience in search of self-endorsing diversions a continuing stream of inexpensively pro-duced pamphlets, broadsides and, crucially for Mandeville, satirical verse. Mandeville made his English debut with two anonymous works in 1703, *The Pamphleteers: A Satyr* and *Some Fables after the Easie and Familiar Method of Monsieur de la Fontaine*. As he was to do throughout his career, in the first work Mandeville defended the revolutionary settlement of 1689 against the attacks of Tory and Jacobite "pample-teers," while the second work was the earliest (rather loose, octosylla-bic verse) English translation of twenty-seven of La Fontaine's *Fables*, to which Mandeville added two of his own in the same style, "The Carp" and "The Nightingale and The Owl." Probably in response to reasonable sales of *Some Fables*, an expanded edition of these poems was printed under Mandeville's name as *Aesop Dress'd: Or a Collection of Fables Writ in Familiar Verse* in the next year. In 1704 Mandeville again drew upon his familiarity with French skeptical and libertine traditions, publishing *Typhon: Or the Wars Between the Gods and Giants: A Burlesque Poem in Imitation of the Comical Mons. Scarron*, a work whose dedication to the "Numerous Society of F[oo]ls" was intended as an invocation of Erasmus, one of the very few Dutch writers or artists whose work Mandeville ever praised. One year later, in 1705, Mandeville sought to advance his career as a fabulist in verse with the publication of *The Grumbling Hive: Or, Knaves Turn'd Honest*, a long 433-line poem written after the manner of Samuel Butler, whose anti-puritan satire *Hudibras* was one of his favorite works. Pitched in the popular "low" style which he had mastered, but attracting hardly any attention from the wider reading public, *The Grumbling Hive* would later serve as the foundation of *The Fable of the Bees*.

---

[7] *A Treatise of the Hypochondriak and Hysteric Passions*, cited by Kaye in *Fable*, I, p. xix.

While Mandeville produced one final volume of poetry, some of it erotic, in the 1712 collection *Wishes to a Godson, with Other Miscellany Poems*, the remainder of his literary output was in prose, most often in the then popular dialogue form in a conversational idiom which he employed for the purposes of philosophical and social commentary. The tone of Mandeville's mature writing is already evident in his first prose volume, *The Virgin Unmask'd: Or, Female Dialogues Betwixt an Elderly Maiden Lady, and her Niece, On several Diverting Discourses on Love, Marriage, Memoirs, and Morals, &c. of the Times* (1709). Here, in ten sexually charged dialogues on virginity, marriage and the designs of men, which include many digressions on history and politics, the luscious and inexperienced Antonia is instructed in the ways of the world by her maiden aunt Lucinda. As he would later do at the beginning of *The Fable*'s second volume of 1728, Mandeville again adopted a female persona in thirty-two numbers of *The Female Tatler* between 2 November 1709 and 29 March 1710. This journal employed the fiction of discussions of a "Society of Ladies," often joined by gentlemen, in order to ridicule the pretensions of Isaac Bickerstaff, the spokesman of Richard Steele in his popular *Tatler*, published between 1709 and 1711. Bickerstaff self-righteously proclaimed that the practice of moral virtue made society possible. In direct contrast, humility, temperance and frugality emerge in the discussions of Mandeville's personae as unpracticed, if much commended, virtues in opulent nations, virtues which flourish precisely because their wealthy members indulge the vices of self-aggrandizement, avarice and prodigality. As one character, the Oxford Gentleman, says, it is absurd because contradictory at once to desire a flourishing trade and the decrease of the vices of pride and luxury – a position Mandeville first enunciated in *The Grumbling Hive*.

By the beginning of the second decade of the eighteenth century, Mandeville had established a decidedly modest literary reputation. Few readers could have known the identity of "B.M.," the initials appearing on the title page of *The Virgin Unmask'd*, or the anonymous author of *The Female Tatler*. Nevertheless, he continued to claim the attention of publishers for the expression of his widening interests, particularly those in medicine and politics. In 1711 he published *A Treatise of the Hypochondriak and Hysterical Passions, Vulgarly call'd the Hypo in Men and Vapours in Women*, also in dialogue form, in which Mandeville's spokesman Philiporo expounds upon the iatromechanical theories of physiology then at the forefront of medical theory. Unlike his competitors – and presumably the officers of the College of

Physicians with whom Mandeville had continuing disputes – Philiporo treats few patients because his scientifically grounded methods demand close and careful observation of patients over long periods of time, in contrast to conventional physicians who engage in profitless speculations about symptoms whose meaning eludes them. Mandeville went on to publish an expanded edition of his medical treatise in 1730, adding to the speeches of its main participants, translating Latin passages for non-learned readers, and reflecting in some detail upon the scientific study of human behavior. The content of these reflections was an important feature of his wider arguments about the analysis of society.

Mandeville's political interests and commitments were not publicly apparent until 1714 (the year before he dropped the copula from his name) when he made his debut as a Whig propagandist. In that year he published *The Mischiefs that Ought Justly to be Apprehended from a Whig-Government*, a dialogue between Loveright, a Whig, and the Tory Tantivy, in which the conventional Whig defense of the revolutionary settlement of 1689, the Protestant succession, and the legitimacy of the Hanoverian line, are primary elements of an uninspired dialogue which concludes with thanks to Providence for sparing the British from popish chains of popery and Stuart tyranny. Many of these same themes reappear in Mandeville's final party political tract, again published under his initials in 1720. As its title implies, *Free Thoughts on Religion, the Church and National Happiness* discourses upon the advantages of Whig governance, explaining that the apparent abuses of politicians, so grumbled at by malcontents, are in fact trivial vices of private persons who in their public roles efficiently administer a benign constitution. In this work Mandeville also adopted an aggressively skeptical view of the religious establishment and of priestcraft generally, stopping short of an outright defense of Deism while arguing for a rationally defensible religion. The humility of bishops, he quipped, must be a very ponderous virtue, since it had to be drawn by a coach and six. Such views evoked the spectre of freethinking – as did the book's title – and despite the patronage of Lord Macclesfield, the Lord Chancellor from 1718 to 1724, Mandeville was never again employed by the Whigs in the cause of political propaganda, something for which his notorious reputation would have in any case permanently debarred him once *The Fable of the Bees* became known as a scandalous book.

Mandeville's masterpiece first appeared under its full title in 1714, when he transformed *The Grumbling Hive* into a small book by adding a preface, "An Enquiry into the Origin of Moral Virtue," as well as twenty prose "Remarks" ranging from single paragraphs to full essays which were meant to elaborate the meaning of his original verses. In these essays, Mandeville first achieved a register adequate for his larger philosophical purposes, but the book in which they were contained seems to have made only a small public impression. In the years immediately following, some other defenders of commercial opulence, like Defoe, employed the phrase, "private vices, public benefits." So did the staunch Whig Matthew Tindal, who defended the regime against critics who complained of growing moral laxity, stating, after Mandeville, that "[p]rivate vices, in this Case, are far from being publick Inconveniences ... vast Numbers of Trades People and Artificers wou'd soon starve, were we oblig'd to live ... in those Times most celebrated for their Frugality; when [there were] no Manufactures, no Trade ... and ... Riches chiefly consisted in ... Cattle ..."[8] Such allusions were quite rare, however, and since Mandeville's name was absent from the book's title-page, his small place in the public's imagination remained confined to readers of his early verse and later political tracts. Only when Mandeville published an enlarged edition of *The Fable of The Bees* in 1723, which included an amplified set of "Remarks" and two new lengthy essays – "A Search into the Nature of Society" and "An Essay on Charity and Charity-Schools" – did he achieve the fame he sought. After the Middlesex Grand Jury's presentment appeared in the press, Mandeville attacked his accusers in *The London Journal* of 27 July 1723, and shortly thereafter published the text of the presentment, together with his own defense, as "A Vindication of the Book, from the Aspersions contain'd in a Presentment of the Grand-Jury of Middlesex, and an abusive Letter to Lord C.," which he then appended to the 1724 editon of *The Fable*. A literary career was belatedly launched, as "Man-devil"[9] joined Hobbes as the eighteenth century's "detested Names, yet sentenced ne'er to die,"[10] while *The Fable of the Bees* quickly acquired an independent identity as an unsubdued mutiny in moral philosophy.

[8] Matthew Tindal, *A Defence of our Happy Establishment: And the Administration Vindicated* (London, 1722), p. 19.

[9] "And if GOD-MAN Vice to abolish came / Who VICE commends, MAN-DEVIL be his NAME," in the anonymous *The Character of the Times Delineated* (London, 1732).

[10] John Brown, *Honour, a Poem.*

The immediate ideological circumstances surrounding Mandeville's spectacular rise to fame have been established by an efflorescence of scholarly interest in the dominant civic humanist language of argument within which the emergence of modern forms of mobile property, public finance and enlarged government power were understood in early-eighteenth-century Britain.[11] *The Fable of the Bees* first came to public attention because it was implicated in an intense controversy about the nature of politics, modern commerce and their contemporary moral consequences. The presentment to the Middlesex Grand Jury claimed that *The Fable* was designed "to run down Religion and Virtue as prejudicial to Society, and detrimental to the State; and to recommend Luxury, Avarice, Pride, and all vices, as being necessary to *Public Welfare*, and not tending to the Destruction of the Constitution ..."[12] This charge, elaborated in the full case against the book published in *The British Journal* on 3 July 1723, was couched in the language of traditional Christian moral preception, laced with puritan idioms. In his "Vindication," Mandeville recognized it at once as the rhetoric of the Societies for the Reformation of Manners, whose campaigns for moral reform and whose program for the education of poor children he had savaged in *The Fable*'s "Essay on Charity and Charity-Schools."

The Grand Jurymen judging the case were Country opponents of the current Court Whig administration. They shared the Tory, and possibly Jacobite, sympathies of the sheriffs who appointed them. These men sought publicly to assert their loyalty to the crown and their moral opposition to Robert Walpole, its chief minister, whose principles they now found politically opportune to claim were enunciated in Mandeville's chargeable book. In his *Free Thoughts* of 1720, Mandeville had argued that "dominion always follows property," and that the Revolution of 1688 had brought the constitu-

---

[11] Most influentially by J.G.A. Pocock, *The Machiavellian Moment: Florentine Political Thought and the Atlantic Republican Tradition* (Princeton University Press, 1975). The paragraphs which immediately follow also rely upon W.A. Speck, "Bernard Mandeville and the Middlesex Grand Jury," *Eighteenth-Century Studies* 11 (1978), pp. 362–374; J.A.W. Gunn, "Mandeville: Poverty, Luxury, and the Whig Theory of Government," in *Beyond Liberty and Property: The Process of Self-Recognition in Eighteenth-Century Political Thought* (Kingston: McGill–Queen's University Press, 1983), pp. 96–119; Reed Browning, *The Political and Constitutional Ideas of the Court Whigs* (Baton Rouge: Louisiana State University Press, 1983); W.A. Speck, "Conflict in Society," in *Britain After the Glorious Revolution* (London: Macmillan, 1969), pp. 135–154; John Brewer, *The Sinews of Power: War, Money and the English State, 1688–1783* (New York: Alfred Knopf, 1989), and Shelly Burtt, *Virtue Transformed: Political Argument in England, 1688–1740* (Cambridge University Press, 1992), pp. 128–149.   [12] *Fable*, I, p. 385.

tion into equilibrium with contemporary property relationships – a thesis which had become the official doctrine of the government party. Mandeville's argument was a elaboration of the government's well-known position, coupled with a satiric attack upon its opponents, who had denounced the government's financial manipulation of placemen in parliament, and came close to questioning its legitimacy as well. Government publicists like Mandeville not only sought to defend the Hanoverian succession against Jacobite claims of usurpation. In championing the new regime, Court Whigs were also obliged to claim as well that its institutions were not signs of what had, for nearly a half-century, commonly been called "corruption": the ability of government through financial reward and the granting of office to manipulate parliamentary institutions. Mandeville's was a telling critique of the opposition's principles. He argued that what was formerly regarded as political unscrupulousness had become inevitable in modern conditions of affluence, and that it was now the function of a well-ordered state to govern men whose growing opportunities for private gain were at the same time prerequisites of contemporary prosperity. Mandeville infuriated his immediate enemies because he defended existing political practices by offering a compelling account of the social place of private impulse to explain their necessity.

In their assault on *The Fable* the Grand Jurors spoke as Old Whigs, in what has been variously called the language of the Commonwealth, of civic humanism or republicanism. They attacked Mandeville in the context of an intense and comprehensive critique of modernity, undertaken in the name of an ideal of virtue practiced in antique Mediterranean republics, particularly republican Rome and the quasi-mythical Sparta framed by Lycurgus' laws. For the Augustans, the primary language of political opposition engaged a vocabulary that opposed virtue to corruption, the dignity of landed to mobile property, and public service to self-interest. Nowhere was this more apparent than in the political press and on the stage, where "Cato" and "Cicero" exposed the duplicities of "Caesar" and "Cataline," names serving as rhetorical markers for the ministers who could not, without risk of prosecution, openly be named. Behind this rhetoric stood a tradition of political analysis ultimately derived from Machiavelli's account of the Roman Republic in the *Discourses*, which was translated into English by Henry Neville in 1674, and then re-issued four times (1675, 1680, 1694 and 1720) by the date of *The Fable*'s prosecution. This mode of argument inveighed against tyrants, found the source of political corruption in self-interest, suspected material affluence as a sign of moral degeneration, and hailed a citizen militia as the necessary guardian of liberty. A commitment to "the liberty of the people" was a constant theme; this literature hardly sought its material betterment, however, since affluence would fan self-interest. Neither did those who spoke as Commonwealthmen encourage popular participation, since political judgement was seen to be embodied in the hero-statesman like Cincinnatus or Cleomenes (the name Mandeville expressly chose for his own spokesman in *The Fable*), whose virtue was thought to derive from their devotion to patriotic principles, and was sustained by an aristocratic, landed, independence from material need.

This cluster of concepts received its decisive English formulation in James Harrington's *Oceana* (1656), a "Machiavellian meditation on feudalism"[13] that became a primary source of British civic humanist principles. Harrington argued that the nobility had been transformed from territorial magnates supporting armies of clients into dependent courtiers, a decline in noble power that accelerated after the dissolution of the monasteries by Henry VIII. The balance of property and thus the balance of power which, for Harrington, followed property, had then come to lie in the freeholders who purchased former monastic lands. Monarchy based upon a landed nobility, what Harrington called "the Gothic Balance," had quickly dissolved. Now the "ancient prudence" of classical republics could be restored in a polity based upon assemblies of independent, armed freeholders. An Agrarian Law would limit wealth and thus luxury; rotation of offices would prevent official corruption; decadent courts would be eliminated; and a natural aristocracy would simultaneously endorse popular sovereignty to ensure liberty.

Central to the civic humanist position was the assumption of a necessary connection between political liberty and landed property. Machiavelli and his Florentine contemporaries had insisted upon this connection,[14] while advancing the complementary thesis that the pursuit of private gain threatened civil liberty. As exemplified in Sallust's explanation of the collapse of the Roman Republic into the

[13] J.G.A. Pocock, *The Ancient Constitution and the Feudal Law: English Historical Thought in the Seventeenth Century* (Cambridge University Press, 1957), p. 147.

[14] See especially Machiavelli, *The Discourses*, trans. L. Walter, ed. Bernard Crick (Harmondsworth: Penguin, 1970), Chapter 19.

despotism of the Empire, it was held that the private scramble for money was one of the major dangers to the maintenance of freedom and public virtue. Instead, land seen as a patrimony that supported men at arms and sustained political independence was understood as the necessary economic foundation of the virtuous citizen. The ideas of moveable wealth, or of land treated as capital floating freely in a volatile market of anonymous risk-takers, conjured up the specter of an easily manipulated public opinion as the measure of one's standing, and of the self-interest and private pleasure through which luxurious nations declined, falling prey to their frugal, independent neighbors. In this way – so those who followed the civic tradition argued – Sparta triumphed over Athens and the Swiss preserved their freedom in the face of the huge, corrupt states on their borders. If the Romans "had kept their purity they [would have] kept their government and their virtue too," Henry Neville said.[15] For Algernon Sidney, the republican martyr, wealth in itself was dangerous, the safest political environment being one in which riches were either banished or held in small regard.[16] Mandeville's contemporaries John Trenchard and Thomas Gordon, whose publisher was charged along with *The Fable*'s, denounced in their influential tract of 1723, *Cato's Letters: Or Essays on Liberty, Civil and Religious, and Other Important Subjects*, the public morality of affluence which they saw as engendering the panic and disaster of the South Sea Bubble less than three years before. Only a frugal population could maintain its freedom, and only a rigorously defended civil liberty stood between civilization and a luxurious decline into arbitrary government.

These were compelling and politically potent doctrines during the first half of the eighteenth century. They were modifications of an allied puritan outlook into less specifically Christian forms of rhetoric, and were put foward in the Age of Anne as a distillation of those Whig principles which the Glorious Revolution supposedly confirmed. Moreover, these ideas helped to make coherent the position of what in the 1720s and after was called "the landed interest," families living on their incomes from rents and who derived few supplementary revenues from office holding, commerce or finance. In the thirty years following 1688 these persons found their political position eroding as rents, mortgages and sales of land rapidly became less profitable. The

[15] Henry Neville, *Plato Redivivus*, in Caroline Robbins (ed.), *Two English Republican Tracts* (Cambridge University Press, 1969), p. 97.
[16] Algernon Sidney, *Discourses on Government* (1698) (London, 1751), pp. 201–202.

new machinery of public credit and government finance, exemplified by the Bank of England and the East India Trading Company, presented great opportunities for profit to individuals eager to invest their newly won surplus capital. This was particularly true of holders of Bank and East India Trading shares, and of those persons handling their affairs on the Stock Exchange. These jobbers, brokers and factors whom the traditional landed classes found so threatening to their status and power, so it was claimed, formed the nucleus of "the moneyed interest" on whose speculation, rather than parliament's grant, the government increasingly depended for its soaring revenues.

Great Britain had recently emerged from wars in Europe against France and her allies in 1689–1697 and 1702–1713 as a major power with Atlantic ambitions, supported by an expanding professional army sustained by a system of public credit and a national debt. These phenomena were seen by the regime's opponents as vastly expanding the crown's already considerable capacities for patronage, thus threatening parliamentary supremacy and also making increasing numbers of individuals directly dependent upon the government for their social and economic fortunes. The "Country" party, as this group was called, opposed the new system, since it directly threatened its members' political power, social standing and self-esteem. It blended the themes of classical republicanism, civic humanism and puritan frugality into an ideological defense of English liberties and the constitution against the supposed intrusion into the public domain of both private wealth and arbitrary influence. It set "virtue" over and against "commerce" and "corruption," "frugality" against "luxury," and the independence of parliament against the apparent desire of the crown for unbalanced dominion. It stressed the role of the independent proprietor against the rentier, speculator and placeman. It identified as threats to liberty and security the manipulators of moveable capital, "stockjobbers" and holders of government notes, self-made urban plutocrats, Huguenots and (particularly Portuguese and Dutch) Jews, all of whom centered their activities in the City of London and lived with that amalgam of unrestrained passion and self-interest which supposedly eroded a devotion to the common good. Sections of the established ruling orders thus felt endangered by *arrivistes*, persons propelled into power by a mysterious finance capital whose imperatives seemed at once to subvert traditional morality and threaten their social standing. Most fervently expressed during the financial crises of 1696, 1710 and 1720, these ideas retained their force

well into the 1760s and beyond. From Andrew Marvell to Bolingbroke and Burke, from *Moll Flanders* to *Roderick Random*, the
vagaries of fortune initiated by the "financial revolution" of the
1690s[17] loomed as a threat to a landed, antique ideal of civic freedom
and public personality.

Setting Mandeville's work within the framework of a multifaceted
British debate about commerce and virtue helps to make historical
sense of much of the remarkably hostile reception *The Fable* initially
received. Rather than an historically implausible moderate Christian
moralism written in the figured contempt of satire,[18] or an ambivalent
commentary upon contemporary habits of mind, at once a moralizing
and cynical,[19] Mandeville's moral skepticism was carefully framed in
a language suited to engender in a large segment of his Augustan
audience a threat to their own self-understanding. By adopting the
Satyr's sneer and at the same time notionally affirming the most
rigorous criteria of the inherited moral tradition, Mandeville successfully fashioned an intuitively compelling picture of a world dramatically transformed by new mechanisms of exchange, a world that
frighteningly demanded from its members the relegation of their civic
ideals to the realm of nostalgia, and the adoption of an intransigently
egoistic morality.

An unintended consequence of this significant advance in our
understanding of the emergence of commercial sociability has been
the marginalization of Mandeville's importance as a *European* thinker
who developed what was regarded by intellectuals in England,
Ireland, Scotland and the continent generally, as a highly articulated,
conceptually challenging, science of man – a project with which the
greatest eighteenth-century students of contemporary society felt
obliged directly to engage. When Mandeville is viewed as a writer
whose primary purpose was merely to intervene in a circumscribed
Augustan conversation about political corruption and social instability, *The Fable*'s central place in the moral imagination of Enlightenment Europe becomes more rather than less puzzling. Furthermore,
when understood as someone who advanced a single, univocal, thesis

[17] P.G.M. Dickson, *The Financial Revolution in England: A Study in the Development of Public Credit* (London: Macmillan, 1967).
[18] Paulette Carrive, *La Philosophie des passions chez Bernard Mandeville*, 2 volumes (Paris: Didier Erudition, 1983), a doctoral thesis abridged as *Bernard Mandeville: passions, vices, vertus* (Paris: Vrin, 1980). Carrive's work contains the most fully documented account of the reception of *The Fable of the Bees.*
[19] Hector Monro, *The Ambivalence of Bernard Mandeville* (Oxford: Clarendon Press, 1975).

of "private vices" leading to "public benefits" for this essentially local purpose, the historical significance of Mandeville's confrontations with his critics, and of his philosophically enriched elaboration of *The Fable*'s claims into a comprehensive social theory, tends to be obscured.[20]

Mandeville was a self-conscious member of the Republic of Letters at the turn of the eighteenth century, and he drew upon a variety of resources at some remove from the native conceptual environment in which he first became known. He recast in an original form arguments from continental traditions of political discourse, natural philosophy and Christian moral psychology with which most of his initial adversaries had only a casual acquaintance. Mandeville was a thinker for whom scraps of quotidian reality provided the most startling information about hitherto unexamined social processes. He introduced into the heart of European social understanding a series of arguments designed to sustain the radically unsettling conclusion that the moral identities of his contemporaries had been permanently altered by a previously unacknowledged historical transformation. These arguments are inadequately captured by seeing in Mandeville's work a proto-Weberian attempt to articulate the "spirit of capitalism,"[21] or as a largely conventional mercantilist exercise undertaken in a modern idiom.[22] They are positively disfigured when anachronistically distilled into a typological history of "economic ideology," in which *The Fable* acquires a pride of place in the purportedly tragic emancipation of economic life from politics.[23] A satisfactory discussion of Mandeville's achievement must recover the sources and strategies of his project as he understood it. It must provide an account of Mandeville's development of this enterprise in the context of those contemporary ideological disputes in which he was embroiled. Perhaps most importantly, it must treat his work with the philosophical seriousness accorded to *The Fable of the Bees* during three generations, from Hutcheson to Kant and Condillac to Malthus. Mandeville provided for eighteenth-century intellectuals a map

[20] M.M. Goldsmith, *Private Vices, Public Benefits: Bernard Mandeville's Social and Political Thought* (Cambridge University Press, 1985).

[21] M.M. Goldsmith, "Bernard Mandeville and the Spirit of Capitalism," *Journal of British Studies* 17 (1977), pp. 63–81.

[22] Thomas A. Horne, *The Social Thought of Bernard Mandeville: Virtue and Commerce in Early Eighteenth-Century England* (New York: Columbia University Press, 1978).

[23] Louis Dumont, *From Mandeville to Marx: The Genesis and Triumph of Economic Ideology* (Chicago University Press, 1977).

– or rather, a sketch from which various maps could then be drawn – not of the economy, but of society itself, understood as a hitherto untheorized entity whose history and structure were now for the first time amenable to systematic analysis.

In approaching the task of comprehensively understanding Mandeville's achievement, I have found it most useful to avoid approaching the development of his thought and its eighteenth-century significance chronologically, and to see it, rather, from a number of distinct yet related perspectives. I hope to show how each of these perspectives emerged from the conceptual environment of ideas and usages in which *The Fable of the Bees* acquired its Enlightenment identity. My aims in what follows are to locate within the context of his own purposes the thought of an author whose work can be said to have epitomized a number of intellectual traditions existing at the time he wrote, and to explain his methods of re-working arguments derived from these traditions for unprecedented purposes. Above all, I intend to recover and clarify the context of controversy through which *The Fable of the Bees* decisively shaped the Enlightenment's encounter with what Mandeville insisted, and his contemporaries found themselves forced – often reluctantly – to agree, were the unique and uniquely disturbing paradoxes of modernity.

CHAPTER I

The foundations of a project

The Fable of the Bees was the Enlightenment's epitome of immoralism. Throughout the eighteenth century, Mandeville was seen as the most formidable modern critic of Christian moral psychology, the exemplary nihilist who applauded illimitable human desire, and the compelling satirist of contemporary codes of propriety. His work, more than any other, called into question fundamental standards of social behavior. To both his few admitted admirers and *The Fable*'s legion of opponents, Mandeville's critique of inherited ideals of conduct was thought never fully to have been answered, not only in his own lifetime, but during the two generations after his death in 1732. Adam Smith, for example, was still revising his attack on *The Fable* in 1790, the last year of his life.[1] Mandeville himself insisted that his distinctive amalgam of philosophy and satire had both a critical and constructive intention: to "pull off the disguises of artful men," as he wrote in response to Bishop Berkeley, and to expose "the hidden springs" of human action to analytic inspection.[2] His project of "anatomizing the invisible part of man" (I, 136) was designed to demonstrate that the vocabularies of formal systems of ethics served the essentially political and socializing purpose of deflecting critical attention from the irreducibly passionate and utterly self-regarding sources of actual human wishes. This claim and Mandeville's elaboration of it were widely disseminated in Europe during the 1720s by the quasi-official journals of the Enlightenment Republic of Letters,[3] and then, most

---

[1] Adam Smith, *The Theory of Moral Sentiments* (6th edition, 1791), ed. D.D. Raphael and A.L. Macfie, (Oxford University Press, 1976), VI.ii.4, "Of Licentious Systems," pp. 485–496.

[2] (Bernard Mandeville), *A Letter to Dion, Occasioned by his Book Call'd Alciphron, or The Minute Philosopher, By the Author of the Fable of the Bees* (London, 1732), p. 8.

[3] For an inventory and summary of these reviews see, André Morize, *L'Apologie du luxe au XVIIIe siècle et 'Le Mondaine' de Voltaire* (Geneva: Slatkine Reprint, 1970), pp. 78–80. For a discussion, see below, pp. 103–104.

notably perhaps, by the efforts of Voltaire, who lived in England during the height of the controversy sparked by *The Fable*, and worked on its translation and commentary upon his return to France, compiling a summary of Mandeville's arguments about the origins of morality in his *Treatise on Metaphysics*.[4] Just as in *Le Mondaine*, his paean to luxury, in the entry *Amour-Propre* in the *Philosophical Diction-ary* Voltaire declared that Mandeville's perspective on the sources of action had become a necessarily unacknowledged feature of educated opinion. "Just as people don't write to prove to men that they have a face," Voltaire said, "there is no need to prove to them that they are egotistical. This egoism is the instrument of our preservation; it resembles the instrument for the perpetuation of the species; we need it, we cherish it, it gives us pleasure, and we must hide it."

Mandeville's most important and disturbing claims derived from his assertion that contemporary moral discourse promoted self-deception. By displacing impulse as the standard unit from which to comprehend social action, the inherited vocabulary of ethics, he argued, thoroughly obscured actual human motives, and at the same time made it impossible to understand the novel conditions of polished sociability under which modern personalities were formed. "Private Vices, Public Benefits," the sub-title of Mandeville's master-piece, thus expressed a paradoxical thesis meant, and immediately taken, as a threat to contemporary self-understanding. While his arguments in *The Fable* relied for much of their persuasive force upon a carefully wrought rhetorical strategy, Mandeville recognized that these arguments depended for their conceptual power upon his ability to invigorate and then defend an ancient insight into the fundamen-tally egoistic sources of human behavior – a thesis still associated in the early eighteenth century with Lucretius (ca.94–ca.50 BC), whose epic *De rerum natura* contained the most detailed classical exposition of the

---

[4] Voltaire, *Traité de métaphysique* (1734–1738), ed. E. Temple Patterson (Manchester Univer-sity Press, 1937) Chapter 8, "L'homme consideré comme un animal social." Not published during Voltaire's lifetime, the work circulated in manuscript, with an abstract sent to Frederick the Great. See Ira O. Wade, *Voltaire and Madame du Châtelet* (Princeton University Press, 1941), pp. 24–33. In the *Lettres philosophiques* (1731), Letter XIII, Voltaire had previously referred his readers to *The Fable* but thought that Mandeville had originally published his ideas under a pseudonym in *Voyages et aventures de Jacques Massé*, a work printed in Rotterdam after 1714 (but dated 1710 on the title-page) and known in freethinking circles. See Aubrey Rosenberg, *Tyssot de Patot and His Work, 1655–1738* (The Hague: Nijhoff, 1972), pp. 91–95, and Lise Leibacher-Ouvrard, *Libertinage et utopies sous le règne de Louis XIV* (Geneva: Droz, 1989), pp. 225–226.

atomist, hedonist and purportedly atheist doctrines of Epicurus (341–271 BC). It was a thesis, moreover, that Mandeville thought had been systematically suppressed on account of its morally subversive implications; suppressed not only in common opinion but in most educated quarters, despite its recent revival within a minority strand of the European philosophical tradition. Situating Mandeville's enterprise within this European context of the philosophical controversy into which he plunged most completely reveals his purposes in writing as he did – as a "naturalist"[5] who sought to lay bare the social mechanisms which conditioned individual human propensities. "Laws and Government," he declared in the first lines of *The Fable*,

are to the Political Bodies of Civil Societies, what the Vital Spirits and Life it self are to the Natural Bodies of Animated Creatures; and as those that study the Anatomy of Dead Carcases may see, that the chief Organs and nicest Springs more immediately required to continue the Motion of our Machine, are ... small trifling Films and little Pipes that are either over-look'd, or else seem inconsiderable to Vulgar Eyes; so they ... may observe ... that [Man's] vilest and most hateful Qualities are the most necessary Accomplishments to fit him for the largest, and according to the World, the happiest and most flourishing Societies ... *Man (besides Skin, Flesh, Bones, &c. that are obvious to the Eye) [is] a compound of various Passions, that all of them, as they are provoked and come uppermost, govern him by turns, whether he will or no.* (1, 3–4; 39)

Mandeville self-consciously appropriated a distinctive tradition of theorizing about the nature of the sciences and their relation to moral reasoning and social practice. Appreciating his attempt to establish foundations for a science of man suited to the conditions of European modernity depends upon recovering the ways he engaged with the texts and the audiences through which this tradition attained its eighteenth-century identity.

EGOISM, POLITICS AND SOCIETY

The Fable of the Bees first gained notoriety when its publisher was charged with having printed a work intended to "run down religion and Virtue as *prejudicial* to Society, and detrimental to the State; and to recommend Luxury, Avarice, Pride, and all kind of Vices, as being necessary to *Publick Welfare*" (1, 385). Mandeville, in short, claimed

---

[5] *An Enquiry into the Origin of Honour, and the Usefulness of Christianity in War*, ed. M.M. Goldsmith (London: Cass Reprint, 1971), p. 5.

that the underlying dynamics of social life were falsified by the Christian view. He argued, by contrast, that the accumulation of riches could not be explained by recourse to genuinely moral virtues. To understand wealth creation, it was necessary to examine the processes through which the innate human desires for power, esteem and sensual pleasure drove men to compete for the tangible satisfactions they so vigorously sought. Similarly, contemporary moral standards themselves, whether found in Biblical injunction or philosophical commentary, could not coherently be accounted for in terms of the received platitudes of orthodox ethical reasoning that Mandeville continually satirized. The commonly held belief in personal rectitude as the source of public good, he claimed in all of his work, derived instead from a longstanding and highly articulated ideological project in which elites laid claim to private virtue in order to disguise their own self-seeking, thereby ensuring the respect of subordinates. The great states of Europe were in fact administered by such persons. All ruling orders sought to channel their wholly private interests into what these elites successfully convinced a politically dependent population were other-regarding public purposes. Moreover, and perhaps most offensively, this duplicitous achievement was in Mandeville's view a necessary prerequisite for the relative social peace and routinely enforced rules of justice which distinguished civilized communities from their barbarous predecessors. Only the "dextrous management of skillful politicians" (1, 339) could serve to stabilize an anthropologically irreducible clash of escalating individual desires, wants whose ungoverned terminus would be anarchy.

According to Mandeville, all civilized nations owed their very foundations not to morally empowered acts of virtuous legislators of the sort populating European national myths, but to the ability of strong, cunning minorities to tame and discipline the fractious passions of savage multitudes (1, 41–57). He sought to reduce to absurdity the idea that polities could have been established from any realistically conceivable process of communal deliberation, or could, as both Pufendorf and Locke had argued, plausibly be represented as originating in acts of rational choice by reflective and articulate rights-bearing subjects. Equally important, Mandeville rejected as contrary to all experience the venerable notion of a moral hierarchy of goods naturally suited to human needs. As William Law, tutor to Edward Gibbon's father, and one of Mandeville's most astute critics, put it, he "enquire[s] whether there be any real Excellency or Worth

in Things, a Pre-eminence of one thing above another[, a]nd ...
shew[s] that there is no such Thing as any real Worth or Excellency in
Things or Actions, but that all is mere Whim and Fancy."[6] Men were,
and would always be, driven by their commonly shared passions,
whose individual intensities were shaped by their inborn temperaments, and whose communal expressions were simply the derivative
functions of given social opportunities. Persons would always and
only seek to act in ways they believed would best serve their individual
interests.

The sociological importance of this psychological truth was for
Mandeville thrown into bold relief in modern conditions of affluence,
which he, virtually alone amongst his contemporaries of the 1720s,
viewed with unambiguous delight. Even before *The Fable* appeared,
one of Mandeville's first literary ventures, *The Grumbling Hive* (1705),
could immediately be identified by English readers as an answer to
the "grumbling" of a number of poetic lamentations published
during the first years of the century which bemoaned the supposedly
corrosive moral effects brought on by an increasing circulation of
money amongst ordinary citizens.[7] Mandeville mocked these jeremiads as little more than self-righteous longings for an idealized and
largely mythical former social order. Well-governed commercial
states in modern Europe, he insisted, were required to confront
recently altered economic conditions that encouraged and rewarded
both aggressive individual enterprise and social mobility. This was
particularly so in Britain, whose continuing prosperity seemed in the
second decade of the eighteenth century heavily to depend on the
confidence shown by investors in the institutions first established in
the 1690s, the Bank of England and the London Exchange, the value
of whose fluctuating shares was an index both of Britain's economic
fortunes and of an upwardly mobile *nouveaux riches*. Rather than
striving to curb the supposed moral corruption encouraged by
widening economic opportunities (which was in reality nothing more
than the utterly normal expression of universal human traits),

---

[6] William Law, *Remarks Upon a Late Book, Entitled, The Fable of the Bees ... In a Letter to the Author* (London, 1724), pp. 55–56.

[7] See, for example, Ned Ward's *The Miracles Performed by Money* (1695), *The Character of a Covetous Citizen, or a Ready Way to Get Riches* (1702) and *To That Celebrated Ideal Mamon ...* (1709), and the anonymous *The Cheating Age Found Out: When Knaves Were Most in Fashion* (1705), which describes money's corrupting effects on 170 different people. For this context see Isaac Kramnick, *Bolingbroke and His Circle: The Politics of Nostalgia in the Age of Walpole* (Cambridge, Massachusetts: Harvard University Press, 1968), p. 201.

politicians, so Mandeville argued, had now expressly to attend to the manipulation of egoism into communally useful purposes. The ruling orders of modern states were obliged to govern subjects whose massively enlarged opportunities for purely personal gain were at the same time prerequisites of national prosperity. Mandeville gleefully dismissed as romantic nostalgia the widely held opinion that the intense scrambles for wealth and power which characterized modern polities provided evidence of a growing corruption of public life. He outraged the audience of *The Fable of the Bees* by offering instead a psychologically compelling account of the positive social function of avarice.

One of Mandeville's most significant achievements in the minds of his Enlightenment readers was his ability to derive universally applicable propositions about the nature of society from apparently recalcitrant local English materials, like the voluntarily supported system of charity schools (I, 253–322) or the collapse of the South Sea Company's shares on the London Exchange (II, 350–355), in whose wake he published the notorious 1723 edition of *The Fable*. Mandeville recognized that a transformation in British public finance had engendered an explosion of moveable capital, creating the foundations of a new social order in which the power of finance necessarily took its place beside the established interests of land and trade. He was among the first to understand that similar transformations were bound to have profound social consequences in the great states of Europe. This was why Montesquieu, like Voltaire a visitor to England during the height of the controversy about *The Fable*, wrote in his journal that he would enthusiastically, if provisionally, accept Mandeville's main arguments, challenging anyone to show that grave and virtuous citizens of any nation in fact contributed more to their societies than the petty and greedy *petit-maîtres* who peopled Mandeville's book.[8]

Mandeville thus meant *The Fable* to have, and succeeded in gaining for it, a wide conceptual purchase. His abstract moral arguments about the primary sources of virtue and justice, rather than the criticism of any particular persons, groups or institutions, inspired the intensely hostile reactions of so many of his immediate contemporaries, notably Berkeley, Francis Hutcheson and William Law. Mande-

---

[8] Montesquieu, *Mes pensées*, cited in J. Didier, *Montesquieu et la tradition politique anglaise en France* (Paris, 1909), p. 225.

ville's compelling subject was the moral and intersubjective demands made upon individuals recently propelled into what he recognized as the novel political and social conditions of commercial societies. In his formulation, the preservation of civil peace required the ruling orders of these opulent nations to develop various stratagems to disguise, and thus officially legitimate, their utterly self-regarding motives. Mandeville understood this demand not so much as a necessary condition of justice, but as a requirement of the prosperity which commercial citizens were coming to expect. As he insisted in his attack on Charity Schools – the part of *The Fable* which enraged his first critics – this essentially political project required the prosperous, and those who sought prosperity, falsely to proclaim their virtuous intentions while all the while encouraging docility and ignorance amongst the lower orders, whose "mean services" and continued deference were required to sustain their opulent living.

Toil must be undergone before man can provide himself with necessaries for his sustenance ... but infinitely more to make life comfortable in civil society, where men are become taught animals ... and the more man's knowledge increases in this state, the greater will be the variety of labour required to make him easy. It is impossible that a society can long subsist, and suffer many of its members to live in idleness, and enjoy all the ease and pleasure they can invent, without having at the same time great multitudes of people that ... will condescend to be quite the reverse, and by use and patience inure their bodies to work for others and themselves besides ... If such people there must be ... would not a wise Legislature cultivate the breed of them with all imaginable care ...? Obsequiousness and mean services are required ... [and] they are never so chearfully nor so heartily perform'd as from inferiors ... [A] wise legislature [would] cultivate the breed of them with all imaginable care. (I, 286–289)

These stark social imperatives clearly applied to Britain, the fiscal-military state which had emerged economically predominant from the recent European wars against France, and whose modern financial and political institutions were now required to support both a growing leisure class and a permanently expanded potential for making war. Mandeville, it should be recalled, defended these institutions in his *Mischiefs that Ought Justly to be Apprehended from a Whig-Government* (1714) and then in *Free Thoughts on Religion, the Church and National Happiness* (1720) by arguing (too radically for the comfort of his patrons) that human nature itself, rather than governmental machinations, engendered supposed corruption; that careful political administration would render common vice innocuous; and that national power was hardly jeopardized by the pleasures of the wealthy. But he employed identical principles to explain the success of both ancient Roman and contemporary Dutch societies, subjects repeatedly revisited both in *The Fable* and its effective extension, *An Enquiry into the Origin of Honour, and the Usefulness of Christianity in War* (1732). Mandeville's thesis about the social necessity of hypocrisy and the civic imperative of dissimulation struck directly, and struck hard, at all claims that British political liberties had their source in the active virtue of an independent ruling elite, just as his denigration of Cato as the slave of his own egoism (I, 209–210; 335–336), and his description of the Dutch as frugal by necessity rather than design (I, 187–191), exposed the vacuity of the moralized descriptions of republican Rome and Holland which then dominated educated opinion.

DUTCH REPUBLICANS AND FRENCH *DÉVOTS*

In order to locate the ideological provenance of Mandeville's arguments it is important to recall the conceptual context in which he began to write. A native of Rotterdam who may have been taught by Pierre Bayle in the city's Erasmian school,[9] Mandeville was immersed in the French Augustinian tradition of analyzing the passions, associated in both England and the continent with Pascal, La Rochefoucauld and the Jansenist theologian Pierre Nicole. He studied medicine at Leiden and remained in contact with the Dutch community in England after immigrating to London in the late 1690s.[10] Mandeville began writing professionally as a translator and fabulist working within the established Aesopian conventions of the genre,[11] and was obviously familiar with the libertine tradition of

---

9   Richard H. Popkin, "Isaac de Pinto's Criticism of Mandeville and Hume on Luxury," *Studies on Voltaire and the Eighteenth Century* 154 (1976), pp. 1705–1714, and Elizabeth Labrousse, *Pierre Bayle* (The Hague: Nijhoff, 1964), II, p. 117, n. 50.

10 See, "In authorem de use interno cantharidum scribentem," a disparaging poem by Mandeville about the College of Physicians prefixed to a medical treatise by a Dutch friend, Dr. John Groenevelt (anglicized: Greenfield), *Uso Interno* (London, 1698), trans. John Marten as "Upon the Author, Treating of the Internal Use of *Cantharides*," in John Greenfield, *A Treatise of the Safe, Internal Use of Cantharides in the Practice of Physick* (London, 1706), and *A Sermon Preach'd at Colchester, to the Dutch Congregation, by the Reverend C. Schrevlius* ..., translated by B.M., MD (London, 1708). Schrevlius was a classicist who published no other sermons. This work is likely a satiric performance by Mandeville himself.

11 *Some Fables after the Easie and Familiar Method of Monsieur de la Fontaine* (London, 1703), and *Aesop Dress'd: Or a Collection of Fables Writ in Familiar Verse* (London, 1704).

social satire with which *The Fable* was almost immediately linked by its critics. He adopted Scarron as a model for the satirical poem *Typhon* (1704),[12] one of his first works, and shortly thereafter published the mildly pornographic *Virgin Unmask'd* in 1709.[13] A physician specializing in the treatment of nervous diseases during his entire professional life, Mandeville was a vigorous critic of Descartes' physiological doctrines, which had formed the basis of his own medical training.[14] Moreover, Mandeville insisted that his anti-Cartesian stance bore directly on the arguments of *The Fable*, in which he dismissed Descartes' physiological views as the speculations of a "vain Reasoner" (I, 181).

It would be difficult to find an English contemporary with a similar intellectual profile during the first quarter of the eighteenth century; more difficult yet to locate a native audience for whom these concerns collectively formed the basis of sustained social commentary. *The Fable*'s power to shock its first British readers, and much of its conceptual force too, was a function of Mandeville's ability to inject novel elements into an already-established discourse on the volatile moral relations between public virtue and the demands of commerce, a discourse which Mandeville had satirized in his early journalism.[15] Many of these elements were distinctive features of a Dutch republican political theory founded on a science of harnessing the passions, a self-described "political science" which Johan and Pieter De la Court formulated in Holland in the 1660s.[16] The De la Courts grafted a reading of Descartes' *Passions of the Soul* (1649) onto the arguments of

---

[12] (Bernard Mandeville), *Typhon: Or The Wars Between the Gods and Giants: A Burlesque Poem in Imitation of the Comical Mons. Scarron* (London, 1704).

[13] For a survey of this genre in England see D.F. Foxon, "Libertine Literature in England, 1660–1745," *Book Collector* 12 (1963), pp. 21–36; 159–177, and 294–307.

[14] See, T.L. Scheurleer and G.H.M. Posthumus Meyes, *Leiden University in the Seventeenth Century: An Exchange of Learning* (Leiden: Brill, 1975), pp. 470–479, on Bucheris De Volder, the staunchly Cartesian professor of Medicine at Leiden, and his contemporaries. Mandeville wrote an orthodox Cartesian thesis, *Disputatio Philosophica de Brutorum Operationibus* (Leiden, 1689), under De Volder's supervision.

[15] J.G.A. Pocock, *The Machiavellian Moment: Florentine Political Thought and the Atlantic Republican Tradition* (Princeton University Press, 1975), pp. 423–461, provides the now standard account. On Mandeville's critical encounter with this moralized civic language in *The Female Tatler* of 1709–1710, see M.M. Goldsmith, *Private Vices, Public Benefits: Bernard Mandeville's Social and Political Thought* (Cambridge University Press, 1985), especially pp. 33–46 and 136–143.

[16] For a discussion of this literature see Richard Tuck, *Natural Rights Theories* (Cambridge University Press, 1979), pp. 139–142; E.O.G. Haitsma Mulier, *The Myth of Venice and Dutch Republican Thought in the Seventeenth Century* (Assen: Van Gorcum, 1980), pp. 120–169, and Haitsma Mulier, "The Language of Seventeenth-Century Republicanism in the United Provinces: Dutch or European?," in Anthony Pagden (ed.), *The Languages of Political Thought*

Leviathan (1651), in which Hobbes distinguished men from social animals like bees by virtue of their political ability to forge agreements and enter into contracts.[17] They found in Descartes a psychological theory of the passions as naturally disposed to desire what is useful for the individual, but in principle subject to rational control.[18] Such control was possible through a reorientation of individual self-seeking so as to direct it to the common good. This goal could only be realized, the De la Courts maintained, in a state founded upon contract, one in which individuals able and willing to calculate their future advantages agreed to form a community. The resulting state would prosper and its citizens remain free if and only if this polity preserved a republican political balance of individual passions and communal interests of the kind classically described by Machiavelli in *The Discourses*. While writing in a Hobbesian idiom of unavoidable pre-political conflict, the De la Courts nevertheless argued that men in the natural state were fully capable of making political calculations about those institutions and societal arrangements which would best serve them collectively.

The native Dutch version of this theory was closely associated with the liberal republicanism of the De Witts, and with the De la Courts' native city of Leiden, where Mandeville studied in the 1680s and 90s. The argument was rendered into English in 1702 as *The True Interest and Political Maxims of the Republic of Holland*, a text in which the crucial distinction between false and prudentially disciplined self-love was articulated in exemplary fables.[19] And it then appeared as *Fables*

---

in *Early Modern Europe* (Cambridge University Press, 1987), pp. 179–195. See, too, E.H. Kossmann, *Politieke Theorie in het zeventiende-eeuwse Nederland* (Amsterdam: North Holland, 1960), pp. 36–58; T. Van Tijn, "Pieter De La Court: Zijn lever en zijn economische denkbeelden," *Tijdschrift Voor Geschiedenis* 64 (1956), pp. 304–370; and H.W. Blom, "Political Science in the Golden Age: Criticism, History and Theory in Dutch Seventeenth-Century Political Thought," *Netherlands Journal of Sociology* 15 (1979), pp. 47–71. For Dutch Cartesianism in this period see, C. Louise Thijssen-Schoute, "La Cartesianism aux Pays-Bas," in E.J. Dijksterhuis *et al.* (eds.), *Descartes et le cartésianisme hollandais* (Paris: PUF, 1950), pp. 183–260.

[17] Thomas Hobbes, *Leviathan*, ed. C.B. Macpherson (Harmondsworth: Penguin, 1968), II.17, pp. 225–226. Amongst bees, Hobbes wrote, "the Common good differeth not from the Private; and being by nature inclined to their private, they procure thereby the common benefit."

[18] See, René Descartes, *Philosophical Works* ed. E.S. Haldane and G.R.T. Ross (Cambridge University Press, 1931), p. 358.

[19] *The True Interest and Political Maxims of the Republic of Holland and West-Friesland* ... (London, 1702), Part II, pp. 248–254, translated from *Consideratien van staat ofte politike weegschaal* (Amsterdam, 1661) and *Politieke discoursen handelende in ses onderscheide boeken* ... (Amsterdam, 1662).

Moral and Political in 1703,[20] supposedly written by Johan De Witt, and published in London by the bookseller John Darby, who was still advertising the work some ten years later, along with his editions of the republican classics of Machiavelli, Milton, Harrington and Sidney. These *Fables* contrasted the luxurious decadence of kings, popes, bishops and courtiers with the frugality and virtue exemplified by the ancient Spartans, and by the Batavian ancestors of the Dutch, the Genoese and Venetians. All persons, the *Fables* taught, strictly adhering to the orthodox republican view, tend to seek their own interest and advantages when they are governed by their vanity and self-love. This debilitating condition of unbridled moral egoism was evident most clearly in absolute monarchies, where the ruling orders sought to conceal their "wants and weaknesses from the eye of men" in order to deceive, manipulate and oppress them. In "well-constituted and Free Republics," by contrast,

such Hypocrisy can be of no use to the Rulers; nay more, in that, if they make use thereof, it often contributes more to their prejudice, than if they guided their Steps in the Paths of Virtue and Honour.[21]

It was strictly necessary for citizens to "make it our business to inquire into all our passions, [of which self-love is the most prevalent,] and so to govern and direct them, that they may tend to our Good, and not to our ill."[22] So governed, men will acquire a "well-grounded self-love" in which reason instructs all members of the community that the way to gain the esteem sought by all is by performing genuinely praiseworthy actions.[23]

In "The Trees Desire a King" (which strikingly resembles Montesquieu's Myth of the Troglodytes in *The Persian Letters*[24]) it was shown how in monarchical governments vice, disorder and sheer self-seeking become elevated into ideals of honor, reducing the citizenry to misery

---

[20] *Fables, Moral and Political, With Large Explications. Translated from the Dutch. In Two Volumes.* (London, 1703), a translation of *Zinryken fabulen* (Amsterdam, 1685), pseudonymously and posthumously attributed to De Witt at the height of French pressure against the Dutch and in the wake of the revocation of the Edict of Nantes. For this context see Fable III, "A Frenchman and a Dutchman in the Kingdom of the Apes," where France is said to be a nation of hypocrites seeking to disguise their animal passions, persons with whom disciplined, moral Dutchmen have nothing in common.

[21] *Fables*, II, pp. 127 and 131.   [22] *Fables*, I, Preface A6.   [23] *Fables*, I, pp. 48–49.

[24] *Fables*, I, pp. 19–25. The resemblance may be more than coincidental, since there is reason to suspect that Montesquieu's story of 1721 was a response to Mandeville's pessimistic and antiutopian inversion of this fable. See Raymond Trousson, *Voyages aux pays de nulle part* (Editions de l'Université de Bruxelles, 1979), pp. 139 and 168–174.

and ruin in the process. "The Boat-Swains Tale" and "The Oak and the Reed"[25] argued that since "all Men are more desirous to procure their own Good ... than that of the public in general [and] cannot lay aside this natural humane affection, it evidently follows that there is a good form of government [a republic] where those who sit at the helm cannot promote their own interests and advantage unless they take care to advance the public."[26] Other fables directly followed from Aesop and adopted the classical Aesopian form of representing animals as human types, but tied this to a Cartesian account of the movement of the animal spirits in the generation of the passions. While the physiologies of humans and animals resemble each other, it was claimed that in man, as opposed to the brutes,

Almighty God has ... join'd our body to a reasonable Soul, and has given it such virtue and power to command the motions of the spirits of a sound and healthy body.[27]

Unlike the other animals, men control the flow of the animal spirits to muscles, sinews and members, and are thus able to perform the actions they wish. Only men can freely choose, for example, to follow the industriousness and thrift of the ant, abjuring the laziness of the fly.[28] They should certainly refuse the example of the bee – as one of the longest fables put it – which represents "a man, who seems to be very choice and prudent in seeking his Delights, and in contenting his sensual Appetite; and who at length is so transported with some new untasted Pleasure, that he forgets himself, and is forever lost in the midst of those ravishing Charms."[29]

It is impossible to tell with certainty whether Mandeville, who translated La Fontaine's Epicurean renditions of Aesop in 1703 and 1704,[30] responded directly to these Dutch *Fables* in his *Grumbling Hive* of 1705 (I, 17–37), a two-penny pamphlet poem in octosyllabic couplets that formed the basis of the first version of *The Fable of the Bees*. But it is clearly the case here that, in contrast to the hive of the De la Courts' imagination, "every Part was full of Vice, Yet the whole

[25] *Fables*, I, pp. 76–82; 286–298. [26] *Fables*, I, p. 80. [27] *Fables*, I, p. 314.
[28] "The Fly and the Ant," *Fables*, I, pp. 51–55.
[29] "The Bee in the Flower, and the Fly in the Honey," *Fables*, I, pp. 359–370, p. 361
[30] Compare, for example, "The Frogs Asking for a King" in *Aesop Dress'd* with "The Trees Desire a King" of *Fables*, I, pp. 19–25. For La Fontaine's Epicureanism and membership in an Epicurean circle headed by Pierre Gassendi, see Ira O. Wade, *The Intellectual Origins of the French Enlightenment* (Princeton University Press, 1971), pp. 404–417.

Mass a Paradise." Deceit and pride rather than virtue and prudence characterized a thriving community.

> Thus Vice nurs'd Ingenuity,
> Which join'd with Time and Industry,
> Had carry'd Life's Conveniencies,
> It's real Pleasures, Comforts, Ease,
> To such a Height, the very Poor
> Liv'd better than the Rich before,
> And nothing could be added more. (i, 26)

Then, as the "mask of hypocrisy" worn by the bees is "flung down," and frugality and moderation are adopted at the instigation of moralists, prosperity and ease vanish. For, as the poem's concluding "Moral" put it,

> Fools only strive
> To make a Great an Honest Hive
> T' enjoy the World's Conveniencies,
> Be fam'd in War, yet live in Ease,
> Without great Vices, is a vain
> EUTOPIA seated in the Brain. (i, 36)

Mandeville sought to render incoherent the De la Courts' language of argument about the beneficent control of impulse for the common good. His hive cast a positive light on precisely those values of self-interest and the dominance of the passions which the De la Courts condemned in bees. The beehive had long been a symbol of the orderliness of absolute monarchies, while in England economic writers commonly used the bee to represent Dutch frugality, discipline and commercial success.[31] Mandeville refused these images and

---

[31] For an example of the genre published as Mandeville was composing the first version of *The Fable* see J. Warder, *The True Amazons: Or the Monarchy of the Bees* (1712), a work reprinted nine times by 1765 and discussed in Ralph Greenleaf, *Order, Empiricism and Politics* (Oxford University Press, 1964), pp. 23–26. On fables and the beehive see J. Glöck, *Die Symbolic der Bienen* (Heidelberg: Groos, 1897), especially pp. 187–195; Stephen Daniel, "Political and Philosophical Uses of Fables in Eighteenth-Century England," *The Eighteenth Century* 23, 2 (1982), pp. 151–171; Annabel Patterson, "Fables of Power," in Kevin Sharpe and Steven N. Zwicker (eds.), *The Politics of Discourse* (Berkeley: University of California Press, 1987), pp. 271–296; Jeffrey Merrick, "Royal Bees: The Gender Politics of the Bee in Early Modern Europe," pp. 7–38, and Roseanne Runte, "From La Fontaine to Porchat: The Bee in the French Fable," pp. 79–90, both in J.W. Yolton and Leslie Ellen Brown (eds.), *Studies in Eighteenth-Century Culture* 18 (1988); and J.A.W. Gunn, "Mandeville and Wither: Individualism and the Workings of Providence," in Irwin Primer (ed.), *Mandeville Studies* (The Hague: Nijhoff, 1975), pp. 98–118. For the bee in English economic writing about the Dutch see, for example, *England's Greatest Happiness* (1677) and *Brittania Languens* (1680), both in J.R. McCulloch (ed.), *Early English Tracts on Commerce* (Cambridge: Economic History Society, 1952).

associations, concentrating instead on the beehive as a symbol of morally unbridled economic activity, a point quickly grasped by John Gay in his poetic riposte to *The Fable*.[32] Mandeville followed La Fontaine's example, incorporating both the skeptical argument about the relation between men and animals in the poet's "Discours à Madame Sablière,"[33] as well as the contentious Gassendian position on the continuity of human and animal drives. The latter was first and most famously enunciated in Pierre Gassendi's "Objections" to Descartes' *Méditations*,[34] and then summarized by his secretary, the physician François Bernier,[35] soon after La Fontaine's *Fables* were published in their entirety. In the same year Bayle brought the ethical significance of the dispute initiated by Descartes over the mental status of animals to the attention of the educated public in an article in his *Nouvelles de la République des Lettres*.[36]

Clearly, Mandeville aimed to demolish the De la Courts' assumption that the passions could only properly be harnessed in a republic and to ridicule the claim that a genuinely civil life could only be led under a republican government, a type of regime he associated with the impoverished rudimentary societies of the antique Mediterranean rather than with supposedly virtuous modern citizens. Mandeville challenged as absurd the supposition that ignorant savages living in the rude conditions preceding the imposition of laws would have been in any position to make the pre-political calculations necessary for "them to agree upon some sort of Government . . . for their common Good" (II, 132), a thesis at the heart of the republican political imagination. Savage man would not "draw consequences from the little which he does know" (II, 211), nor could a community of primitives possibly be able to accept "rules for future behaviour which they would approve of themselves for any continuance" (II, 204). In Mandeville's view, the first unsocial and cognitively undeveloped brutes could never self-consciously have entered into the morally informed agreements which characterized contemporary theories of

---

[32] John Gay, "The Degenerate Bees," in *The Fables of John Gay*, ed. E. Wright (London: Warne, 1889), Fable x, pp. 253–256.
[33] Inserted after Book ix of the Paris, 1679, edition of La Fontaine's *Fables*.
[34] Pierre Gassendi, "Fifth Set of Objections," in René Descartes, *Works*, ii, pp. 139–140.
[35] *Abrégé de la philosophie de M. Gassendi* (Lyons, 1684), vi, pp. 247–259.
[36] See Pierre Bayle, *The Dictionary Historical and Critical of Mr. Peter Bayle. The Second Edition* (London, 1702); 3rd edition, *To Which is Prefaced The Life of the Author, Revised, Corrected and Enlarged, by Mr. Des Maiseaux, Fellow of the Royal Society* (London, 1734), "Rorarius," Remark c, where Bayle quotes from his March 1684 article in the *Nouvelles de la République des Lettres*.

contract. Instead, Mandeville insisted, societies requiring even the most elementary forms of co-ordination and consent had to have been formed by the artful manipulation of the passions of these unreflective primitives.

This last thesis directly connected Mandeville's enterprise to a well-known subversive tradition of continental social theorizing. His was the most potent version of "the doctrine of Pyrrho,"[37] as George Bluett, an early adversary, put it. It was a doctrine, William Law said, which denied "the Power of *Reason* and *Religion* ... ascrib[ed] all human actions to *Complexion, natural Temper, &c.*," and rested upon a description of men as nothing more than complex animals who responded to their impulses.[38] A primary purpose of these and similar attacks on *The Fable* was to discredit Mandeville by linking his writing to the purportedly atheistic doctrines of Bayle and Bayle's allies in the Republic of Letters, and to the Augustinian rigorism of the most prominent Jansenist divines, most of whose major works had been translated into English during the first decades of the eighteenth century.[39] Both groups had shown that a person's apparent practice of Christian virtue in no way provided an observer of these acts with indubitable information about the underlying motives informing them. Since apparently virtuous acts were rewarded by public esteem, it was in the obvious interest of the vicious to mime the conventional behavioral correlates of Christian piety in order to win the approval of their fellows. Forms of egoism, in other words, manifested themselves according to the socially prescribed conventions of propriety amongst skilled social actors. Moreover, if virtue could reasonably be understood as one of the masks available to fallen men in their pursuit of selfish interests, then the difference between virtue and vice would have nothing to do with behavior, particularly in a being whose will employs reason merely as an instrument to further his own designs. Instead, the distinction between an act which

---

[37] (George Bluett), *An Enquiry Whether a General Practice of Virtue tends to the Wealth or Poverty, Benefit or Disadvantage of a People?* (London, 1725), p. 85.

[38] William Law, *Remarks Upon a Late Book, Entitled, The Fable of the Bees ... In a Letter to the Author: To Which is Added, A Postscript, Containing an Observation or Two upon Mr. Bayle* (London, 1724), p. 53.

[39] For Mandeville's relationship to the theory of the passions in seventeenth-century Augustinian moral reflection see Arthur O. Lovejoy, *Reflections on Human Nature* (Baltimore: Johns Hopkins University Press, 1961), Lectures III–V and, building upon Lovejoy's work, Laurence Dickey, "Pride, Hypocrisy and Civility in Mandeville's Social and Historical Theory," *Critical Review* 4, 3 (Summer 1990), pp. 387–431.

stemmed from selfish desire and one whose source was Christian charity would, of necessity, depend entirely upon the judgement of God as He inspected each human heart.

Two unsettling consequences followed from these explorations in moral pessimism. First, it was assumed that the great majority of mankind merely feigned Christian commitments while being, in reality, driven by self-love. Yet the fact that theirs was in principle indistinguishable from true Christian behavior challenged the conventional assumption that believers who feared hell and yearned for salvation were more powerfully motivated toward virtuous action than were pagans, Jews or atheists. Bayle drew the obvious conclusion: any man, atheist or believer, could make a good subject, since civil conduct required only the outward conformity to standards of propriety produced by social pressure and intersubjective expectations, underwritten by law. The rectitude of a citizen required no spiritually enriched conscience.[40] Second, as was famously suggested by Pierre Nicole in his *Moral Essayes*, just as the selfish, and thus necessarily conflicting, wants of individuals could be harnessed to politically beneficial ends, so too could competing social and economic interests be made to obey similar systematic constraints. Social utility and communal benefit could correctly be understood as unintended consequences of certain historically domesticated forms of self-aggrandizement. The seemingly anarchic tendencies of the scramble for wealth, for example, revealed themselves, at a deeper level, to be structured social regularities attending the common pursuit of material gratification. Gross cupidity and never-satisfied material interest created secret social bonds, for the intersubjective sources of commercial interchange in goods and money provided "no less peace, security, and comfort, than if one were in a Republic of Saints."[41]

---

[40] See the contemporary English translation of Pierre Bayle's *Pensées divers sur le comète* (1683), entitled *Miscellaneous Reflections on the Comet* (London, 1708), pp. 212–225.

[41] See particularly, Pierre Nicole, "Of Grandeur," and "Of Christian Civility," in *Moral Essayes: Contain'd in Several Treatises on Many Important Duties* (London, 1696), pp. 83–128 and 137–149. See too the Huguenot Jacques Abbadie, *The Art of Knowing Oneself: Or, An Inquiry into the Sources of Morality* (Oxford, 1695), pp. 126–187, and Jacques Esprit, *Discourses on the Deceitfulness of Human Virtues* (London, 1706), trans. William Beauvoir Preface and pp. 37–38. On this tradition see Lionel Rothkrug, *Opposition to Louis XIV: The Political and Social Origins of the French Enlightenment* (Princeton University Press, 1965), pp. 52–54; Nannerl Keohane, *Philosophy and the State in France* (Princeton University Press, 1980), pp. 283–311, and Dale Van Kley, "Pierre Nicole, Jansenism and the Morality of Enlightened Self-Interest," in Alan C. Kors and Paul Korshin (eds.), *Anticipations of the Enlightenment* (Philadelphia: University of Pennsylvania Press, 1987), pp. 69–85.

This tradition of argument could be termed Pyrrhonist, and so directly associated with the work of Montaigne, Charron, and their antique predecessors Sextus and Carneades, because of its skepticism about any universal ethical principles informing social life across the spectrum of human communities. Bayle himself helped to establish just this association for eighteenth-century readers in his article "Pyhrro" in the *Dictionary*, and Mandeville, both in *Free Thoughts* and *The Fable*,[42] explicitly and through oblique reference, made extensive use of Bayle's discussion. Skeptical social theory was distinguished by a concentration on what Sextus and his followers called *bios* – the common conduct of daily life whose individual sources and social dynamics were conventionally ignored by philosophers. In the hands of libertines and *dévots*, along with Jansenist sympathizers like La Rochefoucauld, this entailed a concerted attempt to reduce the history of actual social practices to that of politics, understood as struggles for self-assertion, dominance and esteem out of which specific codes of ethics and customs were formed. Moral beliefs and shared habits of life differed from place to place because they were the contingent historical products of diverse cultural experiences. The communal expressions of individual self-regard could best be understood, not simply as varied examples of the essential propensity of fallen men to sin, but as dependent features of the discrete practices by virtue of which egoism had been locally disciplined.

Mandeville remodelled the stark Jansenist contrast between divine injunctions and everyday behavior in ways that often made tacit reference to its skeptical sources. For example, his claim in the Introduction to *The Fable* that the arguments that were to follow applied only to fallen men (1, 3–4) was an almost exact paraphrase of La Rochefoucauld's Apology in the Introduction to the 1666 edition of his *Maxims*; and *The Fable's* notorious assertions that men are "worshippers of themselves" and that their wholly self-interested passions require "dextrous management" derive from the same

---

[42] On Mandeville's borrowings from Bayle see E.D. James, "Faith, Sincerity and Morality: Mandeville and Bayle," in Primer (ed.), *Mandeville Studies*, pp. 43–65, and Irwin Primer, "A Bibliographical Note on Bernard Mandeville's *Free Thoughts*," *Notes and Queries* 214 (May 1969), pp.187–188. Similar distinctions are also apparent in Malebranche's contrast in the *Entretiens sur la métaphysiques et sur la religion suivre des entre tiens sur la mort*, (Paris, 1688) between what he termed *sociétés de religion* and *sociétés de commerce*. They informed the discussions of the libertine Club d'Entresol in Regency Paris, of which Montesquieu was a member, and from whose intellectual environment the chevalier Ramsay's skeptical *Essai sur le gouvernement civil* (Paris, 1720) took its shape.

source.[43] Mandeville set out to compare the other-worldly city of the true believer with the motivations and instrumental reason of actors devoid of non-egotistical interests. This aspect of his project closely adhered to the court tradition of anatomizing the passions which flourished in France, especially within the highest aristocratic circles and court society itself in the generation before he wrote. Like La Rochefoucauld's, these French moral anatomies had as their unstated focus of attention a circumscribed and politically insecure noble elite that conceived of itself as arbitrating society's defining cultural standards. Exposing the mundane, purely self-regarding passions which animated members of this community was a critical and potentially subversive act precisely because they understood themselves as constituting the very medium for enacting the operative distinctions and categories of civilized life. Reducing the aspirations of *les grands* to the level of brute emotional necessity threw into doubt the dominant cultural values which their lives symbolically represented.

Mandeville had only a passing interest in the rigorously exclusive social arena of court society, whose threatened habits of life was the compelling subject of La Rochefoucauld and his contemporaries. As Hegel later put it, they merely mocked Tartuffe. *The Fable*'s enquiry centered instead on what was at once a wider, rapidly expanding and relatively novel domain – the social dynamics of monied wealth in modern commercial states, of which Britain and Holland had become the exemplars. Mandeville inherited from his French predecessors what one might call the natural psychology of *ancien régime* social elites. This psychology stressed the centrality of innate human capacities and passions as the determining agents of personality within their local, elite context, which was taken as representative of the human condition itself. La Rochefoucauld, Pascal and Nicole sought to desanctify *all* pretensions to human greatness; but their recurring subject remained the ideal actor of their own tradition – the honored noble warrior capable of remarkable fortitude in the face of shifting fortune – and thus their critique did not extend to society at large.

---

[43] La Rochefoucauld, *Maxims*, trans. Leonard Tannock (Harmondsworth: Penguin, 1959), Maxim 56, describes men as "worshippers of themselves" and compares them to bees. See too, Jean Lafond, "Mandeville et La Rochefoucauld, ou des avatars de l'augustinisme," in Bernhard König and Jutta Lietz (eds.), *Gestaltung–Umgestaltung: Beiträge zur Geschichte des romanischen Literaturen* (Tübingen: Gunter Narr, 1990), pp. 137–150. I owe this reference to Irwin Primer.

Mandeville significantly re-shaped this ideological inheritance by giving equal prominence to the role of the demands made by the social environment in shaping the emotions of all actors into expressive conjunctions of judgement and passion whose local embodiments could only be realized and understood within the established conventions and beliefs of a given public realm. If the demands of pride and the need for esteem were constant and universal features of the human constitution, desires themselves were nevertheless realized or thwarted only in socially structured, rule-governed interactions with others. Mandeville could at once mock both his republican opponents and (in his final work on the origins of honor) the defenders of aristocratic ideals, because of the truth he claimed to have discovered and sustained: that the conditions of commercial modernity had made the Christian saint, the classical citizen and the noble warrior anachronistic mental deposits of long-vanished or quickly eroding social formations.

Mandeville argued that persons in the recently constituted commercial polities on which *The Fable* concentrated were obliged to respond to a revised structure of social priorities if they were to satisfy their impulses. These persons were driven not merely by the universal appetites for authority and esteem, as were all others: in the centers of European commercial societies outward displays of wealth alone were now widely accepted as a direct index of social power. "People, where they are not known," he observed, "are generally honour'd according to their Clothes and other Accoutrements they have about them;"

from the riches of them we judge of their Wealth, and by their ordering of them we guess at their Understanding. It is this which encourages every Body ... to wear Clothes above his rank, especially in large and populous cities where obscure men may hourly meet with fifty strangers to one acquaintance, and consequently have the pleasure of being esteemed by a vast majority, not as what they are, but what they appear to be. (I, 127–128)[44]

The Fable consolidated a revolution in the understanding of the relationship between motives and acts largely begun in France by viewing commerce and sociability as reciprocal and historically decisive features of the modern dynamics of self-regard. Mandeville showed that the aggressive pursuit of wealth had now to be under-

---

[44] Compare, Blaise Pascal, *Pensées* ed. A.J. Krailsheimer (London: Penguin, 1966), Nos. 44 and 89.

stood not as an activity properly confined to marginalized minorities, but as central to the self-definition of urban and commercial populations. The enlarged mechanisms of and opportunities for consumption, which Mandeville described with characteristic relish, emerged in *The Fable* as the distinguishing mark of commercial sociability, and thus a necessarily central concern of public policy and politicians rather than the exclusive domain of moralists and divines. Mandeville claimed that his work for the first time systematically comprehended from the perspective of society itself the consequences of the behavior of persons for whom monied wealth encouraged those forms of excessive self-display that were in effect the vehicles through which they established their identities. While "[i]t is certain," he wrote, "that the fewer Desires a Man has and the less he covets, the more easy he is to himself... and the less he requires to be waited upon, the more he will be beloved and the less trouble he is in a Family ... But ... what Benefit can these things be of ... to ... Nations?" Rather,

the Fickle Strumpet that invents new Fashions every Week ... the profuse Rake and lavish heir, that scatter about their Money without Wit or Judgement, buy everything they see, and either destroy or give it away the next Day, the Covetous and perjur'd Villain that squeezed an immense Treasure from the Tears of Widows and Orphans, and left the Prodigals the money to Spend: It is these ... that we stand in need of ... And it is folly to imagine that Great and Wealthy nations can subsist, and be at once Powerful and Polite without. (I, 355–356)

MEDICINE AND MORALS

Mandeville, then, repositioned many of the materials he first found in Bayle and his Augustinian predecessors in an altered context; and he continued to rely upon their psychological discovery that the passions need not be policed by force alone, but could be harnessed by the artful manipulations of the ruling orders. Nicole put this point quite dramatically in his influential essay, "Of Grandeur."[45] "Left to their own desires," he said, men

are worse than Lions, Bears or Tygres. Every one would devour his neighbour; and it is by means of Policy and Laws that these Wild Beasts are become tractible, and that from them we reap all those human services that might be had from pure Charity.

[45] Nicole, *Moral Essayes*, II, pp. 98–99.

What Nicole called "flattery"[46] could be employed by the "masters of opinion," in Pascal's phrase,[47] to socialize self-love. In the idiom of *The Fable*, "the skillful management of the dextrous politician" could transform private vices into public benefits by channelling pride in socially useful directions. Mandeville learned from these writers that reason could most usefully be understood as an instrumental feature of the individual's purposes, animated by a rampant egoism, rather than as the directive faculty which shaped desire. What, in its recent Augustinian expressions, Christian moral psychology rigorously condemned as sin reappeared in *The Fable* as an ironic, and for Mandeville's chosen audience a bitter, requirement of their own social expectations. For in "civil society," Mandeville said, defending his project,

the Avarice of Some and the Profaneness of Others, together with the Pride and Envy of most Individuals are absolutely necessary to raise them to a great and powerful, and, in the Language of the World, polite Nation. It seems still to be a greater Paradox, that natural as well as moral Evil and the very Calamities we pray against, do not only contribute to this worldly Greatness, but a certain Proportion of them is so necessary to all Nations that it is not to be conceiv'd how Society should subsist upon Earth exempt from all Evil, both natural and moral.[48]

Yet despite his indebtedness to an established discourse for the analysis of the passions, neither were Mandeville's most significant claims ever fully consonant with, nor were they simply derived from, the French *moralistes* and theologians to whom his adversaries so often referred when they sought to discredit him. Initially dependent upon the writings of St. Augustine, their arguments rested upon two important premises. First, they claimed that an unbridgeable gulf divided souls infused with the gift of grace from all others. Both Jansenists and Calvinists insisted that while persons not in receipt of efficacious or purifying grace could lead a serviceable life by following the socially useful principles of *honnêteté*, they could never sufficiently free themselves from vice to escape eternal damnation. The unregenerate were forever bound to the power of their sinful wills, and their acts were devoid of the charity which spiritually distinguished God's elect. The social utility of an action could never for Pascal or Nicole earn the title of virtuous. Virtue was not a social category in their

---

[46] Nicole, "Of Charity and Self-Love," p. 80.   [47] Pascal, *Pensées*, No. 828.
[48] Mandeville, *A Letter to Dion*, p. 21.

view, but rather an absolute quality of purely personal decisions; a matter of individual conscience wholly irrelevant to the requirements of society. Though it was an admirable, if paradoxical, fact that men might succeed in living together amicably by following their interests under the guidance of the sovereign, this in no way implied that one ought to conclude that morality should therefore be understood in terms of social utility alone. For strictly to identify morality with legislation and public prosperity would be to render religion super-fluous and to deprive men of the possibility of salvation.[49] Second, and of equal importance, seventeenth-century Augustinians held that the sinful majority of men were fit subjects for moral instruction (and thus condemnation). Following the orthodox assumption that human beings, as a species, possessed qualitatively distinct spiritual capacities, they argued that men could properly be understood as potential moral beings precisely because human action could *not* be explained primarily in terms of physical organization. While medical and physiological knowledge could, in this view, augment our understanding of and ability to minister to physical needs, it was in principle incapable of significantly altering our moral understanding.

Mandeville's morals, by contrast, rested on what he insisted were scientific foundations, explicitly grounded in a thorough-going naturalistic anthropology. For him, the image of a virtuous but depopulated terrestial Jerusalem was nothing more than an absurd figure of derision (I, 232; 235–238). In this way Mandeville abandoned the Augustinian premises, not only of Calvin and the Jansenists, but also of Bayle.[50] Mandeville chose to call his project an "anatomy" of "the invisible part of man" because he thought that persons living in modern conditions had lost touch with the "natural causes" of their actions (I, 145). Highly polished civilized social actors could hardly "endure to see so much of [their] own nakedness," as one of *The Fable*'s characters put it, because they had thoroughly internalized the codes

---

[49] Jacob Viner, *Religious Thought and Economic Society*, ed. Jacques Melitz and Donald Winch (Durham: Duke University Press, 1978), Chapter 3, usefully explores these distinctions.

[50] For the important divergences between Mandeville and Bayle see Maria Emanuella Scribiano, "La Presenza di Bayle nell'opera di Bernard Mandeville," *Giorale Critico della Filosophia Italiana* 60 (1981), pp. 186–220; Scribiano, *Natura umana e società competitiva: Studio sul Mandeville* (Milan: Feltrinelli, 1980); Pierre Rétat, *Le Dictionnaire de Bayle et la lutte philosophique au XVIIIe siècle* (Paris: Société D'Edition "Les Belles Lettres," 1971), pp. 223–225; and Elizabeth Labrousse, *Pierre Bayle* (The Hague: Nijhoff, 1964), II, pp. 117–125. Mandeville quotes or paraphrases Bayle's *Miscellaneous Reflections on the Comet* or the *Dictionary* in *Fable*, I, pp. 5; 55; 98–100; 167–168, and 214–215; and in *Fable*, II, pp. 55, 104, 216, and 316. In the Preface to *Free Thoughts* he acknowledges his "great use" of the *Dictionary*.

of law and morality which systematically suppressed the instinctual
sources of communal life, thereby erasing them from consciousness.
When critics like Berkeley objected that Mandeville treated persons
as if they were nothing more than animals, repeating a complaint put
into the mouth of Horatio in *The Fable* (II, 139), they astutely captured
a central feature of Mandeville's analytical enterprise. According to
George Bluett, Mandeville's "definitions look more like an account of
some machines, than of the faculties of a human soul . . . *and not those of
the cleverest sort either*. There are several brutes of a much nobler
Make."[51] "You tell [your readers]," William Law accused Mandeville, "that you [like they] are a mere *Animal* govern'd by appetites
over which you have no power; that is, you describe yourself as a
Machine."[52] Law's Calvinist revulsion at the prospect of comprehending the motivations of men in this reductive way was, in addition,
virtually identical to that of Jansenist theologians. Antoine Arnauld
and his colleague Nicole both made generous use of animal metaphors
and analogies to describe the loathsome moral condition of sinners.
But each insisted that the attempt actually to reduce human to merely
animal passions was a false and dangerous tactic of argument, one
most recently employed by skeptics to subvert Christian ethics. It was
an argument intended, like Mandeville's, to applaud the workings of
pride and, in so doing, to justify the literally beastly actions of
unregenerate sinners.[53]

  Mandeville's denial of any innate human propensity for sociability
followed directly from his rejection of the Cartesian contrast between
the springs of animal behavior and the workings of human passions.
In human beings alone, Descartes argued – and Nicole and his
Jansenist colleagues strictly followed him in this[54] – the passions were
under the direction of the rational soul; all other animals behaved as
strict automata. Mandeville took his medical degree at Leiden during

---

[51] George Bluett, *Enquiry*, pp. 55–56.   [52] William Law, *Remarks*, p. 71.
[53] Pierre Nicole, *Visionaires*, Letter VIII, in *Les Imaginaires et Visionaires* (Cologne, 1683), and the
   posthumously published *Traité de l'âme des bêtes* (Paris, 1737). See Leonora Cohen Rosenfeld,
   From Beast-Machine to Man-Machine (Oxford University Press, 1941), pp. 281–299, for
   Jansenist opinion on animal automatism. See too the review of this question in the article
   "L'âme des bêtes" in Diderot's *Encyclopédie ou Dictionnaire raisonnée des sciences, des arts et des
   métiers, par une société de gens de lettres*, ed. D. Diderot and Jean d'Alembert (Elmsford, New
   York: Pergamon Reprint, 1984), I, pp. 342–353.
[54] See Rosenfeld, *From Beast Machine to Man-Machine*, pp. 54–56, where La Fontaine is quoted as
   saying in disgust that "there was hardly a *solitaire* who didn't talk of automata . . . They said
   that animals were like clocks; that the cries they emitted when struck, were only the noise of a
   little spring which had been touched."

a period of intense controversy between Cartesians and their resolutely mechanist opponents on the question of animal automatism. By the time he began writing *The Fable*, he had thoroughly abandoned the pertinent Cartesian views that he had held as a student, and had adopted the position that there was no qualitative distinction between men and beasts. He claimed, *pace* Descartes, that animals, just as men, do feel, that men and animals have nearly identical passions, even including envy (I, 132; 137), and that animals, like men, have calculating minds. This was the skeptical line of reasoning revived by Montaigne, La Mothe le Vayer, Charron and, amongst natural philosophers, most importantly by Gassendi and then by Bernier in his well-known compendium of Gassendi's doctrines. While beasts do not speak our language, so Gassendi argued against Descartes, they have their own forms of discourse. Animal intelligence does not differ from ours in kind; such differences as exist are a function of the varying degrees of physiological complexity in human and other animal organisms. Bayle surveyed the controversy between Cartesians and their opponents on this issue in considerable detail, and he pointedly commented on the vigor of this "Epicurean" challenge which Cartesians had never been able to refute.[55]

Mandeville's distinctive blend of physiological and moral reasoning was, in fact, an unintended outgrowth of the Cartesian program for the sciences. In the *Discourse on Method* Descartes asserted a connection between medicine and morals, laying the foundations of a mechanist physiology whose considerable potential relevance to moral philosophy was almost immediately appreciated, especially in France. *The Passions of the Soul* provided a sketch of this enterprise, but it was one that Descartes never developed adequately. Indeed, his *De L'Homme* was already scientifically outmoded when it appeared posthumously, in 1664. Followers of Gassendi's revived Epicureanism took the project of a medical and physiological analysis of ethical beliefs and moral motivations with absolute seriousness, however,[56] as may be seen in the "philosophical" guide to medical practice of Samuel Sorbière, Sextus' translator,[57] and the author of a short

---

[55] *Dictionary*, "Rorarius."

[56] See Anthony Levi, SJ, *French Moralists: The Theory of the Passions, 1585–1649* (Oxford: Clarendon Press, 1964), pp. 237–245; J.S. Spink, *French Free Thought from Gassendi to Voltaire* (London: Athlone Press, 1960), pp. 215–225; and M. Foster, *Lectures on the History of Physiology* (Cambridge University Press, 1901), Chapter 6.

[57] See Richard H. Popkin, "Samuel Sorbière's Translation of Sextus Empiricus," *Journal of the History of Ideas* 14, 4 (1953), pp. 617–621.

biography which prefaced the most accessible edition of Gassendi's work.[58] Mandeville vigorously adopted this reductive stance as a basis for his own arguments about the wants of men when he asserted an equivalence in kind between human and animal passions. As a central feature of his conjectural account of social formation, he insisted that the consensual regularities imposed by systems of morality formed part of a larger process – the literal domestication of the savage mind.

Mandeville sought to ground his social theory physiologically, arguing early in his writing career that "in knowing the world, was comprehended the understanding of one's Self," which requires "the Study of *Anatomy* and the inward Government of Bodies."[59] He also seems to have understood the scientific disputes in which he partici- pated as a struggle, in great measure, for ideological dominance, in which philosophers of the new science as well as physiologist– physicians like himself engaged their opponents within the larger arena of ethics. All hypotheses, like hoop-skirts, have circumscribed historical careers, governed by their "ability to please" and to generate in others expressions of esteem:

> An Hypothesis, when once it has been a little while establish'd, becomes like a Sovereign, and receives the same Homage and Respect from its Vassals, as if it was Truth it self ... But when another Hypothesis is broach'd ... and being likewise well contriv'd, [it] gets a considerable number of Followers: Then you see all that fought under the Banners of the old Hypothesis bristle up, and every Man of Note amongst them thinks himself personally injured, and in Honour obliged to stand by it with his Life and Fortune. Now all Arts and Sciences are ransack'd, and whatever can be drawn from Wit, Elo- quence, or Learning, is produced to maintain their own Liege Hypothesis, and destroy the upstart one.[60]

These proto-Kuhnian reflections on the history of science were not meant as a serious comment on epistemology, which hardly interested Mandeville, but as a telling example from medicine and physiology themselves of how wholly natural desires dispose human beings to

---

[58] Samuel Sorbière, *Avis à un jeune médecin sur la manière dont il se doit comporter en la practique de la médecine* (Lyons, 1672), and Samuel Soberius, "De vita et moribus Petri Gassendi," in Pierre Gassendi, *Syntagma philosohiae Epicuri* (Amsterdam, 1684).

[59] Mandeville, *The Virgin Unmask'd* (1709) (Delmar, New York: Scholars' Facsimiles, 1975), p. 123.

[60] *A Treatise on Hypochondriak and Hysterik Passions* (London, 1711), p. 125. A revised second edition appeared in 1730 as *A Treatise on Hypochondriack and Hysterik Diseases*. For a similar conception of what would now be termed competing paradigms in social analysis see, *Free Thoughts*, p. 84, and *Fable*, II, p. 92.

seek the approbation of their fellows, thereby necessarily politicizing even scientific activity. Mandeville was a professed adherent of the "empyric" methods he found in Van Helmont and Sydenham.[61] The "upstart" hypothesis to which he first referred in his medical *Treatise* of 1711 was iatromechanism, which explained physiology, pathology and therapeutics in corpuscular and mechanical terms.[62] In the company of others like Boerhave,[63] Mandeville associated this view with Giorgio Baglivi (1668–1707), a professor at the Sapienza at Rome and member of the Royal Society since 1697, whose *De praxis medica* (1696) declared that physicians had become slaves to (especially Cartesian) systems at the expense of clear clinical obser-vations.[64] Baglivi's text was cited repeatedly by Mandeville's spokes-man Philiporo, the "lover of experience," in the *Treatise on Hypochon-driack and Hysterik Diseases*, in which Baglivi's "aphoristic medicine" receives Mandeville's greatest praise. The work itself revolves about a series of aphorisms and has as one of its central premises what Baglivi understood as the Baconian postulate that any larger enquiry into human purposes had to take "nature," in this case biomechanisms, into strict account.[65]

Mandeville's medical investigations were undertaken in the wake of the overthrow of the humoreal aetiology of melancholy and its effective replacement with one which centered entirely on the nervous system.[66] One of the key figures in this transformation was Thomas Willis, the author of *De anima brutorum* (1672), whose second edition of 1683 appeared in the same year as his *Two Discourses Concerning the Soul of Brutes*, just at the time that the Gassendian Walter Charleton chose to lecture on several problems of the "animal oeconomy" before a general audience in the Critlerian Theatre of the London College of Physicians, where he frequently referred to contemporary medical

[61] *Treatise*, pp. 34–37; 52–54.
[62] For the rise to prominence of iatromechanism in physiology and medicine during the generation in which Mandeville wrote, and its subsequent decline, see Theodore M. Brown, "From Mechanism to Vitalism in Eighteenth-Century Physiology," *Journal of the History of Biology* 7, 2 (1974), pp. 179–216. I owe this reference to Stephen Straker.
[63] G.A. Lindebloom, *Herman Boerhave* (London: Methuen, 1968), p. 7.
[64] Translated as *The Practice of Physic* (London, 1696 and 1704), with a second edition, London, 1723.
[65] See, for example, Baglivi's denunciation of "the idols of physicians" in *The Practice of Physic*, Chapter 13.
[66] R.A. Collins, "Private Vices, Public Benefits: Dr. Mandeville and the Body Politic" (D. Phil. thesis, Oxford University, 1988), and Francis McKee, "The Earlier Works of Bernard Mandeville, 1685–1715" (Ph D Thesis, Glasgow University, 1991) explore this subject.

theory.[67] Willis cited Gassendi's authority in arguing that man is a two-souled creature, with the subordinate or corporeal soul containing the life principle.[68] This bodily soul contained in turn two parts, a vital or "flamie" soul rooted in the blood, and a sensitive or "lucid" soul rooted in the brain. An iatromechanist, Willis like Sydenham advocated a physiological psychology which conceived of the passions and related mental phenomena as nothing but the physical and adaptive results of the animal spirits responding to external stimuli within the brain and nervous system. The sensitive soul man shared with brutes, while the rational soul was his alone. Willis argued that brutes must have souls since they learn from experience, and that in man the superior soul governs the corporeal one, which is seated in the middle part of the brain.[69] Willis then quoted Gassendi, claiming that "the acquisition and loss of an habit, stands in the Power of the Brain and Phantasie, [which is] a subject purely corporeal,"[70] and is therefore a proper subject of medical and physiological analysis. Importantly, Willis' argument concerning the processes of learning and habit implied that once this division between rational and corporeal souls had been made, and then put into the service of medical thinking, an increasing proportion of the powers of the putatively rational soul immediately becomes assigned to the sensitive one by physiologist–physicians in sympathy with this physicalist program. Indeed, the shift was endorsed by Willis himself in the second edition of his work.

Mandeville went even farther. He supported Baglivi and the "practical" Sydenham, as opposed to the "speculative" Willis,[71] not because he disagreed with the principles which Willis began to enunciate, but because Mandeville thought that his speculative medicine in fact discouraged close attendance upon patients themselves. In the *Treatise* it is Misomedon, Philiporo's interlocutor, who stays in his closet and reads medical theories, while Philiporo engages in actual practice at the bedside. Willis served as a half-way house for Mandeville as he travelled along the theoretical road to a straightforward physicalist reductionism. Participating in a broad current of

[67] Walter Charleton, *Three Anatomic Lectures* (London, 1683).
[68] See R.G. Frank, "Thomas Willis and His Circle: Brain and Mind in Seventeenth-Century Medicine," in G.S. Rousseau (ed.), *The Languages of Psyche: Mind and Brain in Enlightenment Thought* (Berkeley: University of California Press, 1990), pp. 104–146.
[69] Thomas Willis, *Two Discourses, Concerning the Soul of Brutes*, ed. S. Diamond, trans. S. Pordage (London, 1683) (Gainesville: Scholar's Facsimiles, 1971) pp. 39–42.
[70] Willis, *Two Discourses*, p. 42.   [71] Mandeville, *Treatise* (1730 edn), p. 22.

materialist argument initiated by Locke's suggestion that God could super-add the power of thought to matter,[72] Mandeville argued that there was no verifiable evidence to suggest that the soul was *anything but* material and mortal.[73] Only pride, he provocatively claimed, prevented this hypothesis from being accepted by both physicians and philosophers.[74]

This materialist physiological premise became the foundation in natural philosophy of Mandeville's wider enterprise. His account of social formation began with an examination of cognitively immature "brutes" who populated the "wild state of nature," and then sought to explain how "Savage Man," an "untaught," self-regarding animal, became the tame, sociable creature celebrated by philosophers (1, 46). Mandeville argued that it was precisely the animal impulses naturally disposing men to seek their own satisfactions that made them fit subjects for manipulation by the "lawgivers" who civilized the race as they appealed to the universal appetite of pride. Flattery was the "bewitching Engine" of an ideological project which

extoll'd the Excellency of our Nature above other Animals ... bestow'd a thousand Encomiums on the Rationality of our Souls ... [and] laid before [men] how unbecoming it was the Dignity of such sublime Creatures to be solicitous about gratifying those Appetites, which they had in common with Brutes. (1, 43)

Following the physiological materialists who argued that men were essentially distinguished from one another by their differing temperaments established at birth, Mandeville hypothesized that in the first ages of the race the strong and cunning induced the weak to believe "that it was more beneficial for every Body to conquer than indulge his appetites, and much better to mind the Public than what seemed his private interests" (1, 42). While moral virtue, understood "as the Political offspring which Flattery begot upon Pride" (1, 51), was a mythical and allegorical figure of both the satiric and Augustinian traditions in which Mandeville wrote, it became in his hands an explanatory device put at the service of an unremitting naturalism.

Mandeville argued that the origins of morality, and thus of the

---

[72] For the Enlightenment history of this issue see John W. Yolton, *Thinking Matter: Materialism in Eighteenth-Century Britain* (Minneapolis: University of Minnesota Press, 1983), which stresses the importance of doctors and physiologists in this debate, and *Locke and French Materialism* (Oxford: Clarendon Press, 1991), p. 177, where Yolton points out the association of Mandeville with this tradition of argument.

[73] Mandeville, *Treatise*, pp. 50–51.   [74] Mandeville, *Treatise*, p. 53.

social discipline required for the rule of elites, followed from the discovery by these elites of what he called the "imaginary" reward of praise to which complex animal organisms responded. Flattery was employed to tame men by generating within these prideful creatures a conception of self constituted in part by the opinions of others. Only creatures instructed in the rhetoric of honor and the theology of shame could then introject politically fabricated ideals of virtuous conduct, ideals "by which a rational Creature is kept in Awe for Fear of it Self, and an Idol is set up, that shall be its own Worshiper" (1, 48). *The Fable* meant to explain "the manner in which savage man was broke" (1, 46). Mandeville sought to account for the false but socially necessary belief that virtue was the distinguishing feature of the human race by subsuming socialized men under the larger category of domesticated animals.

Mandeville thus attempted to derive an explanation of moral motivation from the few psychological facts about human nature which were strongly supported by both the claims of experience and scientific inquiry. Moral behavior could suitably be understood to arise from the reactions of an egoistic and necessitous creature to the opinions of others because these opinions have important tangible consequences for one's well-being. Men come to have an interest in keeping their promises, for example, precisely because of their painful realization that others have an interest in their doing so; by virtue of their approval and disapproval of the actions of others, men mete out rewards and punishments. "Men are naturally selfish, unruly and head-strong creatures," Mandeville argued in *Free Thoughts*,

what makes them sociable is their necessity and consciousness of standing in need of others' help . . . and what makes the assistance voluntarily given and lasting, are the gains or profit accruing to industry for services it does to others, which in a well order'd society enables everybody, who in some thing or other will be serviceable to the public to purchase the assistance of others in other instances . . . [H]e that is able to purchase [the chief comforts of life], is in the vogue of the world reckoned the most happy.[75]

If human beings quite understandably seek the approval of their fellows, and thus unwittingly acquire an interest in the continuation of normal intercourse, "politicians" could then seek to promote this

---

[75] Mandeville, *Free Thoughts*, p. 283.

balance by "playing the Passions against one another" (I, 145) once society becomes firmly established.

Mandeville's hypothetical history of social origins, then, was a foundational hypothesis meant to sustain and further encourage a thoroughgoing empirical discussion of the micro-processes of social interaction. In defending his work, Mandeville claimed that *The Fable* rested upon scientific principles, a point he clearly intended to convey to his audience when he cited the work of Gassendi as the philosophical foundation of his "manner of writing" (II, 21). This assertion of influence, repeated by Mandeville in the 1730 editions of his *Treatise on Hypochondriack and Hysterik Diseases*, where he declared himself to be Gassendi's disciple,[76] had a distinct ideological resonance in the early eighteenth century. It was commonly assumed, as Francis Hutcheson put it in his attack on *The Fable*, that "all sects, except the Epicureans, owned that kind affections were natural to men,"[77] while William Law claimed that *The Fable*'s definition of man "seems to suit a *Wolf*, or a *Bear* ... or a *Grecian Philosopher*."[78] Encouraged by the growing influence of Epicurus and Gassendi, Mandeville published at the end of nearly a half-century of anxious debate over the skeptical implications of naturalism,[79] a debate that Richard Bentley, the first Boyle Lecturer, following the views of Robert Boyle himself, sought to represent as a dangerous morally skeptical current within the community of scientists.[80] Gassendi was the first post-Copernican natural philosopher of significance to attempt to rescue the empiricism and stress on pleasure (*voluptas*) in the doctrines of Epicurus from historical obscurity and moral opprobrium. Epicurus, he argued, was a uniquely important source of modern advances in natural philosophy; and contrary to received opinion, Gassendi asserted that

[76] Mandeville, *Treatise* (1730 edition), p. 21, a claim not made in the first edition of 1711.
[77] Francis Hutcheson, *A Collection of Letters* (1723 and 1750) in *Collected Works* (Hildesheim: Olms Reprint, 1971), 7, p. 143.   [78] Law, *Remarks*, p. 2.
[79] See T.F. Mayo, *Epicurus in England (1650–1725)* (Dallas, Texas: Southwest Press, 1934), especially pp. 185–200; R.G. Spiller, *"Concerning Natural Experimental Philosophie": Meric Casaubon and the Royal Society* (The Hague: Nijhoff, 1980), Chapter 5, "Epicurus and the New Philosophy"; and Richard W.F. Kroll, *The Material World: Literate Culture in the Restoration and Early Eighteenth Century* (Baltimore: Johns Hopkins University Press, 1991), Chapters 3–5.
[80] Richard Bentley, *The Folly and Unreasonableness of Atheism, demonstrated from the Advantage and Pleasure of a Religious Life, The Faculties of Human Souls, The Structure of Animate Bodies, and the Origin and Frame of the World* (1692) (Glasgow, 1813), in which Bentley's notes on Lucretius are reproduced. On Boyle's view see J.J. Macintosh, "Robert Boyle on Epicurean Atheism," in Margaret J. Osler (ed.), *Atoms, Pneuma and Tranquility: Epicurean and Stoic Themes in European Thought* (Cambridge University Press, 1991), pp. 197–219.

Epicurus' system of ethics was compatible with Christianity.[81] The naturalistic account of social origins derived from Lucretius and Epicurus gained its importance during the Enlightenment from four major sources: the famous series of quotations from the *Sovran Maxims*, a collection of Epicurus' writings produced by Diogenes Laertius at the close of Book x of the *Lives of the Philosophers*; the dissemination of Gassendi's writings, particularly by Walter Charleton and the Royal Society atomists like Thomas Stanley, whose *History of Philosophy* treated Gassendi as a seminal figure, translated some of Gassendi's work and was arguably conceived along Gassendian lines;[82] Bernier's compendium of Gassendi's ethical doctrines; and Bayle's *Dictionary*, in which Gassendi was credited with the crucial accomplishment of having introduced Sextus to the moderns.[83] By the early eighteenth century these doctrines were commonly regarded as materialist, if not atheist,[84] and associated with physiologists and physicians like Mandeville who enjoyed a reputation for impiety.[85] They quickly assumed an important place on "the stage" of European philosophy according to Leibnitz,[86] were denounced by Christian physicians for their immoralism,[87] and became implicated in a radical current of social theorizing amply discussed in Diderot's *Encyclopédie*.[88] Mandeville

---

[81] Gassendi published his *De vita et moribus Epicuri* in 1647 and the *Philosophae Epicuri Syntagma* in 1649. On the relation of these arguments to contemporary ethics and natural philosophy see Richard Popkin, *The History of Scepticism From Erasmus to Spinoza* (Berkeley: University of California Press, 1979), pp. 99–109; 202–215 and 273–275; Margaret Osler, "Providence and Divine Will in Gassendi's View of Scientific Knowledge," *Journal of the History of Ideas* 44 (1983), pp. 549–560; L.T. Sarasohn, "The Ethical and Political Philosophy of Pierre Gassendi," *Journal of the History of Philosophy* 20 (1982), pp. 239–261; Margaret J. Osler, "Fortune, Fate and Divination: Gassendi's Voluntarist Theology and the Baptism of Epicureanism," in Osler (ed.), *Atoms, Pneuma and Tranquility*: pp. 155–174; and Frederick Vaughan, *The Tradition of Political Hedonism* (New York: Fordham University Press, 1982), pp. 43–51.

[82] Walter Charleton, *Physiologia Epicuro-Gassendo-Charltoniana* (London, 1654) and Thomas Stanley, "The Doctrine of Epicurus," in *History of Philosophy*, Part XIII (London, 1660). In *A Voyage to England* (Paris, 1664) (London, 1702), p. 38, Samuel Sorbière discussed the English dispute between Cartesians and Gassendians. See the angry comments of Thomas Spratt, *Observations on M. de Sorbière's Voyage* (London, 1665), pp. 241–242. For Gassendi's importance in English natural philosophy see Robert Kargon, *Atomism in England from Harriot to Newton* (Oxford: Clarendon Press, 1966), pp. 63–93.   [83] *Dictionary*, "Pyrrho."

[84] David Berman, *A History of Atheism in Britain* (London: Croom Helm, 1988), Chapters 1–2.

[85] See, for example, G. Purshall, *Essay on the Mechanical Fabric of the Universe* (London, 1708). See too, Spink, *French Free Thought*, pp. 224–225.

[86] Gottfried Wilhelm von Leibnitz, *New Essays on Human Understanding*, trans. J. Bennett and Peter Remnant (Cambridge University Press, 1981), IV.2.14.

[87] See, for example, Nicholas Robinson, *The Christian Philosopher* (London, 1741), p. 120, who attacked contemporary physicians "in Favour of Vice and Immorality" as followers of Mandeville.   [88] Diderot, "Epicurus," *Encyclopédie*, v, pp. 783–785.

could be viewed as a dangerous "Epicurean atheist" nearly a generation after he wrote, as well as one of the most important inheritors of continental skepticism, according to William Warburton,[89] precisely because in his hands the naturalism of Epicurus, the "pious atheist" praised by Bayle,[90] appeared to have been given modern scientific foundations.

In *Free Thoughts* Mandeville intended to discomfort his readers with the reflection that Epicurus, "the worst of heritics ... with an hypothesis altogether absurd and contradictory, [is] able to explain what we experience a hundred times better than orthodox Christians do."[91] He then explicitly located *The Fable* within an Epicurean tradition of argument (ii, 210–214), espousing the Lucretian view that nature is not a vehicle for moral improvement but, rightly understood, could be used to liberate us from its tyrannical demands.[92] Mandeville quoted Lucretius in support of the claim that men were not naturally sociable (i, 147–148). He further provided a sketch of Epicurus' views (ii, 252) drawn from Jacques du Rondel, the Calvinist author of the laudatory *La Vie d'Epicure*,[93] and an important authority for both Bayle,[94] and John Digby, Epicurus' most notable English expositor, who emphasized du Rondel's praise of Gassendi and reminded his readers that Epicurus had recommended the study of medicine as the best training for an observer of mankind.[95] *De rerum natura* was considered the most complete system of atheism in print during the early decades of the eighteenth century, not least because the natural philosophy inspired by Lucretius was thought to lead directly to the hypothesis of a wholly deterministic explanation of the universe, to irreligion and to a sybaritic life of morally unbridled passion. It was standardly associated with the radicalism, both philosophic and political, of heretics like Spinoza and Toland, and

[89] William Warburton, *The Divine Legation of Moses* (1738 and 1741) (London: Cadell and Davies, 1811), Book i, pp. 232 and 280–281.

[90] *Dictionary*, "Epicurus."   [91] Mandeville, *Free Thoughts*, p. 112.

[92] See too, Remark o in *Fable*, i, especially p. 147, and compare *Fable*, ii, pp. 309–10 on Epicurean atomism.

[93] Jacques du Rondel, *La Vie d'Epicure* (Amsterdam and Paris, 1679). In a later Latin edition (Amsterdam, 1693), p. 3, du Rondel praised Gassendi as "the most illustrious of the philosophers."

[94] "Pereira," *Dictionary*. Bayle was du Rondel's colleague at the protestant college at Sedan before both emigrated to Holland when the school's operations were suspended in 1681.

[95] John Digby, *Epicurus's Morals, Translated from the Greek by John Digby, Esq. with Comments and Reflections Taken out of Several Authors* (London, 1712), pp. 8 and 125–126.

libertines like Saint-Evremond. Orthodox moralists, moderate clergymen and members of scientific societies themselves reasonably
suspected, with Richard Bentley, that one could not rely upon
Lucretius as a source for natural philosophy without being absorbed
by the immorality and explicit paganism of his work.[96] The reduction
of human to animal was a signal feature of the dangers posed by
Lucretian and Epicurean "atheists," who as Bentley put it, "join the
two notions [of mind and body] together and believe brutes to be
rational or sensitive machines."[97] Available in at least six Latin
editions published since 1675,[98] Lucretius' long poem was famously
translated into English by Thomas Creech in an edition of 1682,
whose notes Bayle praised in the *Dictionary*.[99] When Jean Barbeyrac
published his translation of Pufendorf in 1709, and prefaced it with
with a vastly influential historical sketch of the history of morality and
foundations of natural law, it was the modern revival of these ancient
skeptical views that he found most disturbing.[100] They were doctrines
that Jean Le Clerc, Bayle's unrelenting critic and Barbeyrac's most
esteemed modern authority, claimed to underwrite a perverse "pagan
history . . . in which men live in caves, run in forests like wild beasts,
and [only] afterwards come together . . . [in society]."[101]

The Epicurean provenance of *The Fable*'s most basic and influential
argument, Mandeville's conjectural account of social formation, is
even more striking when compared to the section on the socialization
of mankind in *Epicurus's Morals*, Digby's notorious translation and

[96] See, for example, Richard Bentley, *A Confutation of Atheism from the Origin and Frame of the World* (London, 1697), p. 2.

[97] Richard Bentley, *The Folly of Atheism and (what is now called) Deism* (London, 1693), Sermon VI, p. 13.

[98] Two more English editions were published in 1717 and 1754; Glasgow editions appeared in 1749 and 1759. Three French translations appeared during the seventeenth century. For the French context see Spink, *French Free Thought*, pp. 103–105.

[99] Thomas Creech, *Lucretius his Six Books of Epicurean Philosophy: And Manilus his Five Books* (London, 1700). Creech also translated Plutarch's "The Life of Cleomenes," in *Plutarch's Lives* (London, 1685), IV, pp. 570–627, the name of Mandeville's principal spokesman in *The Fable*. Creech's suicide in 1700 provoked a philosophical scandal in English libertine circles and was the point of reference for Mandeville's discussion of Cato's taking of his own life in *Fable*, I, pp. 209–210 and 335–6. See S.E. Sprott, *The English Debate on Suicide: From Donne to Hume* (La Salle, Illinois: Open Court Press, 1961), pp. 72–76.

[100] Jean Barbeyrac, "An Historical and Critical Account of the Science of Morality and the Progress it has made in the World from the Earliest Times down to the Publication of this Work," in *Samuel Pufendorf, The Law of Nature and Nations . . .*, trans. E. Carew (London, 1749), 5th edition.

[101] Jean Le Clerc, *Sentiments de quelques théologiens de Hollande sur l'histoire critique du Vieux Testament* (Amsterdam, 1685), p. 422.

commentary of 1712,[102] published two years before the *The Fable*'s first edition. As Digby put it,

Epicurus ... had a Notion that ... Primitive Men ... liv'd after a Beastlike manner ... from whence it happened that the *Strongest* always overcame the *Weakest* ... *they*, who had a clearer Sight than *others* made it their *business* to improve the *rest*, and make 'em know, that it was of the last Consequence to make *Laws* ... [Epicurus] looked upon it as a thing impossible that *Nature* should give 'em so perfect an Idea of that *mutual Justice which the Laws enforce*, [and so the first lawgivers] were obliged to have recourse to *Divine Power*, to make their Laws receiv'd with applause.[103]

Digby distinguished the Epicurean from the Pyrrhonist by insisting that only the former knew how to subdue the passions. But he claimed for both the insight, only fully developed by Epicurus, that if "one would be a good *Naturalist*, 'twas in order to become a Moral *Philosopher*."[104] It was precisely as a naturalist that Mandeville had praised Epicurus in *Free Thoughts on Religion*, while prudently distancing himself from the atheistic associations attaching to Epicureanism.[105] Mandeville found that such tactical evasions were no longer necessary after he encountered Gassendi's Christianized interpretations of Epicurus in the 1720s, most probably in Bernier's rendition of Book III of the *Syntagma*, "Three Discourses of Happiness, Virtue and Liberty."[106] Drawing upon Gassendi's work, and wishing to profit from his considerable contemporary reputation, by 1728 Mandeville thought that he had found the philosophical support for the defense of his position. In *The Fable*'s second volume he offered a sustained elaboration of his initial Epicurean account of the civilizing process.

TOWARD A SCIENCE OF SOCIALIZED MAN

The Fable of the Bees should be understood as part of an ongoing theoretical enterprise begun by Mandeville in 1705 with the publica-

---

102 The work is a partial translation of the Baron des Cousture's *La Morale d'Epicure avec des réflexions* (Paris?, 1685), which was favorably reviewed during the following January by Bayle in his *Nouvelles de la République des Lettres*. I owe this point to James Moore.

103 John Digby, *Epicurus's Morals*, pp. 143–144. See too Digby's account of Epicurus' discovery of the importance of imaginative rewards in the civilizing process, pp. 29–30.

104 Digby, *Epicurus's Morals*, p. 80.   105 Mandeville, *Free Thoughts*, pp. 108–109.

106 *Collected from the works of the Learn'd Gassendi, By Monsieur Bernier. Translated out of the French* (London, 1699). See especially, "That Things Profitable and Useful, are sought after for the sake of Pleasure," pp. 91ff., "Of Self-Love," pp. 111ff., and "Of the Origin of Right and Justice," pp. 317ff. Mandeville's reference to his source of support is elliptical in *Fable*, II, p. 21, where he refers to "several dialogues and a Friend." Mandeville may have been led to

tion of *The Grumbling Hive*, and then first elaborated as a satire of a Dutch and English moralized political idiom in 1714. Uniting the physiological presuppositions of his medical *Treatise* with a largely French discourse for analyzing the passions, Mandeville in 1723 produced a satirical version of what he had come to understand as a theory of sociability in commercial societies. This project only achieved what Mandeville regarded as a comprehensive and philosophically secure form, however, as he worked out the consequences of his Epicurean and anti-Cartesian commitments in *The Fable*'s second volume of 1728, which were then further elaborated in what amounted to a third volume, *An Enquiry into the Origin of Honour* (1732). Perhaps as a way of responding to his philosophically minded critics of the 1720s, Mandeville virtually abandoned his earlier satiric mode of writing. This tropic shift in his work was accompanied by a changed mode of address. Mandeville's principal spokesman, Cleomenes, no longer appeared simply as the self-conscious observer of affluent living that readers had encountered in 1723, but as a "student of anatomy and natural philosophy" who "had study'd human nature," and whose stated intention was to explain and defend *The Fable*'s larger naturalistic purposes (II, 16), applying this method to "the whole system of animated beings on the Earth" (II, 247).

Mandeville sought to "put every Reader upon his guard" (II, 21) in 1728 by alerting his audience to *The Fable*'s newly enlarged purpose. He now explicitly set his arguments within a Lucretian evolutionary framework (II, 252), and announced that his understanding of social history was an original extension of the Epicurean view (II, 191) associated in the minds of his audience with Walter Charleton's writing during the previous generation, particularly *Epicurus's Morals* (1656), and with William Temple's *Essay* of 1680 on the origins of government.[107] Mandeville now claimed that the development of the human species as a whole should be understood as driven by processes of competition for scarce rewards (II, 238–240; 247–256). This

---

Bernier after first encountering La Mothe le Vayer's *Cinq Dialoques* (Mons, 1671). On this point see Popkin, *The History of Skepticism*, pp. 90–99. See too La Mothe le Vayer, *The Great Prerogative of Private Life: By Way of a Dialogue* (London, 1678), in which "philosophers" are seen as the only epistemologically "worthy spectators" (p. 102) of the social and political world. La Mothe claims that "paradox" is a medicinal tool in the hands of philosophers (p. 104), especially skeptics (pp. 168–169), and praises Epicurus throughout. He gives a startling anticipation of Bayle's argument that atheists can be good citizens, pp. 386–387.

[107] On Temple's Epicureanism, see Clara Marburg, *Sir William Temple, a Seventeenth-Century Libertine* (New Haven: Yale University Press, 1932).

movement could be described in various ways, as required by Mandeville's immediate rhetorical purpose. When the primary aim is to rebuke man's pride in his rational self-control, Mandeville accounts for the rise and establishment of urban and commercial civilization by parodying seventeenth-century theodicies in the style of Bayle, thus rejecting as unworthy the idea of a divine providence which should infringe on the laws of nature.[108] In this account, communal good is produced out of individual moral evil, but through entirely natural causes, by way of those "Engines it is performed with," the "trifling Films and little Pipes" of the human frame. Providence manifests itself in the workings of our passions over long periods of time, while society emerges independent of any human design in a slow evolutionary process, which "rouses opulent cities and powerful nations from small beginnings" (II, 256). But when Mandeville intends to show what men have accomplished for themselves, he figures society as the creation of political cunning. His naturalism is then put to the service of celebrating human powers in a fashion virtually identical to that of Epicurus, who "shew'd that,"

Civil Society was compos'd of men differently inclin'd ... which made it impossible to expect a perfect union among 'em ... it became necessary that [the most cunning would ensure that] certain laws should be agreed upon, that might restrain and curb ... violence and ambition ... and secure to the mild and gentle, safety and tranquillity.[109]

Once Mandeville stripped away the supposed "moral virtues" upon which civilization is conventionally said to rest, he could then reveal "the wonderful power of political wisdom, by the help of which so beautiful a machine is raised from the most contemptible branches." Men in this view are fit for society in the way that grapes are for wine. They may be combined into a social whole by working on their natural temperaments in a process of human art discovered by intelligence over time (II, 185; 189).

Mandeville proposed that styles of individual behavior in any historical epoch, and the collective fashions in which they participated, should be regarded as biological "phaenomena" or "symptoms" of hidden "natural causes," those elemental drives men shared with the higher animals (II, 91; 138–139). "All passions and instincts,"

---

[108] On this point see J.A.W. Gunn, "Mandeville and Wither: Individualism and the Workings of Providence," in Primer (ed.), *Mandeville Studies*, pp. 98–118; and compare *Free Thoughts*, pp. 282–283.   [109] Digby, *Epicurus's Morals*, p. 157.

he argued, "were given to all Animals for some wise End, tending to the Preservation and Happiness either of themselves or their Species" (II, 92). Gassendi was not invoked simply to buttress these rigorously naturalist views (II, 261–265). Mandeville now explicitly endorsed the foundational Gassendian claim that men and animals shared similar cognitive capacities (II, 166), that their differences could only be discovered by abandoning the "hypotheses" of (Cartesian) philosophers and relying instead upon strict empirical observation,[110] and that the diverse functions of human cognitive capacities could sufficiently be explained only in physiological, rather than moral, terms (II, 159–164). Men differ from bees not because the hive is composed of lower animals, but because the intellectual powers of men could be, and in fact were, "artfully managed" so as to suppress and redirect their primary drives (II, 78–79; 186–188), a civilizing project which is "the joint labour of several ages" (II, 321–322). Even the social function of wealth, Mandeville argued in the concluding discussion of *The Fable*'s second volume, had properly to be explained in terms of the way money "mechanically" works on the passions as an attractive force in polished conditions (II, 354–355).[111]

Mandeville re-shaped his original argument within this amplified naturalistic context. Since men are creatures distinguished from one another only by their innate temperaments (II, 75–77; 122–133), which determine the different perceptions they have of happiness (II, 25), and which depend on the mixture of fluids in our bodies (II, 211–212), it becomes the business of the "politician" to continue the process of socializing the race by devising attractive projects and compelling injunctions which promote stable intercourse. Ruling elites survive and prosper to the degree that they are able on a continuing basis to neutralize inherently antagonistic, unsocial inclinations by playing the passions of individuals against each other (II, 78–79). Mandeville firmly located the achievement of sociability within an evolutionary context. From the premise of a limited set of irreducible desires, he explicitly defended his conjectural history of society as the scientifically most plausible statement of the evolution of the human species. This history could account, he claimed, for the social function of language and the instrumental efficacy of fellow-feeling (II, 177–193), along with the actual application of strict rules of

[110] Compare *Treatise* (1730 edn), pp. 124 and 226.
[111] See too *Fable*, II, pp. 140 and 160–164.

justice, as civilian natural jurists could not.[112] Most importantly perhaps, Mandeville's 1728 revision of his analysis of the passions permitted a theoretical extension of the relation of human sentiments to the functioning of civil societies. Self-love (*l'amour-propre* in the lexicon of the French *moralistes*) was in Mandeville's initial, 1723, account the passion from which all others derived. In the second, 1728, volume of *The Fable*, however, he deliberately employs the philosophically provocative examples of cows, screech-owls, horses, sheep, cats and dogs to introduce what he declared to be a novel hypothesis. The passion of "self-liking," Mandeville now argued, was that feature of animal dispositions which impelled humans alone to over-value themselves in socially decisive ways.

Self-love would first make [this human creature] scrape together everything it wanted for Sustenance, provide against the injuries of the Air, and do everything to make itself and young Ones secure. Self-liking would make it seek for opportunities, by Gestures, Looks, and Sounds, to display the Value it has for itself, superior to what it has for others; an untaught Man would desire everybody that came near him, to agree with him in the Opinion of his superior Worth ... He would be highly delighted with, and love every body, whom he thought to have a good Opinion of him, especially those that by Words or Gestures should own it to his Face. (II, 133–134)[113]

Self-liking serves as a regulating principle of individual actions which promotes social stability by directing men to seek the approval of their fellows.[114]

In the animal kingdom self-love remained in the ascendant, with fear and anger the dominant passions. Accordingly, animals were forever trapped in patterns of behavior which condemned them to repeat the unchanging details of their respective life-cycles. The reverse was the case in formally organized human communities, for in the social realm self-liking rather than self-love governed human behavior. The operations of self-liking would in time enable men to over-ride and control their basic passions of fear and anger. As dramatized by the suicides of Cato and Lucretia in the ancient world, and that of Thomas Creech in modern England, even the instinct of self-preservation could be socially disciplined. Thus self-liking allowed the other passions first effectively anatomized by Bayle and

---

[112] Mandeville, *A Letter to Dion*, p. 43.
[113] See *Honour*, pp. 3–13, for a further elaboration of this notion.
[114] Mandeville, *Honour*, p. 8.

the French *moralistes* to come into play, and also provided the distinctive stimulus for the development of reason and speech. Self-liking made for dynamic and open-ended patterns of behavior which initiated successive historical cycles of emulation, during the first of which the establishment of "morality" signalled the transition from the state of nature to society itself. From this premise, Mandeville could then sketch a naturalistic account of the history of the passions over social time, a discourse on society whose lexicon of terms expresses assumptions supporting arguments about the nature of communal life that depend for their force on a naturalistic reduction of human motivations to a few elementary passions. Men so understood are wholly part of nature, conceived according to the canons of science in an enriched Gassendian project previously hoped for by Walter Charleton, Gassendi's most distinguished English disciple, in his *Natural History of the Passions*.[115]

Self-liking, Mandeville noted, was not merely pride in altered dress.[116] He coined the term in order to answer the need for an emotionally neutral way of describing the workings of the passions in their distinctly human, that it to say, social, context (and, as we shall see, in response to criticism). This need was especially acute in Mandeville's view since his account of social formation depended upon an analysis of passions which had initially been christened by moralists whose purposes were wholly rhetorical rather than scientific.[117] While time and use had permanently inscribed a value-laden terminology about human motivation into educated speech, self-liking was the concept which offered Mandeville a way to employ the moralized vocabulary he had inherited in a non-normative, descriptive fashion. "I now understand what you mean by self-liking," Mandeville has Horatio say to his spokesman Cleomenes,

You are of Opinion, that we are all born with a Passion manifestly distinct from Self-love; that when it is moderate and well regulated, excites in us the Love of Praise, and a Desire to be applauded and thought well of by others,

---

[115] See Walter Charleton, *Natural History of the Passions* (London, 1674; 2nd edition, 1701), p. 94, where Charleton discusses the "contagious" property of "self-estimation" which generates in persons "a better concept of themselves than they really deserve." In the "Epistle Prefatory," where Gassendi is cited as a modern authority and Epicurus is referred to as "our Oracle," Charleton says that "my design was to write . . . neither as an Orator, nor as a Moral Philosopher, but only as a *Natural* one conversant in Pathology." He then praises "the *Ethics of Epicurus*" as "the best *Dispensary* I have hitherto read of Natural *Medicines* incident to the mind of Man," pp. 187–188.   [116] Mandeville, *Honour*, pp. 12–13.
[117] Mandeville, *Honour*, p. 6.

and stirs us up to good Actions; but that the same Passion, when it is excessive, or ill turn'd, whatever it excites in our Selves, gives Offence to others, renders us odious, and is call'd Pride. As there is no Word or Expression that comprehends all the different Effects of this same Cause, this Passion you have made one, *viz.*, Self-Liking, by which you mean the Passion in general, the whole extent of it, whether it produces laudable Actions, and gains us Applause, or such as we are blamed for and draw upon us the ill Will of others.[118]

Mandeville's reconceptualization of egoism, so he said, was not only intended to revive Montaigne's thesis, famously contested by Descartes, that men, like all the animals, imaginatively constitute the world in their own image (II, 131 and 139). He sought in addition to develop a conception of the workings of what he termed this "instinct" in order to comprehend the pervasive force of pride in the shaping of human affairs. Self-liking was the innate mechanism by virtue of which one could explain the decisive power of flattery in first domesticating the species, and then account for those "alterations" in the presentation of the self as an object of approbation which characterized successive historical epochs (II, 138–139). In so naturalizing pride, and providing it with a history, Mandeville completed his project to explain sociability in a language shorn of moralized concepts. In 1723 he had mocked "the short-sighted Vulgar" who "seldom can see further than one Link ... in the Chain of Causes," contrasting these cognitive innocents with "those who can enlarge their View, and will give themselves Leisure of gazing on the Prospect of concatenated Events" (I, 91). Now, in 1728, Mandeville was confident that his own gaze could account for "the Felicity that accrues from the Applause of others, and the invisible wages which men of Sense and judicious Fancy receiv'd for their Labours; and what it was at the Bottom, that rendered those airy Rewards so ravishing to Mortals" (II, 17). When Kant grouped Mandeville with Montaigne and Epicurus as theorists who first discovered the principles governing the "constitution of society" (*bürgerliche Verfassung*),[119] he grasped this striking feature of Mandeville's work, and was plainly indebted to *The Fable*'s naturalistic reconstruction of private vices as public benefits for his conception of unsocial sociability (*ungesellige Geselligkeit*) as the paradoxically propulsive mechanism of human

---

[118] Mandeville, *Honour*, pp. 6–7.
[119] *The Critique of Practical Reason*, trans. T.K. Abbott (London: Longman, 1909), II, Part I, Book I, Chapter 1, "Of the Principles of Pure Practical Reason," p. 129.

history.[120] In his *Project for Perpetual Peace*, Kant reflected on how the natural laws which govern the development of the species engender a productive common order out of colliding individual wills in a form of a competitive economy which strengthens the state, while in his definition of Enlightenment he pointed to "a strange and unexpected pattern in human affairs (such as we shall always find if we consider them in the widest sense, in which nearly everything is paradoxical)."[121] While refusing his satirical tone, Kant appropriated Mandeville's assumption that men in the first phase of human development were fully human only in the biological sense, and that the transformation of this animal into a moral creature capable of subordinating his immediate desires depended upon a "small beginning, but an epoch-making one," when men responded to "a craving to inspire in others esteem for ourselves, through ... [the] repression of that which could arouse in them a poor opinion of us."[122] Mandeville brought home to Kant "the realization of the unintended, but once present, never failing good [which results] from constantly and internally discordant evil." "Animality," Kant wrote, not about bees but about what he called the "spiritual animal kingdom" of mankind,

is ... fundamentally stronger than pure humanity in its expressions, and the domesticated animal is of more use to man than the wild beast only in so far as it is *weakened*. The will of the individual ... always seeks ... not only to be independent, but to dominate other beings ... [Men are] unable to *do without* peaceful coexistence, yet also unable to *avoid* being constantly hateful to one another ... [Mankind is] a coalition always threatened with dissolution, but on the whole progressing towards a ... cosmopolitan civil society.[123]

The dynamics of the rivalry for honor, riches and power, Kant further followed Mandeville in arguing, generate every stage of civilization, while the natural laws which govern the development of the species

[120] Immanuel Kant, *Idea for a Universal History from a Cosmopolitan Point of View*, Fourth Thesis, trans. Lewis White Beck, in Beck (ed.), *Kant on History* (Indianapolis: Bobbs–Merril, 1963), pp. 15–16.
[121] Immanuel Kant, *What is Enlightenment?*, in Hans Reiss (ed.), *Kant's Political Writings* (Cambridge University Press, 1976), p. 59.
[122] Immanuel Kant, *Conjectures Concerning the Beginning of Human History* (1786), quoted in A.O. Lovejoy, *Reflections on Human Nature* (Baltimore: Johns Hopkins University Press, 1961), p. 193.
[123] Immanuel Kant, *Anthropologie in pragmatischer Hinsicht* (1798), in *Werke*, 6th edition, ed. W. Weischedal (Wiesbaden: Insel-Verlag, 1956–1964), pp. 682 and 687. I have modified the translation of Mary J. Gregor, *Anthropology From a Pragmatic Point of View* (The Hague: Nijhoff, 1974), pp. 183 and 188–191.

engender a productive common order out of colliding individual wills.

Mandeville's reputation as the exemplary modern defender of licentiousness was already firmly established in England by the mid-1720s, as the vocabulary of "private vices" and "public benefits" became an established feature of educated speech and popular journalism. It was a reputation greatly enhanced by his determined philosophical opponents, who recognized that Mandeville had issued the most powerful contemporary denial of the claim that morality has an objective foundation.[124] Francis Hutcheson, of whom it was said that he could give no lecture from his chair at Glasgow without criticizing Mandeville, was infuriated by the implications of *The Fable*'s attack on the possibility of benevolence, and sought to dismiss it with the much-repeated, if historically absurd, aside, "that he has probably been struck with some *Fanatick Sermon upon Self-Denial* in his Youth, and can never get it out of his head since."[125] Bishop Berkeley, failing utterly to grasp any of Mandeville's satirical devices, claimed in *Alciphron* (1732) that his unalloyed intention was simply to promote vice. In the following generation only a small segment of *The Fable*'s audience attended to Mandeville's defense and elaboration of his arguments in 1728, while *The Fable* was standardly associated with atheism and uncontrolled greed, a reputation that extended to colonial America and the salons of the Neapolitan Enlightenment.[126] When discussing Mandeville in 1748, a commentator on contemporary religious belief said that irreligion like his threatened to "take possession of all the writers and readers among us."[127] As Johnson quipped to Boswell, by mid-century most readers simply had Mandeville's work on their shelves in the belief that his was a wicked book.

---

[124] See, for example, Gilbert Burnett, *Letters between the late Mr. Gilbert Burnett, and Mr. Hutcheson, Concerning the True Foundation of Virtue* (London, 1735) (originally published in *The Dublin Journal* [1725]); John Clarke, *The Foundation of Morality in Theory and Practice Considered* (London, 1726), and John Balguy, *The Foundation of Moral Goodness; or a Further Inquiry into the Original of our Idea of Virtue, in two Parts*, 2 volumes, (London, 1728–1729). On this subject see, David Fate Norton, "Hume and the Foundations-Problem: Cross-Border Influences," Paper presented at the Cross-Cultural Enlightenment Conference, University of Victoria, April 1993. [125] Hutcheson, *A Collection of Letters*, in *Collected Works*, VII, p. 169.

[126] See, for example, J.E. Crowley, *This Sheba, Self: The Conceptualization of Economic Life in Eighteenth-Century America* (Baltimore: Johns Hopkins University Press, 1974), pp. 14–15, and Richard Bellamy, "'Da Metafisico a mercatante': Antonio Genovese and the Development of a New Language of Commerce in Eighteenth-Century Naples," in Pagden (ed.), *The Languages of Political Theory*, pp. 281–290.

[127] Philip Skelton, *Ophiomaches, or Deism Reveal'd* (London, 1748), II, pp. 347–348.

Largely because of his scandalous reputation, Mandeville's revised and expanded arguments about the physiological sources of the passions most often entered British intellectual life through a suppression of their subversive source. *The Fable*'s second volume was more than an unacknowledged classic, however, as can be seen, for example, from the iatromechanist physician La Mettrie's paraphrase of Mandeville in his hedonist and materialist anti-Stoic discourse, *Anti-Sénique* (1747), and from the Sorbonne's condemnation of *De l'esprit* because Helvétius' attempt thoroughly to naturalize ethics in the service of political ends was seen directly to derive from Mandeville's.[128] Chamfort, the most celebrated aphorist during the final days of the *ancien régime*, grouped Mandeville with Montaigne, La Bruyère, La Rochefoucauld and Helvétius as the most important moralists and *politiques* who viewed human nature as odious and ridiculous.[129] Adam Smith openly, though regretfully, acknowledged *The Fable*'s importance in the constitution of Enlightenment social understanding. A vigorous critic of Mandeville's ethical arguments, Smith nevertheless recognized that no matter "how destructive ... this system may appear, it could never have imposed upon so great a number of persons, nor have occasioned so general an alarm ... had it not in some respects bordered on the truth."[130] When he reviewed Rousseau's *Discourse on the Origins of Inequality* (1755) for *The Edinburgh Review* in 1756, Smith told his audience that "whoever reads this ... work with attention, will observe, that the second volume of the *Fable of the Bees* has given occasion to the system of Mr. Rousseau."[131] Indeed, Rousseau's conjectural history of humanity, while strenuously denying *The Fable*'s conclusions, was perhaps the most influential single text which openly injected Mandeville's expanded naturalism into the wider Enlightenment debate on the sciences of

---

[128] Adrien Claude Helvétius, *De L'Esprit* (Paris, 1757), Discourse II, Chapter 24 paraphrases the 1750 French translation of *The Fable*, II, p. 261. In a Letter of 13 August 1760, Voltaire commented to Helvétius on the latter's indebtedness to Mandeville. See *Voltaire's Correspondence*, ed. Theodore Besterman (Banbury: Voltaire Foundation, 1972), XXII, Letter 9141. See too, Paul Sackmann, *Bernard de Mandeville und die Bienenfabel-Controverse* (Freiberg: Siebeck, 1897), pp. 211–212, and F. Grégoire, *Bernard de Mandeville et La "Fable des Abeilles"* (Nancy: Georges Thomas, 1947), p. 205.

[129] Chamfort (Sébastien Roch Nicholas), *Maximes et pensées*, ed. Claude Roy (Paris: Union Générale d'Editions, 1963), p. 33.

[130] Adam Smith, *The Theory of Moral Sentiments*, ed. D.D. Raphael and A.L. Macfie (Oxford University Press, 1976), p. 495.

[131] Adam Smith, "Letter to the Edinburgh Review," in *Essays on Philosophical Subjects*, ed. W.P.D. Wightman and J.C. Bryce (Oxford University Press, 1980), p. 250.

man. Rousseau modelled his theory of the emergence of culture on an Epicurean account of social evolution,[132] and he explicitly confronted Mandeville's arguments while attempting to provide a natural history of morals founded, as was Mandeville's, upon the modern sciences and medicine.[133] In the process, Rousseau directed Kant's attention to *The Fable* and probably alerted the Sorbonne's censors when they condemned Helvétius two years after Rousseau's *Discourse* was published amidst considerable controversy. Within a generation, almost every significant Enlightenment intellectual, from Voltaire to Turgot, Gibbon and Smith had pronounced on the problem of the morally paradoxical nature of material progress. This problem, which was a staple of Enlightenment anthropology in France,[134] formed a starting point in Scotland for the project of constructing a "natural history" of man.[135] Late in the century it became a central feature of German reflection on modernity, notably in Kant and then in Schiller's *Letters on the Aesthetic Education of Mankind*.[136]

Hume, who characterized his own philosophical activity as akin to that of an "anatomist,"[137] and who was himself accused of Epicureanism, served as a decisive figure in this discussion, most influentially amongst his Scottish colleagues and successors like Smith. While he

[132] Jean Morel, "Recherches sur les sources du *Discours sur l'Inégalité*," *Annales de la Société Jean-Jacques Rousseau* 5 (1909), pp. 163–164; Roger D. Masters, *The Political Philosophy of Rousseau* (Princeton University Press, 1968), pp. 170–176, and Vaughan, *Political Hedonism*, pp. 119–129.

[133] Jean-Jacques Rousseau, *Discourse on the Origin and Foundations of Inequality* (New York: St. Martin's Press, 1964), trans. Roger D. Masters, notes D through J.

[134] Michèle Duchet, *Anthropologie et histoire au siècle des lumières* (Paris: Maspero, 1971), pp. 323–357.

[135] See Paul Wood, "The Natural History of Man in the Scottish Enlightenment," *History of Science* 28 (1989), pp. 89–123; George Davie, "Berkeley, Hume and the Central Problem of Scottish Philosophy," in Nicholas Capaldi, David Fate Norton and Wade Robson (eds.), *McGill Hume Studies* (San Diego: Austin Hill Press, 1979), pp. 43–62; and M.M. Goldsmith, "Regulating Anew the Moral and Political Sentiments of Mankind: Bernard Mandeville and the Scottish Enlightenment," *Journal of the History of Ideas* 49, 4 (1988), pp. 587–606.

[136] For Mandeville's reputation in Germany see, Bernhard Fabian, "The Reception of Bernard Mandeville in Eighteenth-Century Germany," *Studies on Voltaire and the Eighteenth Century* 15, 2 (1976), pp. 693–722.

[137] David Hume, *A Treatise of Human Nature*, ed. L.A. Selby-Bigge (Oxford: Clarendon Press, 1955), III.iii.6. Hume angered his teacher Francis Hutcheson when he wrote in a distinctly Mandevillian idiom that "there are different ways of examining the Mind as well as the Body. One may consider it either as an Anatomist [Hume] or as a Painter [Hutcheson]; either to discover its most secret Springs and Principles or to describe the Grace and Beauty of its Actions ... [When one] pull[s] off the Skin, and display[s] all the minute Parts, there appears something trivial, even in the noblest Attitudes and most vigorous Actions." Hume to Hutcheson, 17 September 1739, in *Letters of David Hume*, ed. J.Y.T. Greig (Oxford: Clarendon Press, 1932), p. 32.

sought to distance himself from "certain philosophers who delight so much to form mankind of this particular [selfishness], [since they] are as wide of nature as any accounts of the monsters we meet with in fables and romances,"[138] and while he attempted to reduce the controversy surrounding *The Fable* to a purely literary squabble,[139] Hume named Mandeville as one of "the late philosophers in England, who have begun to put the science of man on a new footing."[140] Hume's analysis of his early psychosomatic illness, and of the role of the animal spirits in the operation of the passions, relies heavily on Mandeville's physiological claims in the *Treatise on Hypocondriak Passions*, which Hume studied with care.[141] Likewise, as we shall see later, while Hume prudently refrained from alluding to *The Fable* when articulating a view of the passions as pre-conceptual and pre-linguistic, he fully exploited Mandeville for the purposes of his own science of morals, claiming that the passions have a strict correspondence in men and animals, that identical qualities give rise to pride in each, "and it is on beauty, strength, swiftness, or some other useful or agreeable quality that this passion is always founded."[142]

The recognition, as Hume put it, that "pride and humility are not merely human passions, but extend themselves over the whole animal creation,"[143] was a cardinal presumption behind a European-wide enterprise in which *The Fable* served as a decisive exemplar. Its aim was to include the entirety of civilized intercourse within the category of the drives of individuals, scientifically considered. In *The Fable*'s anatomy of human motives, the social order could for the first time analytically be isolated and comprehensively understood as a complex, but rule-bound, conjunction of the facts of nature. This science of socialized man would seek to map the unintended consequences of self-interested action and have as its primary objective the discovery of stabilizing social mechanisms inherent in communal expressions of self-regard. Mandeville conceived the goal of this project as the explanation of sociability, and thus of moral standards, in a vocabul-

---

138 *Treatise*, III.ii.2.
139 David Hume, "Of the Dignity and Meanness of Human Nature," in *Essays Moral, Political and Literary* (Indianapolis: Liberty Press, 1985), pp. 80–81.
140 *Treatise of Human Nature*, p. xvii.
141 John P. Wright, *The Sceptical Realism of David Hume* (Manchester University Press, 1983), pp. 190–191.   142 *Treatise*, I.i. 12.
143 *Treatise*, II.i.12. A claim for which Hume was abused by John Brown in *An Estimate of the Manners and Principles of the Times* (1757), II, pp. 20–21, who associated Hume with Mandeville.

ary shorn of moralized concepts. His reduction of society to the action of individual agents – which was only ideal and morally normative in modern natural law – came to be accepted as methodologically prescriptive for an entire program of social inquiry. *The Fable* served in the two generations after Mandeville wrote as a fitfully acknowledged, often suppressed, but indelibly inscribed foundation for this enterprise. His naturalization of pride generated a systematic, though not final, vocabulary for the constitution of a human science. As Bentham said of the *The Fable*'s effect at the century's end, Mandeville's work had "broken the chains of ordinary language" in the discourse of educated persons.[144] It is a fitting paradox for so paradoxical an author that Mandeville's project of establishing a science of unsocial yet socialized man on the ruins of an exhausted language of morals should have been of such signal importance to the major inheritors of this tradition.

[144] Jeremy Bentham, *Introduction to the Principles of Morals and Legislation* (1800), Chapter 10, "Motives," Section XIII.

CHAPTER 2

Self-love and the civilizing process

Mandeville's commitment to a developmental perspective on the "anatomy of the human frame" had immediate consequences. Most important was the realization during the 1720s that his initial understanding of contemporary European civility and opulence depended for its force not only upon the naturalistic analysis of sociability for which he first became notorious but upon an historically plausible reconstruction of the progress of pride as the human race matured from its primitive beginnings over the course of social time. All forms of social life, Mandeville had claimed in *The Fable*'s Preface of 1723, were in fact nothing more than various structures within which the "symptoms" and "symbols" of instinct were politically regulated in the interests of peace and security. But this challenge to morally grounded conceptions of society was exceptionally difficult to argue convincingly in the absence of an evolutionary consideration of morals and justice; the more difficult since, by Mandeville's own testimony, "all the symbols of [pride] are not easily discovered; they are manifold and vary according to age, humour, circumstances, and often constitution, of the people" (1, 138). Having adopted that aggressively evolutionary stance which characterized his writing in the wake of *The Fable*'s stormy reception after 1723, Mandeville explored this problem for the ten remaining years of his working life. In the second volume of *The Fable*, and again in its supplement on "Honour," he defended his original postulates by attempting to demonstrate that what Epicurean predecessors like Walter Charleton had called a "natural history of the passions" was a practical project of social intelligibility rather than a merely notional artifact generated by a physiologically informed theory of the emotions. Kant made the relevant observation: *The Fable*'s speculative anthropology laid the foundations for a conjectural, but scientifically defensible, history of humanity from its rude and unreflective beginnings to its polished and self-consciously purposive social arrangements. Mandeville's attempt to sketch this history provided the framework within which his most telling arguments achieved their eighteenth-century importance.

THE HISTORY OF PRIDE

When anatomizing the behavior of savage man, Mandeville claimed that he went directly "to the Fountain Head, human nature itself... [for] when Things are very obscure, I ... make use of Conjectures to find my Way" (II, 128). Historical conjecture was required for an understanding of the first primitives, since "we have so few Examples of human Creatures, that never convers'd with their own Species, that it is hard to guess, what man would be, entirely untaught" (II, 189). But in the absence of adequate anthropological evidence of pre-social creatures – despite the flood of European reports of tribal communities in the Americas since the sixteenth century[1] – Mandeville reasoned that the character of savage man could best be established by observing the behavior of children prior to their induction into "the Rules and Decorums" of established society. Given his belief in the innate character of the passions and their pre-conceptual primacy in determining human behavior, this conventional Epicurean postulate was a natural one for him to accept.

Children could above all be seen as domineering in their relations with other creatures, both human and animal; they expressed in an unmediated fashion "the love of Dominion and that usurping Temper all Mankind are born with" (I, 281). This universal propensity for "taking everything to be our own" (II, 223–224) is "the never-failing consequence of Pride," common to all Men and fully apparent to any unprejudiced observer of their offspring (II, 204). Like the brutes they so closely resemble, persons in their earliest years have everywhere shown themselves to be devoid of reasonable notions of right and wrong. Children – and by direct implication their savage ancestors – naturally follow the demands of their untaught passions, expressing wild anger and aggressive rage when their instincts are frustrated, "something implanted in the Frame, the Mechanism of the Body, before any Marks of Wit or Reason are to be seen in them" (II, 280).

---

[1] Mandeville treated the subject of contemporary Amero-Indian societies in *The Female Tatler* (London, 1709–1710), especially No. 262 (November 1709).

Like savages, children are "stubborn and obstinate," and fond "of following their own Will" (II, 280–281). Devoid of both reason and speech, as are children at birth, men in their historical infancy are similarly little more than barely individuated bundles of raw passions, possessing so rudimentary a form of self-awareness that they take inanimate objects to possess identical feelings as those they themselves experience (II, 209).

In the "state of simplicity" which characterized the original human habitat, men had few desires and no appetites "beyond the immediate Call of untaught Nature." Chief among these was lust, which drove men to multiply "much faster than can be allowed in any regular society" (II, 201). The "love of Ease and Security" which continued to characterize the species was thus first frustrated by the ensuing competition for increasingly scarce resources caused by population growth, a struggle which constantly thwarted the innate desire of men to ameliorate their condition (II, 180) and, most importantly, energized the root passion of fear by the immediate prospect of extinction (II, 230). Fear drove men and their families to seek safety in numbers, forming the first communities (II, 230). In socialized conditions parents act as civilizing agents, establishing "good discipline" amongst these little beasts, "and break in us the Spirit of Independency we are all born with" (II, 280–281). But parents of primitive households could scarcely educate their offspring into the rigors and rewards of society. The enforcement of parental discipline was an impossible task for savages, even in their first communal state, for they were "no better qualified, [and] could teach their children but little" (II, 201). While these children would have been expected to aid in the hunt, and would of course seek to imitate their parents, they could acquire via such activities only the most rudimentary skills and habits, since "all the Instructions [these children] receiv'd would be confined to things immediately necessary" (II, 203). Thus, the savage family could serve neither as an instrument of socialization nor, as Filmer had notoriously proposed, a model for the origins of government, for persons "who never had been taught to curb the working of [their] Passions, would be very unfit for such a task" (II, 203). Children would remain essentially ungovernable because parents in the most primitive ages of the race remained unable to govern themselves. While pity and compassion, "the most gentle and the least mischievous of our Passions," would be stirred involuntarily by the crying of infants (II, 286), this "fraility" in human nature and the emotional affection parents naturally have for their children (II, 201) could at best only moderate the more powerful demands of pride. Expressed in the desire for superiority, pride would encourage the head of a family to "look upon his Children as his Property, and make such use of them as is most consistent with his Interest" (II, 201). While society could be understood in its first appearance in the world as an amalgam of these private families, "to produce a Man fit to govern others, much more was required" (II, 231).

As men first attempt to live in groups, new and more complex passions begin to emerge. Once born, they are reinforced through a long and gradual process of social intercourse, in which "envy, avarice and ambition begin to catch hold" (II, 271). At the same time, self-love and the drive to dominion, unrestrained by any moral sense or the penalties of a legal order, impel savage man to "have every thing he likes, without considering whether he has any Right to it or not; and he will do everything he has a mind to do, without regard to the Consequences it would be to others" (II, 270–271). And since others behave similarly, an unregulated series of conflicts of wants and desires is the natural result of the enlarged repertoire of passions of these newly united brutes, who are then forced to the fundamental discovery that other men, rather than wild beasts, have become their primary enemies. In an unplanned and wholly unexpected fashion, men naturally come to realize that the greatest threat to their ease, security, and even to life itself, is the presence of each other.

The strongest, most agile and courageous would naturally prevail in the ensuing struggles, arising as they did from the expression of randomly distributed physical attributes. Success in these first primitive wars, therefore, depended "only upon the different Frame, [and] the inward Formation of either the Solids or the Fluids" (II, 122). The fittest warriors then "would naturally divide Multitudes into Bands and Companies, that would all have their different Leaders, and of which the strongest and most valiant would always swallow up the weakest and most fearful" (II, 267). This "second step to society" (II, 266), as Mandeville called it, was the decisive result of the dangers men posed, and were seen to pose, to one another. Their quarrels arose not merely, nor even primarily, from disputes over increasingly scarce resources. Such disputes became the local occasions for the war of all against all, since the innate drives to superiority and domination inherent in the human frame would necessarily have manifested themselves in inter-species conflict, even in the most benign conditions that "the most luxuriant Imagination could Fancy" (II, 309). Natural dangers of the environment could be overcome much more easily than the untamed desires of the human constitution – passions which are, ironically, multiplied and given even freer rein in the ill-mastered environment of the first human groups. Self-interested and aggressive men had now to seek ways to redress and regulate the destructive, because anti-social, effects of their own natures. For Mandeville, these creatures can be understood as singularly suited for society in the crucial sense that they, and they alone, could productively address these life-threatening problems; theirs was a uniquely human potential which could only be realized once "great Numbers of them are joyn'd together and [then] artfully manag'd" (II, 188). Primitive man was thus "more fit for Society than any other Animal we know" (II, 177), not because of any principle of sociability or benevolence unique to his nature but, paradoxically, because the superabundance of his desires produces chaos and pain in his dealings with his fellows. These radical discomforts are the unbearable conditions from which his self-love demands release.

While Mandeville assumed with Hobbes that fear was the only human passion which naturally disposed men to peace, he rejected the Hobbist thesis that social order and the principles of contract could coherently be reconstructed primarily from this passion, just as he denied that superior strength alone could sufficiently account for the various forms of submission required in any stable political order. For it was evident that

> to be governable implies an Endeavour to please, and a Willingness to exert ourselves on behalf of the person that governs: But . . . no Creature can labour for others, and be easy long, whilst Self is wholly out of the Question. Therefore a Creature is then truly governable, when, reconciled to Submission, it has learn'd to construe his Servitude to his own Advantage; and rests Satisfy'd with the Account it finds for itself in the labours it performs for others. Several kinds of Animals are, or may, with little Trouble, be made thus governable; but there is not one Creature so tame, that it can be made to serve its own Species, but Man; yet without this he could never have been made sociable. (II, 184)

As a condition of avoiding "the Discords occasioned" by the "unruly passions" of fear and anger (II, 267–268), men had to be "managed" in order that they would pursue their interests in more circumscribed, less blatantly self-gratifying, and less destructive ways. The formation of ordered society thus depended on the readiness of men to find satisfaction in "labouring for others," and the development of this preparedness in turn required a shift in the valences of the most fundamental human instincts. Otherwise, every man would remain "incurably adverse to Society, and more obstinately Conscious of his Savage Liberty, than any other creature would be" (II, 300).

Only government could establish a stable background of social expectations within which the primordial drives of fear and anger would sufficiently be tempered. And for this "third and last Step to Society" to occur, so Mandeville argued, an expansion of both the imaginative and cognitive potentials associated with articulate speech and "the invention of letters" was required, since peace rested upon the force of established government, and "no Government can subsist without Laws; and no Laws can be effectual long, unless they are wrote down" (II, 269). Political organization was thus the defining characteristic of the highest stage of human intercourse, the stage in which "the Execution of [laws] is facilitated by general Approbation, [so that] Multitudes may be kept in tolerable Concord among themselves" (II, 300). In political society fear for the first time becomes the foundation of an *internalized* form of social obedience, while a legal order, the "antidote" to the ill-consequences of human nature (II, 283), insures that anger can be channelled through, and legitimated by, the repressive, but communally sanctioned, instruments of the state.

The first Care therefore of all Governments is by severe Punishments to curb [man's] Anger when it does hurt, and so by increasing his Fears prevent the Mischief it might produce ... The only useful Passion then that Man is possess'd of toward the Peace and Quiet of a Society, is his Fear, and the more you work upon it the more orderly and governable he'll be. (I, 206)

The taming of fear and anger by the first expressions of "the State's Craft" produces harmony from competing vices (I, 24). Instruments of government open the way not merely for the political discipline upon which complex communities necessarily depend but also for the psychological freedom to refine and elaborate brute appetites, so that politically organized populations "sooner became sensible to Grief and Joy ... with greater difference as to the Degrees, than they are felt in other creatures." And as appetites slowly become more nuanced and elaborate, men are "render[ed] ... more industrious to please [themselves] ... than [are] ... Animals of less Capacity" (II, 300).

In politically organized, if socially rudimentary, communities men learned and then became habituated to respond to the ever-pressing demands of self-love in ways less immediate and more calculable than those operative amongst the first primitives. Envy, avarice and ambition, the original sublimations of anger and self-love required for civilized living, appear in organized polities as fundamental characteristics of the human constitution. These inter-related changes in psychological organization promoted the superiority of human understanding within the animal kingdom, most especially that singular capacity required for the "general approbation" upon which government itself rests. An expanded constellation of passions could now conscript newly developed cognitive powers as "so many Tools, Arguments, by which Self-love reasons us into Content, and renders us patient under many Afflictions," a disposition "of infinite use to a Man, who finds himself born in a Body Politick, and it must make him fond of Society" (II, 300). Indeed, only this type of emotionally mature person could plausibly submit to "the Number of Clauses and Proviso's ... prodigious beyond Imagination [that are required] to govern a large flourishing City well" (II, 321). Over time, these constraints of law and custom would become habitual, precisely because the latter have come to be experienced as secure opportunities for gratifying the expanded and reconstituted desires which characterize civilized men as opposed to savages. Political society thus governs itself through the global introjection of law. Finally, "when once [these laws] are brought to as much Perfection as Art and human wisdom can carry them, the whole Machine may be made to play of itself with as little skill, as is required to wind up a Clock" (II, 323).

Durable social conditions created by law allowed those inventions and improvements which characterize civilization to flourish. With basic material needs satisfied on a stable basis, and the most pressing demands of self-love answered (II, 175), men became increasingly susceptible to management and control through the agency of self-liking. In nature, "destitute of all outward ornament," a man would have "infinitely less Temptation, as well as Opportunity of shewing this Liking of himself, than he has when civiliz'd" (II, 132). Now men could internalize codes of manners and morals through the instruments of public approbation and disapproval; but this step could be accomplished only once the development of communicative competence rendered possible the perfection of techniques of persuasion and dissimulation. As creatures of unreflective instinctual response, savages could never have been disciplined without the development of language and the consequent refinements in the arts of flattery. In the absence of the deceptions made possible by speech men could never successfully "hide and stifle" their appetites and desires. They would never be "ashamed of confessing themselves" (I, 45), think "to disapprove of their natural inclinations, or prefer the good of others to their own" by offering "a reward for the Violence, which by so doing they of necessity must compel themselves" (I, 42). Language, the primary instrument of self-liking, makes hypocrisy possible, since only persons who value their psychic as well as their physical well-being could be persuaded to adopt the repressive moral standards civilization requires by attaching public approbation and disapproval to, respectively, their performance and neglect. Thus, just as they answer the passion of self-liking, verbal signs serve as the psychological rewards men receive in winning the esteem of their peers. They are "the Raptures enjoy[ed] in the Thoughts of being liked," and "equivalents that overpay the Conquest of the strongest Passions" (I, 68). Through the agency of self-liking, language becomes empowered as the mechanism by which an individual is recompensed for the pain of self-denial. Speech is the means by which the suppression of instinct can be stabilized through the social disciplining of pride – the most socially beneficial passion – as it regulates anti-social instincts in civilized conditions by exciting the need for esteem.

Mandeville's conjectural narrative thus describes a progressive development in pride's history amongst men as they formed in groups. In constructing this notional history he was able to supply a cultural framework within which to comprehend his primary object of concern: the decisive shift to those modern, affluent conditions of communal life in which the instinct to dominate was successfully sublimated in the materially productive, socially useful and artfully mannered forms of intercourse, those styles of civility that both Mandeville and his ideological opponents designated by the term "politeness." A fundamental aspect of this process was the reconstitution of anger, not merely during the initial processes of domesticating the savage but, more crucially, in the increasingly intricate intersubjective relationships which characterize socially complex forms of life. For once propelled out of the savage state, "if we examine [man] as a Member of a Society and a taught Animal, we shall find him quite another Creature."

As soon as his Pride has room to play ... he is roused from his natural Innocence and Stupidity. As his Knowledge increases, his Desires are enlarg'd, and consequently his Wants and Appetites are multipl'd: Hence it must follow that he will be often cross'd in the Pursuit of them, and meet with abundance more disappointment to stir up his Anger in this than his former Condition, and Man would in a little time become the most hurtful and noxious Creature in the World, if let alone . . . The first Care therefore of all Governments is . . . to curb his Anger when it does hurt, and so by increasing his Fears prevent the mischief it might produce. (1, 205–206)

If the invention of morality, and with it the production of guilt, were the initial means by which savages became subject to self-control, it was evident to Mandeville that in contemporary polities the "tye of society" no longer depended on claims of strict moral discipline upon individuals long ago released from the regimens required for mere survival. In primitive social conditions "virtuous" codes of conduct necessarily required "extraordinary pains to master some . . . natural appetite[s]," for without stark and publicly enforced demands for self-control in fundamentally insecure material environments, unmediated expressions of natural desire, especially anger, would instantly threaten social stability itself. In advanced conditions of material security, and especially of affluence, the demand for severe self-deprivation in the name of a higher morality was, however, merely a vestigial mental deposit of primitive social arrangements. What in fact distinguished modern conditions from all previous forms of communal life was the degree to which the secure and affluent, fearing neither God nor the Devil, could indulge their appetites without being counted as immoral by their peers (1, 55; 198–223).

Mandeville's most immediate purpose in distinguishing contemporary from primitive forms of sociability was to provide a further demonstration for his claim that, in the psychic economy of commercial populations accustomed by habit to the emotional rigors of civilization, "courage," the archetypal expression of selfless virtue in the republican canon, had in fact become separated from its natural basis in anger. Both republicans and divines were blind to the fact that new personality types had emerged with the appearance of the stable structures of modern civil society; and that, as a consequence – or so Mandeville argued – the virtuous citizens of both classical and Christian pedigree had become unintended casualties of the civilizing process, save in the fantasies of moralists.

The Reason why there are so few Men of real Virtue, and so many of real Honour, is, because all the Recompense a Man has of a virtuous Action, is the Pleasure of doing it, which most People reckon but poor Pay; but the Self-denial a Man of Honour submits to in one Appetite, is immediately rewarded by the Satisfaction he receives from another, and what he abates of his Avarice, or any other Passion, is doubly repaid to his Pride. (I, 222)

The Fable pointed directly to what Mandeville claimed had been a previously unacknowledged revolution in the history of morals. First rechristened as "valor," the rudiments of primitive courage were then codified in the morality of "honor" by ruling elites during the course of post-medieval European history. Psychologically, honor could obviously be understood as a welcome, because less repressive, substitute for virtue as the primary social tie, especially amongst men of exalted pride. Socially, however, this transformation was possible only in conditions of relative material security, where public exhibitions of self-love would not immediately and uncontrollably enrage one's fellows, thereby threatening the well-being of the community. In contrast to the ancient standards of virtue, modern codes of honor make fewer demands of self-denial upon the individual.

A man of honour must not cheat or tell a Lye; he must punctually repay what he borrows at Play, though the Creditor had nothing to shew for it; but he may drink, swear and owe Money to all the Tradesmen in Town, without taking notice of their dunning. A man of Honour must be true to his Prince and Country ... but if he thinks himself not well used, he may quit it, and do them all the Mischief he can. A Man of Honour must never change his Religion for Interest, but he may be as Debauch'd as he pleases, and never practise any. He must make no Attempts upon his Friend's Wife, Daughter, Sister, or any body that is trusted to his Care, but he may lie with all the World besides. (I, 222–223)

As "honour gives [a man] large grains of allowance, and virtue none," periods of relative affluence allow pride a wide latitude in its search for demonstrable signs of public approbation. And this search is precisely what unconsciously converts the individual's self-love to socially beneficial purposes.

In the wake of a critique of noble heroism as an ideological disguise for aristocratic self-interest amongst a faded warrior caste – which both he and his audience associated with near-contemporary moralists like La Rochefoucauld, and with the fiction of Cervantes (I, 218) – Mandeville reflected upon contemporary codes of honorable conduct.[2] In this literature, honor in its "literal Sense," as Mandeville put it, was exposed as nothing more than "a Means which men ... have

[2] See *Honour*, p. 95.

found to please and gratify one another," all the while seeking to protect their inherited symbols of social dominance. However, he engaged this tradition of criticism expressly intending to demonstrate the general social utility of these demystified ideals. The "Principle of Courage, Virtue and Fidelity" constituting the ideology of noble honor was, he understood, not simply an instrument for the promotion of the interests of a privileged elite. Instead, Mandeville insisted that the establishment of aristocratic ideals "did an abundance of Good throughout the World, by taming Monsters" (I, 218). These norms were "an Invention of Politicians, to keep Men Close to their Promises and Engagements, when all other Ties prov'd ineffectual; and the Christian Religion itself was often found insufficient for that Purpose."[3] The reform and extension of this ancient code of conduct into "a new standard" of "modern honour" during "the last century" signalled a crucial transformation to modernity. In the radically altered social conditions of the seventeenth century, princes, state administrators and their associated clerisies recognized that the methods employed by the medieval Church to tame expressions of courage, in that way policing violence, had lost their psychological force.[4] Substantially reformed civilizing codes were required to discipline unprecedently larger masses of men, most particularly those whose imaginations had been released from the superstitions supporting priestly injunction and whose enlarged opportunities for worldly satisfaction diluted the material austerity and moral rigor of their ancestors. Thus, Mandeville argued, the invention of modern honor did not merely take place at a "much later Date" than the invention of virtue; it was "the greater achievement by far." The ideal of honorable conduct is a distinct "improvement in the Art of Flattery"[5] as a weapon of social discipline, one by virtue of which

the established Pride that is inseparable from those that are possessed of Titles already, makes them often strive as much not to seem unworthy of them, as the working Ambition of others that are yet without, renders them industrious and indefatigable to deserve them ... [While] all the Recompense a Man has of a virtuous Action is the Pleasure of doing it ... the Self-denial a Man of Honour submits to in one Appetite, is immediately rewarded by the Satisfaction he receives from another, and what he abates of ... any other Passion, is doubly repaid to his Pride. (I, 221–222)

---

[3] *Honour*, pp. 29–30.   [4] *Honour*, p. 15.   [5] *Honour*, p. 42.

By distinguishing the forms of honorable conduct which characterized the moral history of the post-medieval world, Mandeville was
able conceptually to identify those novel social disciplines by means of
which citizens in commercial societies could sublimate their most
violent passions, thereby unintentionally promoting political stability, and venting the primary demands of self-liking in materially
productive and psychologically rewarding ways. While the narrowly
restricted martial elites in pre-modern landed societies were immediately disposed to the relatively simple and violent – but emotionally
direct – pleasures of domination, commercial civilizations depended
for their continuity upon maintaining an acceptably muted face of
pride amongst considerably larger populations under conditions of
increasing mobility, extensive civil intercourse and heightened prosperity. Revised "methods of making ourselves acceptable to others,
with as little prejudice to ourselves as possible" (II, 147), were required
as the "bond of society" amongst persons whose wealth and security
enabled them to distinguish themselves by, and thus take delight in,
the "tokens and badges" of affluent living instead of the trophies of
conquest and the submissions of war. Social pretense had now largely
supplanted physical aggression. Clothes, ornaments, equipages,
servants, furniture, buildings and titles had come to offer the psychological satisfactions necessary to stifle the violent, "odious part of
pride" (II, 126). Through the agency of flattery, the social legislation
of a once rude and recently reconstituted warrior caste, tamed and
made polite by social forces beyond its control, together with the
elaborate codes of decorum which distinguished all modern elites,
licensed the emotional compensations for living with others that
previously could be gained only by the prospect of force. Increasingly
internalized as they were formally codified, these rules for the
satisfaction of pride through public approbation

are no more than the various methods ... by which artifice we assist one
another in the enjoyments of life, and refining upon pleasure; and every
individual person is rendered more happy by it, in the Fruition of all the good
Things he can purchase, than he could have been without such Behaviour.
(II, 147)

For the first time in social history the standards of refined civility, now
"to be observ'd everywhere, in speaking, writing and ordering
Actions to be performed by others," enabled persons consistently to
gain the "applause" of their fellows with minimal physical risk.

As with all post-primitive social forms, commercial societies were shaped by "the alterations, that are made in the Behaviour of Men by their being civilized," wherein they learn "useful Cautions, Shifts and Stratagems ... that oblige them to act as they do *viz.*, The Passions within, that, unknown to themselves, govern their Will and direct their Behaviour" (II, 139). But commercial societies were historically unique in one crucial respect: material affluence and political security enabled their members to satisfy self-regarding impulses in ways that largely transcend the conflict between the individual's pursuit of his own pleasure and the blatantly repressive demands of social discipline that previously characterize every society. As never before, men could indulge themselves in the world of commerce because in it they were free to compete in wholly non-violent ways for the most valued "tokens" of public approbation. The "good manners ... civility and politeness" which had come to characterize the social habits of modern elites were in fact regulatory devices governing an unprecedented, but in Mandeville's view already dominant, process of conspicuous consumption of "symbols" for the promotion of self, the relentless accumulation of emblems that could be acquired by wealth alone in a commercial market of marks of esteem.

Modern manners thus comprised the last stage in the history of pride, and "the best way to manage it" (II, 78). The habituation to "politeness" through the "artful education ... [of the] strictest Rules of good Breeding" (II, 79) had effectively, albeit unconsciously, domesticated the violence of an expanding elite within recent history, while redirecting its energies to the productively liberating (because economically expansive) end of luxury consumption. For, "when his noble and polite manner is become habituated to him, it is possible, he may in time forget the Principle he set out with, and become ignorant, or at least insensible of the hidden Spring that gives Life and Motion to all his Actions" (II, 79). Once men were able to distinguish themselves by mannered social pretense underwritten by the marks of wealth, the stern and self-denying morality of virtue which first made communal life possible was effectively reduced to a nostalgic remnant of the politically defeated and downwardly mobile. The decorous intercourse of contemporary elites, then, was at once the initial target of Mandeville's satiric voice as he exposed the hypocrisy of its supposedly other-regarding pronouncements, and the terminus of his enquiry into the history of pride which concluded with the achievement of polished civility – commercial society's successful surrogate for self-denial.

HUTCHESON'S POLEMIC AND HUME'S CRITIQUE

Mandeville distinguished three decisive causes in the long, slow progression to civility: the banding together of savages for their mutual defense against animals; the stimulation of man's innate pride and courage through threats and attacks of other men; and the invention of language and letters, by means of which laws would remain stable and trustworthy instead of being subject to the errors and insecurities necessarily associated with societies governed by oral traditions. Each stage in the civilizing process was accompanied by an "invention" or further refinement of "morality," understood in Mandeville's history as the norms of conduct formally enacted or tacitly designed by the ruling elites, which governed every polity in order to stabilize forms of intercourse amongst beings whose radical egoism and constitutional asociability remained an ever-present threat to society itself.

This conjectural history of the passage from barbarism to commerce, developed mainly in *The Fable*'s second volume, could immediately be read as an extension of the "Vindication" of Mandeville's book, first published in the *London Journal* shortly after *The Fable* was charged in 1723, and subsequently bound together with all future editions of the work (1, 384–412). In this essay Mandeville not only defended his book from the Middlesex Grand Jury's charges of immorality, but emphasized anew his claim that it "describes the Nature and Symptoms of human Passions, detects their Force and Disguises; and traces Self-love in its darkest Recesses ... beyond any other System of Ethicks" (1, 405). *The Fable* was meant to show that

> the Multiplicity of [human] Wants depend [... upon] all those mutual Services which the individual Members of a Society pay to each other; and that consequently, the greater Variety there was of Wants, the larger Number of Individuals might find their private Interest in labouring for the good of others, and united together, compose one Body. (1, 403)

Mandeville's most important self-defense was his claim that the elements of the social system apparent to a conventional, pre-scientific and therefore theoretically innocent observer of contemporary society, like Cleomenes' interlocutor Horatio, constituted a seriously defective basis for representing the "hidden springs" of "all civil commerce." Such an observer "seldom can see further than one Link ... in the Chain of Causes; but those who can enlarge their View, and will give themselves Leisure of gazing on the Prospect on concatenated Events, may in a hundred Places see Good spring up and pullulate from Evil, as naturally as Chickens do from Eggs" (1, 404). Historical anthropology provided a foundation for Mandeville's thesis about the unintended social consequences of self-regarding individual actions. By demonstrating that society and history were causally bound together through a previously unravelled succession of events, now deciphered in *The Fable* via a thought experiment analogous to those classically undertaken in the physical and medical sciences, the history of pride substantially supported the intensely contested argument that persons had become civil in ways unknown to themselves.

Mandeville's physiological model of the passions licensed the foundational presumptions of this hypothetical history: men everywhere and at all times had identical psychological structures; these structures were expressed in basic impulses which predisposed individuals to be strictly self-seeking agents who desired only their own satisfactions. Consequently, the social development of the race must be understood to have resulted from the largely unplanned, though, because physically derived, not random consequences of persons pursuing the amoral and heterogeneous ends which answered the pull of their passions at any given moment in their life histories. The narrative constructed from these premises described a stadial history of the race's progress from instinct to morality and then to law. It charted the course of the most immediate needs of body and mind, needs which were at first both paramount and psychologically transparent, because unmediated by social symbolism. Beginning in conditions of bare subsistence and primitive survival, this story culminated in the commercial polities of contemporary Europe. While the fundamental passionate repertoire of the human frame remained undiminished, these passions were now effectively harnessed, redirected from violent ends to seek "tokens" of public esteem and, during the long course of the civilizing process, made largely unconscious to the social actors themselves.

Now Mandeville's model of the civilizing process entailed two distinct forms of explanation. He sought on the one hand to show that forms of social life advanced as a result of individual actions motivated by nothing but self-regard, since the desire of all persons to satisfy their wants and of "meliorating their condition" (II, 284)[6] without regard

---

[6] See too *Honour*, p. 16.

for the common good could be shown to engender material and technical progress. So viewed, the history of mankind was a decidedly ironic progression in which pure selfishness moderated only by prudence unintentionally engendered affluence and civility. On the other hand, Mandeville's narrative of the history of the race rests somewhat equivocally upon the workings of a hidden hand of nature or Providence which, on the level of society, resolves a universal conflict of individual desires for relatively scarce rewards. For he insisted that both the stability and effective operation of any and every society necessarily depended upon the "work of politicians over several ages." By their legislative tact and ideological cunning, ruling elites played, and would of necessity continue to play, the critical managerial role of directing constitutionally resistant egoists to participate in common social endeavors.

These two forms of social explanation were not easily harmonized, even in the light of Mandeville's reminder that "the work of politicians" should be understood as an evolutionary and often unconscious process taking place "over several ages." One form of explanation depends on the presumption of a continued expression of pure selfishness by all persons at every moment in the history of society; the other seems to invest in the consciousness and will of "politicians" a detached perspective on wider social needs that Mandeville denied to the strictly self-regarding egoists who populate *The Fable*. The tension between the two was only partially resolved by refinements to the initial arguments out of which Mandeville constructed his conjectural history of pride. His sketch of the civilizing process was shaped by a narrative in which the decisive moments of social evolution, such as the transformation in the notion of honor that occurred in the seventeenth century, could be understood as rationally comprehensible responses by groups of individuals seeking only to maximize their utilities in conditions of increasing security, affluence and knowledge. At the same time, however, such important shifts in belief and practice, Mandeville argued, finally proved successful and socially significant primarily because of the stabilizing work of ruling elites who sought by political intervention either to protect or extend their historically acquired powers. "Politicians" are significant historical actors in Mandeville's history in respect of their ability effectively to contain strife in periods of social transition by providing communally useful and ideologically satisfying rewards to hungry egoists largely unaware of the manipulations being performed on their pride. These devices include the "farces and ceremonies" to which the Roman Church subjected great princes in the High Middle Ages, thereby containing their enlarged resources for bellicosity.[7] They make themselves abundantly evident in commercial societies, where the impulse of even larger bodies of powerful men forcibly to dominate others becomes effectively re-chanelled by law and custom in politically harmless displays of the signs of social power conveyed by the instruments of wealth.

Mandeville's attempt to resolve the explanatory tensions between a stark methodological individualism and a resort to Providence embedded within his work, and at the same time to defend *The Fable* from the criticism of moralists who accused him of licensing impiety, produced its own unintended consequences. In the measure that his genealogy of morals conceptually established the possibility of a wholly secular and strictly naturalistic account of the evolution of mankind from conditions of need and use, it also underscored Mandeville's own foundational hypothesis about the formation of formally organized society. Mandeville not only claimed that the "invention of morality" constituted "the last step to society;" he also argued that the rudiments of political life itself could only have been established by the ideological intervention of a cunning minority who first made men governable by "flattering" violent and unruly primitives so that they would constrain their passions and willingly obey rules of justice designed by these political elites for their own advantage. "It is evident that the first Rudiments of Morality, broach'd by Skilful Politicians to render Man useful to each other as well as tractable were chiefly contrived that the Ambitious might reap the more Benefit from, and govern vast Numbers of them with the greater Ease and Security" (I, 46–47).

It was this foundational argument that drew Francis Hutcheson's anger, first vented in letters to *The Dublin Journal* in February of 1726,[8] and which remained the occasion of later attempts by the Presbyterian minister and professor of Moral Philosophy at Glasgow to ridicule and demolish *The Fable*.[9] Mandeville's claims that all motivations are

[7] *Honour*, pp. 49–51.

[8] Reprinted as J. Arbuckle (ed.), *A Collection of Letters and Essays on Several Subjects, lately Publish'd in the Dublin Journal* (London, 1729), 2 volumes, in *Collected Works*, ed. Bernhard Fabian (Hildesheim: Olms Reprint, 1971), VII, and in Francis Hutcheson, *Reflections on Laughter and Remarks on the Fable of the Bees* (Glasgow, 1750).

[9] David Fate Norton, *David Hume: Common-Sense Moralist, Skeptical Metaphysician* (Princeton University Press, 1982), pp. 65–70.

necessarily self-regarding, that the rules of morality derived from convention, and that they were a necessary but secondary effect of the civilizing process, directly challenged Hutcheson's lifelong enterprise of providing a philosophically consistent and psychologically egalitarian conception of man's natural sociability, and of an account of the benevolent nature of his social passions. Hutcheson contended that actions and values were properly to be judged according to what Shaftesbury had first called a "moral sense," universally distributed rather than the exclusive property of a cultivated elite, and which functioned in a way analogous to the natural human sensibility to beauty and perfection. Crucial insights into the beauty of virtue, Hutcheson argued, were equally available to all; as possible for the rude but sturdily independent inhabitants of a "republick of farmers" as for the "virtuoso" who represented the learned in an economically advanced trading state.[10] And the most fundamental prescription of the moral sense, so Hutcheson claimed, was the production of the greatest pleasure for the greatest number. Thus, *pace* Mandeville, pointing out the various ways in which moral actions seem to serve our personal ends fails to show that these actions are founded in or motivated by considerations of self-interest, since principles of morals, far from being contrary to private interest, are founded in a fundamental sociable principle of human nature.

Hutcheson attempted to harness these arguments with natural law theory as it was coming to be interpreted within the Scottish academic tradition. *An Inquiry into the Original of Our Ideas of Beauty and Virtue* (1725), his first work, was intended to encourage this moral perspective on the study of human nature by systematically comprehending the ultimate ends and pleasures of human life in ways superior to what he regarded as the narrowly interest-based interpretations of the Grotian natural law tradition, associated with Hobbes and Pufendorf, then with Locke's *Two Treatises of Government*, and most recently, as he insisted in his *Essay on the Nature and Conduct of the Passions and Affections* (1728), with Mandeville's account of the manner in which self-love shapes moral conduct. In Hutcheson's view, this tradition was defective because of its unjustifiably limited concentration on the means by which sociability could be said to have been achieved. As he said in the following year, "[h]ence it is that the old notions of *natural*

---

[10] Francis Hutcheson, *A System of Moral Philosophy* (Glasgow, 1755), in *Collected Works*, v–vi, ii.xiii.7, vi, p. 74.

affections, and kind *instincts*, the *sensus communis*, the *Decorum*, and *Honestum*, are almost banish'd out of our books of morals ... All must be *interest*, and some selfish view."[11] Hutcheson's over-riding objective was to establish the foundations of a common moral consciousness without reducing this sentiment either to self-interest narrowly considered, or to those merely physiological sources posited by skeptics and freethinkers. He sought, in other words, to re-infuse an essential and enlarged moral characteristic, seen as embedded in the human constitution, into the conception of sociability developed in modern natural law, one which transcended and thereby gave ethical coherence to a merely empirical condition.

The first volume of Mandeville's *Fable* provided Hutcheson with an ideal target in this project of reconstruction, as he announced on the title-page of the *Inquiry*. Mandeville's widely circulated arguments could easily be taken as a *reductio ad absurdum* of the skepticism inherent in the minimal moral compass of the constellation of "selfish theories" Hutcheson sought to criticize. *The Fable* deeply offended Hutcheson because in it Mandeville appeared not only to rejoice in human depravity as the source of national prosperity and individual happiness; also, he directly asserted that unalloyed competitive individualism worked in the interests of society as a whole and, moreover, that it should rightly be seen as the propulsive mechanism in the development of sociability itself. Hutcheson saw the task of "laying the foundations of morality" in human nature as a project which entailed the art of convincing people to act virtuously. The moralist was obliged to "preach" morality, so Hutcheson argued. He would promote virtuous conduct by demonstrating to men that it was in their best interests to act virtuously, in accordance with their nature, which is "not the ordinary condition of mankind ... but the condition our nature can be raised to by due culture."[12] Most pointedly, Hutcheson was outraged by Mandeville's attempt to show that the smooth operation of modern systems of exchange and specialization could be understood solely by virtue of a self-contained analysis of the workings of self-regard, and required no effort of benevolent public-spiritedness, kept alive by Presbyterian homilies and professorial disquisitions.

For Hutcheson then, *The Fable*'s comprehensive reduction of

---

[11] Hutcheson, *A Collection of Letters*, p. 103.
[12] Hutcheson, *A System of Moral Philosophy*, I, p. 77.

virtues to passions, and its claim that all systems of sociability could be derived from this reduction, constituted an ideal point of departure. Against Mandeville, he sought to establish the virtues as embedded features of human constitutions deriving from a moral sense through which men naturally perceive both pleasure and beauty. This moral principle was, Hutcheson repeatedly argued, superior to, because more basic than, either the passions of interest or self-love which were at the heart of Mandeville's licentious doctrines.

[A] certain turn of mind or temper, a certain cause of action, and plan of life is plainly recommended to us by nature; and the mind finds the most joyful feelings in performing and reflecting upon such offices as this sense recommends; but it is uneasy and ashamed in reflecting upon a contrary course . . . What is approved by this sense we count as right and beautiful, and call it virtue; what is condemned, we count base and deformed and vicious.[13]

Hutcheson quoted Aristotle on the peculiar human fitness towards certain ends, and concluded his first polemic against *The Fable* by arguing that this teleological perspective was the necessary foundation of any subsequent inquiry into the processes of sociability. "We must therefore search accurately into the constitution of our nature," he insisted, "to see what sort of creatures we are; for what purposes nature has formed us; what character God our Creator requires us to maintain."[14]

While he rightly pointed to the various ambiguities embedded in the motto, "private vices, public benefits," and strove throughout his career to convince his readers that Mandeville's immoralism was nothing but an empty play on words,[15] the sentimentalism which informed Hutcheson's campaign against *The Fable* was nevertheless grounded in a moral discourse complementary to Mandeville's. Both he and Mandeville argued that actions are expressions of passions; reason alone could provide no independent standard for action. For Hutcheson as for Mandeville, the truth of no principle of morality could be established without first examining the facts of human nature. Each agreed that these facts pointed to the irreducibility of the passions as the springs of action, and that persons are constituted in intersubjective contact with others. Given these premises, Hutche-

---

[13] Hutcheson, *A Short Introduction to Moral Philosophy* (1747), in *Collected Works*, IV, I.x, p. 17. See too *A Collection of Essays*, p. 136, and *A System of Moral Philosophy* in *Collected Works*, v, p. 58.
[14] Hutcheson, *Short Introduction*, I.i, in *Collected Works*, IV, p. 2. See too pp. 13–14, and *An Inquiry into the Original of our Ideas of Beauty and Virtue*, in *Collected Works*, I, pp. 197 and 275.
[15] Hutcheson, *A Collection of Letters*, pp. 132–133.

son's argument against Mandeville ultimately came precariously to rest on a single, fragile claim: that "a social feeling or sense of partnership with mankind" not only could restrain and direct egoistic desires, but that the history of society itself, and the stability of social institutions, could plausibly be understood as the product of just such restraint and direction. And it was around this claim against Mandeville that Hume, Hutcheson's pupil and friend, broke with his former teacher and developed Mandeville's arguments in a new direction.

Hume's very sympathy with Hutcheson's conviction that sentiment rather than pure rational agency guided men in their moral judgements led him to take issue with Hutcheson on Mandevillian grounds. In Hume's view, Hutcheson's conception of the natural sentiments lacked any satisfactory way of accounting naturalistically, as Mandeville had attempted to do, for the ways in which interest and self-love could be restrained. For Hume, the causes of animal passions lie solely in the body, while with humans they can be placed in the mind or in external objects; but as far as the body is concerned, the same qualities cause pride in the animal as in the human. Humans and animals share "all the internal principles" to produce either pride or humility. The causes are the same and so is their mode of operation. It was precisely the inadequacies of Hutcheson's tacit assumption that the rudiments of a complete system of ethics were imprinted in the unique features of human character – a view Mandeville explicitly sought to demolish – which drove Hume to reconsider the construction of moral rules from Mandeville's perspective on morals as derivative features of the civilizing process.

Hume took the position that we praise actions not by virtue of their execution, but only according to the motives which produce them, since we habitually regard actions themselves as signs which indicate the motives which caused an individual to act. However, following the line of argument developed by Bayle and amplified by Mandeville, Hume went on to claim that it would be a mistake to think with Hutcheson that we give our approval to persons because we are naturally pleased on each occasion that we are confronted with actions we deem virtuous. This would be absurd, again as Mandeville had indicated, because

[t]he first virtuous motives, which bestow a merit on any action, can never be a regard to the virtue of that action, but must be some other natural motive or principle. To suppose that the mere regard to the virtue of the action may

be the first motive, which produced the action, and rendered it virtuous, is to reason in a circle.[16]

Each time moral questions are considered, the source for the categories of virtue and vice must be sought elsewhere, in some motive of human nature which is logically distinct from the sense of its morality. Hume argued that the fact that people do occasionally act from what they genuinely experience as a sense of duty or morality only occurs, as Mandeville stressed, in a state of civilization, where all human actions are strongly conditioned by the power of education, habit and custom, in the ambience of which a moral sense becomes second nature. And even if one concedes to Hutcheson that *some* benevolent sentiments derive from a natural motive (something Mandeville sought to account for with his conception of "pity," which Hutcheson ignored), the rules of justice which compelled one to repay a debt, for example, had no plausible natural source capable of accounting for their universal and unconditional applicability. For this reason these rules had to be deemed "artificial," in the sense that they do not arise directly from human emotions, nor fully accord with them, but are inculcated through our interaction with existing social institutions. As Hume wrote to Hutcheson,

I cannot agree to your sense of *Natural*. 'Tis founded on final Causes; which is a consideration, that appears to me pretty uncertain and unphilosophical. For pray, what is the End of Man? Is he created for Happiness or for Virtue? For this life or for the next? For himself or for his Maker? Your definition of *Natural* depends upon solving these Questions, which are endless, and quite wide of my Purpose. I have never call'd Justice unnatural, but only artificial.[17]

It was precisely the question of accounting for this artificiality, for the prudential and conventionalist nature of the central features of civilized sociability, that set Hume's project apart from Hutcheson's and allied it with Mandeville's. So it seemed to the governors of Edinburgh University, who denied Hume the chair of Ethics and Pneumatical Philosophy because he "sapp[ed] the Foundations of Morality, by denying the natural and essential Difference betwixt Right and Wrong, Good and Evil, Justice and Injustice; making the Difference only artificial, and to arise from Human Conventions and

---

[16] Hume, *Treatise*, III.ii.1.   [17] Hume, *Letters*, I, p. 33.

Contracts."[18] Indeed, in the Conclusion to Book III of the *Treatise of Human Nature*, Hume made the connection patent. Repeating what he had written privately to Hutcheson about their philosophical differences, and trading upon Berkeley's attempt to dismiss Mandeville as a "minute philosopher," Hume wrote:

The anatomist ought never to emulate the painter; nor in his accurate dissection and portraitures of the smaller parts of the human body, pretend to give his figures any graceful and engaging attitude or expression. There is even something hideous, or at least minute, in the views of things which he presents; and it is necessary the objects should be set more at a distance, and be more covered up from sight, to make them engaging to the eye and imagination. An anatomist, however, is admirably fitted to give advice to the painter; and it is even impracticable to excel in the latter without the assistance of the former. We must have an exact knowledge of the parts, their situation and connection, before we can design any elegance or correctness.

Of all of Mandeville's contemporary critics, Hume most clearly understood the broad implications of Mandeville's project of naturalistic social explanation. At the same time, he deftly isolated the crux of *The Fable*'s foundational claim, that men could have been made moral, and subject to political discipline, merely by being, as Hume put it, "talked at." Hume agreed with Mandeville that "though [the historical] process of the sentiments be *natural*, and even necessary, it is certain that it is ... fowarded by the artifice of politicians, who in order to govern men more easily, and preserve peace in human society, have endeavoured to produce an esteem for justice."[19] Yet "some philosophers," he said, alluding to Mandeville,

have represented all moral distinctions as the effect of artifice and education, when skilful politicians endeavoured to restrain the turbulent passions of men, and make them operate to the public good, by the notions of honour and shame. This system, however, is not consistent ... [for] had not men a natural sentiment of approbation and blame it could never be excited by politicians; nor would the words *laudable* and *praiseworthy*, *blameable* and *odious*, be any more intelligible than if they were a language perfectly unknown to us.[20]

In effect, Hume did not object to Mandeville's speculative anthropology and hypothetical history as immoral or ill-conceived, as virtually all previous critics had done. Rather, he accepted Mande-

---

[18] Quoted in Ernest Campbell Mosner, *The Life of David Hume*, 2nd edition (Oxford: Clarendon Press, 1980), p. 630.   [19] Hume, *Treatise*, III.ii.2.   [20] Hume, *Treatise*, III.iii.1.

ville's naturalistic assumptions and then insisted that, in a crucial respect, *The Fable*'s argument was insufficiently naturalistic. While setting the infant sciences of man on a new scientific footing by demonstrating that any compelling account of action and belief had to proceed from a detailed anatomy of the passions, Mandeville, Hume claimed, had then asserted the "impossible," that the actions of politicians "should be the sole cause of the distinction we make betwixt vice and virtue. For if nature did not aid us in this particular, it would be in vain for politicians to talk of *honourable* or *dishonourable*, *praiseworthy* or *blameable*."[21] If men were not directly responsive to moral language, the "speeches" of politicians would have fallen on deaf ears. Hume's (Mandevillian) point was clear enough. For any comprehensive understanding of social progress to be philosophically defensible, in that it followed the "experimental method" of the sciences, it would have to account for accepted conventions of politics and the emergence of rules of justice strictly in terms of the unforeseen consequences produced by the passions of individuals. Moral rules, Hume agreed with Mandeville, should be understood through a conjectural anthropology of morals which attempts to describe the necessary features from which our moral judgements, or those of any society, arise. But such an anthropology must attempt to explain the way in which the actions of individuals unintentionally lead over time to uniform and orderly patterns of moral behavior. Here, Hume argued, Mandeville had failed. The success of *The Fable*'s project, in Hume's view, depended upon the purging from its narrative all vestiges of the purely voluntarist and historically mythological remnants that disfigured Mandeville's enterprise.

Hume wished to lay the foundations of an empirical and secular "science of morality" which, like Mandeville's, dispensed with the religious hypotheses which underlay natural law, but one which also avoided the licentious implications of *The Fable*'s "selfish system."[22] Justice, Hume argued, could only have been defined by "conventions" arising from the progress of the passions. But although these conventions were "artificial," in the sense that there was no elemental

---

[21] Hume, *Treatise*, III.ii.2.

[22] See Duncan Forbes, *Hume's Philosophical Politics* (Cambridge University Press, 1975), pp. 68–72; James Moore, "Hume's Theory of Justice and Property," *Political Studies* 24 (1976), pp. 103–119; and Moore, "The Social Background of Hume's Science of Human Nature," in David Fate Norton, Nicholas Capaldi and Wade L. Robinson (eds.), *McGill Hume Studies* (San Diego: Austin Hill, 1976), pp. 23–41.

or original instinct for law, as there was for hunger or resentment, they were not arbitrary features of human evolution, as Hume took Mandeville to have suggested. The re-direction of socially destructive passions by the understanding of a naturally inventive species to the common ends of the group was the spontaneous and unplanned product of social intercourse. As such, they could be considered as "natural laws" entirely consistent with the passionate repertoire of the individuals who first banded together in families and, "by a slow progression," improved as society enlarged.[23] Law and justice were themselves aboriginal, "palpable and evident" features of any form of social life. This point was obvious even to the most savage members of the human race, Hume contended, precisely because the languages of morals and of law which characterized every community were, contrary to Mandeville, wholly reflexive, unanticipated expressions of the understanding which arose from the natural sentiments. "Experience," Hume said, "soon teaches us [a] method of correcting our sentiments, or at least correcting our language, where the sentiments are more stubborn and unalterable."[24] Thus, in the process of exposing weaknesses in *The Fable*'s argument, Hume was the first to recognize that in denying that the emergence of moral language was a strictly unplanned, natural consequence of human evolution, a thesis shared by Grotius and Pufendorf as well as Hobbes, Mandeville had put foward his most radical and unsettling challenge to the moral legitimacy of civil society. And in ways Hume never fully anticipated when he published *The Treatise* in 1740, *The Fable*'s discussion of the origin of language, and thus of moral discourse, became a primary vehicle through which this challenge became a central feature in the Enlightenment's confrontation with the consequences of its own discoveries about modernity.

RHETORIC AND THE EMERGENCE OF CIVILITY

As we have seen, the invention of language and letters was the decisive "third and last step to society" in *The Fable*'s conjectural history of the progress of pride. Mandeville was far less interested in verbal and written discourse as cognitive instruments designed for the improvement of knowledge, than in the first formation of language as a stage in the civilizing process and in language use as the primary vehicle for

---

[23] Hume, *Treatise*, iii.ii.2.   [24] Hume, *Treatise*, iii.iii.1.

the continuous promotion of sociability. He reasoned that although the race began with solitary brutes endowed with the capacities for reason and speech, these potentials would have had to remain wholly dormant until they were called forth unselfconsciously in unanticipated circumstances of need and desire. Mandeville was thus committed to a naturalistic view of the origin of language, one directly opposed to the orthodox doctrine that language had been given ready-made to man by God, or was the immediate result of a specific aptitude infused by God into Adam and then passed to his progeny. Drawing upon scripture, this view presumed that language not only resulted from divine instruction, but that all existing languages derived from a time, before the flood and the confusion of Babel, in which words conveyed the essential quality of things and language was in natural accord with the creation of which it was a part.[25]

The claim that languages were human and conventional rather than divine and natural already had, at the time Mandeville wrote, prestigious support in Locke's demolition of the Adamic presumption that names contained the knowledge of things. But Mandeville had few longstanding epistemological interests, and while he alluded to Locke's authority on this question (II, 190), the intricate arguments of Book III of *The Essay Concerning Human Understanding* were of little immediate concern to him. Mandeville was less interested in the foundations of meaning than in the vagaries of use. In approaching the original function of settled articulate language, he expressly denied that "the design of speech is to make our thoughts known to others" (II, 289), dismissing as absurd the claim central to natural law theories (and all contractarian modes of political argument) that promises acquired their legitimacy in the free traffic of verbal exchange. Mandeville first made this point in his tale of the merchant and the lion, one of the most contentious parts of *The Fable*'s first volume (I, 176–181). A member "of the Breed that rang'd in *Aesop's*

---

[25] See Paul Kuehner, *Theories on the Origin and Formation of Language in Eighteenth-Century France* (Philadelphia: University of Pennsylvania Press, 1944) and Lia Formigiari, *Linguistica e anthropologia nel secundo settecento* (Messina: Editrice La Libra, 1972). The most valuable discussions of the philosophical presuppositions of this eighteenth-century debate on language origins are Hans Aarsleff, "Leibniz and Locke on Language in the Eighteenth Century and the Debate in the Berlin Academy Before Herder," in *From Locke to Saussure* (Minneapolis: University of Minnesota Press, 1982), pp. 42–83 and 146–209, and David E. Wellbery, *Lessing's "Laocoon": Semiotics and Aesthetics in the Age of Reason* (Cambridge University Press, 1984), pp. 1–42. See too, G.A. Wells, "Condillac, Rousseau and Herder on the Origin of Language," *Studies on Voltaire and the English Language* 230 (1985), pp. 233–246, and Pierre Juliard, *Philosophies of Language in the Eighteenth Century* (The Hague: Nijhoff, 1970).

Days," the lion spoke several languages, and thus could understand and communicate with the merchant, washed up on the shores of Africa who, at his mercy, "pleaded his Cause with abundance of good Rhetorick." But the merchant's "Flattery and fine Words made very little impression" on the hungry beast, nor did his "Arguments of greater Solidity," since the lion, the only participant in the dialogue to speak with nature's voice, understands that the "Vain and Covetous Animal" pleading before him primarily employs speech as an instrument of self-promotion. Just before the merchant "fainted away" with fear at the prospect of being devoured, the lion suggests that he too might follow the "Maxims of Men," with whom "nothing is more sacred than that the Reason of the strongest is ever the most prevalent." Later, in *The Fable*'s second volume, Mandeville extended the implications of this tale:

If by Man's speaking to be understood you mean, that when Men speak, they desire that the Purport of the Sounds they utter should be known and apprehended by others, I answer in the Affirmative. But if you mean by it, that Men speak, in order that their thoughts may be known, and their Sentiments laid open and seen through by others, which likewise may be meant by *speaking to be understood*, I answer in the Negative. The first Sign or Sound that ever Man made, born of a Woman, was made in Behalf, and intended for the use of him who made it; and I am of Opinion, that the first Design of Speech was to persuade others, either to give Credit to what the speaking Person would have them believe; or else to act or suffer such Things, as he would compel them to act or suffer, if they were entirely in his power. (II, 289)

Since he understood language as an essentially social instrument, Mandeville sought "the first Motive and Intention that put Man upon speaking," for it is through public speech "that a very considerable, if not the greatest part of the attribute [of sociability] is acquired" (II, 189). He wished to explain how, lacking any instinct for language and unable to develop it purposively, the first primitives could have made themselves understood. In his formulation, articulate language had its origins in the need to express emotion rather than in any desire to transmit knowledge. Once even the rudest primitive came in continuous contact with others, "Self-liking would make it seek for Opportunities, Gestures, Looks, and Sounds, to display the value it had for itself, superior to what it had for others . . . He would be highly delighted with, and love every body, whom he thought to have a good Opinion of him, especially those, that by

Words or Gestures should own it to his Face" (II, 133–134). The initial purpose of expression, then, was to voice what Mandeville called men's "Wants and their Will" (II, 290), a project of persuasion and deception in which words cannot be conceived apart from the voices which utter them. The origin of language thus raised for Mandeville the question of moral and political authority, since language use had as its object the self-regarding interests of speakers in pleasing themselves as they symbolically or in brute fact dominated their respondents.

The "wild couples" living in nature were at first speechless brutes, having no inclination towards verbal expression yet nonetheless endowed with a capacity to communicate by the "dumb Signs" of an aboriginal language of gesture.

[F]or it is more natural to untaught Men to express themselves by Gestures, than by Sounds ... To express Grief, Joy, Love, Wonder and Fear, there are certain Tokens, that are common to the whole Species. Who doubts that the crying of Children was given them by Nature, to call Assistance and raise Pity ...? How universal, as well as copious, is the Language of the Eyes, by the help of which the remotest nations understand one another at first Sight, taught or untaught ... and in that Language our wild Couple would at their first meeting say more to one another without guile, than any civiliz'd Pair would dare to name without blushing. (II, 286–287)

Uniformly endowed with common gestural signs of their primitive mental states, savages would naturally comprehend each other's expressions of emotion,[26] since a specific gesture is the reflexive result of a desire upon our bodies (II, 158–159). This original state of communicative competence permitted savages an unselfconscious understanding of each other's needs, facilitating the development of social relationships. A conventional language of verbal signs originated in reflection upon these gestural regularities and in the convenience, recognized only after at least "a dozen generations," of marking and symbolizing needed objects not immediately present to sensation. The longer men lived together "the greater Variety of Sounds they would invent, as well for Actions as [for] things themselves," a process accelerated by the ability of the young to invent new sounds owing to the greater flexibility of their organs of speech. "Every Generation" would improve upon these sounds, "and this

---

[26] Compare Lucretius, *De rerum novarum*, trans. W.E. Leonard (New York: Dutton, 1957), Book v, lines 1010ff.

must have been the Origin of All Languages, and [of] Speech itself"
(II, 288). Reason and reflection would then polish and perfect verbal
languages so as to increase their precision and increase as well the
ability of the more sagacious to employ words in the service of their
own veiled ends.

Mandeville's was one of the earliest anti-Adamic and evolutionary
sketches of the development of language. In the conceptual architec-
ture of *The Fable*, however, this argument was not meant to stand
independently. Instead, it was intended to supplement "An Enquiry
Into the Origin of Moral Virtue" (I, 41–57), which Mandeville later
recognized was the work's most radical and influential part.[27] There,
it will be remembered, he argued that "all untaught Animals are only
solicitous of pleasing themselves, and naturally follow the bent of their
own Inclination" (I, 41). In "the State of Nature" only those
creatures having the fewest appetites and the least self-understanding
were fit to live together in peace. No species of animal is less socially
inclined than man, that creature of almost infinite selfish desires who
is too headstrong and cunning to be subdued by force alone. Yet "no
creature besides himself can ever be made sociable," and no animal is
more in need of society than this one, by nature the least sociable.

Mandeville set about exploring this paradox while posing another:
those impulses which dispose men to seek only their own satisfactions
at the same time make them fit subjects for manipulation by others
adept at the arts of persuasion. The "Lawgivers and other wise men"
who civilized the race convinced their fellows "that it was more
beneficial for every Body to conquer than indulge his appetites, and
much better to mind the Publick than what seemed his private
interest." They "bestow'd a Thousand encomiums on the Rationality
of [their] souls" (I, 43), and through the "Aerial Coin of Praise" (I, 55)
contrived imaginary rewards in place of "real" ones. Men continued
to follow their inclinations of course – they could hardly do otherwise
– and sought only their own pleasures. The transformation into
sociability begins not with an impossible alteration of human nature,
but with the substitution of imaginary for real objects of desire.
Indeed, because men are self-reflective, knowingly seeking pleasure
and self-consciously anticipate its rewards, they can be manipulated and controlled. No man was "either so savage as not to be
charmed with praise, or so despicable as patiently to bear contempt."
Flattery was thus the "bewitching engine" employed to tame men by

---

[27] *Honour*, Preface.

encouraging within them a conception of self which had as part of its content the opinion of others. And once the arts of flattery "insinuated themselves into the Hearts of Men," they could be instructed in the rhetoric of honor and shame, in the ideals of public service, and in the purely verbal rewards of praise.

The multitudes were convinced by "arguments" of those seeking to rule that a supposed conquest of impulse was the highest principle of moral judgement. This standard served to divide mankind into a majority incapable of self-denial, and the lofty few representatives of the species who repressed their passions in exercises of public spirit. "This was (or at least might have been) the manner after which savage man was broke" (1, 46). The "first rudiments of morality" were framed by Mandeville as cunning political inventions which rendered men tractable so that the ambitious might more easily command the rest. Mandeville thus conceived of the civilizing process as beginning in rhetoric. A sustained verbal performance by the strong subdued the innocent through their own consent

to call every thing which, without Regard to the Public, Man should commit to gratify any of his Appetites, VICE ... And to give the Name of VIRTUE to every Performance by which Man, contrary to the impulse of Nature, should endeavour the Benefit of others, or the Conquest of his own Passions out of a Rational Ambition of being good. (1, 48)

While "the Heroes who took such extraordinary Pains to master some of their natural Appetites" (1, 45) were more than compensated for these repressions by a vast increase in their power over others, and through the ensuing public "applause" that gratified their self-love (1, 55),

those who wanted a sufficient Stock of either Pride or Resolution to buoy them up in mortifying ... what was dearest to them ... would yet be asham'd of confessing themselves to be those despicable Wretches that belong'd to the inferior Class, and were generally reckon'd to be so little remov'd from Brutes; and that therefore in their own Defence they would say, as others did, and hiding their own Imperfections as well as they could, cry up Self-denial and Publick-spiritedness as much as any. (1, 45)

This "invention of Lawgivers" was an already-established allegorical figure of the tradition of analyzing the passions in which Mandeville wrote.[28] An ironic reversal of republican arguments about the

---

[28] Arthur O. Lovejoy, *Reflections on Human Nature* (Baltimore: Johns Hopkins University Press, 1961), pp. 175–178.

civilizing function of eloquence, classically put forward by Cicero and Quintillian,[29] it served on the one hand as a hypothetical point of origin, a founding moment deduced from the trajectory of civilized intercourse. On the other hand, as Mandeville made clear, civilization had to be understood as a slow and gradual consolidation of this original ideological achievement, one in which praise became a political token of esteem "by which a rational Creature is kept in Awe for Fear of it Self, and an Idol is set up, that shall be its own Worshipper."[30]

Mandeville's speculations about the origin of language, then, were intended directly to supplement his account of the foundations of civilization and morality. The passage from conditions of innate, gestural communication to the circumstances surrounding articulate discourse he conceived as the movement from nature to artifice. Moral virtues became "the Political Offspring which Flattery begot upon Pride" (I, 51) through the purely conventional speech acts of naming and agreement. They marked not so much the progress of cognition as the construction of an intricate framework of deception and self-deception in which men who commanded words commanded the assent of others as well. As their vocabularies and stock of idioms grew, the polished manipulators whose moral anatomy Mandeville sought to lay bare were precisely those inhabitants of societies where natural forms of gestural expression had been reduced to remnants of public speech and theatrical contrivance. Amongst materially backward people – like his southern European contemporaries who retained powerful gestural components in their communicative practices, and so still exchanged natural "tokens" of feeling "without guile" – men were at the same time startlingly less successful in the repressive but materially rewarding disciplines of modern commercial life.

Mandeville's account of language as the agent of socialization aimed to arouse concern over the apparent contradiction between the march of civilization and articulate speech on the one hand, and, on the other, the decay of naturally expressive forms of sympathy. He employed a specific strategy of argument to achieve this effect. Mandeville sought to implicate the reader of *The Fable* in his own

---

[29] See especially *De inventione*, I, 2, and *De oratore*, I, 8. In the *Institutio oratoria* (modelled on the opening of *De inventione*), Quintillian claims (II.xvi.9–10) that the founders of cities could not have brought wandering multitudes together to form peoples without "the highest powers of oratory."   [30] *Honour*, p. 41.

applause for the spectacular ability of modern societies to create wealth, and then through irony to detach him from the moral justifications of these societies by exposing their rhetorical strategies for concealing sheer self-interest. The profound impact of *The Fable* was due in part to Mandeville's having adopted the ancient distinction between language as a mechanism of rational argument and speech as a method of seduction, a distinction refined by the Jansenist moralists to whose understanding of the passions he was indebted.[31] In his own account of the foundation of moral virtue Mandeville then dissolved forms of argument into the modes of rhetoric through which men were seduced, and seduced themselves, into the shackles of self-denial. Articulate language was the vehicle through which the deceptions required for the pleasures of civilization arose, and were then maintained on the ruins of transparent gestural understanding.

A subversive feature of Mandeville's approach to language as an instrument of social discipline was its pagan philosophical provenance.[32] While Thomas Stanley had previously combined the accounts of language and society given by Lucretius and Diogenes Laertius in a brief passage in his *History of Philosophy*,[33] Mandeville's was the first extended modern adaptation of the Epicurean thesis that ordinary language was the product of convention, that laws were originally established as the direct product of these conventions, and that, as Diogenes famously paraphrased Epicurus, "there never was an absolute justice, but only an agreement made in reciprocal intercourse in whatever localities now and again from time to time, providing against the infliction of suffering or harm."[34] *Pace* Plato in the *Cratylus*, Epicurus denied that the problem of whether names were first given in accordance with the nature of things (as in onomato-

---

[31] See, for example, Blaise Pascal, *Réflections sur la géométrie en général. De l'esprit de géométrique et de l'art de persuader*, in *Œuvres complètes*, ed. Jean Mesnard (Paris: Gallimard, 1954), pp. 576–604, especially 592–602, and Wilber Samuel Howell, *Eighteenth-Century British Logic and Rhetoric* (Princeton University Press, 1971), pp. 322–330, for the importance of the Port-Royal *Logic* of Antoine Arnauld and Pierre Nicole. Mandeville was unaware of the most significant contemporary engagement with this tradition, that of Vico. For this see Paulo Rossi, *The Dark Abyss of Time: The History of the Earth and the History of Nations from Hooke to Vico* (University of Chicago Press, 1984), trans. Lydia D. Cochrane, especially pp. 246–250; Michael Mooney, *Vico in the Tradition of Rhetoric* (Princeton University Press, 1985), pp. 171–186 and 210–216, and Frank Manuel, *The Enlightenment Confronts the Gods* (New York: Atheneum, 1967), p. 167, who suggests that Vico was probably acquainted with *The Fable*.

[32] For the history of these questions see Rossi, *The Dark Abyss of Time*, Part III, "Barbarism and Language," especially pp. 195–222. [33] Stanley, *The History of Philosophy*, pp. 591–592.

[34] *The Lives of the Philosophers*, x.150.

poeia) or through pure convention, perhaps by the act of some person or persons, was essentially logical in nature. In his view it called instead for an empirical and historical answer. In a short passage Epicurus proposed that while at a first, primitive stage in the evolution of mankind natural naming might have been used, later on people in a given region would conventionally decide on certain words to facilitate communication. Lastly, when the need arose for abstract terms to signify universally applicable concepts, the few who required them invented suitable names.[35] This conventionalism did not preclude a founding belief in the natural origins of language, since the complex economy of pleasure and pain which structured human behavior was for Epicurus grounded in primitive elements of feeling whose reflexive signs in gesture and sound might be viewed as natural, irreducible atoms of linguistic experience. But Epicurean conventionalism, especially in its revived European form associated with Gassendi, Charleton and their followers, threw doubt upon the metaphysical reality, as opposed to the social utility, of those general concepts invented by minorities skilled in the manipulation of language. As Mandeville pointedly noted, these included the "Chimeras and Surmises" of religion whose dogmas were articulated by priests to answer primitive fears (II, 213–214). John Digby put this point well in 1712 in commenting upon the Epicurean maxim, "The Wise Man Shall not study Eloquence in the Exposition of his Discoveries," in *Epicurus's Morals*:[36]

'Tis unworthy [of] the Wise Man, to be over-studious in the knowledge of Words . . . 'tis making a Criminal Medley of Things Real, and those that have their Existence, but in the Imagination. The Philosopher therefore must not imitate the ways of the Orator whose Profession . . . is to persuade . . . by the means of his Expressions . . . and to charm (as one may say) his Auditory in favour of the Fable . . . Epicurus will have it that the Figures of *Rhetoric* are altogether useless in the explication of the Precepts of Wisdom.

Lucretius' discussion of language in *De rerum natura* supported this skeptical view of the function of speech as an instrument of social mystification.[37] This discussion was the notoriously heretical source of Père Richard Simon's influential critique of the Biblical account of language origins,[38] versions of which circulated in anti-religious

---

[35] *Epistula*, 1.75–76, in *Epicurus, the Extant Remains*, trans. C. Bailey (Oxford: Clarendon Press, 1926).   [36] Digby, *Epicurus's Morals*, pp. 29–30.

[37] *De rerum natura*, Book V, lines 1028–1090.

[38] Richard Simon, *Histoire Critique du Vieux Testament* (Amsterdam, 1678), Book I, Chapters 14 and 15. Lucretius is quoted twice at Chapter 15, pp. 92–93.

accounts of the formation of society and language during the early eighteenth century,[39] and the source of a thesis of Mandeville's that enraged William Law, because it "make[s] the Harrangues ... of Philosophers *the Origin of moral Virtue*."[40] Epicurus argued that language arose as an expression of need by savages confronted with the pressing demands and conflicts engendered by love, families and stable dwellings. Lucretius expanded this formulation of the beginnings of society amongst rude, pleasure-seeking primitives to include an account of the development of language as a distinctive feature of the rise of human culture from its most rudimentary state to a full-blown civilization. After painting a picture of life amongst the first savages, he presents as the decisive steps toward civilized life the formation of families, the growth of friendships and of the feeling that the strong should protect the weak. Only then does language appear, as "convenience moulded the names of things," amongst creatures who required the use of words at a relatively late stage of their natural histories. And only after the invention of language, Lucretius continues, could those processes unique to civilization, the formation of the city-state, and the invention of religion, be secured.

Lucretius asked why language started in the first place. He sketched a possible answer in terms of its usefulness for creatures naturally endowed with the means to speak, but for whom the appurtenances of civilization which language made possible would have been wholly unnecessary before these creatures began to experiment with their natural powers, came into continuous contact with one another, and then confronted those problems of communal life insoluble without massively expanded powers of communication. Lucretius could thus reasonably be understood to have provided the historical framework for Epicurean naturalism, supplying a narrative context within which language was assigned a place – indeed the most important place – in the purely human inventions and discoveries which gradually transformed the human condition from a mere struggle for existence to the establishment of secure and civilized patterns of social life. This was, at any rate, Mandeville's understanding of Lucretius' primary importance, which he seems only to have fully appreciated in *The Fable*'s second volume of 1728 (II, 285–291), following his encounter with the revived Epicureanism of Bernier and

---

[39] Ira O. Wade, *The Clandestine Organization and Diffusion of Philosophic Ideas in France from 1700 to 1750* (Princeton University Press, 1938), pp. 100–103.
[40] William Law, *Remarks*, p. 13.

Gassendi. Mandeville's discussion of language origins and the place of language in the civilizing process flows directly from the account given in Book v of *De rerum natura*, while incorporating within it the radical Epicurean postulate that "the natural Ambition and strong Desire Men have to triumph over, as well as persuade others, are the occasion" (II, 291) of both the insecurities of the savage state and of civilized living itself.

THE FRENCH CONNECTION

Mandeville's insistent focus on rhetoric as an agent of dominion rather than on language as a cognitive instrument at first placed *The Fable* at some remove from the epistemological concerns informing the two-generation Enlightenment debate about language and language origins which began shortly after his death in 1732. The *philosophes'* enquiry self-consciously derived from the *Essay Concerning Human Understanding*, a source Mandeville only acknowledged in passing, in which, as Voltaire put it in *The Philosophical Letters*, "Locke proves ... that all our ideas come to us through the senses ... and shows the imperfections of all the languages spoken by men, and our constant abuse of terms."[41] What so impressed Voltaire and his contemporaries was Locke's discussion *Of Words*: his anatomy of the links between claims to knowledge and language, and his subsequent analysis of the system of sensible signs by which features of the world were designated.[42] Locke sought to show how the "imperfections and abuses" of words, a consequence of the way language is learned, were primary sources of epistemological confusion. This enterprise was for Locke a major part of the reform of knowledge he directly associated with the new science of Boyle and Newton, one of whose primary aims, as the Royal Society's historian Thomas Spratt put it, was to clear away "many mists and uncertainties [that] ... specious *Tropes* and *Figures* have brought to our Knowledge," and "return back to a close, naked, natural way of speaking."[43]

Locke's own thinking followed closely from this philosophically prophylactic stance. He directed his arguments against the theory of

---

[41] Voltaire, *Lettres philosophiques* (Paris, 1733), Letter XIII.

[42] John Locke, *An Essay Concerning Human Understanding* (Oxford University Press, 1975), ed. Peter H. Niddich, especially III.1–10 and II.19.

[43] Thomas Spratt, *History of the Royal Society* (1667), ed. Jackson I. Cope and Harold D. Jones (St. Louis: Washington University Press, 1958), p. 114.

knowledge and the conception of the nature of man implied by the Adamic fable of language origins, a conception entailing in his view the false doctrine of innate ideas and which licensed the use of an intensely figural language of description at odds with the scientific study of nature. Locke saw the philosophically ungoverned history of language acquisition as the source of the "abundance of empty unintelligible noise and jargon" whose reform was the business of critical thinking. This intrinsically historical project would trace the conditions under which men "often suppose their words to stand [not for ideas alone but] also for the reality of things."[44] Languages were neither "natural," in the sense of God-given or innate, nor were they creations of what with quiet sarcasm Locke called philosophers. A language of verbal signs arose instead from "ignorant and illiterate people ... by those sensible qualities they found in them."[45] The conventions of cognitive primitives, rather than some mythical moment of divine instruction, inaugurated articulate speech. Voltaire summarized this accomplishment:

[a]fter so many deep thinkers had fashioned the romance of the soul, there came a wise man who modestly recounted his true history. Locke has revealed human reason in man, as an accomplished anatomist explains the springs of the human body.[46]

Yet despite his avowal of an "historical, plain method," Locke's own approach to the problem he formulated, the invention of signs and significations, was almost wholly conceptual. Rather than a comparative inquiry into the history of languages, his point of departure was a generalized examination of existing language use within a community already possessed of a system of thought. On that basis Locke sought to account for the formation of an individual's ideas; sought to account for them, therefore, in these already established conceptual conditions. While the *philosophes'* projects of epistemological reconstruction self-consciously adopted Locke's approach to the relation between words and things, they added a more conspicuously genetic perspective to his program for rehabilitating the understanding through an analysis of language. The *Essay* injected an historical dimension into their conception of language as a replication of the processes of thought. It secured the notion of language as a transcript of mental operations whose recovery and

---

[44] *Essay*, III.2.5.   [45] *Essay*, III.6.25 and III.10.4.
[46] Voltaire, *Lettres philosophiques*, Letter XIII.

subsequent improvement philosophy in its reformed state was now equipped to achieve. "The language of a people," Diderot wrote as he described the *Encyclopédie*'s purposes,

gives us its vocabulary, and its vocabulary is a sufficiently faithful and authoritative record of all the knowledge of that people; simply by comparing the different states of a nation's vocabulary at different times one could form an idea of its progress.[47]

Turgot saw this study as a form of "experimental metaphysics." In "analyzing and comparing words," he wrote, "by tracing them from their origins to the different meanings they have since taken on, we could follow the thread of ideas and see the [cognitive] stages ... through which men have passed."[48] An empirically grounded investigation of cognitive processes, this project treated language as a developing set of devices used to mark, externalize and communicate what Turgot, following Locke, called "ideas," the term denoting mental representations in both the rationalist and empiricist traditions of the seventeenth and eighteenth centuries.[49] Verbal expression formed a diachronic record of human "reasoning in which grammar and even the greatest part of logic are only rules."[50] The examination and study of this record, a veritable history of cognition, would expose those features of thought, "subject to so many errors," which demanded enlightened criticism and reform.

It was this comparative and anthropological perspective which characterized the Enlightenment's intense concern with language origins, particularly in France, and which distinguished most eighteenth-century reflection on this question from Locke's. Stemming from the *Essay*, a program of hypothetical historical enquiry supported by a rapidly growing body of knowledge about comparative grammar and language use was, from the 1740s, directed toward the philosophical goal of the improvement of knowledge. As both Diderot and Turgot emphasized, this program took Condillac's *Essai sur l'origine des connaissances humaines* (1746) as its paradigmatic statement.

---

[47] *Encyclopédie, ou Dictionnaire raisonée des sciences, des arts et des métiers, par une société de gens de lettres* (Elmsford, New York: Pergamon Reprint, 1984), v, p. 637.
[48] Anne Robert Jacques Turgot, *Reflections sur les langues*, in *Œuvres de Turgot* ed. Eugène Daire and Hyppolyte Dussard (Paris: Guillaumin, 1844), 2 volumes, II, p. 753.
[49] See, for example, Ian Hacking, *Why Does Language Matter to Philosophy?* (Cambridge University Press, 1975), pp. 15–33 and 163–170.
[50] Turgot, "Etymologie," *Encyclopédie*, v, p. 108.

Locke argued that words were a repertoire of representational instruments which "signify only Mens peculiar Ideas, and that by a perfectly arbitrary [rather than divine] Imposition."[51] Under philosophical inspection language revealed the limits of whatever is taken to be knowledge by exposing to rational inquiry the jumble of error and myth which infused the signifying process during the course of its history. Condillac strictly followed Locke in arguing that "figures and metaphors . . . have become an ornament to discourse . . . and thus it is that by the abuses of them, they have been the first and principal cause of the decline of languages."[52] Condillac radicalized this argument in a decisive way, however. He took signification itself as a replication of cognition and then saw in the development of signs – in the origin and history of language – the record of the mind coming to its current epistemological maturity. Men are by nature social creatures, he assumed, endowed with reason and a capacity for reflection. They are, furthermore, uniformly endowed with identical gestural expressions of their primary mental states, like fright, joy and surprise; and this species-wide emotional inheritance combines with sociability and reason to form a rudimentary, pre-linguistic epistemological condition. The subsequent emergence of articulate speech is the moment after which the higher mental faculties of imagination, contemplation and memory are then derived from sensation. Language, Condillac argued, formed the continuous thread in the development of consciousness itself, which philosophy was meant further to refine by bringing language use into accord with scientific knowledge.

The *Essai* could be understood to be a "supplement to Mr. Locke's," as its English translator put it,[53] because Condillac offered a genetic account of the passage from sensation to understanding which the *Essay* only implied. The invention of signs appeared in Condillac's argument as the factor which initially enabled men to distance themselves from the tyranny of immediate sensation. Primitives could perform the first genuinely cognitive acts only when they began to reflect upon their own activity of calling forth perceived objects by means of signs. Rather than being a secondary, neutral and merely transmissive mental instrument, language was instead conceived by Condillac as the primary tool without which intricate cognitive

---

[51] *Essay*, III.2.8.
[52] *Essai*, II.13, in *Œuvres philosophiques de Condillac*, ed. Georges Le Roy (Paris: PUF, 1947), I.
[53] These are the words of the title-page of the Thomas Nugent translation, *An Essay on the Origin of Human Knowledge: Being a Supplement to Mr. Locke's Essay* . . . (London, 1756).

procedures and, consequently, the acquisition of knowledge, would be impossible. The creation of signs was thus the first substantial achievement of human freedom from within the otherwise determined flux of sensation and imagination. Reason and a capacity for reflection triggered by signs then permitted men systematically to communicate, remember and organize into knowledge the associations between invented signifiers and their corresponding signifieds. With the origin of language, in other words, men passed from the realm of mere nature into the wholly human domain of culture, at which point the history of signification became the history of the knowing mind.

The structure of Condillac's argument posed a dilemma. If the invention of signs was the prerequisite for reflection, signing seemed possible only by virtue of a prior reflective act, one in which nature would paradoxically produce culture out of itself. As the Scots critic Hugh Blair put this problem when he reviewed the debate on the origins of language in 1783, "either how Society could form itself previously to Language, or how words could rise into a language previously to Society formed, seem to be points [of] equal difficulty."[54] Condillac devoted some of the richest sections of the *Essai* to this issue, exploring what he called "the language of action," a preconventional language whose development marked the transitional stages between sensation and autonomous cognition. He imagined two inarticulate children, "wandering in the desert," whose undeliberated cries of pain and pity, and even more whose expressive gestures of need and assistance, were the first communicative performances.[55] Condillac credited William Warburton's *Divine Legation of Moses* (1738 and 1741) with this insight into instinctual gestural competence.[56] He then followed the English Bishop's model of the development of signification through mixed gestural and metaphorical discourse to a precise language of conventional verbal signs, arguing *mutatis mutandis*, as Warburton had, that writing proceeded from pictures through hieroglyphs to characters.[57]

---

[54] Hugh Blair, "The Rise and Progress of Language," in *Lectures on Rhetoric and Belles Lettres* (London: Strahan and Cadell, 1790), fourth edition, 3 volumes, I, pp. 122–148, p. 126.

[55] *Essai*, II.1.1.

[56] William Warburton, *The Divine Legation of Moses* (1738 and 1741) (London: Cadell and Davies, 1811), Book IV, pp. 116–214. The first three Books were translated by Etienne Silhouette as *Dissertations sur l'unions de la religion, de la morale, et de la politique* (London?, 1742), 2 volumes; most of the last Book was translated by Leonard de Malpines as *Essai sur les hieroglyphes des Egyptiens* (Paris, 1744), 2 volumes, which Condillac reported that he read while working on Part II of the *Essai*. See, *Essai*, II.1.13.   [57] *Divine Legation*, IV, p. 393.

"Speaking by action," the innate ability of primitives to communicate with one another posited in the *Divine Legation*, was so close to what in *The Fable* were called "dumb signs" that the omission of any reference to Mandeville in Warburton's discussion of language at first seems surprising. Mandeville saw gestures as richly textured significations amongst savages, while in Warburton's account men employed a "language of action" in order to supplement their rude sounds, and which, he too implied, followed unconscious syntactic rules that transformed vocalizations into meaningful language. One of Warburton's ideological objectives, however, was to refute Mandeville's Epicurean and anti-Adamic conventionalist arguments about language origins, and to re-assert Biblical authority against them.[58] For he recognized that these arguments were part of a forceful and, at the time that he wrote, highly influential moral theory with radically heterodox implications.

Because Warburton wished to dissociate himself from his ethical and theological opponents, he made no mention of *The Fable*'s discussion of language, despite its similar, sometimes indeed identical, claims about the centrality of gesture in the history of human communication; nor did Warburton choose to emphasize that he, following Mandeville, claimed that "ancient mysteries" of the first complex human communities were invented by rulers.[59] Instead, Warburton employed the standard rhetorical tactic of placing Mandeville's work in an apparently unrelated context, one in which his "very popular book" would be "tested, unmasked and proven wrong."[60] Warburton cited *The Fable* in a section of the *Divine Legation* dealing with ethics, not language. Repeating phrases from Hutcheson's polemic of 1726,[61] Warburton first misdescribed Mandeville's argument, and then tendentiously claimed that since private vice cannot be essential to public benefits it is only productive of the latter in an incidental way. Private vice must contribute to public benefit only by those accidental properties that may also be present in things not vicious. Accordingly, Warburton concluded, Mandeville's "execrable paradox" was empty: a state may become rich and powerful without the assistance of vice at all. Warburton sought to caricature and then dismiss Mandeville as the most important

---

[58] *Divine Legation*, IV, p. 393.   [59] *Divine Legation*, IV, pp. 309–311.
[60] *Divine Legation*, I, Section VI, p. 111ff.
[61] Francis Hutcheson, *A Collection of Letters*, in *Collected Works*, VII, p. 133.

contemporary instance of an author who, employing Bayle's principles, "forged a scheme of religion independent o[f] morality."
Mandeville, he continued, exemplified Bayle's "Epicurean atheist,
who denied the providence of God," and who, moreover, so influentially asserted "an unheard-of impiety, wickedly advanced, and
impudently avowed, against the universal voice of nature; in which
moral virtue is represented as the invention of knaves; and Christian
virtue as the imposition of fools."[62]

Condillac followed Warburton not only in attributing great
importance to gesture in the history of communication, but also by
tactically effacing the idea's subversive source in *The Fable of the Bees.*
The hypothetical creators of words, Condillac's "two children ...
wandering in the desert," were modelled upon Mandeville's "wild
couple." As in *The Fable* these youths were able to create new words
because of the flexibility of their tongues. Condillac argued as well
that primitives first spoke in cries and gestures common to the race,
urged on by natural sympathy, *The Fable*'s "pity." Echoing Mandeville, he then emphasized the slow and accidental character of the
emergence of verbal expression in the face of natural gestural
competence, whose persistence, as in Mandeville's account, hindered
the growth of verbal signs.[63]

Condillac acknowledged none of these borrowings from Mandeville, who was in the process of achieving wide notoriety in France just
as Condillac was planning the *Essai.* Mandeville became known on
the European continent in a different way from England, not merely
via reviews of *The Fable* upon the appearance of its two volumes, but
through the four French and German translations of *Free Thoughts* in
the 1720s, and then early in the next decade through the French
translation of Berkeley's *Alciphron,* which branded Mandeville a
freethinker in the spirit of Bayle.[64] Rather, Mandeville was first seen
in Europe as a libertine, and only later rediscovered as a social
theorist. This advance reputation excited interest in *The Fable* in
radical philosophical circles in France, where an established tradition
of libertine political and social argument was firmly in place. With the

---

[62] *Divine Legation,* I, pp. 232 and 280–281.
[63] *Essai,* II.I.I. F.B. Kaye pointed out these borrowings in "Mandeville on the Origin of
Language," *Modern Language Notes* 34 (1924), pp. 136–142. See Rüdiger Schreyer, "Condillac, Mandeville and the Origin of Language," *Historiographica Linguistica,* I, 2 (1978), pp. 15–
43, for a detailed comparison which takes issue with some of Aarsleff's claims.
[64] *Alciphron, ou le Petit philosophe; en sept dialogues: contenant une apologie de la religion chrétienne contre
ceux qu'on nomme esprits forts* ... (Paris: Rolon, 1734), 2 volumes, trans. E. de Joncourt.

publication in 1724 of the French translation of *Free Thoughts on Religion*, the prosecution of *The Fable*'s London publisher and the printing of the "Vindication of the Book," Mandeville acquired a considerable reputation.[65] A 25-page notice of *The Fable* in the *Bibliothèque Anglais*, which also commented on Bluett's attack, appeared in 1725, as did another in the *Journal de Savans* in 1726. In 1729, shortly after the publication of the *Fable*'s second volume, the *Bibliothèque Raisonnée* offered a 44-page review and commentary that included translated excerpts, while in 1733 the *Bibliothèque Britannique* reported on *The Origin of Honour* in a 52-page critical summary of the work, which culminated by emphasizing Mandeville's "outrageous thesis" that "particular vices tend to public advantage."[66] During the 1730s Mandeville's early French reputation as a freethinker whose views were closely allied to the libertine writings of the Regency was thus enlarged to include a consideration of his social doctrines. This view was much encouraged with the help of Jean-François Melon's commentary on Mandeville's economic ideas, along with his contempt for the supposed virtue and self-sufficiency of antique republics.[67]

Condillac composed his *Essai* in the wake of this growing interest in Mandeville amongst the French reading public and, most immediately, of *The Fable*'s first French translation in 1740.[68] So great was the demand for Mandeville's book that another commercially profitable translation was issued ten years later. Unlike in Britain, where the full import of the second volume of *The Fable* was sometimes blunted by the contention surrounding the scandal provoked by the Middlesex Grand Jury in 1723, *The Fable*'s French version was printed and read as a single, unified treatise. The *Mémoires de Trévoux*, a Jesuit journal and the most prestigious organ of contemporary Catholic philosophy, thought the translation important enough to have three critical essays

---

65 Bernard de Mandeville, *Pensées libres sur la religion, l'église, le gouvernement et le bonheur de la nation* (Amsterdam, 1724), 2 volumes, trans. J. Van Effen. Another translation appeared in Amsterdam in 1725, and a German translation followed in 1726. See Carrive, *La Philosophie des passions chez Bernard Mandeville*, pp. 112–114.

66 *Bibliothèque britannique ou histoire des ouvrages des savans de la Grande Bretagne* (1733), p. 2.

67 Jean-François Melon, *Essai politique sur le commerce* (Bordeaux, 1734), and see André Morize, *L'Apologie du luxe au XVIIIe siècle et 'Le Mondain' de Voltaire* (Geneva: Slatkine Reprint, 1970), pp. 120–122.

68 Bernard de Mandeville, *La Fable des Abeilles, ou les fripons devenus honnêtes gens, avec le commentaire, où l'on prouve que les vices des particuliers tendent à l'avantage du Public, traduit de l'anglais sur la sixième [1732] edition* (London?: Aux Depens de la Compagnie, 1740), 4 volumes, trans. J. Van Effen.

devoted to it. The last of these pieces, a 135-page article alerting readers that the "Enquiry into the Origin of Moral Virtue," printed at the end of the French translation, was in fact the subversive foundation of the entire book, one with distinct scientific pretensions, which "arranges the components of societies in the way Descartes constructed worlds."[69] At the appearance of *The Fable*'s second translation in 1750 the semi-official *Mercure de France* claimed that Mandeville's theses had become almost classical in France – a point repeated by Diderot and Voltaire in the next decade[70] – and that he was held in high esteem in the opinion of the enlightened public. Condillac published his *Essai* in 1746, at the height of *The Fable*'s French vogue, and within a year of its being placed on the Index of Prohibited Books in May of 1745, when it was also condemned by the Sorbonne, and then ritually burned by the public hangman. His lifelong aversion to public controversy, along with a circumspect adherence to orthodox belief,[71] readily encouraged Condillac's prudential suppression of Mandeville's significance for his own theorizing.

Condillac's larger purposes, moreover, differed significantly from Mandeville's. The *Essai* had as its primary objective a theory of language formation from which Condillac derived his stadial history of the growth of knowledge, not of society. Keyed to the development of language use, that history described a passage from figurative and metaphorical poetic understanding, including music and dance as modes of information transfer, to prosaic forms of description and analysis.[72] Condillac intended to chart the career of the language of action as it was transformed by words into a precise cognitive instrument. The sciences themselves, he held, were no more than well-made languages which provide the ideals for our daily speech. Yet Condillac's intense regret at the loss of poetic power entailed in this movement of consciousness was only partly balanced by a conviction that the progressive refinement of language constituted a profound

[69] *Mémoires de Trévoux* (1740), pp. 940–981, 1506–1536 and 2103–2147, p. 2107.
[70] See Dennis Diderot, *Œuvres complètes* (Paris: Garnier, 1875–1877), ed. J. Assézat, x, p. 299, and Voltaire's entries "Abeilles" and "Amour-Propre" in the *Dictionnaire Philosophique*. Diderot's own epistemological and social radicalism were linked to Mandeville by Adrien Pluquet in *De la sociabilité* (Paris, 1767), 2 volumes, I, p. 30. For this association see, Robert Mauzi, *L'Idée du bonheur dans la littérature et la pensée française au XVIIIe siècle* (Geneva: Slatkine Reprint, 1979), pp. 599–600.
[71] See, for example, *Essai*, II.I, where Condillac affirms the "extraordinary assistance" of God in granting Adam the capacity for speech.
[72] For example, *Essai*, I.3–8; 13–16, and IV.32–39.

philosophical advance. This nostalgia sharply contrasted with Mandeville's uncompromising modernism, which viewed philosophy's history from the perspective of politics and scorned what he considered any romantic longing for the infantile barbarisms broken by civilization. Unlike Condillac, Mandeville saw in the rhetorical agility of those in command a renewable ideological resource that could be used to tame the passions of men by playing on their need for self-regard. For him the very opacity of the political goals of rhetoric was the source of language's power to civilize; the history to which he referred described a progress of ideology masked as a sequence of moral injunctions. Condillac, on the other hand, deferred any consideration of these issues. Viewing language as a privileged conceptual treasury whose analysis made transparent the thinking process of language users, he described the history of language use as a narrative of conceptual progress in which refinements of logic and science displaced the felt but figural significations of more primitive attempts to know.

ROUSSEAU IN MANDEVILLE'S SHADOW

Rousseau's enormously popular and philosophically influential *Discourse on the Origin and Foundations of Inequality* of 1755[73] elevated the question of language origins into an Enlightenment controversy about the ethical consequences of the progress of civilization. His interrogation of Condillac's argument injected Mandeville's morals into the heart of European social theory. Before he studied the *Essai*, Rousseau was already acquainted with *The Fable*'s argument about the social utility of luxury consumption, probably first encountering it in Melon's enthusiastic summary, which was later cited with approval by Montesquieu in *The Spirit of the Laws*. Rousseau lamented that Melon was "the first to publish the poisonous doctrine whose novelty brought him more followers than the soundness of his reasoning."[74] In the prize-winning *Discourse on the Sciences and Arts* of 1750, Rousseau had drawn attention to Mandeville's "paradox" about luxury, "so worthy," he bitterly remarked, "of being born in our time," and voiced the fear that virtue would be destroyed if men "must get rich at

---

[73] Jean-Jacques Rousseau, *Discourse on the Origin and Foundations of Inequality* (New York: St. Martin's Press, 1964), trans. Roger D. Masters; hereafter, *Second Discourse*.
[74] Jean-Jacques Rousseau, Letter to Bordes, *Œuvres complètes* (Paris: Gallimard, 1964), ed. Jean Fabre, II, p. 71.

any price."[75] As Rousseau said in response to a critic of his work, "I am not afraid to be alone in my century to fight those odious maxims which only tend to destroy and debase virtue, and to make for rich people and wretches, that is to say only for wicked men."[76] Shortly after publishing the *Second Discourse* he wrote another short "refutation" of Mandeville's opinions, this time inspired by a similar exercise of the abbé de Saint-Pierre in the 1730s.[77] Condillac's *Essai*, however, provided Rousseau with the foil he needed for expanding upon and giving philosophical expression to these anti-modernist sentiments.

Following Condillac, who "perhaps gave me the first idea of it,"[78] Rousseau saw the progress of knowledge toward ever greater distinctions in thought as a movement into speech; a transition from perception and imagination to the manipulation of conventional signs; from a collection of expressive–gestural signals and tropic designations which were the beginnings of language to the abstract discourse of philosophy which underwrote the sciences. He wished "to consider how many ideas we owe to the use of speech; how much grammar trains and facilitates the operations of the mind."[79] But for Rousseau, with Mandeville and against Condillac, the record of cognitive progress mapped by the development of language was the secondary effect of a forgotten social history. He argued that an examination of this record would reveal that the appearance of articulate speech involved a rupture between nature and culture, ended the isolation of individuals and all but crippled their power to express themselves without cunning and artifice.[80] The history of

---

[75] Jean-Jacques Rousseau, *Discourse on the Sciences and Arts* (New York: St. Martin's Press, 1964), trans. Roger D. Masters, p. 51.   [76] Letter to Bordes, p. 88.

[77] Jean-Jacques Rousseau, "Contre l'opinion de Mandeville," in *Œuvres complètes*, III, pp. 672 and 682, in response to Saint-Pierre's *Ouvrages de morale et de politique* (Rotterdam, 1733–1741), XVI, pp. 143–156.

[78] *Second Discourse*, p. 120. In *The Confessions*, Book VII, Rousseau claims to have been the first to recognize Condillac's true intellectual worth. Rousseau had previously tutored the son of Condillac's brother, and the two dined together weekly along with Diderot while Condillac was composing the *Essai*, for which Rousseau asked Diderot to find a publisher. See *The Confessions* (London: Penguin, 1954), trans. J.M. Cohen, pp. 324–325.

[79] *Second Discourse*, p. 119.

[80] Jean Starobinski, *Jean-Jacques Rousseau: la transparence et l'obstacle* (Paris: Gallimard, 1971), pp. 168–200 and 356–379 gives the best account of these ruptures and of Rousseau's arguments about language. See too Jacques Derrida, "Genesis and Structure of the *Essay on the Origin of Languages*," in *Of Grammatology* (Baltimore: Johns Hopkins University Press, 1976), trans. G. Spivak, pp. 165–268, and Michèle Duchet and Michel Launay, "Sychronie et diachronie: l'Essai sur l'origine des langues et le second *Discours*," *Revue Internationale de Philosophie*, 21 (1967), pp. 421–442.

language, in other words, was above all for Rousseau, as for Mandeville, a decisive part of the history of morals. His attempts to recover
the repressed deposits of this history were not only meant to show "the
innumerable difficulties and infinite time which the first invention of
languages must have cost,"[81] but how the evolution of language was
implicated in the aberrant course of social development.

Rousseau's audience recognized that his hypothetical history of the
emergence of culture was modelled on an Epicurean account of the
evolution of human nature, laced with Lucretian allusions.[82] He
supplemented the classical, particularly Platonic, sources of his
theorizing with a philosophical statement of Lucretian naturalism,
enriched by what he understood to be contemporary scientific
practice. Rousseau intended to write a strictly natural history of
morals, an anthropologically informed complement to Buffon's *Histoire naturelle*, one in which the emergence of language marked a
decisive transition to civil life.[83] He sought to describe in a rigorously
naturalistic fashion the passage from a conjectural state of nature to
that of civil society because his objective was to highlight the radical
discontinuities between any scientifically plausible description of
elementary, asocial human requirements and the insatiable desires of
socialized men. While Rousseau explicitly distanced his imagined
savages in the state of nature from those in *The Fable* by enhancing the
role of pity in their hearts, "which Mandeville understood so well,"
his speechless brutes with elementary cognitive endowments were
striking analogues of Mandeville's primitives, whose physical
impulses and self-love conditioned their behavior.[84] Like the creatures
in *The Fable*, the isolates inhabiting Rousseau's natural state "did not
require a language much more refined than that of monkeys ... For a

---

[81] *Second Discourse*, p. 120.
[82] Jean Morel, "Recherches sur les sources du *Discours sur l'Inégalité*," *Annales de la Société Jean-
Jacques Rousseau* 5 (1909), pp. 163–164. See too Roger D. Masters, *The Political Philosophy of
Rousseau* (Princeton University Press, 1968), pp. 170–176, and Vaughan, *Political Hedonism*,
pp. 119–129.
[83] *Second Discourse*, notes D through J, and especially p. 152: "For the poet it is gold and silver, but
for the philosopher it is iron and wheat which have civilized men and ruined the human
race." See too Christopher Frayling and Robert Wolker, "From the Orang-Utan to the
Vampire: Towards an Anthropology of Rousseau," in R.A. Leigh (ed.), *Rousseau After Two
Hundred Years* (Cambridge University Press, 1982), pp. 109–132, and Michèle Duchet,
Anthropologie et histoire au siècle des lumières (Paris: Maspero, 1971), pp. 323–357.
[84] *Second Discourse*, p. 131, and see Malcom Jack, "One State of Nature: Mandeville and
Rousseau," *Journal of the History of Ideas* 39 (1978), pp. 119–124.

long time inarticulate cries, many gestures and some imitative noises composed the universal language."[85]

Rousseau's "formidable" and "humiliating" hypothesis about the origins of language amongst bare hominoids[86] sought to distance the sources of speech from basic human needs by representing the first men as living in an epoch of satisfaction and perfect communicative immediacy. Gesture, exclamation and glance he understood as unmediated physical expressions of sentiment, as "paintings of the passions" rather than conventional, and thus deliberated, signs of information. Following Mandeville, Rousseau tied the problem of language origins to that of the origins of societies, and then linked the process of social formation to cognitively creative acts amongst the first language users. Rousseau thus secured a theoretical foundation from which he could point to the gulf between nature and culture in Condillac's argument, with which he otherwise agreed, since Condillac "assumed what I question – namely a kind of society already established among the inventors of language ... [I]f men needed speech in order to learn to think they had even greater need of knowing how to think in order to discover the art of speech."[87] Rousseau declared the question of language origins "insoluble," as if further to emphasize the chasm between biological impulse and the deformed habits of a socialized second nature.[88] The first agreements among men, including the conventions required for speech, could be traced to no set of natural necessities. Any account of the passage to civility would thus have to depend upon "hypothetical and conditional reasonings like those our own physicists make every day concerning the formation of the world."[89] These conjectures were the philosophical corollaries of scientific theories which bring the apparently random forces of nature – what Rousseau in Lucretian fashion called natural "accidents" – into a productive conceptual order. The modes of language use were an essential feature of this theoretical project of genetic reconstruction, since language and socialization formed the crucially dependent variables in the emergence of civility.[90]

---

[85] *Second Discourse*, p. 144.   [86] Bauzée, "Langue (Gramm.)," *Encyclopédie*, IX, p. 250.
[87] *Second Discourse*, pp. 120 and 121–122.   [88] *Second Discourse*, p. 126.
[89] *Second Discourse*, p. 103.
[90] Rousseau directly addresses this problem in the *Second Discourse*, Part II, and in its intended supplement, the *Essai sur l'origine des langues*, completed in 1761 but published posthumously in 1781. I refer to the Charles Porset edition (Bordeaux: Ducros, 1970).

Two histories of language, or rather two models of socialization connected by a set of perverse and radically deforming speech acts, anchored Rousseau's conception. Originating in cries for help, articulate speech emerged from its more naturally expressive gestural sources only with the formation of the first, pre-political communities in which mutual dependencies called forth a common idiom.[91] While the physical needs that were directly expressed in cry and gesture promoted no social impulses, speech marks the emergence of love, hatred, pity and anger," passions which compel men to seek one another's company. In the course of this transition self-love generates a sense of extended selfhood, a disposition toward regarding others as parts of something radically other than oneself. And with this newly born individuality the need for a language of communication and for concepts of mutuality arise, by means of which individuals can both relate with others and distinguish themselves from them. Language is in this sense "the first social institution."[92] Like Condillac, Rousseau understood the original language as figural, poetic and musical; following Mandeville and Warburton he saw in its gestural survivals the sources of the compelling, pre-analytical power of elementary need.

A simple and methodical language of analysis only slowly developed when men found it necessary to form general, abstract ideas under whose description similar objects could be comprehended. Language mediated by concepts thus necessarily creates a distance between nature and men, whose experience is no longer literally direct and, because conceptually mediated, drives a wedge between reason and feeling. People now may view themselves as others view them, or as they wish to appear to others, and must therefore to some degree be shaped by an objectified self-understanding which language makes possible. Yet the practice of supporting speech with gesture, Rousseau argued, must have continued to infuse human communication with the possibility of undivided expressions of self long after it was strictly necessary for the transmission of information. This gestural mother-language persisted at the sacred centers of early communal life because through it one could directly come into contact with the most elemental needs. The Jewish prophets and Greek lawgivers spoke in what Mandeville had called "the language of the eyes." These founders of peoples communicated, Rousseau

---

[91] *Second Discourse*, p. 148.   [92] *Essai sur l'origine des langues*, pp. 27 and 43.

claimed, "more effectively to the eye than to the ear," for each intuitively grasped that the force of vocal discourse was to encourage calculation rather than genuine human bonds.[93] This language of action continued through the long period of agriculture and metal-lurgy – the happiest era of social life – in which essentially unreflective collectivities, bound by convention rather than by laws and formal agreements, experienced a communal identity by way of their customs and modes of expression: their songs, dances and speech. For in these environments the figurally enriched modes of gesture, pantomime, song and dance, while promoting the first egoistic comparisons between men during their leisure hours, nonetheless permitted them almost unmediated transmissions of feeling.[94]

As the birth of society was signalled by the emergence of language, its decline is triggered by "the most deliberate project that ever entered the human mind," that is, the effort to separate in an auditor's imagination reality and appearance through the seductive manipulation of words. In a heightened Mandevillian moment of rhetorical duplicity "the speech of the rich [man]" inspires com-moners with "maxims" as advantageous to him as the natural order of things served to his detriment, and so makes "his defenders out of his adversaries."[95] An ideology of mutual benefit and protection comes to mask the dominance of the propertied whose power it sanctifies.

The first person who, having fenced off a plot of ground, took it into his head to say this is mine and found people simple enough to believe him, was the true founder of civil society. What crimes, wars, murders, what miseries and horrors would the human race have been spared by someone who ... had shouted to his fellow men: Beware of listening to this imposter.[96]

It is important to notice that the first individual represented by Rousseau in his hypothetical history of humanity is also the first person he permits to speak, and that the speech of this person is undertaken expressly in order to deceive. The success of this lawgiver who, in Rousseau's narrative, inaugurates the socialization of the race depends upon others lacking a counter-discourse, on the absence of a mode of communication which could resist the power of abstract argument and expose his calculating reason as the vehicle of self-

---

[93] *Essai sur l'origine des langues*, p. 8. Compare Condillac, *Essai*, IV, 39: "the eye [is now, in modern times] the seat of expression; there it is that the able actor paints the emotions of his soul ... Hence our theatres are much smaller and better illuminated than those of the ancients."
[94] *Second Discourse*, p. 149.   [95] *Second Discourse*, pp. 158–159.
[96] *Second Discourse*, pp. 141–142.

interest. Rousseau described the history of language itself as an irreversible process of separation between music and speech, the figural and the analytic, feeling and calculation. Just so, the passage into political society embodies for him the disfiguring incoherence between authentic expression and a discourse of feigned other-regarding desire. Language proves to be the decisive instrument by which men forge the chains which will then enslave them.

Rousseau's politics sought to recover the lost, primal eloquence of communities before their rhetorical fall, a mode of speaking which could command the affections without appealing to interest.[97] Antique leaders, he imagined, ruled precisely in this way. They governed by employing non-verbal powers of symbol and music to evoke civic emotions through a silent repertoire of signs in order that the public mind would speak in the unmediated language of the individual heart.[98] Even the sonorous, prosodic, harmonious oratory favorable to ancient liberty had little to do with contemporary speech. Unless modern tongues voiced the hopes of unlettered peoples, these languages, "made for murmuring on couches,"[99] were little more than instruments designed for deception. In place of their promiscuous public speech, flowing from and addressed to instrumental reason, Rousseau evoked in *The Social Contract* the discourse of Moses and Lycurgus, archetypical legislators who could "win over without violence and persuade without convincing,"[100] moral giants who spoke with the elemental force of a primal language and founded polities in sacred oratorial acts. The Romans, whose republican virtue Rousseau wished to revive, similarly mastered a pre-articulate language of signs before they perfected a civic rhetoric. Their dress, ornaments, buildings and ceremonies silently impressed duty on the hearts of citizens, just as silence shields the electorate of Rousseau's ideal state from the rhetoric of interest politics as they reflect in isolation upon all questions concerning the common good.[101]

If Rousseau expressly wished to dramatize the true legislator's need of a repertoire of signs in order to arm model citizens against the

[97] See the discussion of this point in Bronislaw Baczko, "La Cité et ses langues," in Bronislaw Baczko (ed.), *Rousseau After 200 Years* (Cambridge University Press, 1982), pp. 87–108.

[98] *Essai sur l'origine des langues*, p. 35; and see, too, *Emile* (New York: Free Press, 1979), trans. Allan Brown, Part IV. Rousseau was cited on this point by Duclos in "Declamation des anciens," *Encyclopédie*, IV, pp. 686–691.   [99] *Essai sur l'origine des langues*, p. 199.

[100] *The Social Contract*, Book II, Chapter 7.

[101] *Essai sur l'origine des langues*, 33–35; *Social Contract*, Book IV, Chapter 2.

seductions of civilization, he did so against the background of a growing despair over the habits of his civilized readers, who followed a different axis of signification. They lived "in the opinion of others,"[102] and were, as a consequence, unknowing victims of their own applause. Civilization had even mastered gesture, transforming naturally expressive acts into duplicitous forms of theatrical art, a view made famous not only in Rousseau's polemical attack against the theatre in his *Letter to D'Alembert*, but in the article on "Language" in Diderot's *Encyclopédie*, where, in effect, it was paraphrased:

If men ... finally found the art of communicating their thoughts with precision, with finesse, with energy, they learned as well to hide them or disguise them behind false expressions.[103]

The modern self had become a heteronomous residue of its reflection in the signs of strangers, themselves in constant need of public reminders of their own identities. Since "this Age of Reason has stuffed its maxims with disdain for the duties of men and citizens," countervailing maxims were needed – if not for the impossible resurrection of virtue in a Paris committed to the distortions of modern luxury and bereft of non-dissimulating communication, then for lawgivers to tame vice by manipulating that public opinion which imparted to fully socialized, deracinated metropolitans the sentiment of their own existence.[104]

Rousseau was convinced that the "dangerous doctrines" of "Lucretius and ... Mandeville had more than succeeded."[105] At the same time, his own prescriptions for the maladies of civilization tended heavily to rely upon Mandeville's diagnosis of modern life, for which the satirist had "achieved distinction": a commercialized form of social obligation which places everyone in positions of mutual constraint by the "knots of self-interest." In such a society the vicious are required to assume the mask of virtue, and persons must cultivate agreeable talents in order to win the approval upon which their worldly success depends.[106] Rousseau viewed what he regarded as Mandeville's ideological triumph as a human tragedy. Yet his account of the trajectory of human history closely followed *The Fable*'s

[102] *Second Discourse*, pp. 179.
[103] Chevalier de Jaucourt, "Langue," *Encyclopédie*, IX, pp. 249–266.
[104] *Narcisse, ou l'amant de lui-même*, in *Œuvres complètes*, ed. Jean Starobinski (Paris: Gallimard, 1964), Preface, pp. 966 and 972, and *Second Discourse*, p. 179. See, too, Charles E. Ellison, "Rousseau and the Modern City: The Politics of Speech and Dress," *Political Theory*, 13, 4 (November 1985), pp. 497–534.   [105] *Narcisse*, Preface, p. 966.   [106] *Narcisse*, p. 967.

narrative account of the progress of society – a point upon which Voltaire gleefully remarked, and one, as we have seen, which Adam Smith was quick to notice.[107] Sometimes even paraphrasing Mandeville without acknowledgement,[108] at other places Rousseau offered his readers examples drawn from *The Fable* to support his claim that now "the reason of each individual dictates to him maxims ... in which each man finds his profit in the misfortune of others."[109] Mandeville, "the most excessive detractor of human virtues,"[110] stood as the compelling anti-type of Rousseau's project. For unlike Condillac's, or any other sustained reflection upon contemporary habits, only in *The Fable* was the development of language inextricably bound to the process of socialization and to the most dissonant moral registers of modernity. Moreover, Rousseau found a means of confronting modernity on its own ground in Mandeville's anatomizing, as he called it, of the passions of civilized men to reveal the natural sources of the manipulative duplicities of modern life. Rousseau not only discovered in Mandeville the exemplary defense of licentiousness in the most advanced commercial societies, but employed the Epicurean and contemporary scientific hypotheses upon which *The Fable*'s arguments rested as a presupposition which sustained the most dramatic elements of his own anti-modernism.

In the work which first brought him public acclaim, Rousseau voiced republican outrage at peoples who had lost their simplicity and so spoke in the artificially fabricated, elegant language "of the rhetoricians who govern you."[111] Mandeville's naturalistic model for understanding the rhetoric of modernity then offered him both a method of conjecture for the recovery of a supposedly pre-discursive human condition, and an ideological target for his attack upon the

---

[107] Voltaire, "Luxe," *Dictionnaire philosophique*, and Adam Smith, "Letter to the Edinburgh Review," in *Essays on Philosophical Subjects* ed. W.P.D. Wightman and J.C. Bryce (Oxford University Press, 1980), pp. 250–254.

[108] Compare, for example, the end of "The Third Dialogue" of *Fable*, II where, following a description of the improvements in material techniques which encouraged greater interdependence and an improvement in the social arts, Mandeville says of men: "When they are thus far advanced, it is easy to conceive the rest" (in *La Fable des abeilles* ... [1740]: "Parvenues à un aussi haut point, il n'est pas difficile de concevoir le reste.") with Rousseau's paraphrase at an identical point in the hypothetical history of the *Second Discourse*: "Les choses étant parvenues à ce point, il est facile d'imaginer la reste." *Discours sur l'origine et les fondements d'inégalité parmi les hommes*, ed. Jean Starobinski (Paris: Gallimard, 1964), p. 174.

[109] *Second Discourse*, p. 194, and see note 1 for Rousseau's use of the examples of shipwrecks and the great fire of London drawn from *The Fable*.   [110] *Second Discourse*, p. 130.

[111] *Discourse on the Sciences and Arts*, p. 45.

morally corrosive maxims of modernity. Rousseau's longing for a return to an imagined utopia of communicative immediacy prompted his adoption of the strategies of his chosen adversary. By so doing he gave eloquent testimony of the power during the Enlightenment of Mandeville's argument that the tropes of civilized discourse comprised a rhetoric of dominion. "There reigns in the world," Rousseau wrote, while apologizing for his own rhetorical success,

a multitude of little maxims which reduce simple minds by their false air of philosophy ... This is one of them: "Men have all the same passions; above all self-love [*amour-propre*] and interest lead them; in this they are all alike ..." In Europe, government, laws, costumes, interest all are part of ... the necessity of mutually deceiving without end; everything makes them need vice; it is necessary for them to become wicked in order to be sages.[112]

A more succinct description of the beliefs of "the rich man" as he won over his innocent neighbors merely by speaking, or of Mandeville's thesis that polished sociability is founded upon the exchange value of deceit, could scarcely be imagined. Nor would Mandeville have to depart from what Rousseau called his "cold and subtle style" in order to agree with Rousseau that "the good man is he who has no need to deceive anyone, and [only] the savage is that man."[113] For as Rousseau reflected upon the intersubjective imperatives of contemporary civilization, it increasingly seemed to him that only a few remote Corsicans and isolated Swiss mountain villagers, supposedly unsullied by the temptations of modernity, could hope to speak in a transparent discourse of unalienated practical reason – a thought anticipated in *The Fable*'s satire of the fantasies of republican moralists, and one which, when given new life by Rousseau a generation later, could only have evoked Mandeville's knowing sneer. Rousseau's engagement with *The Fable* injected into the highest levels of Enlightenment social theory the proposition that what he, along with Mandeville's first adversaries, called moral corruption was a necessary adjunct to the progress of civilization. Flourishing modern societies depended for their continuing prosperity on the heightened indulgence of self-regard. Rousseau's admitted failure to defeat this argument, save in the minds of those already captivated by the myths of ancient virtue which *The Fable* had done so much to discredit, threw into the sharpest relief the force of Mandeville's most disconcerting

[112] *Narcisse*, Preface, 969n.   [113] *Second Discourse*, p. 130; *Narcisse*, Preface, p. 970 n.

discovery: that for commercial peoples, addicted to the benefits of material progress, there was no escape from the moral demands of modernity, one of whose baleful symptoms was a regressive nostalgia for the vanished simplicities of a supposedly halcyon, virtuous, past.

CHAPTER 3

Performance principles of the public sphere

Rousseau portrayed the antique ideals of frugality, civic virtue and martial independence as the only morally sound and therefore politically defensible alternatives to the vision of modernity he found in *The Fable of the Bees*. The corruption of contemporary commercial societies, Rousseau argued, followed inexorably from their illegitimate political foundations, a passage Mandeville had sketched with a perverse glee, and one to which Rousseau compulsively returned. *The Fable* haunted Rousseau's moral imagination, rendering him oblivious to Mandeville's satiric purposes. Rousseau simply passed over in contemptuous silence Mandeville's frequent assertions that the forms of commercial sociability were at the same time foundations of politically enlightened polities which respected the rights of their citizens, and which more than any others in recorded history provided expanding opportunities for an individual's worldly happiness. Rousseau became one of Mandeville's most influential readers precisely because he could so creatively accept, isolate from their ironic context, and then magnify those features of *The Fable*'s argument in which it was baldly asserted that "What we call Evil in this World . . . is the grand Principle that makes us sociable Creatures" (1, 369).

In his attack on Mandeville, Rousseau chose to ignore one of *The Fable*'s most sociologically astute insights. The appearance of a new commercial ruling elite – what Mandeville and his British contemporaries called the "monied interest" of stockjobbers and officeholders whose relations with government were those of mutual dependence – sprang from conditions in which the notion of virtue itself was being redefined. The anti-commercial, austerely civic or Augustinian senses with which Rousseau continued to employ the concept had already undergone considerable transformation during the period in which Mandeville wrote. (Rousseau was undoubtedly made aware of this shift in public usage by his then friend Diderot's 1745 translation of

116

Shaftesbury's *An Inquiry Concerning Virtue and Merit.*[1]) While, like Rousseau, some of Mandeville's contemporary adversaries, for example William Law and Bishop Berkeley, still adhered to standards of morality whose ideal agents were the classical citizen or the Christian saint, *The Fable*'s primary targets – indeed, Mandeville's intended audience – comprised a distinctly different order of persons. He pointedly addressed the "fashionable part of Mankind in all countries of Christendom," the *beau monde* "for whom Ease and Pleasure are the Chief ends of their education," but for whom elite social forms were no longer overwhelmingly aristocratic in tone and inclination. These persons cherish "the Comforts of life, as well as the Lessons of Human prudence, [they] avoid Pain and Trouble in order to enjoy as much of the World, and with as little Opposition, as it is possible" (II, 11). Mandeville recognized that the habits of a recently enlarged social stratum were themselves in the process of being reformed and codified into an ideology of "manners," into an informal code of acceptable moral rules for persons living, not in landed or aristocratic independence, but within the public and intersubjective worlds of commerce, the arts and cultivated leisure. Theirs was a world in which the newer forms of property – shares on the exchange, places conferred by the state, moveable capital which instantly could be traded, and so on – were at once the material foundation of wealth and the social basis of personality. In this world, Mandeville pointedly noted, the "Decency of Fashion" is "the chief, if not the only Rule, all modish People walk by." Here, though "Virtue... is a very fashionable Word,"

they mean nothing by it, but a great Veneration for whatever is courtly or sublime, and an equal Aversion to every thing, that is vulgar or unbecoming. They seem to imagine, that it chiefly consists in a strict Compliance to the Rules of Politeness, and all the Laws of Honour, that have any regard to the Respect that is due to themselves. It is the Existence of this Virtue, that is often maintain'd with so much Pomp of Words ... Whilst the Votaries of it deny themselves no Pleasure, they can enjoy, either fashionably or in secret ... [and] can only condescend to abandon the outward Deformity of Vice, for the Satisfaction they receive from appearing well-bred. (II, 12)

MANNERS, MORALS AND THE EARL OF SHAFTESBURY

When Mandeville published these words in the Preface to *The Fable*'s second volume, he could count on his readers to recognize that "the

[1] *Essai sur le mérité et la vertu* (Paris, 1745).

rules of politeness" with which he equated "virtue" amongst an established oligarchical elite had acquired an importance much greater than the mere "points of small morals" that Hobbes, for example, had dismissed as largely irrelevant to civil polities, being in his view nothing more than social decencies, "as how one man should salute another, or how a man should wash his mouth, or pick his teeth before company."[2] Nor were the rules to which Mandeville referred merely a codification of the *politesse*, featured in Renaissance courtesy books like Castiglione's *The Courtier*, that developed in seventeenth-century Parisian salons and then became the social legislation of a French aristocratic elite for whom the norms of acceptable conduct at Versailles would be labelled immoral in urban and commercial settings.[3] As the French exile Saint-Evremond put it during the last decade of the seventeenth century, "the only study in the courts of princes is how to please, because a man makes his fortune there by being agreeable. This is the reason why courtiers are so polite. On the contrary, in towns and republics where men are forced to take pains to get their living, the last of their cares is to please, and this it is that makes them so clownish."[4] For Mandeville and his intended audience, by contrast, "politeness" had come to refer precisely to the manners of "the Town" rather than of the court, to acceptable forms of behavior by monied commoners rather than the titled alone, particularly in the West End of London, which served as the exemplary site for Addison and Steele's enormously influential discussions of the relation of morals to manners during the the first decades of the eighteenth century.

The French language of politeness with which Mandeville, unlike most of his contemporaries, was directly familiar, focused on the distance between genuine moral virtue and the techniques for self-presentation in everyday life, which contemporary *moralistes* like Nicole denounced as corrupting judgement.[5] These techniques were nevertheless the constituent elements of "the art of pleasing in

[2] Hobbes, *Leviathan*, 1.10. p. 160.
[3] For the role of this French language of politeness, see Maurice Magendie, *La Politesse Mondaine et les théories de l'honnêteté, en France au XVIIe siècle, de 1600 à 1660* (1925) (Geneva: Slatkine Reprints, 1970); Norbert Elias, *The Court Society* (Oxford: Blackwell, 1983), and Peter France, *Politeness and Its Discontents* (Cambridge University Press, 1992). For its transmission to England see L. Charlanne, *L'Influence française en Angleterre au XVIIe siècle* (Paris, 1906), Chapter 3.
[4] Saint-Evremond, *Works* (London, 1728), ed. Pierre Desmaizeaux, II, p. 426.
[5] Pierre Nicole, *Essais de morale* (Paris, 1675), I, pp. 289–290.

company," and necessary for a gentleman, as the Huguenot refugee Abel Boyer put it in his well-known translations of a variety of French treatises on manners. Borrowing from La Rochefoucauld, Boyer defined *politesse* as "a dextrous management of our Words and Actions, whereby we make other people have [a] better Opinion of us and themselves."[6] It should be remembered that Mandeville mined the same source when exploring "the dextrous management of ourselves" (I, 68). His perspective on the conditions under which forms of politeness had become acceptable norms of public behavior was shaped by this essentially French discourse, one in which the arts of self-presentation and the maximization of social opportunities occurred in an intersubjective social domain wholly governed by the demands of self-love. But for Mandeville, unlike Nicole, La Rochefoucauld and Boyer, the distance between appearance and motivation, between social and moral identity, was the ideal conceptual space within which to examine the hidden dynamics of commercial sociability.

While Mandeville most fully refined this morally skeptical outlook on manners in *The Fable*, many of the characteristic elements of his point of view were already prominent features of his early journalism, particularly the essays he published between 1709 and 1710 in *The Female Tatler*, one of the many papers which exploited the market of urban and readers to whom Steele and Addison so successfully appealed in *The Tatler* and *The Spectator*.[7] Members of "a society of ladies," Mandeville's *personae* in this journal took as their primary object of ridicule Steele's Isaac Bickerstaff, Esq. In *The Tatler*, this gentleman posed as a social legislator who proposed standards of virtuous conduct to a London populace consumed and confused, as he saw it, by the vagaries of fashion. This "Censor of Great Britain" would haul offenders against propriety before an imaginary tribunal over which he presided, much in manner of the Societies for the Reformation of Manners, whose program Bickerstaff praised, and whose members actually had brought homosexuals, drunkards, prostitutes, gamblers and other "promoters of vice" before the courts. Mandeville's object in these essays was not simply to heap scorn upon

---

[6] Abel Boyer, *The English Theophrastus* (London, 1702), p. 106. Boyer was a popular writer who also published translations of French authors as *Characters of the Virtues and Vices of the Age* (London, 1695), *Letters of Wit, Politicks and Morality* (London, 1701), and *Choice Letters of Gallantry and Friendship* (London, 1701).

[7] See, especially, Goldsmith, *Private Vices, Public Benefits*, pp. 35–46, and 136–143.

these social guardians who, he never tired of pointing out, themselves derived considerable benefit (and, in the case of Steele, a profitable audience) from the society whose habits they criticized. He wished also to show that well-intentioned proposals for the stamping out of vice were either misconceived or a sham, and that the atheism and libertinism so feared by the Societies and Steele were most easily found, not amongst ordinary persons or the rabble, but within the refined and monied classes themselves.

In *The Spectator*, Addison wondered if the "Politeness which reigns among the unthinking part of Mankind, and treats as unfashionable the most ingenious part of our Behaviour," would "undermine Morality" as it "recommends Impudence as Good Breeding."[8] Steele too feared that within the polite society he addressed, the debased currency of "ambition," "wealth" and "luxury" would drive "the Taste of Good-will, of Friendship, of Innocence" out of circulation.[9] He suspected that this "most polite Age is in danger of being the most vicious," because the mannered posturings upon which he commented so often concealed transgressive behavior. In *The Christian Hero* (1701) Steele sought to instruct his readers how a life devoted to honor and worldly esteem could accord perfectly with Christian principles, if only persons would discriminate between genuine refinement and its vicious simulacrum. Both writers attempted to provide revised and semi-official regulations for what they hoped would be a reformed, though increasingly opulent, elite – one whose propriety incorporated ethics into etiquette, and for whom standards of polite behavior amongst autonomous individuals were consonant with the dictates of morality. In what might fairly be considered an announcement of *The Spectator*'s program, Steele put the matter as follows:

I lay it down therefore for a Rule, That the whole Man is to move together; that every action of any Importance, is to have a Prospect of publick Good; and that the general Tendency of our indifferent Actions ought to be agreeable to the Dictates of Reason, of Religion [and] of good Breeding.[10]

At the heart of Mandeville's mature argument was the thesis that the growth of commerce, increased consumption and the expansion of a class of leisured commoners were all civilizing agents. Together they

---

[8] Donald F. Bond (ed.), *The Spectator*, 5 volumes (Oxford University Press, 1963), No. 231.
[9] *Spectator*, No. 6.   [10] *Spectator*, No. 6.

enlarged the consciousness of one's dependence on others and at the same time promoted effective restraints on arbitrary government. But in direct opposition to Addison and Steele, Mandeville celebrated rather than bemoaned the contradictions of modern societies, where the polish and civility that necessarily accompanied commercial opulence had created a decidedly secular world in which publicly-proclaimed standards of propriety paid mere lip service to the Christian or antique ideals that the triumph of modernity had rendered vestigial. Nothing exemplified this point for Mandeville so forcefully as the examination of "Good Manners," which have "nothing to do with Virtue or Religion; instead of extinguishing, they rather inflame the passions," which "the Man of Sense and Education ... hides ... with the greatest Dexterity ... [and] enjoys a Pleasure altogether unknown to the Short-sighted" (1, 79).

Mandeville's purpose in satirizing the attempts by moralists like Addison and Steele to refine the tastes of a commercially oriented metropolitan elite, and then equate this class-bound conception of cultivation with the dictates of morality, was not, like Swift's, utterly to delegitimize the norms of contemporary sociability. Even when he adopted an obviously Swiftian pose, as in his *Modest Defence of Publick Stews* (1724), in which, under the pseudonym of "Philo-Porney," he proposed public brothels as the most efficient protectors of female virtue, Mandeville's purposes differed. He sought to show that modern patterns of politeness served the socially beneficial end of encouraging opulence, that the goal of opulent living had become a necessary feature of the policy of modern states, whose governments were obliged to encourage and direct the pursuit of strictly private ends; and that a society genuinely committed to a strict regard for religion and virtue could achieve few of the benefits accompanying commercial prosperity. Addison's and Steele's attempt to discipline and moralize modern social habits was, for Mandeville, nothing other than an example of the hypocrisy required of persons for whom a "philosophy of manners" had become the effective substitute for, rather than a refinement of, a coherent moral theory. Once a monied elite became enmeshed in the transactional obligations which defined commercial societies, it was sheer pretense to claim that these persons lived or could live according to the standards of Stoic or Christian ethics. As Mandeville had written in *Free Thoughts*, the very practices of commerce, typically referred to as "fair-dealing," amply characterized "the arts of cunning and deception," practices which "modern deists," as he pointedly called them, now sought to re-define as virtues by proclaiming the coincidence of morality and self-interest.[11]

Mandeville's critique of the ideology of politeness, then, was largely in place by the time he published *Free Thoughts* in 1720, six years after *The Fable* first appeared as a self-contained book. But in 1723, when he brought out the amplified edition of what would later be known as *The Fable*'s first volume, Mandeville not only included "An Essay on Charity and Charity-Schools," dedicated to the Societies for the Reformation of Manners and the probable cause of the prosecution of his publisher, but he appended a theoretical excursus, "A Search into the Nature of Society" (I, 323–369). In this essay, Mandeville announced that the Earl of Shaftesbury's *Characteristics* (1711, revised 1714) was the text which most clearly embodied those illusions which *The Fable* targeted. He claimed that "[t]he attentive Reader ... will soon perceive that two Systems cannot be more opposite than his Lordship's and mine" (I, 324). In *The Fable*'s second volume of 1728, Horatio, the foil of Mandeville's spokesman Cleomenes, who could not "endure ... my own [moral] nakedness" (II, 108), begins by maintaining Shaftesbury's position, but finally accepts Mandeville's after participating in six dialogues, the form Shaftesbury thought most suited to polite argument. Interestingly enough, however, Mandeville had previously praised Shaftesbury as "one of the most polite authors of the age."[12] He had in fact agreed with Shaftesbury's defense of limited monarchy and religious toleration, along with the third Earl's denunciations of superstition, religious fanaticism and the political pretensions of Tory and Jacobite clergymen. Moreover, in *Free Thoughts* Mandeville had borrowed quotations from the *Characteristics* without attribution, and many of his religious views in the tract, as well as in *The Fable*, seemed so much like Shaftesbury's that in *Alciphron* (1732) Bishop Berkeley attacked both authors as prominent enemies of Christian belief.[13]

In the 1720s, however, the *Characteristics* presented Mandeville with hitherto unavailable polemical opportunities for promoting his argument. Shaftesbury's posthumous reputation was at its zenith during this decade, while *The Tatler* and *The Spectator* had already

---

[11] Mandeville, *Free Thoughts on Religion, The Church and National Happiness* (1720) (London, 1729), 2nd edition, p. 280.   [12] Mandeville, *Free Thoughts*, p. 266.

[13] For an examination of this relationship see Irwin Primer, "Mandeville and Shaftesbury: Some Facts and Problems," in Primer (ed.), *Mandeville Studies* (The Hague: Nijhoff, 1975), pp. 126–141.

begun to recede into the mists of literary and journalistic history. In choosing Shaftesbury as his adversary, Mandeville could now not only offer the first systematic summary of his argument in "A Search into the Nature of Society," but also could firmly locate this argument in the minds of his readers as the most telling of those systems "of improved selfishness" devised by "speculative men" whose reductionist moral psychology Shaftesbury had strongly criticized as a perverse attempt to "new-frame the human Heart."[14] One of the aims of the *Characteristics* was "to recommend MORALS on the same foot, with what in a lower sense is calls manners and to advance philosophy ... on the very Foundation of what is call'd agreeable and polite."[15] Shaftesbury set the "polite arts" and "polite learning" of a contemporary social elite against the pedantry of previous rude ages. He insisted not only that genuinely to philosophize was itself "to carry good-breeding a step higher,"[16] but also that modern forms of civility, embodied in the behavior of an enlightened "public," were in fact the most heightened expressions of a natural sympathy common to the species. Such feelings were the most authentic signs of the moral sentiments, those quintessentially human passions that were refined by free social intercourse.

All Politeness is owing to Liberty. We polish one another, and rub off our Corners and rough sides by a sort of amicable collision. To restrain this, is inevitably to bring a Rust upon Mens Understanding. 'Tis a destroying of Civility, Good Breeding, and even Charity it-self, under the pretence of maintaining it.[17]

Unlike the posturing practices of courtiers, now happily "banished [from] the town," Shaftesbury claimed that urban and urbane politeness was at once the "true standard" and finest expression of a society characterized by "liberty and commerce."[18] Within this society, the "mere goodness" inherent in human nature, while falling

---

[14] "*Sensis Communis*: An Essay on the Freedom of Wit and Humour," in Anthony Ashley Cooper, Third Earl of Shaftesbury, *Characteristics of Men, Manners, Opinions, Times etc.*, ed. John M. Robertson (London: Richards, 1900), 2 volumes, I, p. 78. Shaftesbury's probable targets were Hobbes and the reputed atheists Charles Blount and John Toland. On Shaftesbury's importance for the ideology of politeness see particularly Lawrence Klein, "The Third Earl of Shaftesbury and the Progress of Politeness," *Eighteenth-Century Studies* 18, 2 (Winter 1984/5), pp. 186–214, and "Liberty, Manners and Politeness in Early Eighteenth-Century England," *Historical Journal* 32, 3 (1989), pp. 583–605.
[15] *Characteristics*, II, "Miscellany III," p. 257.
[16] *Characteristics*, II, "Miscellany III," p. 255.
[17] *Characteristics*, I, "An Essay on the Freedom of Wit and Humour," p. 46.
[18] *Charateristics*, I, "An Essay on the Freedom of Wit and Humour," p. 45.

short of the selfless virtue of pure benevolence, is nevertheless promoted as never before:

Now as to that passion which is esteemed peculiarly interesting, as having for its aim the possession of wealth, and what we call a settlement or fortune in the world: if the regard towards this kind be moderate and in a reasonable degree [, as politness requires]; if it occasions no passionate pursuit; nor raises any ardent desire or appetite; there is nothing in this case which is not compatible with virtue, and even suitable and beneficial for society. The public as well as the private system is advanced by the industry which this affection excites.[19]

No single work was more important than the *Characteristics* in articulating the moral foundations for what has been called "the social theory of elite hegemony" in eighteenth-century Britain,[20] or for naturalizing those modes of mannered display through which the governing classes publicly dramatized their right to rule.[21] Shaftesbury amplified and then standardized into a gentlemanly public discourse the principles first made popular by Addison and Steele. He effectively articulated a view of morality which did not clash with, but was instead embedded in, the refinements and material aspirations of a commercial world – a world whose only predecessor, he claimed, was Athens, that polity standing at a considerable remove from the rude severities of Sparta, republican Rome or, for that matter, an England governed by puritan saints or their self-appointed successors. The considerable success of the *Characteristics* made it possible for Mandeville in 1723 to cast Shaftesbury's arguments as the archetypal example of what he had already defined as moral self-delusion.

The imaginary Notions that Men may be virtuous without Self-denial are a vast Inlet to Hypocrisy, which being once made habitual, we must not only deceive others, but likewise become altogether unknown to our selves ... [I]t will appear, how for want of duly examining himself this might happen to a person of Quality of Parts and Erudition, one every way resembling the Author of the Characteristics himself. (1, 331)

The social virtues so eloquently examined by Shaftesbury, Mandeville went on, were exactly those features of the Earl's own dissembling character, qualities he shared with members of an elite who

---

[19] *Characteristics*, 1, "An Inquiry Concerning Virtue or Merit," p. 326.
[20] J.C.D. Clark, *English Society, 1688–1832* (Cambridge University Press, 1985), pp. 93–119.
[21] E.P. Thompson, "Patrician Society, Plebeian Culture," *Journal of Social History* 7, 4 (1977), pp. 382–405.

skillfully hide "the different Motives they act from" (1, 350). By 1723, "Shaftesbury" had become for Mandeville the symbolic exemplification of the rule that reason is moved in whichever way passion draws it, and that, as with Steele's Bickerstaff, but with considerably greater sophistication, the primary purpose of his arguments was to justify private inclination by shrouding it in encomiums of praise.

Mandeville's attack on Shaftesbury, then, was a stratagem for accomplishing a number of polemical objectives. First, the attack enabled him to offer a summary of and commentary upon the theory of sociability originally outlined in the prose "Remarks" to *The Grumbling Hive* by placing his own views in a supposed absolute contrast to the arguments of the *Characteristics*. Second, by naming Shaftesbury as his primary target in "A Search Into the Nature of Society," Mandeville himself set the theoretical agenda for future criticisms of *The Fable*. In choosing the most esteemed moralist of his generation as his primary target, Mandeville placed his own critique of "politeness," and of the conception of a moral sense as a form of hypocrisy, within the most publicly visible arena of philosophical controversy. By invoking a strictly naturalist argument directly to attack Shaftesbury's claims that man's natural bent is towards society, that polished passions were compatible with altruism and benevolence, and that these moral sentiments procured social benefit, Mandeville was able to place upon his opponents the burden of demonstrating that his reduction of fellow-feeling to self-regard was false. He openly challenged those who agreed with Shaftesbury to make the author of *The Fable* "see, why this [supposed] Love of Company, this strong Desire after Society should be construed so much in our Favour, and alleged as a Mark of some Intrinsic Worth in Man not to be found in other Animals" (1, 340–341).

In "A Search into the Nature of Society" Mandeville encouraged his adversaries to take the arguments of *The Fable* in a systematically reductionist sense. In this essay he could plausibly be construed as claiming that the "human frame" is constituted by a compound of passions, whose relative strengths and immediate valences depend primarily upon the innate differences between individual constitutions, established at birth. Each passion could then be understood as an animal appetite, in the sense that its satisfactions depend upon the achievement of some goal or object independent of the feelings, beliefs, attitudes and passions of other persons, save when these impede or prevent an individual from satisfying the ruling passion currently motivating him. "I demonstrate," Mandeville said, "that the Sociableness of Man arises only from Two things, *viz*. The multiplicity of his Desires, and the continual Opposition he meets with in his Endeavours to gratify them" (1, 344). An individual must take the feelings and desires of others into account when pursuing his ends, not because he is concerned with these states of feeling in a way intrinsic to the satisfaction of his own wants, but because they are potential obstacles to the attainment of his satisfactions. Despite the apparent concern which their manners imply they have for their fellows, social actors remain oblivious to the specifically human needs of others, for their desires (passions) are independent of the consciousness of other people, save in a purely instrumental way. The primary passion of pride – the expression of the innate desire to dominate – demands that we attempt to establish ourselves in positions of superiority with respect to others, but not that others esteem us highly because our actions are genuinely meritorious. Mandeville starkly challenged his critics to prove that modern manners and morals should not be treated as ideological instruments designed by their users to elicit the "praise" contingently required from other persons in order to satisfy one's need for approbation.

BISHOP BUTLER AND THE PURSUIT OF HAPPINESS

It was precisely this challenge to contemporary moral reasoning that was taken up by Joseph Butler, the most important of Mandeville's immediate philosophical adversaries, in his *Sermons*, published in 1726, three years after the appearance of the first volume of *The Fable*. Butler never mentions Mandeville by name. But a considerable part of his philosophical activity was concerned, whether directly or indirectly, with the refutation of Mandeville's ideas. Butler frequently paraphrased parts of *The Fable*, and the allusions to Mandeville in the *Sermons* and *The Analogy of Religion* are unmistakable, even when he is discussing Hobbes or Bayle. Butler's opposition to Mandeville was one of the strongest determinants of his interests as a philosopher, and he might never have directly addressed many of the dilemmas of ethical naturalism had *The Fable* not attained notoriety as a morally subversive book.

Butler intended to demolish Mandeville's major arguments on their own conceptual ground, emphasizing that he, like Mandeville, began his inquiries into morality from a study of human nature rather

than from abstract moral principles. Butler argued that our experience of the world compels us sharply to distinguish human from
animal behavior, especially when considering the morally decisive
question of the relationship of desire to action. Animals, Butler
claimed, always follow the bent of their nature, for in animals passions
or appetites are strictly ordered according to their relative strengths at
any given moment. Consequently, the actions of animals always flow
from their strongest immediate appetite or inclination. It is clearly
apparent, even to the most skeptical observer of animals, Butler
claims, that some of these actions are not for the creature's own good,
often leading to extreme pain or even death. The nature of animals
then, is distinguished, and their actions shaped, by impulses over
which they lack rational control. Humans, on the other hand, can act
naturally *or* unnaturally because human nature contains principles
which are superior to other factors, such as the strength of a given
desire. It would therefore be unnatural, Butler argues, if a *man*,
"foreseeing [in] the ... design of action ruin,"[22] should still follow his
strongest desire; and this bow to prudence on a person's part would,
pace Mandeville, be thoroughly consonant with what Butler calls the
principle of "reasonable and cool" self-love with which all persons are
differentially endowed.

The consonance rather than the opposition of self-love and the
prudential rational direction of human action follows for Butler from
the fact that self-love is a "general" rather than a particular passion,
as it was so often mistakenly regarded by "selfish theorists" like
Hobbes and Mandeville who seek to reduce human to animal
motivations. Self-love is the desire to seek whatever it is that makes
one happy, and "happiness or satisfaction consists only in the
enjoyment of those objects, which are by nature suited to our
particular appetites, passions and affections."[23] The object of self-
love, then, is happiness, understood as the long-term good or interest
of the moral subject.[24] Whatever particular actions lead to happiness,
the happy person is he whose life largely fulfills the particular
appetites, passions and affections implanted in him; and there may
well be, given the inherent differences in human constitutions, a
different order of preferences in various persons within a universally

---

[22] Joseph Butler, *The Works of Joseph Butler*, ed. J.H. Bernard (London: Macmillan, 1900), 2
volumes, I, "Sermon II," Section 10.　　[23] Butler, "Sermon IX," Section 9.
[24] Butler, "Sermon IX," Section 8.

shared human nature. As these persons have different life-projects, their self-love must be understood as (what we would now call) a second-order affection, a framework for other particular desires embodied within it. Thus self-love *is* a desire, but a desire that a person's primary desires should be satisfied to the extent required for his happiness in the long term. From this distinction, Butler argues, it follows that the due exercise of self-love in any given individual requires his self-knowledge, that is, a knowledge of what mode of life will be a happy one for him, given the particular desires that he has. Correctly understood, self-love is at once an affection, or passion, *and* a rational principle, since it requires the capacity to distinguish between various objects of desire, and as such it may be designated as "cool and reasonable" rather than "violent," as compared to our often impetuous immediate desires for particular objects.

Butler refers to the difference between self-love and particular desires as a difference between "internal" and "external" objects. His purpose in so proceeding is to offer an argument aimed at refuting Mandevillian hedonism, particularly the omnibus and, Butler thought, widely accepted claim, adopted from Epicurus by way of Gassendi, "that things profitable and useful are sought after for the sake of pleasure."[25] As Mandeville put it in *The Fable*, "it is impossible that . . . mere fallen Man should act with any other View but to please himself" (1, 348).

There is a strange affection in many people of explaining away all particular affections, and representing the whole of life as nothing but one continued exercise of self-love. Hence arises that surprising confusion and perplexity in the Epicureans of old, Hobbes, the author of *Reflections, Sentences et Maximes Morales* [La Rochefoucauld] and this whole set of writers; the confusion of calling actions interested which are done in contradiction to the most manifest known interest, [our happiness,] merely for the gratification of a present passion.[26]

For Butler, this "account of human nature" is more than mistaken. It is dangerously perverse, "because there is raised upon [it] a general scheme which undermines the whole foundation of common justice and honesty."[27]

Mandeville's doctrines, Butler argues, rest on a willful confusion

---

[25]   *Three Discourses of Happiness, Virtue and Liberty. Collected from the Works of the Learn'd Gassendi, By Monsieur Bernier. Translated out of the French* (London, 1699), p. 91.

[26]   Butler, "Sermons," Preface, Section 35.   [27]   Butler, "Sermon v," Section 2.

about the difference between self-love and particular desires, a difference revealed when internal and external objects of the passions are properly distinguished. When we have particular desires, we want not the pleasure of getting what we want, but the object itself, because of the "prior suitableness" between desires and their specific objects. Indeed, there would otherwise be, contrary to all experience, no enjoyment of one thing more than another, and the pleasures all persons receive in the acquisition of certain things rather than others would be inexplicable.

That all particular appetites and passions are towards *external things themselves*, distinct from the *pleasure arising from them*, is manifested from hence; that there could not be this pleasure, were it not for that prior suitableness between the object and the passion: there could be no enjoyment or delight from one thing more than another, from eating food more than from swallowing a stone, if there were not an affection or appetite to one thing more than another.[28]

   On the other hand, the objects of self-love differ from the objects of the particular passions precisely in being wholly internal. One can see this by attending to the distinction between the desire for happiness – the object of self-love – and the momentary desire for sexual gratification that was one of Mandeville's favorite examples of the undiminished passions hidden in polished society. Acting on the desire for sexual gratification with a certain person at a particular time may well be detrimental to one's happiness and health, in which case the fulfillment of this desire would thus run counter to self-love. And simply because this desire is a person's own, it does not follow that any action proceeding from it aims at some internal state of his, as opposed to an object in the world, just as the desires for beer and petticoats – two more of Mandeville's preferred examples – do not necessarily aim at good health or comfort. Selfish theorists like Mandeville either ignore or collapse this distinction. But without it, Butler argues, these theorists are forced to treat all persons as having the single goal of pleasure, and remain unable to account for what it is that gives one person pleasure from one thing rather than from another. For all objects are implicitly treated by selfish theorists not as the chosen objects suitable to satisfy a particular passion, but only as goods which serve an instrumental function in the achieving of a qualitatively undifferentiated good, indiscriminately labelled "pleasure." More-

[28] Butler, "Sermon xi," Section 6.

over, among the desires which motivate individuals may well be found those that increase the happiness of others; indeed, even desires for their happiness which, if fulfilled, would contribute to one's own. So benevolence may well be no more contrary to self-love any more than any other desire, since even if we did, counterfactually, always choose to follow self-love, this might lead us to indulge our desires to do good to others.

An unprejudiced observation of our thoughts and actions, and of the behavior of others, will show, so Butler argues, that the principles he characterizes are present in human nature. The person who, like Mandeville, denies that we act from reasonable self-love, benevolence or conscience, at least some of the time, challenges what appears patently obvious to virtually all actors themselves. But in fact, and despite their appeals to experience, Butler claims that selfish theorists argue from nothing more than dogmatic premises to explain away this problem. Egoists hold that all motives are selfish, while hedonists claim that all motives can be reduced to a single desire for our own pleasure. Both "prove" that conscience and benevolence are fictions essentially by asserting baseless "general hypoptheses" about the passions. But the problem of establishing whether or not a man's "inward frame" includes good will is a "question of fact or natural history, not provable immediately by reason," and one, in addition, which our "inward perceptions" affirm.[29] Indeed, conscience is neither an affection nor a passion at all, but a rational property vital to our nature, "a principle of reflection in men, by which they distinguish between, approve and disapprove their own actions." It is the only faculty by which we "reflect on our own nature" and the motives and actions proper to it.[30] Conscience has the distinctive character of approving and disapproving of our actions and passions, judging objects as virtuous or vicious in themselves, rather than merely as leading to a certain vicious result.[31] Conscience thus judges intentions. It is our capacity for moral judgement, and the "magisterial" authority of conscience, superior to all other principles, whose dictates are at once the laws of God, the following of which will be for our own good, and "by Nature a rule to us."[32] Conscience at once asserts itself without being consulted, and is unaffected by the

---

[29] Butler, "Sermons," Preface Sections 35–42, and "Sermon IX," Section 5–18.
[30] Butler, "Sermon I," Section 8.   [31] Butler, "Sermon II," Section 8.
[32] Butler, "Sermon II," Sections 13–14.

strength of the motivating passion for action. It is the faculty by which we evaluate the actions of others as well as our own. What is more, a great number of actions performed in various circumstances and in respect of different objects makes it wildly improbable that we unfailingly seek what we take to be our immediate advantage, for we frequently act – act knowingly – against our interests. This happens, Butler argues, when we follow a particular desire because it is stronger than self-love, even though self-love should presumably over-ride the desire and stop us. Indeed, for Butler, as against Mandeville, most people can be seen to have *too little*, rather than an over-abundance of self-love, since

they have not cool and reasonable concern enough for themselves to consider wherein their chief happiness in the present life consists; or else, if they do consider it ... they will not act conformably to what is the result of that consideration.[33]

Butler's conception of morality accommodates those other-regarding actions which Mandeville argued were psychologically implausible by invoking a wholly natural and rational principle of ordering of the desires which promote self-love. Thus he presents virtuous and benevolent actions as the result, not of what Mandeville claims is an impossible exercise of self-denial, but of a prudent calculation of our own long-term interests which may fully accord with the dictates of morality.[34] Self-love in this account is not antithetical to benevolence: the desire for our own happiness *requires* us to satisfy particular passions, and among these, experience suggests, are desires to do good to others.[35] This experience accords perfectly with the commonly held and correct belief that "principles in the heart of man carry him to society."[36] Mandeville fails to recognize this truth because of his confused presumptions about egoism and hedonism. But, in fact, the pursuit of the good of others is fully consonant with the dictates of self-love, even though benevolence, implanted in men by a loving God, is a principle distinct from it.[37] Indeed, "self-love, ... though confined to the interest of the present world, does in general perfectly coincide with virtue."[38]

It is not surprising that Mandeville found the argument that the

---

[33] Butler, "Sermon I," Section 14.   [34] Butler, "Sermon IX," Section 19.
[35] Butler, "Sermon IX," Section 3.   [36] Butler, "Sermon II," Section 2.
[37] Butler, "Dissertation on the Nature of Virtue," in *Works*, II, Sections 1–2.
[38] Butler, "Sermon XI," Section 7.

practice of virtue, rather than being indissolubly linked to self-denial, is in fact in our best interests, to be an evasion of his main point. Butler sought to show that the claims of conscience and morality are not ideological artifacts designed to mask wholly selfish motives, but rather could be seen to follow from the dictates of self-love, properly understood. Yet what Butler claims to be a "rational principle" of ordering desire,[39] a principle of conscience consonant with the practice of benevolence, is scarcely different from Mandeville's assertion, following Bayle, that reason is a calculating instrument employed by human agents driven by complex and sometimes competing passions to seek their own satisfactions. And if the practice of virtue is to be taken, as Butler suggests, as the surest course to the maximal satisfaction of desire, rationally conceived, this would merely be an injunction, in Mandeville's sense, prudentially to follow the dictates of morality as they are currently constituted in the society in which one lives, because by so doing one can reasonably anticipate public approbation. From Mandeville's perspective, Butler's arguments simply refuse to ask the central ethical question of how acts could possibly be distinctly moral if they are in fact indistinguishable from self-interested ones. Instead, Butler can be seen as giving philosophical expression to what was already a conventional Augustinian truism at the time that he preached: that nature works in an almost perfect harmony with morality,

so we find that means very undesirable often conduce to bring about ends in such a measure desirable as greatly to overbalance the disagreeableness of the means ... and in general, that those things which are objected against the moral scheme of Providence, may be upon the the whole, friendly and assistant to virtue, and productive of an overbalance of happiness.[40]

While a minority of Mandeville's opponents called for the outright suppression of his book because, like Bishop Berkeley[41] and Edmund Gibson, the Bishop of London,[42] they claimed that *The Fable* not only promoted atheism but actively encouraged criminal behavior,[43]

---

[39] Butler, "Sermon I," Section 9.
[40] Joseph Butler, *The Analogy of Religion, Natural and Revealed to the Constitution and Course of Nature,* in *Works,* II, I.vii Section 6.
[41] George Berkeley, *Alciphron; or, the Minute Philosopher; containing an apology for the Christian Religion against those who are called Free-Thinkers* (London, 1732), 2nd Dialogue.
[42] Edmund Gibson, *Pastoral Letter to the People of His Diocese* (London, 1726).
[43] See too John Therold, *A Short Examination of the Notions Advance'd in a (Late) Book, intitled, The Fable of the Bees ...* (London, 1726).

Butler recognized that Mandeville's arguments were intended neither to encourage any significant alteration in the behavior of ordinary persons nor to subvert the power of the English state Mandeville so unambiguously supported. Butler clearly understood that the subversive feature of Mandeville's enterprise was his attempt thoroughly, and perversely, to redescribe the inherited moral tradition in ways which effectively licensed forms of self-aggrandizing behavior when this behavior obviously, albeit unintentionally, contributed to public happiness and prosperity. By explicitly removing intention as the primary ground from which to judge the soundness of an entire category of acts, Mandeville's genealogy of morals threatened to expose as incoherent both Christian and humanist principles of moral responsibility. It was "a way of thinking" so bizarre, William Law said, "as to make the History of the curing People in Bedlam, a true Account of the *Origin of Reason*."[44] Mandeville's "strange ... Assertion[s]," according to the prominent literary critic and moralist John Dennis, "make all the Writers of Politicks, from Plato down to Machiavelli, contemptible ignorant Fools. For it has been the Business of all those Writers to shew, That Vice is always attended by Corruption, and is the Pest and bane of every Free Community."[45]

What then was Mandeville's primary offense in the minds of his contemporaries? It consisted, as John Hervey put it, of challenging the accepted moral tradition by way of publicly exposing some unpleasant truths about the necessary workings of moral compromise in opulent nations.[46] Mandeville effectively gave voice to an already presupposed, but rarely acknowledged, view among educated metropolitans that selfishness, if tactfully pursued, was in fact a species of ethically trivial activity, despite typically being deemed "evil." *The Fable*'s notoriety made it impossible further to elide this issue. It was a short step for moralists like Butler to seek to domesticate Mandeville's exposure of the hypocrisy inherent in publicly supporting the rigorous standards of Christian ethics, while privately attempting to satisfy desire. He did so by offering a positive demonstration that the workings of self-love were consonant with benevolence. This was the view classically expressed in Pope's Epistle I of his *Moral Essays*, and

---

[44] William Law, *Remarks Upon a Late Book, Entitled, The Fable of the Bees* ... (London, 1724), p. 12.
[45] John Dennis, *Vice and Luxury Public Mischiefs: Or, Remarks on a Book Intitled, The Fable of the Bees* ... (London, 1724), p. 13.
[46] John Lord Hervey, *Some Remarks on the Minute Philosopher in a Letter from a Country Clergyman to his Friend in London* (London, 1732), pp. 22–23, and 42–50.

often repeated by Mandeville's critics, like the popular writer John Brown[47] and Archibald Campbell, professor of Church History at St. Andrews. Campbell claimed to have learned from his Scottish colleague Francis Hutcheson's attack on *The Fable* that,

it is impossible that *Self-interest* can ever be inconsistent with *Virtue*, but only the *deceitful shadow* of it, which I own, is grasped at by every deluded Imagination, to his own ruin, and the great Disturbance of the World.[48]

Butler's general discussion of pleasure and its relation to particular desires would, moreover, have little import for Mandeville's argument, because the future Bishop of Durham presumed that all motivations were *conscious* ones – a point Mandeville, following the line of Jansenist moral psychology,[49] explicitly denied. One of *The Fable*'s objects was to expose the ways in which men conceal their desires from *others*, and in this project of exposing hypocrisy the figure of "the dissembling Courtier" (I, 132) or the member of the *beau monde* who refused to "distinguish the real from the Counterfeited" (I, 404) served Mandeville's intentions. Men were hypocrites when they performed actions deemed virtuous solely in the anticipation of public applause (I, 55). But *The Fable*'s larger and more conceptually ambitious purpose of "anatomizing the invisible Part of Man" (I, 145) was intended to encompass all persons who successfully concealed their desires from *themselves*, because these repressions, first constituted during the training of children by their nurses and parents (I, 72), and subsequently refined and reinforced by the pressures of social injunction (I, 73), were the necessary requirements of civilized living. They were performed "without reflection, and Men by degrees, and Great Length of Time, fall as it were into these Things spontaneously" (II, 139). Butler sought to deny that there was any necessity for selfish theorists like Mandeville to "pull off the Masque[s]" (I, 307) persons wear in order to conceal their desires from others, since these desires – including the desire to be well regarded – derived from natural sources which accorded with morality when rationally governed. Because Butler presumed that a person's desires and motives were transparent to his consciousness, he had no response whatsoever

---

[47] John Brown, *Essays on the Characteristics of the Earl of Shaftesbury* (London, 1751; New York: Garland Reprint, 1970), Part II.

[48] Archibald Campbell, *An Enquiry into the Origins of Moral Virtue* (Edinburgh, 1733), p. 452.

[49] See, for example, E.D. James, *Pierre Nicole, Jansenist and Humanist* (The Hague: Nijhoff, 1972), pp. 38–43 and 124–125 on Nicole's notion of *pensées imperceptibles*; and compare *Fable*, I, p. 139.

to Mandeville's claim that polished societies heavily rested on the forms of *self*-deception which the repression of instinct fostered, and thus upon a "want of self-understanding" (I, 280).

Nevertheless, Butler's criticism of Mandeville did present an important challenge to the arguments of the first volume of *The Fable*, since he effectively distinguished between two significantly different senses of pleasure which Mandeville initially overlooked. By distinguishing the pleasure to be gained by possessing a particular object or engaging in a particular activity from the general desire for happiness constituted by the sum of these pleasures over the course of a life, Butler thought he had demonstrated Mandeville's argument that all acts were self-regarding and motivated by an undifferentiated desire for pleasure to rest on a facile play of words. He claimed that, because of a conflation of these two senses of pleasure, Mandeville's main point was voided of content, since it was logically inconceivable that a person should have things other than particular objects in mind when desire presses upon him. It would be impossible for a Mandevillian egoist to act in the purely instrumental ways anatomized in *The Fable*. If, even amongst model egoists and hedonists, certain particular goods or acts had no privileged position in relation to the passions, then the acts of these persons would, absurdly, be nothing more than random and self-stultifying attempts to satisfy an incoherently imagined need.

More than any other contemporary, Butler distilled in trenchant philosophical form the major moral objections levelled by most of Mandeville's first significant British critics, along with a host of outraged minor divines, against *The Fable*'s assertion that the "moral virtues are the political offspring which flattery begot upon pride" (I, 51). Conventional expressions of moral outrage at Mandeville's attempt to decompose ethical injuctions into instruments of social discipline were, however, effectively anticipated by Mandeville in *The Fable*'s first volume. He pointed to the accusations of immorality he foresaw by future opponents as examples of a blindness to "the real Sentiments of our Hearts before others" (I, 68), which civilization required. In the Preface to *The Fable*'s second volume Mandeville dismissed these writers as mere defenders of the hypocritical ethical standards he had exposed, as persons who, if they had "seen with better Eyes ... would easily have perceiv'd, unless they were too well pleas'd with their Pride ... they wanted nothing but Sincerity" (II, 6). As well, Mandeville easily reduced to absurdity the claims of antagonists like Berkeley (who seems hardly to have read Mandeville's work) that *The Fable*'s purpose was in fact to promote immorality and atheism, and held them up to ridicule as "silly People who imagine that the Good of the whole is consistent with the Good of every Individual."[50]

Butler, on the other hand, confronted Mandeville on his own ground. He defended orthodox Protestant ethics on the basis of moral psychology. Appealing first to experience, Butler then argued that *The Fable*'s anatomy of the passions was incoherent because of its repeated confusions about the nature of those pleasures which, Mandeville insisted, motivated all actors. Mandeville dismissed many of these criticisms as stemming from an ignorance, or at least an "insensibility" to the unconscious "hidden Spring that gives Life and Motion to all ... actions" (II, 79). But he took quite seriously Butler's major objection, which he placed in the mouth of Horatio, the foil of Mandeville's spokesman Cleomenes in *The Fable*, that

What is all this but the Old Stories over again, that every Thing is Pride, and all we see, Hypocrisy, without Proof or Argument ... which is so clashing with daily experience, that the very reverse is true?

Butler thus helped Mandeville to understand that he was obliged to engage his opponents on two distinct grounds. Obviously, he had effectively to redescribe everyday experience (II, 67–75) so that it could plausibly be seen as evidence supporting "what I argue for, and must insist upon ... the Possibility that all these [actions which appear as other-regarding] might be perform'd by a man from no other Views, and with no other Helps, than those I have named" (II, 77). And indeed, much of the material in the six dialogues which constitute *The Fable*'s second volume is devoted to placing heroism, the administration of the state, wealth creation, religious observance and the rules of propriety in the appropriate descriptive framework of the workings of pride, one which, Mandeville pointedly insisted, "helps us to explain the Phaenomena that occur ... which cannot be accounted for any other way" (II, 92). Very likely in reaction to Butler's criticism,[51] Mandeville realized that his notion of pride had to be reconceptualized, and that Gassendi's modernized Epicureanism offered the firmest foundation for this project. Mandeville, as will be recalled, shared Gassendi's view that motives for action could be

---

[50] Mandeville, *A Letter to Dion*, p. 49.
[51] See Kaye's comment in *Fable*, II, pp. 129–130, n. 1.

reduced to desires, and that desires themselves could further be reduced to desires for pleasure, which in turn had physiological sources. But if it was incoherent to believe that one could desire an internal state of mind (like pleasure), and then act in a particular way that would effectively answer this general, second-order, desire, then Mandeville's attempt to provide a scientific foundation for the claim that men were only self-regarding pleasure-seekers would be beside the point: there would be no way for these creatures to satisfy the desires which supposedly motivated them.

Butler's modern commentators have pointed out that his thesis that we cannot coherently desire what he called internal objects of the passions, and so are unable to satisfy them through particular actions, overlooks the fact that persons do often desire certain kinds of internal states, like thrills or the cessation of pain, and that we can and sometimes do satisfy these desires, just as persons can successfully seek to be surprised.[52] Even health, it could be said, is this kind of state, which would reasonably explain why a diabetic would choose to have a meal even though there is a more immediately absorbing activity at hand. While Mandeville was of course generally unconcerned with the task of providing counter-examples to Butler's arguments in a spirit of academic philosophical debate, he did address Butler's challenge in *The Fable*'s second volume, published within three years of the appearance of the *Sermons*.

Butler claimed that Mandeville's moral theory did nothing more than baldly assert that actions are done "to gratify an inclination in a man's self." Mandeville was therefore unable, according to Butler, to distinguish between "totally different" kinds of acts; unable, crucially, to provide "different words [i.e., terms] ... to express the difference, between the principle of an action, proceeding from cool consideration that it will be to my own advantage; and an action ... by which a man runs upon certain ruin, to do evil or good to another."[53] An understanding of "self-liking," the source of pride (II, 131), Mandeville argued, answers this objection. Properly understood, self-liking is precisely that term which refers to the second-order desire Butler discussed, attention to which would effectively regulate and grade a person's first-order desires for particular objects. It is an "Instinct ... by which every individual values itself above its real

---

[52] See, particularly, Austin Duncan-Jones, *Butler's Moral Philosophy* (Harmondsworth: Penguin, 1952), and Terence Penelhum, *Butler* (London: Routledge, 1985).
[53] Butler, "Sermon II," Sections 10–11.

Worth," one which makes us "so fond of the Approbation, Liking and Assent of others; because they strengthen and confirm us in the good Opinion we have of ourselves" (II, 130). Creatures always living in the same circumstances, with only slight variations in their way of living, would have little occasion or temptation obviously to express this passion. But those with diffident temperaments would only rarely respond to this instinct in manifest ways. For "[w]hilst Men are pleas'd, Self-liking has every Moment a considerable Share, tho' unknown, in procuring Satisfaction they enjoy" (II, 135–136). Yet it is "the Principle on which the Love [of other members of the species] is built" (II, 131), and one which becomes most crucially and demonstrably active in modern commercial environments, where a flood of "outward Ornaments" emerges as the publicly agreed-upon symbols of one's inherent worth.

Self-liking endows all creatures with a general desire for superiority. It is thus the source of the "Thirst of Dominion" which merely natural, physical capacities rarely can provide amongst humans, even in rudimentary environments (II, 132). Accordingly, this passion increasingly predisposes persons as they become socialized animals to satisfy their need for esteem instrumentally and symbolically, especially through the rituals of manners and conventions of language, understood as socially inscribed devices for the acquisition of praise. Even in the most primitive of societies, self-liking would dispose an individual to

seek for Opportunities, by Gestures, Looks, and Sounds, to display the Value it has for itself, superior to what it has for others; an untaught Man would desire every body that came near him, to agree with him in the Opinion of his superior Worth ... He would be highly delighted with, and love every body, whom he thought to have a good Opinion of him, especially those, that by Words or Gestures should own it to his face. (II, 133–134)

Self-liking, then, is the principle which shows how the appetites and affections which Butler contrasted with self-love in fact derive their motive force from self-regard. Desires for particular objects become intense because these objects acquire what Butler calls their "suitableness" to the passions of a given person. This suitableness has however to do with the place of these objects in the current social hierarchy of symbols of esteem, not with the objects themselves.

Attempts to gratify self-liking can, of course, fail, either for want of wit or reasonable opportunity; but, Mandeville continues, it is so necessary to the Well-being of those that have been used to indulge it; that they can taste no pleasure without it, and such is the deference, and the submissive Veneration they pay to it, that they are deaf to the loudest Calls of Nature, and will rebuke the strongest Appetites that should pretend to be gratify'd at the Expense of that Passion. (II, 136)

Thus, once he attended to Butler's views, Mandeville had little difficulty explaining why persons at given moments can be "deaf to the loudest calls of nature," as Augustine had classically pointed out in his discussion of Lucretia's taking her own life in preference to being thought an adulteress (I, 208–210). These desires and aversions, aroused by what helps or endangers self-preservation, can be suppressed by individuals living in relatively secure environments in the imaginative context of their anticipation of the pleasures flowing from an increase in self-regard. Self-liking may, coherently, motivate an action that redounds to one's own immediate disadvantage, not only because of miscalculation or bad luck, but because of one's intense hope for greater future reward. And just as merely animal desires can easily be over-ridden by socialized creatures whose self-liking has been enlarged during the civilizing process, so too can the want of this passion, for the ultimately bio-physiological reasons Mandeville had discussed in his medical *Treatise*,[54] lead to melancholy, "the extinction of hope" and finally to suicide, following from the "wish ... for the Dissolution of our Frame" (II, 136).

THEATRUM MUNDI

In responding to Butler's challenge to his account of the wholly passionate sources of action, Mandeville did not stop at refining his original conception of the passions as distinct but interdependent features of self-love. Also, he enriched an already-powerful argument which directly implied that if moral judgements were nothing other than expressions of feeling (even if, as Butler claimed, benevolence and self-love were not necessarily opposed), then the operative traditions of Christian moral psychology could not be enlisted to explain the status and workings of human desire. These judgements had to be set in a different problem-space from the one typically assumed by Mandeville's contemporaries. Mandeville effectively

---

[54] Mandeville, *A Treatise of the Hypochondriak and Hysterick Diseases* (London, 1730), 2nd edition, enlarged, p. 226.

redescribed the scene of moral activity as an arena which (*pace* Butler) was not populated by rationally endowed, undivided consciousnesses enquiring into those choices which directly affected their own souls, and the good of their community. The moral actor described in *The Fable* was, by contrast, an intersubjectively defined, socially situated participant in a communal drama; a person driven by passions who of necessity competed with those around him in a public market for tokens of esteem. This individual's desires alone formed the premises of his practical reasoning, while the material and symbolic rewards of the social order to which he happened to belong constituted inescapable features of his own identity. They were socially defined prizes whose acquisition and loss were signs of no intrinsically moral qualities, but merely an index of the ethically indifferent process governing the rise and fall of individuals and groups in which he was obliged to participate.

Mandeville's genealogy of morals thus placed the question of what it was that made a desire and its consequent action moral in the inescapably historical context of the socialization of the race. Moral codes themselves were, in his account, not expressions of universal ethical principles, but historically inscribed products of the cunning of elites as they established their dominance during the stages of the civilizing process. First locating the "origin of moral virtue" within this context, he then recast the notion of "the rational ambition of Being Good" (I, 49) as a psychologically implausible standard of virtue designed to manage irreducibly passionate egoists through shame and guilt. Mandeville was therefore free to argue that the actual workings of desire in any given community could in principle be accounted for by a sociology of its members' emotions – by placing the expression of supposedly moral sentiments in the context of responses to locally generated opportunities for private satisfaction. And once he was able to demonstrate that a good action (socially considered) need not be the action of a good man, but the unintended result of his "private vice," Mandeville could also make the telling point that what Butler and other contemporaries termed "happiness" was conceptually independent of the officially sanctioned moral standards which supposedly regulated public life. Hence social action could be strictly conceived in terms of an individual's search for pleasure and the degrees to which he managed to satisfy his desires. And since these desires had self-liking as their foundation, which in its all but most elementary manifestations depended upon public esteem and approbation, Mandeville could do more than explain why persons so often spoke and acted in ways which *appeared* moral (since in so doing they would be publicly rewarded); he could further argue that both speech and action could most usefully, and without self-deception, be understood instrumentally. Behavior in public was a species of performance designed to win approval, a series of performances whose success depended upon no genuine moral standard, but on how well a social actor could satisfy his desires within the given, socially structured conventions of rewards and punishments.

This conception of the dynamics of public life in highly developed social environments fully harmonized with Mandeville's seminal discussion of the origins of morality in "An Enquiry Into the Origins of Moral Virtue." From this discussion, he drew the conclusion that the majority of men were unselfconscious participants in societies whose techniques of persuasion and dominion remained unknown to them. They genuinely believed in those standards of propriety through which ruling elites promoted that docile conformity required of the multitudes in all well-governed states. What characterized the behavior of these elites themselves, however – most obviously, for Mandeville, amongst the expanding *beau monde* in commercial societies – was what he termed "hypocrisy" rather than commitment. Since

we cannot prevent the Ideas that are continually arising within us, all Civil Commerce would be lost, if by Art and prudent Dissimulation we had not learn'd to hide and stifle them ... In all Civil Societies Men are taught insensibly to be Hypocrites from their Cradle. (1, 348–349)

The desire for "applause" rather than the demands of duty could now be seen to govern the actions of persons for whom wealth and breeding alone provided a ready access to the symbols of public esteem. This process remained invisible to most observers, for

the Man of Sense and Education never exults more in his Pride than when he hides it with the greatest Dexterity; and in feasting on the Applause, which he is sure all good Judges will pay to his Behaviour, he enjoys a Pleasure altogether unknown to the Short-sighted. (1, 79)

Mandeville insisted that any discussion of contemporary morals and manners had to account for the dramatic social fact that modern social elites were only notionally committed to the foundations of the moral codes which they publicly endorsed. In reality their behavior could not be understood by reference to their manifest beliefs, which they announced in order to win public approval, but rather by an examination of the socially sanctioned devices through which these persons sought to master the performative requirements of the roles they played in order to maximize their satisfactions. As Mandeville's spokesman Cleomenes declared: "In the very Politeness of Conversation, the Complacency, with which fashionable People are continually soothing each other's Frailties, and in almost every part of a Gentlemen's Behaviour ... there was a disagreement between the outward Appearances, and what is felt within, that was clashing with Uprightness and Sincerity" (II, 17). Styles of behavior deemed virtuous, polite and honorable served as a model for this histrionic quality of social transactions:

When *A* performs an Action which, in the Eyes of *B*, is laudable, *B* wishes well to *A*; and, to shew him his Satisfaction, tells him, that such an Action is an Honour to Him, or that He ought to be Honoured for it: By saying this, *B*, who knows that that all Men are affected with Self-liking, intends to acquaint *A*, that he thinks him in the Right to gratify and indulge himself in the Passion of Self-liking. In this sense the Word Honour, whether it is used as a Noun or a Verb, is always a Compliment we make to Those who act, have or are, what we approve of; it is a term of Art to express our Concurrence with others, our Agreement with them in their Sentiments concerning the Esteem and Value they have for themselves ... So that the Highest Honour which Men can give to Mortals, whilst alive, is in Substance no more, than the most likely and most effectual Means that Human Wit can invent to gratify, stir up, and encrease in Him, to whom that Honour is paid, the Passion of Self-liking.[55]

In locating the space of moral approbation within the context of what he pointedly described as a "Comedy of Manners" (I, 79), Mandeville followed the lead of Nicole, La Rochefoucauld and Bayle. He adopted the stance of the skeptical observer of worldly folly who recognized that the content of actions standardly understood as virtuous can, from this detached perspective, be redescribed as enacting a drama of performance; and that once so redescribed, these actions immediately lose their distinctly moral character, conceptually transformed as they are into features of merely prudential attempts to win the approbation ("applause") of the locally circumscribed audience to whom they are directed. By subsuming the moral codes governing public behavior under the headings of what he repeatedly called mere "ceremonies" and "customs," Mandeville

[55] Mandeville, *Honour*, pp. 8–9.

sought to place the "general practices" of polite society in a theatrical context, within whose histrionic conventions the inter-subjective negotiations of public life necessarily took place.

For Bayle the image par excellence of a world characterized by passionate human striving without end was a "spectacle of mario- nettes," which most charitably could be seen as a diversion for the Creator.[56] In the *Maxims*, La Rochefoucauld followed his teacher Jacques Esprit in setting the habits of the court within a conceptual environment of histrionic falsity, of deceitfulness and covert exhibi- tionism, in which masks must always be worn. Players "end by disguising ourselves from ourselves." Here, sadly for his worldly prospects, "a wise man thinks it more advantageous not to join the battle than to win."[57] Theatrical conventions themselves provided Nicole with the most telling metaphors through which to depict the duplicities governing social exchange amongst an unregenerate elite. "We are like those dancers at a masked ball," he wrote,

who hold one another by the hand affectionately without recognizing one another, and part a moment later, never to see each other again ... To see how men use one another one might think of human life and the affairs of the world as a serious game where any moves are permitted to seize the goods of another at our own risk, and where the lucky players despoil with all honour, the more unfortunate or less skilled."[58]

For each of these writers, the ancient figure of the *theatrum mundi* served their social criticism as a compelling device for the represen- tation of and response to grave spiritual uncertainties about the constitution of a stable, authentic and thus morally responsible self. Public life understood as little more than a theatre of outward display and moral dissimulation at once provided for them instantly comprehensible metaphors for the depiction of elite, particularly aristocratic, social space, and compelling idioms for the examination of an individual sinner's actions within it. Trading on the rhetorical symbiosis of the vocabularies of stage and society in Western lan-

---

[56] Pierre Bayle, *Nouvelles Lettres sur l'histoire du Calvinisme*, XVI, ix, p. 278b, cited by Elizabeth Labrousse, *Pierre Bayle* (The Hague: Nijhoff, 1964), II, p. 122, who provides a useful discussion of this point.

[57] La Rochefoucauld, *Maxims*, 119 and 549. See Jacques Esprit, *The Falsehood of Human Virtue* (London, 1691), p. 40, for a description of the court as the stage where affectation "acts her masterpieces."

[58] Pierre Nicole, *Essais de morale*, p. 421. In his *Traité de la comédie* (1667), ed. Georges Couton (Paris: Société D'Edition "Les Belles Lettres," 1961), pp. 49–59, Nicole argues that these passions are inherent in and promoted by theatrical entertainments themselves.

guages, they were particularly responsive to the stress placed by
aggressively demythologizing accounts of the body politic on the
classical association of the person with the figure of the masked actor.
As Hobbes put it in *Leviathan*,

> The word Person is latine ... as *Persona* in latine signifies the *disguise*, or
> *outward appearance* of a man, counterfeited on the Stage; and sometimes more
> particularly that part of it, which disguiseth the face, as a Mask or Visard:
> And from the Stage, hath been translated to any Representer of speech and
> action, as well in Tribunalls, as Theatres. So that a *Person*, is the same that an
> *Actor* is, both on the Stage and in common Conversation; and to *Personate*, is
> to Act, or Represent himself, or an other.[59]

Heightened fears about exposing one's true character to the world,
and dilemmas about being revealed to others, were at the heart of
the French moralists' concerns as they concentrated upon a court
society characterized by what they took to be the rampant growth of
unbelief, by merely ceremonial religious observance and by the
spread of immorality. All could adopt a theatrical perspective on this
morally suspect world because each in his own fashion adhered to the
Augustinian view that motives alone determined the quality of any
act, and that regardless of one's success in concealing his motives from
those around him, God would always penetrate behind the curtain of
the world's theatre and judge individuals accordingly.[60]

Mandeville, as we have seen, embraced this French inflection
recently given to the Augustinian language of morals. It served the
critical purpose of enabling him to expose the irreducible gap between
natural impulse and virtuous action, while employing the rigorous
moral rhetoric shared by his opponents. By speaking in their language, Mandeville could satirically pose as an advocate of the most
severe ethical standards, and then from an elevated rhetorical
position insist that "be we Savages or Politicians, it is impossible that
Man, mere Fallen Man, should act with any other View but to please
himself ... [for] we are always forc'd to do what we please, and at the
same time our Thoughts are free ... it is impossible we could be
sociable Creatures without Hypocrisy" (1, 348–349). This mock-
Augustinian stance enabled Mandeville to situate the distance
between motive and act within the theatrical perspective which

---

[59] Hobbes, *Leviathan*, "Of Man," 1.14, pp. 217–218.
[60] For a discussion of the central place of theatricality in Augustinian ethics see E.J. Hundert,
"Augustine and the Sources of the Divided Self," *Political Theory* 20, 1 (1992), pp. 86–104.

served his French predecessors. In so doing he was able to place in a socially relevant contemporary context the ancient insight that actions on the stage and in society each have as part of their content the possibility of being variously performed and understood as features of a role. Like Nicole and La Rochefoucauld, he could then show that the meaning of these performances can never be transparent, an actor's overt professions notwithstanding, since roles are filled by persons who must, as a condition of success, perform them in certain socially specified ways to the exclusion of others. Not only do public acts invite, but they always demand, interpretation by members of the audience, members who by their responses alone certify success or failure. As in Gay's *The Beggar's Opera* (1728), to which Mandeville compared his own unmasking efforts (II, 6), actors may play the roles of criminals, who themselves play roles as "gentlemen," "merchants" and "ladies" before an audience meant to read their own values into these impostures. Public life portrayed as a theatre of deceit dramatically served to reveal Mandeville's intentionally unsettling claim that moral evil, like hunger, was inseparable from the pleasures of gluttony, which a gentleman would hypocritically strive to conceal. For "everything is evil, which art and experience have not taught us to turn into a blessing" (I, 345). Indeed, "things are only Good and Evil in reference to something else, and according to the Light and Position they are placed in" (I, 367).

For Mandeville's French predecessors, the metaphor of world-as-stage derived from the Stoic conception of the theatre as a paradigm of human life, a trope standardized in Latin literature by Petronius' *Satyricon*. Its zone of applicability was later extended to the entire sublunary world in John of Salisbury's influential *Polycraticus* (1159), a discourse on "the frivolities of courtiers and the footprints of philosophers" much reprinted during the sixteenth and seventeenth centuries, especially in France.[61] The metaphor was intended to expose the artificial, because merely conventional, boundaries placed on acceptable public behavior and to throw into skeptical relief the formal regularities of social existence. Like the popular medieval imagery of the Wheel of Fortune and the Ship of Fools, the theatrical metaphor was a literary device employed by moralists to unmask worldly

---

[61] Ernst Robert Curtius, *European Literature and the Latin Middle Ages*, trans. Willard Trask (London: Routledge and Keegan Paul, 1953) pp. 140–142. "Totus mundus agit histrionen" ("All the world plays the actor"), taken from Petronius' *Satyricon*, ran above the newly erected Globe Theatre in London in 1599.

ambition and pretense. For Bayle and Nicole, as for Jacques in *As You Like It*, the reminder that "all the world's a stage" served the traditional and essentially conservative function of recalling to individuals the fact that they are subject to the scrutiny of a higher power into whose care their souls were entrusted. Within the conceptual ambit of the theatre, men could be viewed as puppets in a drama of which they remained unaware, as unwitting actors who inhabited roles which had an illusory, because merely secular, importance. For this very purpose Don Quixote announced "that there is nothing that shows us more clearly, by similitude, what we are and what we ought to be than do plays and players." He told Sancho Panza, who had already heard "this fine comparison ... many times before," that "in the comedy that we call life," we "play ... all the characters that a drama may have – but when it is all over, that is to say when life is done, death takes from each the garb that differentiates him, and all are at last equal in the grave."[62]

The metaphor of the *theatrum mundi* retained its conventional ethical force for Mandeville's seventeenth-century Augustinian predecessors because it served to underwrite their deeply held assumption of the existence of a moral identity independent of and prior to a person's status and occupation. The allegorical figure of the world as a stage functioned for the French *moralistes* as an instrument of social intelligibility in the restricted though important sense that it reasserted the central Christian doctrine of the spiritual role-nakedness of all persons, regardless of the social stations to which they may have been assigned by birth or good fortune. The word *play*, as Huizinga long ago noted,[63] for the most part had carried with it the connotations of a game, and referred to the sets of gestures involved in all sorts of bodily activities, like playing an instrument or plying a skill. Unless quite specifically and unusually qualified, the notion of "playing a part" essentially involved the accomplishment of a task, a sense commonly extended to the notion of one's social as distinct from spiritual role as that part given to an individual to play either well or badly.

Mandeville's purposes in emphasizing the theatricality of public life, and the context within which he portrayed commercial societies as theatrical worlds, were significantly different. In the revived

---

[62] Miguel de Cervantes, *Don Quixote*, trans. J.M. Cohen (Harmondsworth: Penguin, 1958) II, iii, 12.

[63] Johan Huizinga, *Homo Ludens* (London: Routledge and Kegan Paul, 1949), pp. 38–39.

Epicurean tradition, the metaphor of society as theatre served not so much to expose the vanity of human aspirations from a celestial perspective as to highlight the distance between genuine knowledge and mere appearance in the minds of social actors themselves. Thomas Burnaby's well-known translation of the *Satyricon* in 1694 was so understood by contemporary Epicureans like Saint-Evremond,[64] while the enemies of Lucretius and Epicurus as heralds of irreligion typically pointed to the efflorescent London stage as a sign of the moral degeneracy of the age.[65] The *theatrum mundi* became a conceptually enabling device by the early eighteenth century with which philosophical radicals could examine the gulf between the detached observer of the world and the mass of men who remained imaginatively ensnared by its public rituals. "The Wise Man," as Epicurus put it in a maxim rendered into English by John Digby, "shall reap more Benefit, and take more Satisfaction in the public Shews, than other Men."

He there observes the different Characters of the Spectators; he can discover by their looks the effect of the Passions that moves 'em, and amidst the Confusion that reigns in these places . . . he has the Pleasure to find himself the only person undisturb'd, and in a State of Tranquillity.[66]

Digby's translation was meant to evoke the famous passage that begins Book II of *De rerum natura*, where Lucretius writes of the pleasure of beholding a ship in peril at sea from the safety of the shore. The passage not only illustrates the pleasure (literally, the sweetness) of watching suffering or danger from a safe distance, but compares this delight to that which the true philosopher experiences in his security from worldly illusion. As Bacon rendered Lucretius in his essay "Of Truth":

It is a pleasure to stand upon the shore, and to see ships tossed upon the sea; a pleasure to stand in the window of a castle, and to see a battle and the adventures thereof below: but no pleasure is comparable to standing on the vantage ground of Truth and to see the errors, and the wanderings, and tempests, in the vale below.

---

[64] Saint-Evremond, *Works*, I, p. 158.
[65] Most famously by Jeremy Collier, *A Short View of the Immorality and Profaneness of the English Stage* (London, 1698), and Sir Richard Blackmore, *Creation: A Philosophical Poem* (1712), the most thoroughgoing anti-Epicurean document of the eighteenth century. Blackmore's poem is printed in his Preface to *Prince Arthur* (1695), in J.E. Springarn (ed.), *Critical Essays of the Seventeenth Century* (Oxford University Press, 1909), III, p. 230.
[66] John Digby, *Epicurus's Morals*, p. 52.

Mandeville adopted a Baconian perspective when he interpreted this passage, a perspective he identified with that of modern scientific inquiry. In the fashion of Bacon, Mandeville engaged in "serious satire" by writing a "treatise into the inner nature of things," to take the titles of two of Bacon's works, in order to describe "what men do, and not what they ought to do."[67] He understood the false beliefs of his contemporaries, particularly those socially stabilizing myths Bacon had called the *idola* of the marketplace, as conceptually distorting ideological residues generated by commercial society's unwritten conventions. The wise man became a student of this society by virtue of his ability to stand aloof from those public spectacles through which these myths were enacted. "To me," Mandeville said, alluding to Lucretius,

> it is a great Pleasure, when I look on the Affairs of human Life, to behold into what various and often strangely opposite Forms the hope of Gain and thoughts of Lucre shape Men, according to the different Employments they are of, and Stations they are in. How gay and merry does every Face appear at a well-ordered Ball, and what a solemn Sadness is observ'd at the Masquerade of a Funeral! But the Undertaker is as much pleas'd with his Gains as the Dancing-Master ... [Likewise,] those who have never minded the Conversation of a spruce Mercer, and a young Lady his Customer ... have neglected a Scene of Life that is very Entertaining ... Reader[s] [should] ... examine these People separately, as to their Inside and the different Motives they act from. (1, 349–350)

A dominant line of eighteenth-century moral argument followed the view taken in the abbé Du Bos' seminal work on aesthetics, *Critical Reflections on Poetry and Painting* (1719), in which Lucretius' words were cited in support of an argument placing the audience of theatrical entertainments at a safe imaginative remove from the performances enacted before it.[68] Du Bos argued, in a manner similar to Shaftesbury, that an enlightened "public," can properly assess the value of a spectacle because its sentiments are refined by education and exper-

---

[67] Francis Bacon, *Of the Proficience and Advancement of Learning*, in *The Works*, ed. J. Spedding, R.L. Ellis and D.D. Heath (London: Longman, 1963, reprint), III, p. 430, quoted in Dario Castiglione, "Mandeville Moralized," *Annali della Fondazione Luigi Einaudi* 17 (1983), pp. 239–290, to whose analysis of Mandeville's relationship to contemporary traditions of satire I am indebted.

[68] J.B. Du Bos, *Réflexions critiques sur la poésie et sur peinture* (Paris, 1719), I, ii; English translation, London, 1748. On Du Bos' importance see D.G. Charleton, "J.B. Du Bos and Eighteenth-Century Sensibility," *Studies on Voltaire and the Eighteenth Century*, 266 (1990), pp. 151–162, and Peter Jones, *Hume's Sentiments: Their Ciceronian and French Context* (Edinburgh University Press, 1982), Chapter 3.

ience to form a kind of sixth sense, *le sentiment*.[69] An audience is thus enabled to form disinterested judgements (*sans intéret*),[70] particularly about those powerfully moving expressions of emotion which, on the stage as in society, could not effectively be conveyed in words.[71] In a directly related vein, one of Addison's purposes in *The Spectator* was to help constitute just such a public, a "Fraternity of Spectators," as his spokesman announced in one of the early numbers, composed of "every one that considers the World as a Theatre, and desires to form a right Judgement of those who are actors in it."[72] These "impartial spectators"[73] would be able to "consider all the different pursuits and Employments of Men, and ... will [be able to] find [that] half [of] the[ir] Actions tend to nothing else but Disguise and Imposture; and [realize that] all that is done which proceeds not from a Man's very self is the Action of a Player."[74]

One of Mandeville's primary purposes was to expose this view as self-serving nonsense. It was itself an example of the "Practical Part of Dissimulation" (II, 77) and hypocrisy which contemporary doctrines of politeness, and supposedly refined aesthetic prejudices (II, 40), were meant to conceal by describing the "Arts of rendering ... Behaviour agreeable to others, with the least Disturbance to themselves" (II, 11). Members of the expanding *beau monde* who constituted the elite of commercial rather than court societies could never, Mandeville insisted, strictly adhere to the codes of polite intercourse promoted by Addison, Steele and Shaftesbury, while at the same time remaining independent and undeluded moral agents. These individuals were required to adopt highly stylized public personae as they regularly confronted virtual strangers, especially in the widening urban spaces whose rituals had become the privileged subjects of popular art – the coffee house, club, square, park and, as Voltaire pointedly remarked, the Stock Exchange, where material interest alone formed a social bond, and promoted civilized intercourse amongst unrelated persons with otherwise incommensurable habits and beliefs.[75] "In populous cities," Montesquieu said, directly alluding to Mandeville, "men are motivated by an ambition of distinguishing themselves by trifles – strangers to one another, their vanity redoubles because there is

---

[69] Du Bos, *Réflexions*, II, xxii.   [70] Du Bos, *Réflexions*, II, xxi.
[71] Du Bos, *Réflexions*, III, xiii and xvi.   [72] *Spectator*, No. 10.   [73] *Spectator*, No. 274.
[74] *Spectator*, No. 370.
[75] Voltaire, *Lettres philosophiques*, Letter VI. In *Fable*, I, 343, Mandeville claims that traders would have no more civility "than Bulls" had not interest brought them together.

greater hope of success."[76] "The more people communicate with each other," he continued, citing *The Fable* as his authority, "the more easily they change their manners, because each becomes to a greater degree a spectacle to the other."[77] Along with other contemporary observers, Mandeville was quick to notice that the enlarged public at London's theatres themselves (II, 39), which were and would remain the most commercially successful public entertainments in Europe during the eighteenth century, provided a microcosm, in the esteemed critic John Dennis' words, of a new and frightening social world, a world in which people who had risen from obscurity and who had recently made their fortunes from speculation could pretend to polite habits and aspire "to a condition of distinction and plenty."[78] As Dennis wrote in his attack on *The Fable*, Mandeville's work embodied the threat of moral degeneration posed to British society by the newly monied.[79] When Mandeville's adversary William Law attacked Dennis for defending the moral propriety of the stage, he observed that the patrons at London's theatres were convinced of their right to judge a play simultaneous with its production. They thus enlarged the idea of performance to include the auditorium as well as the stage, in Law's view ample evidence that one "must ... abhor the Thoughts of being at a Play, as of being a player your self."[80]

Mandeville enthusiastically adhered to the ancient view, enriched by an Augustinian perspective, that theatricality had a necessarily hostile relationship to all forms of moral intimacy, and that individuals would become divided personalities to the degree that the social

[76] Montesquieu, *The Spirit of the Laws*, trans. A.M. Cohen, B.C. Miller and H.S. Stone (Cambridge University Press, 1989), VII.1.

[77] Montesquieu, *The Spirit of the Laws*, XIX.8.

[78] John Dennis, *A Large Account of the Taste in Poetry* (London, 1702), in *The Critical Works of John Dennis*, ed. Edward Niles Hooker (Baltimore: Johns Hopkins University Press, 1939), I, p. 293. See too for example, the comments about the social composition of London audiences by Henri de Valbourg Misson, *Mémoires et observations faites par un voyage en Angleterre* (The Hague, 1698), pp. 63–64.   [79] Dennis, *Vice and Luxury Public Mischiefs*.

[80] William Law, *The Absolute Unlawfulness of Stage-Entertainment Fully Demonstrated* (London, 1726), p. 9. On the subject of the theatrical behavior of the socially enlarged London theatre audience of the early eighteenth century see Harry W. Pedicord, "The Changing Audience," in Robert D. Hume (ed.), *The London Theatre World, 1660–1800* (Carbondale, Illinois: Southern Illinois University Press, 1980), pp. 239–241; 242–246, and Leo Hughes, *The Drama's Patrons: A Study of the Eighteenth-Century London Audience* (Austin: University of Texas Press, 1971), pp. 97ff. See too, for example, Alexander Pope's satire of the stage in his "Project for the Advancement of the Stage," in *Peri Bathous* (1728), and Pope's lament about raucous audience behavior and the decline of public taste in *First Epistle of the Second Book of Horace* (1732), II, 312–313.

pressures of civil society required them to adopt the strategic poses of actors in public life. But he abandoned entirely the effective, and originally Platonic, corollary of this view, that is, that public theatrics were necessarily destructive of the political body and the social fabric. Mandeville abandoned it since a genuine sense of duty could hardly be expected of persons whose public professions were always mediated by masks of propriety, just as the classical figure of the masked actor, the *hypocrates* who merely impersonates by playing a role, could never be relied upon to treat his fellows as brothers. Instead, Mandeville celebrated theatrical relations as inherent attributes of political and economic life, especially in advanced societies. One could, for example, best understand the failure of the British state to enforce social discipline amongst the swelling London populace by viewing the "festival atmosphere" of the procession from Newgate to Tyburn as a "spectacle" in which crimes the law purportedly punished were transformed into acts of popular heroism by the official mismanagement of what in effect was a "public theatre."[81] It is the business of the skillful politician to "extract good from the very worst, as well as the best" by assigning appropriate social roles to those individuals most competent to play them (I, 49–52; 208–210). The management of appearances in fact lay at the heart of governing egoists, whether these be devout believers, which "Popes ... by a Stratagem of the Church ... have made great Men the chief Actors in ... childish Farces," common soldiers captivated by Cromwell's zealous professions of faith, which he "made use of ... accordingly," or members of the educated classes, who "conform to all Ceremonies that are fashionable," and "make a Shew outwardly of what is not felt within, and counterfeit what is not real."[82]

On a more mundane, but socially decisive, level, Mandeville argued that the envy and emulative propensities characteristic of fallen men had, in commercial societies, become the propulsive features of civil life itself, despite the standard disapproval of self-indulgence which remained the prevailing moral orthodoxy. In nations shaped by commerce, the selfishness which characterized all persons everywhere took the form of man as a consuming and

---

[81] Bernard Mandeville, *An Enquiry into the Frequent Executions at Tyburn* (London, 1725), Augustan Reprint Society, Publication No. 105 (Los Angeles: William Andrews Clark Memorial Library, 1964), pp. 21, 26 and 40.
[82] Mandeville, *Honour*, pp. 107, 149, 162 and 189.

displaying animal, a creature whose boundless appetites are systematically directed by the desire for esteem to an expanding world of available goods. An ethos of public display fired an economy of conspicuous consumption, which in turn depended upon the promotion of unstable fashion and social fantasy. As Mandeville first put it in *The Grumbling Hive*:

> Envy it self, and Vanity
> Were Ministers of Industry;
> Their darling Folly, Fickleness
> In Diet, Furniture and Dress,
> That strange ridic'lous Vice, was made
> The very Wheel, that turn'd the Trade.
> Their Laws and Cloaths were equally
> Objects of Mutability ...   (I, 25)

Here, even a "poor common Harlot ... must have Shoes and Stockings, Gloves, the Stay and Mantuamaker, the Sempstress, the Linnen-draper, all must get something by her, and a hundred different Tradesmen dependent on those she laid her Money out with, may touch part of it before a Month is at an end" (I, 88).

Little wonder that for Mandeville's adversaries like George Bluett, a society so understood as an aggregation of purely self-interested individuals competitively bound to one another by greed, vanity and imagination, immediately evoked the image of a perverse masquerade.[83] Mandeville had previously exploited this image in his satiric defense of government politics, when he had a fictional opponent of the Whigs charge them with being "admirably qualified for Poetry and the Stage: you first forgo Harpies, Sphinxes, Dragons, and Chimeras, that never were in Nature, and then put them off [as] Realities upon the People."[84] He insisted that under modern conditions public life was of necessity theatrical, resembling in considerable detail the masquerades put on by Count Heidegger, the Flemish adventurer whose spectacles featuring masks, cross-dressing and purportedly illicit liaisons at The Haymarket were the toast of London society, and the object of fear and revulsion amongst

---

[83] George Bluett, *Enquiry*, pp. 216–218. Masquerades, as Bluett pointed out (pp. 143–149), had for some time been the fashion in London society, and were denounced by a number of Mandeville's other clerical and lay adversaries. See, for example, the description of these events by Addison, in *Spectator*, Nos. 8 and 14, as a "libidinous Assembly" of "Assignations and Intrigues."

[84] Mandeville, *The Mischiefs that Ought Justly to be Apprehended from a Whig-Government* (1714) (Los Angeles: William Andrews Clark Memorial Library Reprint, 1975), pp. 1–2.

contemporary moral reformers.[85] As he mockingly said of one o
Bishop of London's sermons against immoral practices, his w
"most edifying Anti-Heidegger Discourse."[86]

HENRY FIELDING AT THE MANDEVILLIAN MASQUERADE

Mandeville's most anxiety-provoking claim was neither that his
contemporaries were immoral, nor that the springs of their actions
could be shown to contradict their professed ideals. It was rather that
fiction and fantasy profoundly influenced the fashioning of selves in
commercial society, and that the primary stabilizing forces of this
society were those inherent in the essentially theatrical relations
through which it regulated itself. Mandeville expressed in heightened
form the legitimation anxieties of a recently disenchanted community, one in which the content of inherited moral commitments had
become detached from the tacit picture of the world inhabited by
individuals unavoidably situated in a community whose practices
stand at some remove from its professed beliefs. Mandeville was a
dangerous author because his argument threatened to subvert the
historically moralized structures of deference and obedience upon
which traditional society rested. "Suppose every body knew as much
as the Author of *The Fable of the Bees* and that Virtue and Vice were
but Bugbears invented for the uninterrupted indulging of the Appetites of some cetain Persons," the anonymous author of *The True
Meaning of the Fable of the Bees* asked his readers, "or suppose they had
made the Discovery that it was in the Essence of the *Politician* to
consult nobody but himself. How would you keep People in awe?"[87]

Mandeville's anatomy of the passions, and his theatrical account of
their harnessing as social instruments, demanded from his readers a
dramatically altered perspective on the conventions of civil life. As we
have seen, *The Fable* exemplified for a significant segment of his
audience the triumphant principles of a recently debased public
sphere, where the sentiments of love, honor, friendship and civic
virtue were all too plausibly redescribed, and then celebrated, in

---

[85] See, particularly, Terry Castle, *Masquerade and Civilization* (Stanford University Press, 1986),
pp. 1–56. For the unsettling relationships between the theatre, theatricality and commerce
see Jean-Christophe Agnew, *Worlds Apart: The Market and the Theatre in Anglo-American
Thought, 1550–1750* (Cambridge University Press, 1986).

[86] Mandeville, *A Modest Defence of Publick Stews*, Dedication.

[87] Anon., *The True Meaning of the Fable of the Bees* (London, 1726), p. 27.

terms of pure social contrivance. In taking Mandeville as his imaginative point of departure, no writer more than Henry Fielding exemplifies how large *The Fable*'s arguments loomed in the Enlightenment's understanding of the modern moral subject. As with Sterne's appropriation of Locke's epistemology, Fielding's confrontation with Mandeville's morals embodied a central feature of eighteenth-century public consciousness.[88]

Fielding self-consciously adopted a position in diametric opposition to those "political philosophers,"[89] particularly Mandeville and La Rochefoucauld, who represented man as a "depraved, and totally bad" creature.[90] He ascribed their "ugly picture of human nature" to "the deformity of their own minds."[91] In *Tom Jones* Fielding condemned "that modern doctrine" which alarmed the world by declaring "that there were no such things as virtue or goodness really existing in human nature, and ... deduced our best actions from pride."[92] The greatest, because the most influential, representative of this modern doctrine of cynical egoism was "that charming fellow Mandevil ... who hath represented human nature in a picture of the highest deformity."[93] Fielding occasionally invented disreputable characters who express Mandeville's views, like Thwackum and Square in *Tom Jones*, while his apostrophe to vanity in *Joseph Andrews* is in fact a summary of *The Fable*.[94] Likewise, Fielding's "Modern Glossary" of vice in *The Covent-Garden Journal* is a compendium of Mandeville's arguments about the role of self-love,[95] in which *The Fable*'s discussion of dress as a primary mark of social worth is similarly satirized.[96] Throughout his career, Fielding alternatively sought to ridicule or demolish Mandeville's psychological views,[97] even when

---

[88] Eva Tabor, *Skepticism, Society and the Eighteenth-Century Novel* (New York: St. Martin's Press, 1987), pp. 54–77, discusses *The Fable*'s place in the eighteenth-century literary imagination, and suggests that Mandeville served as an important point of departure for Richardson as well.

[89] Henry Fielding, *Champion*, 22 January 1739/40, in *The Complete Works of Henry Fielding* ed. W.E. Henley, (London: Heinemann, 1903) xv, 162.

[90] *Champion*, 11 December 1739, xv, 94; and Preface to *Miscellanies*, in *Complete Works*, XII, 243.

[91] *Champion* 11 December 1739, 95, and *The History of Tom Jones a Foundling*, ed. Sheridan Baker (New York: W.W. Norton, 1973), VIII, 15.   [92] *Tom Jones* VI, 1.

[93] *Covent-Garden Journal*, 21 14 March, 1752.

[94] *The History of the Adventures of Joseph Andrews and his Friend Mr. Abraham Adams. Written in Imitation of the Manner of Cervantes, Author of Don Quixote*, ed. Martin C. Battestin (Boston; Houghton Mifflin, 1961), I, xv.   [95] *Covent-Garden Journal*, 14 January, 1752,

[96] *Covent-Garden Journal*, 25 April, 1752.

[97] See Bernard Harrison, *Henry Fielding's Tom Jones* (London: Sussex University Press, 1975), pp. 39–48 and 70–88.

his diagnosis of contemporary social ills, like the increase of robbery in London, was virtually identical to Mandeville's.[98] As Captain Booth says of Mandeville in *Amelia*,

He hath left out of his system the best passion which the mind can possess, and attempts to derive the effects of energies of that passion from the base impulses of pride or fear. Whereas it is certain that love exists in the mind of man as that its opposite hatred doth; the same reasons will equally prove the existence of the one as of the other.[99]

Were Fielding's opposition to Mandeville confined to these essentially doctrinal remarks, his views would simply be part of the general chorus of complaint which *The Fable* continued to elicit in the two generations after its publication. But as Hazlitt said, Fielding sought to offer an imaginative picture of the "moral, political and religious feeling" in the England of George II.[100] He attempted directly to counter the world which Mandeville described because it riveted the imagination of his contemporaries, a world in which distinctions between the real and the merely apparent, the felt and the feigned, are features of an ensemble of dispositions whose articulation is entirely public. Because Fielding fully accepted Mandeville's challenge to orthodox ethical reasoning as a defining focus of his fiction, he is important for an understanding of *The Fable*'s significance in forging a language of social intelligibility. Fielding sought to depict the public sphere as a spectacle of competing characters dominated by ruling passions, an imaginative realm in which he, like Mandeville, could count on his readers' consciousness of role distance as a pervasive category of their own social perceptions. Fielding wished to reveal and decipher the code which underlay this spectacle, and then claim for his enterprise a moralizing function which vitiated the premises upon which Mandeville's understanding of it was based. He sought imaginatively to reveal that "there is in some human Breasts, a kind and

---

98 Compare, particularly, Fielding's analysis of public executions in *Covent-Garden Journal*, 28 March, 1752, and *An Inquiry Into the ... Recent Causes ... of the Increase in Robbers* (1751) (New York: AMS Press Reprint, 1975), p. 121, with Mandeville's in *Tyburn*. See too Hélène Desfond, "Tyburn chez Mandeville et Fielding, ou le Corps Exemplaire du Pendu," in Paul-Gabriel Boucé and Suzi Halimi (eds.), *Le Corps et l'âme en Grand-Bretagne au XVIIIe siècle* (Paris: Sorbonne, 1985), pp. 61–70.

99 *Amelia*, III, 5. Similarly, in V, 5, the hypocrite Miss Mathews mentions her approval of Mandeville's doctrines, which show "that religion and virtue are mere names."

100 P.P. Howe (ed.), *The Complete Works of William Hazlitt*, cited in Homer Goldberg, *The Art of Joseph Andrews* (Chicago University Press, 1969), p. 260.

benevolent Disposition, which is gratified by contributing to the Happiness of others."[101]

Fielding accepted the fully theatricized public domain which Mandeville had portrayed as his representative subject, in which "the Hypocrite may be said to be the player, [as] ... indeed the Greeks called them both by one and the same name." As the narrator of *Tom Jones* says, departing from the telling of his hero's story to reflect on the colonization of public discourse by theatrical metaphor, the "comparison between the world and the stage,"

has been carried so far and become so general that some words proper to the theatre and which were at first metaphorically applied to the world are now indiscriminately and literally spoken of both: thus stage and scene are by common use grown as familiar to us, when we speak of life in general, as when we confine ourselves to dramatic performances; and when we mention transactions behind the curtain, St. James's is more likely to occur to our own thoughts than Drury-Lane.[102]

Readers of *Tom Jones* were told that the characters of the novel should be considered actors in a double sense. Their performances enact roles understood as such by the generalized "audience" of society, a public divided into the socially segregated "boxes, stalls and balconies" where theatrical responses form essential aspects of the spectacle on view. Fielding's conceptual object was to situate these spectators as the central characters "at this great drama." His fictions were meant to serve as appropriate vehicles for the representation of their consciousness, aware of the possibility of detachment from any particular social embodiment, and for the understanding of character as a circumscribed feature of this self-awareness. Like Mandeville, Fielding conceived of his readers as the audience at a drama in which they participated, and as persons who would be provided with sets of instructions necessary to decode its rules. The aesthetic instrument of this educative art was "the exactest copying of nature," a representational strategy requiring the writer to describe "not men but manners; not an individual but a species."[103]

The "comic prose epic" was intended by Fielding to be a mechanism for decoding "the ridiculous," by which he meant the figure whose source of action is affectation, and whose affectation derives

---

[101] *Tom Jones*, VI, I.
[102] *Tom Jones*, VII, I: "A Comparison between the World and the Stage."
[103] Henry Fielding, *Joseph Andrews*, Preface.

from vanity and hypocrisy. His claim that such figures demanded a new genre for their portrayal was part of a broader aesthetic enterprise of unmasking those "appearances," as a contemporary guide to manners put it, which "give things in some measure a second existence."[104] Fielding saw in the "rational and useful pleasure" which flowed from what he called the imitation of nature a singularly effective device for exposing deceit within a growing and socially heterogeneous urban public whose relationships were guided by newly emerging and still volatile standards of propriety. In this metropolitan setting, which promoted wholly consensual forms of intercourse between once formally stratified groups, personalities themselves appeared as mobile as the forms of property which occasioned their existence. Mandeville had most clearly articulated this vision in *The Fable*, and Fielding provided an exemplary history of the fugitive transformations of identity the modern city encouraged in his character Wilson's autobiographical narrative at the structural center of *Joseph Andrews*. Here the hero's disastrous pilgrimage through London's corrupting temptations can only be redeemed by love, "where vanity has no votary."[105] Fielding also evoked *The Fable* when he observed that men now "employed their utmost abilities to invent systems by which the artful and cunning . . . may be enabled to impose upon the rest of the world."[106] He took as his point of departure Mandeville's claim that this public had, in the process of its formation, acquired fresh emotional commitments as it self-consciously engaged in altered social practices. It could no longer be relied upon, Fielding thought, to respond to the inherited forms of communal moral instruction, clerical injunction and classical tragedy, toward which its responses had "soured." Yet, as the success of *The Fable* demonstrated, this burgeoning reading public seemed immediately responsive to the voice of satire (that staple genre of an exploding publishing industry) in which rhetorical inversions of character pointedly elevated newly crafted behavioral styles into objects demanding self-reflection. While vanity and hypocrisy had always encouraged the "affecting [of] false characters, in order to purchase applause,"[107] Fielding realized that the swelling opportunities for the conspicuous consumption of marks of esteem had within

---

[104] Stephen Philpot, *Polite Education* (London, 1759), p. 59.   [105] *Joseph Andrews*, III, 3.
[106] Henry Fielding, "An Essay on the Knowledge and of the Characters of Men," *Works* (London: Heinemann, 1903), XI, pp. 173–216, p. 175. Hereafter, "An Essay."
[107] *Joseph Andrews*, Preface.

living memory propelled these vices to the forefront of an altered public consciousness. They became the artist's privileged subjects because in their fictive representations his audience would recognize themselves.

Aimed at this public of sensible spectators, Fielding's epic comedies were meant to block the reader's natural tendency to remove himself as an object of satiric representation. If satire was, as Swift put it, "a glass, wherein beholders do generally discover everybody's face but their own,"[108] the comic prose epic would further empower the moralizing function of comedy by creating a mirror of the reader's actual purposes, one in which he could not help but view himself. In this project of compelling self-recognition, Fielding saw his own aesthetic as continuous with vernacular traditions of critical social realism, epitomized by Hogarth's "comic history-paintings." Hogarth served as Fielding's visual model because his pictures "express the affections of men on canvas" by investing the figures represented with consciousness, making them *"appear to think."*[109] They were intended, Hogarth said, to absorb the spectator by placing before him outwardly referring dramatic images.

> I wished to compose pictures on canvas, similar to representations on the stage ... I have endeavoured to treat my subjects as a dramatic writer; my picture is my stage, and men and women my players, who by means of certain actions and gestures, are to exhibit a *dumb* show.[110]

Like Hogarth, Fielding sought to show his protagonists completely losing themselves in the metaphors entailed by the roles they adopted.[111] He exploited the dramatic tensions between, on the one side, a classical order of representation and, on the other, the demotic energies which found no place within the inherited hierarchy of literary genres. On the title-page of *Joseph Andrews* Fielding informed his readers that the work before was "Written in Imitation of The *Manner* of Cervantes." This message carried a particular meaning, just as it had for Mandeville, since, on the dominant contempor-

---

[108] Jonathan Swift, *The Battle of the Books*, in *Prose Works*, ed. H. Davis (Oxford University Press, 1939), I, 140.   [109] *Joseph Andrews*, Preface.

[110] William Hogarth, *The Analysis of Beauty* (London, 1753), quoted in Robert Halsband, "Stage Drama as a Source for Pictorial and Plastic Art," in Shirley Strum Kenny (ed.), *British Theatre and the Other Arts, 1600–1800* (Washington: Folger Shakespeare Library, 1984), pp. 149–170, 155.

[111] On this point see Ronald Paulson, "Life as Journey and as Theater: Two Eighteenth-Century Narrative Structures," *New Literary History* 8, 1 (1976), pp. 43–58.

ary understanding, *Don Quixote* was the most formidable satire of social institutions in print. Sir William Temple thought the book to have caused the decline in esteem shown to the Spanish aristocracy, a view disseminated by Defoe in his *Memoirs of Captain Carleton* (1728), whose hero is told by a Spanish gentleman that any man behaving in a noble style "found himself the jest of high and low . . . after the world became a little acquainted with [Cervantes'] notable history . . ."[112] The 1742 English edition of *Don Quixote* was prefaced by the translator's interpretation of Cervantes as a satirist and reforming social critic, to which Pope's editor and Mandeville's adversary Bishop Warburton added an essay defending this form of vernacular literature's serious religious intentions.[113] Like Cervantes, Fielding would seek to undermine the approval given to certain styles of social behavior by exposing through ridicule their dramaturgical conventions, and then extract spiritual significance from the acts of these now naked actors – "stripped," as Quixote put it, "of their players' garments."[114] Fielding wished to devise a morally informed genre of satiric writing specifically suited to expose the theatrically patterned hypocrisies of contemporary private aspiration. Such books, he said, would record "the history of the world . . . at least that part which is polished by laws, arts and sciences; and of that from the time it was first polished to this day."[115]

Fielding understood that his audience, unlike Cervantes', was composed not so much of elite consumers of printed texts but of literate, middling inhabitants of a post-chivalric culture in which the standard literary genres had lost much of their compelling power. An "exact copy of nature" would suitably represent these readers as a species of self-conscious observers of actual and, he said, metaphorical theatrical acts within roles that were adopted provisionally, as the play demanded. He saw the engagement of an individual's self-regarding passions with the larger imperatives of commercial societies as the site for understanding modes of self-presentation within the contemporary structures of everyday life. "The passions, like

---

[112] Cited in Walter L. Reed, *An Exemplary History of the Novel* (University of Chicago Press, 1981), p. 124, a study of the Quixotic motif. See, too, A.P. Burton, "Cervantes the Man Seen through English Eyes in the Seventeenth and Eighteenth Centuries," *Bulletin of Hispanic Studies* 45 (1968), pp. 1–15, and E.A. Peters, "Cervantes in England," *Bulletin of Hispanic Studies* 24 (1947), pp. 226–238.

[113] William Warburton, "A Supplement to the Translator's Preface, Communicated by a Learned Writer, Well-Known in the Literary World," in Miguel de Cervantes' *Don Quixote*, trans. Henry Jarvis (London, 1742).   [114] *Don Quixote*, III.iii.   [115] *Joseph Andrews*, III, 1.

managers of a playhouse," Fielding wrote, "often force men upon parts without consulting their judgements,"[116] and so compel them to "suffer ... private mortification [to] ... avoid public shame."[117] In polished societies, where "the art of thriving ... points out to every individual his own particular and separate advantage to which he is to sacrifice the interest of all others,"[118] economic opportunity had become the motive force driving self-regard into the foreground of self-reflection. Joseph Andrews reports that Lady Booby "held my hand, and talked exactly as a lady does to her sweetheart in a stage play, which I have seen in Covent Garden." The lady responds to what the reader knows is Joseph's genuine naiveté, itself the product of an uncritical reading of his sister's letters, as if this too must be a pose, whose "pretended innocence cannot impose on me."[119] When Joseph says that he has never done anything more than be kissed, Lady Booby gives the appropriate response of the seasoned theatre-goer: "Kissing," she says, "do you call that no crime. Kissing, Joseph, is as a prologue to a play."[120] Fielding took care to provide his characters with appropriate theatrical analogues, drawn from a familiar history of the stage, whose actors he named. He similarly invested these characters with a repertoire of dramatic styles through which they establish public identities, and in whose confusion "persons know us in one place and not in another and not tomorrow."[121] For in life as on the stage, "it is often the same person who represents the villain and the hero; and he who engages your admiration today, will probably attract your contempt tomorrow."[122]

Fielding's object was to translate the signs and concepts formerly at home in Quixote's moral and discursive environment into the codes of a monied and mobile culture where they bore altered intersubjective meanings. The comic prose epic would be a "physic for the mind." It would render the actions of men as performances necessarily undertaken within discrete behavioral styles. The artist would represent these forms of public personality stereotypically in order to expose their unwritten protocols. Once in conscious possession of these rules, the audience could, as Shaftesbury and Du Bos had argued, emotio-

---

[116] *Tom Jones*, VII, 1.   [117] *Joseph Andrews*, III, 1.   [118] "An Essay," p. 177.
[119] *Joseph Andrews*, I, 6.   [120] *Joseph Andrews*, I, 8.
[121] See especially, *Joseph Andrews*, II, 13: "A Dissertation Concerning High People and Low People ..."   [122] *Tom Jones*, VII, 1.

nally detach itself from the roles persons played, precisely because the performative requirements of these roles had been revealed as merely the outward conformity of otherwise free moral agents to pre-scripted social demands. Fielding sought to disperse the passionate attachments which these stylized social performances were meant to engender in an audience for whom styles of behavior had become objects of dramatic art. He wished to re-create Addison's impartial spectator, the participant–observer who could, in effect, systematically separate the form of an act – its socially specified and easily mimed behavioral requirements – from its ethical import and the moral sources of action upon which men ought properly to be judged.

Fielding feared the demise of the classical ideal of virtuous self-sacrifice in the name of the public good because, as he put it using Mandeville's idiom, this standard of moral propriety was fast becoming in the minds of his audience a "political maxim" by which the cunning advanced their private interests. Yet he sympathized with this response, believing that

it is impossible that any man endowed with rational faculties, and being in a state of freedom, should willingly agree, without some motive of love or friendship, absolutely to sacrifice his own interest to that of another ... Thus, while the crafty and designing part of mankind, consulting only their own separate advantage, endeavour to maintain one constant imposition on the others, the whole world becomes a vast masquerade where the greatest part appear disguised ... a very few only showing their own faces, who become by so doing, the astonishment and ridicule of all the rest.[123]

Like Mandeville, Fielding here deployed one of the most ubiquitous Augustan images of social subversion and the decay of public identity;[124] and it is important to notice that in exposing to ridicule the moral duplicities of this "vast masquerade" he was also intent on showing how even those honest souls for whom love bridged the gulf between motive and act still necessarily followed the theatrical imperatives which governed communal behavior. Suppose these individuals were distinguished by genuinely moral, other-regarding sentiments. As social creatures they nevertheless were obliged to act

123 "An Essay," pp. 177–178.
124 Fielding's first publication, a poem, "The Masquerade" (1728), in Claude E. Jones (ed.), *"The Female Husband" and Other Writings* (Liverpool University Press, 1960), was inscribed to "C—T H—D—G—R," and criticized his entertainments, "Because that thing, which we, in English, / Do virtue call, is always took / To hold its station in the look" (lines 200–202). See Terry Castle's discussion of this theme in *Amelia* in *Masquerade and Civilization*, pp. 177–252.

within the formal conventions demanded by all social roles, to appear in one of "those disguises" worn on "the greater stage" of society.[125] Just as Joseph Andrews mistakenly takes his sister's letters as the appropriate prompt-book for his own performances, so even the virtuous Parson Adams enacts the role of a Quixote of the ethical, a good man often deluded by the maxims of his classical education.

Fielding's avowed purpose was to reveal the person behind the public mask, and it is of some significance that he frequently does so by creating contexts which strain his characters' scripts beyond their capacity for successful enactment. Near the end of *Joseph Andrews*, Parson Adams, after his essential goodness has been firmly established, rebukes Joseph for being "too much inclined to passion," citing Abraham's readiness to sacrifice Isaac as his exemplary text. In the midst of this discourse the Parson receives news that his youngest son has drowned. Adams then "began to stamp around the room and deplore his loss with the bitterest agony," to which Joseph responds by attempting to give him comfort with "many arguments that he had several times remembered out of [Adams'] own discourses, both in public and private (for he was a great enemy to the passions, and preached nothing more than the conquest of them by reason and grace) ..." But, overcome with grief and rage against his son's senseless death, Adams "was not now at leisure to hearken to his advice. 'Child, child', said he [to Joseph], do not go about impossibilities."[126] Adams, whom the reader knows as an admirer of Addison's *Cato*, "the only English tragedy I ever read," and one of the few plays "fit for a Christian to read,"[127] is the good man whose stoicism has reached its limit. At the moment when he can no longer contain his passions, he, Joseph and Fielding's audience are made to confront the inadequacies of what was perhaps the most thoroughly inscribed Augustan role, that of the virtuous citizen, even when played by a person whose life so closely embodied its ideals. Fielding wished to show that even the best of men, Adams and Cato, must inhabit roles that shape the performance of emotional response, and thereby create a curtain behind which their passions remain hidden from view.

Yet if one maintains that all men are players, and that even the highest forms of moral sensibility remain extrinsic to the performative demands of the ethical act, how then can the theatrically embodied persons who appear on society's stage truly be known, save perhaps in

---

[125] "An Essay," p. 178.   [126] *Joseph Andrews*, IV, 8.   [127] *Joseph Andrews*, III, 5, and III, 11.

those rare and privileged moments when the force of circumstance may lead to a collapse of dramaturgical ingenuity? This was the question Fielding inherited from Mandeville, and he explicitly sought to resist the force of Mandeville's motto, "private vices, public benefits," in order to deny the morally skeptical conclusions of *The Fable* because of their licentious and atheistic implications. Fielding argued instead that the true scene of meaningful human action, and thus of morals, was not the mere backdrop of conventional social arrangements in which, he agreed with Mandeville, the skillful deceived less talented players. It was rather a universe of supposedly natural signs of divine inscription, a world populated by beings whose very features revealed their genuine sentiments. In such a moral universe, even the most practiced performer could be unmasked, for

however cunning the disguise which a masquerader wears; however foreign to his age, degree or circumstances; yet if closely attended to he very rarely escapes the discovery of an accurate observer; for Nature, which unwillingly submits to the imposture, is ever endeavouring to peep forth and show herself; nor can the cardinal, the friar, or the judge, long conceal the sot, the gamester or the rake.

In the same manner will those disguises which are worn on the greater stage generally vanish, or prove ineffectual to impose the assumed for the real character upon us, if we employ sufficient diligence and attention in the scrutiny.[128]

Fielding was committed to the Augustinian view that truly moral acts could only be performed by genuinely virtuous actors. He believed as well that goodness was a property of the soul, given through grace, though not by the *Deus absconditus* of La Rochefoucauld, Nicole and Esprit, whose workings could nowhere be seen with any certainty. Rather, Fielding thought that the purposes of an Enlightenment God "peep forth" from the "Nature" in which He inscribed them. This precept, he said, gave him the courage to "defy the wisest man in the world to turn a true good action into ridicule."[129] For even if in their theatrically encoded performances all persons became fit subjects for satire, Fielding was convinced that the property of virtue was Nature's stamp, "imprint[ed on men with] sufficient marks,"[130] and permanently available for the properly instructed to decipher.

---

[128] "An Essay," p. 178. The characters Fielding names are stock figures of the Restoration stage.
[129] *Joseph Andrews*, Preface. [130] "An Essay," 179.

Just as Mandeville and his philosophical adversaries took the passions to be, in Abel Boyer's words, "Nature's never-failing Rhetoric, and the only Orators that can master our Affections,"[131] contemporary artists and critics similarly concentrated on the representation of the passions as the crucial element in the portrayal of character.[132] A true "painting of the passions" was taken, as in Fielding's own criticism, to be the highest praise one could bestow on any attempt to depict the vicissitudes of human nature. It was thought to be the artist's business to know the best way of representing each passion so as to make his audience respond appropriately, while an intricate set of rules provided for artists the affective conventions through which the passions could be portrayed. These conventions were drawn in part from classical authorities, but they primarily derived from recent formulations of a grammar of passions which could be represented pictorially. The most important of these guidebooks was the *Conférence de M. Le Brun sur l'expression générale et particulière* (1667). Chancellor of the Académie Royale de Peinture et de Sculpture, Charles Le Brun codified the principles of Cartesian philosophical psychology in a catalogue of instructions, accompanied by drawings, on how properly to depict the influence of each passion on the human face.[133] Each of Le Brun's illustrations was accompanied by a caption specifying the means by which the face could be drawn to express an emotion like contempt, the subject of Figures 8, 9 and 10.

Contempt is expressed by the eyebrows knit and lowering towards the nose, and at the other end very much elevated; the eye very open and the pupil in the middle; the nostrils drawing upwards; the mouth shut, with the corners somewhat down, and the under-lip thrust out further than the upper one.

The pervasive influence of Le Brun's treatise extended beyond the audience of painters to whom it was addressed. Translated into English in 1701, *A Method to Learn to Design the Passions* was reprinted throughout the century. An expensive edition appeared as late as 1813, near the time when Wordsworth thrilled at the perfectly

---

[131]   Abel Boyer, *The English Theophrastus: or the Manners of the Age* (London, 1702), p. 301.

[132]   Brewster Rogerson, "The Art of Painting the Passions," *Journal of the History of Ideas*, 1 14, (1953), pp. 68–94, is a rich discussion of this subject. See too Lawrence Lipking, *The Ordering of the Arts in Eighteenth-Century England* (Princeton University Press, 1970), especially pp. 38–65.

[133]   For a discussion of Le Brun see Stephanie Ross, "Painting the Passions: Charles Le Brun's *Conférence sur L'Expression,*" *Journal of the History of Ideas*, 45, 1 (1984), pp. 25–47.

expressive face of the Magdalene in the Louvre.[134] The most important non-pictorial consequence of the idea that there were universal
and invariant norms of expression was its effect on theatrical practices, a transmission encouraged by Shaftesbury's arguments affirming the parallels between the pictorial and dramatic arts[135] and then
codified into principles of literary criticism.[136] In contemporary
acting treatises, like those of Thomas Betterton and Aaron Hill, the
stage was conceived as if it were a *tableau vivant* where actors drew upon
a standardized gestural "language" for the expression of the passions.
Audiences engaged with actors in a contract of performance and
response wherein they were presumed to be thoroughly familiar with
nature's rhetoric of emotional representations. Fielding began his
literary career as one of the most popular playwrights for the London
stage, while his friend and performing ideal, Garrick, said that a great
actor, "by calling in the aid and assistance of articulation, corporeal
motions and ocular expression, imitates, assumes, or puts on the
various mental and bodily emotions arising from the various
humours, virtues and vices, incident to human nature . . . [because he
knows] each humour and passion, their sources and effects."[137] These
details of facial aspect, gesture and tone of voice already began to be
catalogued in 1724 in the *Thesaurus dramaticus*, an account of the
"poetical beauties" of the English stage, while betterton's authority
supported the view that the actor had to master the rules of posture
and tone; above all, he must command his face.

Your Eye-brows must neither be immovable, nor always in Motion . . . but
generally they must remain in the same Posture and Equality, which they
have by Nature, allowing them their due Motion when the Passions require

134 William Wordsworth, *The Prelude*, ed. J.C. Maxwell (Harmondsworth: Penguin, 1971), IX,
     lines 76–80. For Le Brun's importance for the plastic arts see Alastair Smart, "Dramatic
     Gesture and Expression in the Age of Hogarth and Reynolds," *Apollo* 82 (1965), pp. 90–97,
     and Alan T. McKenzie, "'The Countenance You Show Me': Reading the Passions in the
     Eighteenth Century," *The Georgia Review* 32 (1978), pp. 758–773.
135 Anthony Ashley Cooper, Earl of Shaftesbury, *A Notion of the Historical Draught of the Judgement
     of Hercules* (1732), in Benjamin Rand (ed.), *Shaftesbury's Second Characteristics* (Cambridge
     University Press, 1914), pp. 29–62. This point is discussed in Ronald Paulson, *Hogarth: His
     Life, Art and Times* (New Haven: Yale University Press, 1972), I, pp. 103–104. On the
     representation of the passions on the eighteenth-century stage see William Worthen, *The
     Idea of the Actor* (Princeton University Press, 1984), Chapter 2, and the works cited therein.
136 See, for example, Henry Home, Lord Kames, *Elements of Criticism* 6th edition (Edinburgh,
     1785), 2 volumes, Parts I–VII, "Emotions and Passions."
137 David Garrick, *An Essay on Acting* (1744), in Toby Cole and Helen C. Chinoy (eds.), *Actors on
     Acting* (New York: Crown, 1954), p. 133.

it; that is, to contract themselves, and frown in *Sorrow*; to smooth and dilate themselves in *Joy*; to hang down in *Humility*, &c.[138]

Fielding worked within this set of conventions in his satiric dramas of the 1730s, the more successful of which, like *Pasquin* and *The Tragedy of Tragedies*, employed devices such as the play within a play so as not to allow the audience to forget that it was in the theatre. Fielding's interpolated narratives, and his digressions on style and form, similarly distanced the reader of his fictions by reproducing in the novel the theatre's rhetorical demands.[139] He expected his audience to be familiar with established dramatic conventions and assume a theatrical perspective on the characters he portrayed. These characters he in turn depicted within self-consciously theatrical settings where the rules of gesture and facial expression guide the meaning of the performance. When, for example, Partridge is taken by Tom Jones to see Garrick's *Hamlet*, he not only thinks that the best actor plays Claudius, but that the king does not look like a murderer. He also believes that "I could act as well as [Garrick] myself," unaware of the meaning of his own testimony that he only knew King Hamlet was a ghost when Hamlet responded to it, so great were the expressive powers of Garrick's glance. When Partridge then misquotes Juvenal's line, "*fronti nulla fides*," he becomes the doubly satiric example of the person who consistently misreads the face and thus the meaning of the player.[140] In *Joseph Andrews* Fielding describes Mrs. Slipslop, who "flung herself into the chaise, casting a look at Fanny as she went, not unlike that which Cleopatra gives Octavia in that play," fully expecting his reader to be familiar with the characteristics signifying contempt.[141] When Fielding (correctly) quotes Juvenal in discussing the method of understanding character, he points out that the adage, "no trust is to be given to the countenance," was written by the poet in the context of his, and of Fielding's own, rhetorical question, "what place is not filled with austere libertines?"[142] The theatrical transposition of Le Brun's pictorial aesthetic offered Field-

---

[138] Thomas Betterton, *The History of the English Stage* (London, 1741), p. 98.
[139] The third-person narrator's virtual omniscience in *Joseph Andrews* is enhanced by his persona as a director who "imitate[s] the wise conductors of the stage," offering set-pieces of humor or satire to impede the reader's absorption in the tale before him. Brian Corman, "Congreve, Fielding and the Rise of Some Novels," in Shirley Strum Kenny (ed.), *British Theatre and Other Arts, 1600–1800* (Washington: Folger Shakespeare Library, 1984), pp. 257–270, discusses these points.   [140] *Tom Jones*, XVI, 5.
[141] *Joseph Andrews*, II, 13, p. 135. The play referred to is Dryden's *All For Love*, III, 1, in which Cleopatra and Octavia meet.   [142] "An Essay," pp. 178 and 181.

ing a way to answer this question by equipping him with principles of unmasking the stage managers of their own public demeanors.

Nature "imprint[ed] sufficient marks in the countenance to inform an accurate and discerning eye," and in the "Essay" (and again, at the end of his life, in *The Journal of a Voyage to Lisbon*) Fielding sought to "set down some few rules" to guide the discernment of men of open dispositions, the sure indication, he said, "of an honest and upright heart."[143] He sometimes thought that these principles, drawn from Le Brun and cited with Shaftesbury's authority, offered a way for the morally worthy to remain impartial spectators of their own social drama. These persons could achieve the critical distance necessary to comprehend the global character of theatrical behavior. Then, by judging dissimulation with charity, they could reduce the anxieties generated by their own performances, and begin a morally informed process of harmonizing public representations with private insight. "A single bad act no more constitutes a villain in life, than a single bad part on the stage," the narrator says in *Tom Jones*:

Thus the man as well as the player may condemn what he himself acts; nay it is common to see vice sit as awkwardly on some men as the character of Iago would on the honest face of [the popular actor] Mr. William Mills.[144]

Like Tom Jones, who knows that "appearances ... are often deceitful," but who is seldom so deceived, and unlike Jonathan Wild, author of "Maxims for the Great Man," the hypocrite's handbook, it could be hoped that good men, no matter how ordinary, might know their fellows and in that knowledge forgive them.

Yet, as the self-regarding passions drove the players of a theatricized world, they similarly distorted the judgement of its spectators, "for as affectation always overacts her part, it fares with her as with a farcical actor on the stage ... while the truest and finest strokes of Nature, represented by a judicious and just actor, pass unobserved and disregarded."[145] Although in possession of the rules by which to decipher nature's inscriptions, men nevertheless remained vulnerable to the passionately distorted images of their own creation and failed to encounter the man performing behind the mask. Even in a world of

---

[143] Compare this quality with mere "good Breeding[,] the latter being the Art of conducting yourself by certain common and general Rules, by which Means, if they were universally observed, the whole world would appear (as all Courtiers actually do) to be, in their external Behaviour at least, but one and the same Person," in Henry Fielding, *The Covent-Garden Journal*, 55, 18 July, 1752.   [144] *Tom Jones*, VII, 1.   [145] "An Essay," p. 187.

natural signs "a more reliable guide" was needed for their decoding. This guide, Fielding said, is to be found in "the *actions* of men."[146] One cannot help but think this advice would give small relief to his discerning reader, so intimately acquainted by Mandeville's *Fable*, and by Fielding's own fictions, with the endlessly interpretable, because never unmediated, transactions between audience and masquerade, reader and player, in what Fielding himself described as a mere pantomime of critical communication.[147] As the century's greatest mime told a philosopher who, like Fielding, sought to defend the principles of virtue and penetrate by reason the masks of vicious actors, "the man who must have a manual won't ever go far, [for] society offers many more [poses] than ... art can imitate."[148]

THE DISCOURSE OF THE PASSIONS AT ITS LIMITS

Fielding's dilemma arose from the traditions of moral psychology informing eighteenth century techniques for representing the person. He assumed that the modern writer's task was to classify and embody the visible signs of the invisible powers from which action sprang, critically distancing the reader from his own motives by satirically rendering their effects. As he said early on in *Joseph Andrews*: "passions operate differently on the human mind, as diseases on the body, in proportion to the strength or weakness, soundness or rottenness, of the one and the other."[149] In his fictional practice, Fielding combined the "various atoms" which comprise "all human particles" – passions, dispositions, social position, education, habit, occupation – in different ways, in order to discover, as he says of the human spectacle in *Tom Jones*, what their result would be. The rhetoric of the theatre eminently suited these purposes. Fielding exploited the power of the metaphorical equation of the world as a stage as it became common lexical currency for social comprehension by persons experiencing a dislocation of the traditional nexus between status and economic power, and whose expanded opportunities for profit and social

[146] "An Essay," p. 188.
[147] *Joseph Andrews*, III, 10: "A Discourse Between the Poet and Player."
[148] Rameau's nephew to "Lui," in Denis Diderot, *Rameau's Nephew*, trans. L.W. Tancock (London: Penguin, 1966), pp. 76 and 120. It is worthy of note that Rameau was referring to Noverre, the greatest contemporary teacher of dance, and that the dancing master was one of Mandeville's and Fielding's preferred images for the representation of deceit, a point made about Fielding by Claude Rawson in "Gentlemen and Dancing-Masters," in *Henry Fielding and the Augustan Ideal Under Stress* (London: Routledge, 1972), pp. 3–34.
[149] *Joseph Andrews*, I, 7.

promotion in an increasingly mobile world heightened the distance between private perceptions and the requirements of public performance. The relatively stable system of expression, pose, gesture and plot within which Fielding and his contemporaries wrote permitted him to depict for an enlarged and diverse reading public those universal features of the human drama whose representations were previously confined to the socially elevated. As Fielding said, his novels sought to embody the spirit of the epic under modern, prosaic conditions.

The response which Diderot placed in the mouth of Rameau's nephew highlights how these representational practices, contingent upon particular assumptions about what constitutes psychological realism, became problematic during the course of the eighteenth century.[150] Fielding already had an inkling of this shift when he rejected those "immense Romances of the modern Novel ... [which,] without any assistance from Nature or History, records persons who never were, or will be, and facts which never did nor possibly can happen."[151] His point, here famously made against Richardson, was that the narrative of a given identity could only successfully be charted against the background of its governing passions. Such a life could only move and instruct an audience if it were placed in imaginative contact with precisely these unvarying characteristics of human nature, publicly expressed on the dramatic surface of social action. Mandeville began from identical premises, as did Prévost, d'Holbach and Helvétius. Hume and Gibbon wrote their histories from a similar perspective. So did Smollett, whose fictions, like Fielding's, are populated with Mandevillian figures of wickedness. Like these writers, Fielding thought it absurd that the peculiarities of a character's emotional response, historical or fictive, could, or should, compel the reader somehow to "identify" with him – a usage, it is worth noting, which did not become common until late in the generation after Fielding's death.[152] Like Mandeville, Fielding

---

[150] Alasdair MacIntyre, *After Virtue* (Notre Dame University Press, 1981), pp. 35–48, gives a brilliant account of the relation between Rameau's masquerades and eighteenth-century moral philosophy. For the decay of the behavioral styles represented by Fielding see Charles Pullen, "Lord Chesterfield and Eighteenth-Century Appearance and Reality," *Studies in English Literature, 1500–1800* 8 (1968), pp. 501–515, and Michael Curtin, "A Question of Manners: Status and Gender in Etiquette and Courtesy," *The Journal of Modern History* 57 (September 1985), pp. 395–423.   [151] *Jospeh Andrews*, Preface.

[152] *Oxford English Dictionary* (1977 edition), *s.v.* "identify," and see Marion Hobson, *The Object of Art: The Theory of Illusion in Eighteenth-Century France* (Cambridge University Press, 1982), p. 208. Compare, Samuel Johnson on biography in *Rambler* 60, 13 October 1750.

wanted to encourage the reader's conceptual distance from his creations, not the suspension of disbelief. He wished to dissect the theatrical demands of all roles, so that in an encounter with the performance of them spectators could detach, not identify, themselves remaining self-consciously free moral agents. The standard observation that Fielding gives us only the surface of characters, and the attendant critical regret that his characters have no convincing "inner" lives, assume without argument that this inner life is a permanent human attribute rather than an emergent intersubjective property. In other words, it assumes that inwardness is a feature of the self that Fielding, along with his contemporaries, lacked the imagination to grasp, rather than an historical consequence of the disintegration of assumptions upon which his writing depended.[153]

Fielding's understanding of social action as theatrical rests on the assumption, made explicit by Mandeville and later bemoaned by Rousseau,[154] that contemporary societies were distinguished by the encouragement given their members to conduct their lives in ways designed for self-misrepresentation. The modern reign of fashion was at once an instrument of and spur to these deceptive practices, depending as it did upon an explosion of mobile wealth and its associated ideology of manners, recently elevated by Shaftesbury to the status of moral philosophy. Social actors, most especially those recently propelled into the higher orbits of society, were seen repeatedly to conceal their intentions because the exposure of these wholly self-regarding purposes would make their achievement impossible. From this perspective, hypocrisy emerged at once for Fielding as a defining feature of human conduct, as it did in much of eighteenth-century thought, while the astute social observer in his fictions assumed the role of an impartial spectator – a detached decoder of ubiquitous practices of concealment. Fielding unmasks the intentions of men in order to give full sense to their performances, conceived as elements of social practices which cannot, in principle, be understood from the point of view of the fully engaged participant in public life.

As Fielding stressed time and again, the awareness of others as

---

[153] See, for example, the now classic statement of this position in Ian Watt, *The Rise of the Novel* (London: Peregrine Books, 1963), pp. 282 and 286.

[154] "When we are purely spectators," Rousseau wrote in his polemic against the theatre, "we immediately take the side of justice," but when we enter into theatrical relations, "only then [do] we prefer the evil that is useful to us to the good that makes us love." In *Politics and the Arts: Letters to M. D'Alembert on the Theater*, trans. Allan Bloom (Glencoe: The Free Press, 1960), p. 24.

beholders who were complicit in accepting the necessity of representing themselves as their fellows wished to see them engendered within an elite metropolitan community a commonly shared psychological perspective on the sources of social conduct. In the language that Addison and Shaftesbury did so much to construct, persons of refinement were both actors and spectators in relation to their own lives, lives understood as moral careers that are shaped by the techniques of politeness for monitoring and controlling one's public persona. A primary object of this language was to normalize the relations of persons self-conscious of the apparent gulf between inherited standards of propriety and contemporary requirements for social success. It is for this reason that writers, like Hume, who employed this language, so often expressed perplexity about identity and moral agency, and strenuously devoted their intellectual energies to the discovery of those features of a self which could be said to possess undistorted moral sentiments.[155] Mandeville articulated the assumptive background against which this language developed. He did not simply deny that exclusively moral sentiments could coherently be imagined for persons driven by self-regard. Mandeville's most significant ideological accomplishment consisted in providing an argument about the centrality of the passions which effectively set the terms in which the eighteenth-century language of sociability addressed the problem of moral autonomy. As he put it, "we need not look for ... the Origin of Politeness ... any further than in the Self-Liking, which I have demonstrated every individual Man to be poss'd of" (II, 138). Modern sociability, Mandeville continued, has "nothing to do with Virtue or Religion ... It is a Science that is ever built on the same steady Principle in our Nature,"

and we shall find, that Luxury and Politeness ever grew up together, and were never enjoyed assunder; that Comfort and Delight upon Earth have always employ'd the Wishes of the *Beau Monde*; and that, as their chief Study and greatest Solicitude, to outward Appearance, have ever been directed to obtain Happiness in the World, so what would become of them in the next seems, to the naked Eye, always to have been the least of their Concern. (II, 146–147)

After the controversy begun by the prosecution of *The Fable*'s publisher, virtually all socially engaged British critics, philosophers

---

[155] See especially Hume, *Treatise*, I.iv.7, where he gives his famous account of personal identity as nothing but a heap of perceptions. At the same time, at *Treatise*, II.i.5, Hume continues to speak of "self, or that individual person, of whose actions and sentiments each of us is intimately conscious."

and theologians of the following two generations were obliged to confront Mandeville's claim, expanded from its source in Bayle, that reason's essential practical role is to answer those questions which the passions provide the only motives for asking – questions concerning the existence and nature of those objects which the passions impel all persons to want or to be. If reason's purpose is to prescribe means for the achievement of the ends set by the passions, and judges those means only in terms of their efficacy, then, as Mandeville insisted, any plausible account of morals would have to be undertaken within the context of a hierarchy of indelible desires. An epistemology of sense impressions and ideas, wedded to a psychology of passions, shaped in the eighteenth century a conception of personality moulded solely through interaction with the objects it encounters. Within this conceptual space, where the person is understood as a strictly arranged ensemble of dispositions, all actions may coherently be considered in terms of the divided personality's need to establish an "outward appearance" for the approval of others, while attempting to satisfy its hidden impulses. When Hume asserted that "reason is, and ought only to be the slave of the passions and can never pretend to any other office than to serve and obey them,"[156] he effectively distilled this precept into a principle, and drew from it an account of the development of morals founded upon the intersubjective, histrionic relationships Mandeville located at the heart of commercial sociability. "In general," Hume said, evoking Epictetus' comparison of the world and the stage,[157] "the minds of men are mirrors to one another,"

not only because they reflect each other's emotions, but also because those rays of passions, sentiments and opinions may often be reverberated, and may decay away by insensible degrees. Thus the pleasure which a rich man receives from his possessions being thrown upon the beholder, causes a pleasure and esteem; which sentiments again, being perceived and sympathized with, encrease the pleasure of the possessor; and being once more reflected, become a new foundation for pleasure and esteem in the beholder ... But the possessor has also a secondary satisfaction in riches arising from the love of esteem he acquires by them, and this satisfaction is nothing but a second reflection of that original pleasure, which proceeded from itself. The secondary satisfaction of vanity becomes one of the principal recommendations of riches, and is the chief reason we either desire them for ourselves or esteem them in others.[158]

[156]   Hume, *Treatise*, III.iii.3.
[157]   Epictetus, *Encheiridion*, trans. W.A. Oldfatter (London: Heinemann, 1946), 2 volumes, 17.
[158]   Hume, *Treatise*, III, ii, 5.

Beginning his inquiry from the spectator's point of view, and presuming with Mandeville that the individual's judgements are governed by the compound of his passions, Hume not only viewed the self as a kind of theatre, "where several perceptions successively make their appearance, pass, re-pass, glide away, and mingle in an infinite variety of postures and situations;"[159] he sought to show that the individual's limited sympathies for the welfare of others could be furthered and fully accounted for in terms of an essentially self-interested beholder's responses to the postures and demands of his fellows. Montesquieu had previously made a related point in *The Persian Letters*, when his Persian visitors to Paris saw in the theatre and its audience the model of contemporary European culture, one in which individuals are obliged continually to interact with other social actors in order to secure public approbation, and may advance their private ambitions only by respecting the rules of civility.[160] Similarly, for Adam Smith, social life of necessity resembles a masquerade,[161] for the approbation and disapprobation of oneself which we call conscience is a mirror of feeling – a social product which is an effect of each of us judging others as a spectator while finding others as spectators judging ourselves. We then come to judge our own conduct, Smith argued in direct opposition to the "indulgent and partial spectator" of Mandeville's "licentious system,"[162] when "we examine it as we imagine an impartial spectator would."[163] Men require mirrors, for without society, a man "could no more think of his own character ... than of the beauty or deformity of his own face," and the only mirror in which he can view his character "is placed in the countenance and behaviour of those he lives with."[164]

We begin ... to examine our own passions and conduct, and to consider how these must appear to [others] ... We suppose ourselves the spectators to our own behaviour, and endeavour to imagine what effect it would, in this light, produce upon us. This is the only looking-glass by which we can, in some measure, with the eyes of other people, scrutinize the propriety of our own conduct.[165]

[159] Hume, *Treatise*, i.iv.6.
[160] E.J. Hundert and Paul Nelles, "Liberty and Theatrical Space in Montesquieu's Political Theory: The Poetics of Public Life" in *The Persian Letters, Political Theory*, 17, 2 (May 1989), pp. 223–246.
[161] Smith, *Theory of Moral Sentiments*, VII.2.4.10.   [162] Smith, *Theory of Moral Sentiments*, VII.2.4.
[163] Smith, *Theory of Moral Sentiments*, III.4.6.   [164] Smith, *Theory of Moral Sentiments*, III.1.3.
[165] Smith, *Theory of Moral Sentiments*, III.1.5. Compare Shaftesbury, *Characteristics*, I, p. 257, where the mind is referred to as "a spectator or auditor of other minds." See too Charles L. Griswald, Jr., "Rhetoric and Ethics: Adam Smith on Theorizing the Moral Sentiments," *Philosophy and Rhetoric* 24, 3 (1991), pp. 213–237; Jonah Barish, *The Anti-Theatrical Prejudice*,

All of these writers, like so many of their Enlightenment contemporaries, not only accepted Mandeville's initial challenge that the abiding problem posed by commercial sociability was to show how individuals could be thought of as moral if they were irreducibly prideful and vain, and that the world of commerce depended upon the encouragement of these propensities. Engaged in this challenge, they were obliged as well to confront the argument, most clearly associated with *The Fable*, that character was in essence a social artifact, a construct existing only in an intersubjective space of the demands of others, and within which a person's public identity was of necessity devised. Once Mandeville's challenge was addressed in the idiom of the passions which *The Fable* elevated into a dominant vocabulary amongst post-Protestant (or post-Augustinian), pre-revolutionary intellectuals, persons could immediately be understood as actors pressured by circumstance and goaded by opportunity to perform in ways designed to elicit that public approbation demanded by their dominant passions. And until the vocabulary of the passions was succeeded by a language of the emotions – the language of Rousseau's *Confessions* and *The Sorrows of Young Werther*, of Romantic poetry, Hegel's *Phenomenology* and the nineteenth-century novel, which presumes that feelings rest on judgements or stimulate other feelings which enable the modification of passion itself, the language in which persons began to understand themselves as moved by integrated patterns of feeling which shaped a unique identity – Mandeville's *Fable* would retain its central place on the horizon of social understanding.[166]

(Berkeley: University of California Press, 1981), pp. 243–255, and Joseph J. Spengler, "Smith Versus Hobbes: Economy Versus Polity," in F.R. Glahe (ed.), *Adam Smith and The Wealth of Nations* (Boulder: Colorado Associated University Press, 1978), p. 43, who points out that Smith's "invisible hand" was compared by Fontenelle in *Pluralité des mondes* (1686), a work Smith knew, to "that of an Engineer who, hidden in the pit of a French theatre, operated 'the Machines of the Theatre' in motion on the stage."

[166] John Stuart Mill captured some of this contrast in his 1838 essay on Bentham, whose assumptions about human psychology Mill also associated with both Hume and Helvétius. "Self-consciousness," Mill wrote, "that dream of the genius of our time, from Wordsworth to Byron, from Goethe to Chateaubriand, and to which this age owes most . . . of its cheerful and its mournful wisdom, never was awakened in [Bentham] . . . He had never been made alive to the unseen influences which were acting on himself, nor consequently on his fellow creatures . . . he knew still less of the influence by which these feelings are formed; all the more subtle workings both of the mind upon itself, and of external things upon the mind, escaped him." J.S. Mill, "Bentham," in Gertrude Himmelfarb (ed.), *Essays on Politics and Culture* (New York: Anchor, 1963), pp. 94–95.

CHAPTER 4

A world of goods

When, early in his literary career, Mandeville wrote *The Grumbling Hive*, he satirized his contemporaries for trumpeting their commitment to classical or Christian ideals of virtue while glorying in recent English prosperity. Employing the beehive as a symbol of productive activity for his own satiric purposes, he divided the poem into two parts. The first part stresses the economic benefits that follow when a society can accommodate a certain amount of (relatively unselfconscious) moral corruption amongst its members. In the second part, Mandeville contrasts this public felicity with an imagined society in which disastrous economic consequences follow when the lives of citizens are purged of immoral and immoderate behavior. Yet even in the wealthy hive, the "knaves" populating it are hypocrites who "boast ... of their honesty" while engaging in duplicitous social practices. Mandeville's obvious and intentionally transgressive point in the poem is that commercial societies seem naturally to entail forms of artifice and imposture which should be understood as the moral price of commercial prosperity. As we have seen, he gave theoretical expression to this common concern amongst observers of British public life in the early eighteenth century, that, as one of them noted, "Greatness is so Theatrical, and the actors change so often that really I was at a loss where to fix."[1] Mandeville later put the point starkly in the body of *The Fable*: "it is impossible we could be socialized creatures without hypocrisy," the necessary ingredient of all "civil commerce" (I, 349).

FROM HYPOCRISY TO EMULATION

In the 1723, and even more pointedly in the 1728 volume of *The Fable*, however, Mandeville altered some of his original views about

---

[1] E. Phillips, *An Appeal to Common Sense: Or, Some Considerations Offer'd to Restore Publick Credit. As Also the Means of Reviving It* (London, 1720), p. 4.

moral evil. Vice he now most often associated with pride and envy rather than with avarice and greed. This shift of emphasis probably resulted from his having to defend *The Fable*'s dominant assertion of irreducible egoism by answering critics like Butler, Hutcheson and Law, who claimed to defeat Mandeville's arguments by explaining social actions through an appeal to the natural benevolence of mankind. Mandeville's critics also argued, as we have seen, that no peaceful and prosperous society could possibly be sustained by pure egoists competing for scarce satisfactions; they argued, indeed, that Mandeville could only make such an absurd claim by perversely suspecting the most obviously innocent and benevolent actors of hidden and vicious intentions. "It is a suspicion," William Law wished to convince his readers, "thus founded against all the appearances of truth, and is forced to make those the proofs of the absence of a thing, which are the natural signs of its presence."[2] Assaults like these had an immediate rhetorical design. They were meant to blunt *The Fable*'s force amongst the educated public by treating Mandeville as little more than a minor Hobbesian acolyte with a Grub Street talent for churning out conceptually nonsensical satirical wit. Hutcheson's first attacks on Mandeville, which appeared in the pages of *The Dublin Journal* in 1725, were brought together and posthumously published in 1750 under the title *Reflections on Laughter* for this polemical purpose,[3] expressing a collective hope nearly twenty years after his death that Mandeville finally could be dismissed as a wicked but ultimately risible author whose pernicious doctrines were philosophically vacuous. Hutcheson's Scots colleague, Adam Ferguson, while echoing *The Fable*'s charge that the "standard of felicity" amongst commercial moderns "flatter[s] their own imbecility under the name of *politeness*," adopted the same tactic in the 1760s. "It is pleasant," he wrote of Mandeville,

to find men, who, in their speculations, deny the reality of moral distinctions, forget in detail the general positions they maintain, and give loose to ridicule, indignation, and scorn, as if any of these sentiments could have place, were the actions of men indifferent; and with acrimony pretend to detect fraud by which moral restraints have been imposed, as if to censure a fraud were not already to take part on the side of morality.[4]

---

[2] William Law, *Remarks,* p. 43.

[3] Francis Hutcheson, *Reflections on Laughter and Remarks on The Fable of the Bees* (Glasgow, 1750).

[4] Adam Ferguson, *An Essay on the History of Civil Society 1767*, ed. Duncan Forbes (Edinburgh University Press, 1966), p. 33.

For his part, Mandeville seems never to have been less than secure about his own rhetorical agility. Critics who attempted to demolish with ridicule saw their own assertions effectively reduced to parody and held up for derision in the "Vindication of the Book," where Mandeville mocked the *"Scribblers"* who attacked him (1, 390), and did so again in both *The Fable*'s second volume and its supplement on "Honour." Yet in addition to these purely polemical objectives, Mandeville was intensely concerned in these works to answer those critics who bracketed *The Fable* with *Leviathan*, the work of Hobbes he seems most to have admired but which he thought had exhausted the analogy between natural and political bodies.[5] Mandeville distinguished his work from Hobbes' by elaborating and refining his claim that consistent common experience confirmed that men care immeasurably more about the opinions rather than the welfare of others. *Pace* Hobbes, Mandeville argued that in polished as opposed to predatory societies envy and the hypocrisy to which it gave rise were naturally self-limiting rather than a socially destructive passions – a conception Montesquieu was known to have transposed in his discussion of the stabilizing role of noble honor in monarchies in *The Spirit of the Laws*.[6] Instead of encouraging men to engage in bouts of physical aggression and to invade the property of others, as Hobbes had claimed, Mandeville argued that in conditions of modern opulence envy would instead be directed into politically harmless and socially beneficial channels. In fine: the emergence of commerce had unintentionally contributed to the stability of the modern state.

It is important to keep in mind that Mandeville's seminal claim about communally beneficent hypocrisy in commercial settings ran counter to most informed opinion during most of the eighteenth century, not only to Hobbes.[7] Mandeville's immediate contemporaries like Hutcheson and Law, and later Ferguson, Rousseau and Smith, all worried that once the arts of dissembling, economic self-interest and envy were aroused by the informal as well as the formal institutions of commerce, these intensely self-regarding types of activity could not reasonably be expected to remain confined to economic affairs. They feared that the drive for profit, accumulation,

---

[5] Bernard Mandeville, *A Modest Defence of Publick Stews* (London, 1724), p. 57.
[6] Montesquieu, *The Spirit of the Laws*, III.7. See Melvin Richter, *The Political Theory of Montesquieu* (Cambridge University Press, 1977), pp. 43–44.
[7] A point usefully explored by Thomas Horne, "Envy in Commercial Society," *Political Theory* 9, 4 (1981), pp. 551–569.

and material superiority would corrupt and then finally dominate all other aspects of communal life. It was classically argued and still widely believed in the eighteenth century that as private interests took precedence over public duties nations largely comprised of persons consumed with self-regard in their struggle for material advantage were threatened with civil incapacity. Public morals would wither amidst an anarchic scramble for wealth as an instrument of dominance, a struggle that could only be contained, as Plato imagined in the final Book of *The Republic*, by a despot. In *The Discourse on the Origins of Inequality* Rousseau, who, as we have seen, took Mandeville's *Fable* as commercial society's most truthful and self-incriminating expression, followed this line of thought. He argued that despotism was the inevitable consequence of modernity, a conclusion in his view supported not only by classical authorities but most recently by Montesquieu's observation in *The Spirit of the Laws*, where it was argued that mere avarice threatened to supplant lofty ambition in societies circumscribed by petty commercial concerns.[8] Indeed, when Mandeville directly addressed contemporary British politics in the wake of the collapse of the South Sea Company's shares, he also assumed that talent in trade and knowledge of commercial dealings in no way prepared a person for a full civic identity. Unlike virtually the whole of his initial audience, however, Mandeville remained pointedly undisturbed by the prospect that in commercial societies, which by their nature required an intensified specialization of social functions, a man may "have good notions of *Meum* and *Teum* of private persons, and yet not be able to determine anything concerning the property of nations."[9]

Mandeville seems always to have believed that British politics could safely be left in the hands of enlightened Whig elites. He argued neither that the manipulative practices of these elites, nor the hypocrisy which characterized the commercial populations they governed, in any way threatened social peace, as the dominant strand of Western political argument had maintained. Like his critics, Mandeville understood hypocrisy as the socially constituted ensemble of techniques necessary for the fabrication of disguises civilized persons don in order to conceal their avarice from one another. For persons inextricably bound by the web of commercial relations,

---

[8] Montesquieu, *The Spirit of the Laws*, III.3.
[9] Bernard Mandeville, *Free Thoughts*, pp. 390–391.

hypocrisy is the requisite mask for hiding avaricious economic vanity from the moralizing gaze of one's fellows (1, 72–80 and 131–132). Mandeville repeatedly argued that *from any given individual's point of view*, hypocritical practices may correctly be seen as devices employed to conceal a person's vicious motives. This was, he knew, the point of view consistently adopted by the moralists he proposed to satirize; and it was one, moreover, whose conclusions he seldom tired of repeating himself. As he put toward at the end of his career, "[t]o make a Shew outwardly of what is not felt within, and counterfeit what is not real, is certainly Hypocrisy, whether it does good or hurt." Indeed, Mandeville went on, we can reasonably include all that comes under the headings of morality, modern manners and politeness in this category.[10]

But amongst Mandeville's most historically important theoretical achievements was the recognition that the individual's point of view, while instinctive in naturally self-regarding creatures, in fact tends often to conceal the social significance of his actions. The first-person perspective encourages the apparently obvious but false belief that what is morally good or materially beneficial for an individual actor must needs be so for society as a whole. Similarly, we unreflectively tend to believe that an individual vice must be communally vicious. Since every person is "an entire individual, a wonderful machine, endowed with thought and will independent of anything visible from without ... every body looks upon his own dear person, as an individual, if not independent being which he is obliged in every way to gratify and take care of, very often forgetting they are members of society."[11] The scientific student of society, by contrast, is obliged to regard actions from an altered and counter-intuitive perspective, a perspective consistently alert to the ironic disjunction between the truth of a belief held by an actor – the passions from which his action may spring – and, most significantly, its social consequences. He evaluates the deeds of persons by different criteria,

the Usefulness and dignity of their callings, their capacities, with all qualifications required for the exercise or performance of their functions ... In this view we have no regard for the persons themselves, but only the benefit they may be of to the publick ... they are only look'd upon as parts and members of the whole society.[12]

---

[10] *Honour*, p. 202. [11] Mandeville, *Free Thoughts*, pp. 282 and 285.
[12] Mandeville, *Free Thoughts*, p. 282.

As Mandeville put it to Bishop Berkeley, "to understand the Nature of Civil Society, requires Study and Experience ... They are silly People who imagine that the Good of the whole is consistent with the Good of every Individual."[13]

The Fable's conceptually significant and radical claim regarding the function of hypocrisy proceeds from this methodological insight: *from the point of view of society itself* the vice of hypocrisy in fact serves a hidden positive purpose, the familiar Mandevillian objective of pride being managed for public benefit "by playing the Passion against itself" (II, 78–79). "The more pride [men] have and the greater value they set on [gaining] the esteem of others, the more they'll make it their study to render themselves acceptable to all they converse with" (II, 65). Mandevillian pride, then, should be seen from his own dual, evolutionary perspective. Pride begins its career as the egoistic and hedonistic desire to enhance one's self-esteem. This desire initially empowers "flattery" to tame men by encouraging the internalization of elementary forms of social discipline. Then, after they have become moralized in the latter stages of the civilizing process, pride appears as the consequent desire of persons for some form of *dependence* on the approbation of others. The passion which highlights human hypocrisy and the role of theatrical appearance, the pride of polished moderns can at the same time be employed by politicians to direct individual actions into socially beneficial channels by appealing to the need of civilized egoists to gain public approval. As was the case with honor, the previous "tye of society," hypocrisy in commercial nations masks the emulative striving arising from envy. Hypocrisy, disseminated amongst all but the poorest ranks, thereby curbs rather than encourages violent and communally baneful forms of immoderate behavior. As Voltaire perceptively noted, Mandeville effectively disturbed one of his audience's most deep-seated moral intuitions by explaining in detail the positive consequences of envy. By taking emulation rather than aggression as envy's primary expression, Mandeville, so Voltaire thought, achieved his greatest insight: he "is the first who sought to prove that envy is a very good thing, a very useful passion" for society.[14] Mandeville showed how, without any

---

[13] Mandeville, *A Letter to Dion*, p. 49.
[14] Voltaire, "Envie," *Questions sur l'encyclopédie* (1771), in *Œuvres complètes de Voltaire*, ed. Louis Moland (Paris: Garnier, 1878), II, pp. 537–538, added to all later editions of the *Dictionnaire philosophique*.

formal encouragement, hypocrites discover socially useful methods of "making ourselves acceptable to others" (II, 147).

What is chiefly aim'd at in a refined Education is to procure as much Ease and Pleasure upon Earth, as that can afford: Therefore Men are first instructed in all the various Arts of rendering their Behaviour agreeable to others, with the least Disturbance to themselves. Secondly, they are imbued with the Knowledge of all the elegant Comforts of Life, as well as the Lessons of human Prudence, to avoid Pain and Trouble, in order to enjoy as much of the World, and with as little Opposition, as it is possible: whilst thus Men study their own private Interest, in assisting each other to promote and encrease the Pleasures of Life in general, they find by Experience, that to compass those Ends, every thing ought to be banish'd from Conversation, that can have the least Tendency of making others uneasy. (II, 11)

The modish and powerful follow fashion as their chief rule. As Mandeville argued both in his attack on Shaftesbury and in the Introduction to *The Fable*'s second volume, it is from the rules of polite sociability that they acquire their notions of virtue; not, as standardly claimed, the other way round (II, 12). So the difference between being and appearing, which for Mandeville remains the most psychologically significant characteristic of public life in commercial societies (I, 127–130), is at the same time the most visibly obvious and socially significant consequence of the spread of modern manners since the seventeenth century. A regime of polished intercourse had accompanied the growth of commercial relations and the decline of those aristocratic concepts of honor which hitherto tamed the warrior class (I, 122). The unintended social consequence of this transformation, Mandeville argued, was that just as the arts of flattery and thus hypocrisy reached new stages of perfection with the expansion of commerce in the course of recent history, so too did exceedingly subtle and efficiently self-regulating forms of social discipline. Although Hume regarded Mandeville's philosophical arguments as seriously flawed, he endorsed the practical and political implications of this insight when he argued, in the first *Enquiry*, that "those who prove or attempt to prove, that such refinements rather tend to increase industry, civility, and arts, regulate anew our moral as well as political sentiments."[15]

As we have seen, contemporaries less committed than Hume to

---

[15] David Hume, *Enquiry Concerning the Principles of Morals*, ed. L.A. Selby-Bigge (Oxford University Press, 1902), p. 181.

adopting Mandeville's scientific perspective on society were often scandalized by the licentious premises of these novel assertions. But they would not have been wholly surprised by the more narrowly economic implications of Mandeville's thesis. During the first decades of the Restoration many English economic writers began to understand that material possessions beyond those necessary to sustain a frugal existence were desired more for their aesthetic effects and approbative power than for the actual material needs they satisfied. Like Mandeville, these writers examined the psychology of envy, desire and imaginary wants, extending their investigations of market relations well beyond the conventional limits of trade viewed as merely the exchange of commodities.[16] The aggregate demand for economic goods, both Nicholas Barbon and Sir William Petty reasoned, would be intensified in wealthy trading nations primarily because of the esteem they attracted and, also perhaps, the consequent self-respect they appeared to engender in their possessors. "The meaner sort," Sir Dudley North claimed in his *Discourses on Trade*,

seeing their Fellows become rich, and great, are spurr'd up to imitate their Industry. A Tradesman sees his Neighbour keep a Coach, presently all his Endeavours is at work to do the like, and many times is beggered by it; however the extraordinary Application he made, to support his Vanity, was beneficial to the Publick, tho' not enough to answer his false Measures as to himself.[17]

John Pollexfen saw evidence of this process in London at the end of the 1690s. "From the greatest Gallants to the meanest Cook-Maids," he remarked, "nothing was thought fit, to adorn their persons, as the Fabricks of India."[18] Once the implications of such observations were accepted, a process of burgeoning consumption could be seen as in principle endless under appropriate legal and political conditions, endless since goods in the economic realm, void of lasting psychological satisfaction, would quickly lose their luster in the face of other novelties supplied by trade and manufacture.

Mandeville gave his readers little indication of having carefully studied the reflections of late seventeenth-century pamphleteers on the domestic social implications of an enlarged foreign trade. They

---

[16] Joyce Oldham Appleby, *Economic Thought and Ideology in Seventeenth-Century England* (Princeton University Press, 1978), pp. 158–198.
[17] Sir Dudley North, *Discourses on Trade* (London, 1690), p. 15.
[18] John Pollexfen, *A Discourse on Trade, Coyne, and Paper Credit* (London, 1697), p. 99.

were primarily concerned with detailed considerations of government policy, a subject to which Mandeville paid only infrequent attention. Yet, as was long ago pointed out by Marx,[19] and then in some detail in the classic study of mercantilism,[20] the amoral and proto-utilitarian assumptions of many neo-mercantilist writers, who treated the pursuit of self-interest as the sole motive required to understand economic behavior, bear a striking resemblance to Mandeville's. When *The Fable* was branded "Hobbist," it was Mandeville's affinity with the work of these writers that his critics often had in mind. Here, Mandeville's critics had an important point, although not the precise one they wished to make. Mandeville effectively incorporated the insights of his seventeenth-century predecessors into a comprehensive account of the wider social implications of modern prosperity. According to his picture, first the great and then all monied persons throughout the social spectrum do not derive their primary social satisfactions from a naked ability physically to subdue competitors. Rather, such satisfaction as they attain comes from the attention conspicuous displays of articles of consumption are able to draw from others in an economically expanding world of newly available goods. To this thesis Mandeville added a philosophically significant caveat: it is either blatantly hypocritical or simply conceptually fruitless to attempt to understand the relatively recent explosion of emulative behavior in an expanding commercial market for material marks of esteem within the terms provided by the inherited moral tradition. Instead – so he argued – envy and emulation must properly be conceived from a naturalistic perspective, as strong impulses resulting from the passion for dominance "playing" against pride, while changing "its symptoms" in a way unimagined by Hobbes. The expansion of commerce makes products available which markedly reduce the primitive powers of select individuals to compel approbation and obedience by "Looks and Gestures" backed simply by force. As it does so, "costly Equipages, Furniture, Buildings, Titles of Honour, and everything that Men can acquire" rapidly become the primary "Marks and Tokens" of esteem (II, 126). Commerce thus transforms the rules of dominion. "While ... wallowing in a Sea of

---

[19] Karl Marx, *Capital* (Moscow: Foreign Languages Publishing House, n.d.) I, p. 616, n. 2.
[20] Eli F. Heckscher, *Mercantilism*, trans. Mendel Shapiro (London: Allen and Unwin, 1955), II, pp. 286–315. See, too, J.A.W. Gunn, *Politics and the Public Interest in the Seventeenth Century* (London: Routledge, 1969), pp. 205–265, p. 21, and John Brown, *Essays on the Characteristics of the Earl of Shaftesbury* (1751) (New York: Garland Reprint, 1970), p. 140.

Lust and Vanity," civilized men in advanced societies remain psychologically compelled "to put a favourable Construction upon [their]
most glaring Vices" (1, 149). For the first time, however, these persons
are obliged to gear their public performances to the hidden imperatives of a mobile world of goods, in which relations with others are
rarely brutal and immediate, but instead are commonly mediated by
the unstable imaginary values embodied in their very possessions. In
such a world, Mandeville's relentless critic John Brown recognized to
his horror when he attacked *The Fable* some thirty years after its
publication, "*moral* Beauty and Deformity, *Virtue* and Vice, could
have no other Law, that that of Fancy and Opinion."[21]

LABOR AND LUXURY

Brown, who authored the popular *Estimate of the Manners and Principles
of the Times* (1757) – a veritable encyclopedia of conventional worry
about contemporary immorality which was reprinted at least a dozen
times within a year of its appearance – detested Mandeville's glorifi-
cation of excess. His unmitigated abhorrence flowed from a realization that *The Fable* had dramatically placed into circulation the
question of what happens when large numbers of individuals are
required to engage with, and are powerfully moved by, the imagery
produced through the display and manipulation of commodities. For
Brown, the luxurious practices these fantasies encouraged signalled
the imminent "destruction" of the "Desire of Rational Esteem," just
as some of Mandeville's first readers, like William Law, feared that he
had perversely but successfully celebrated the fact that persons in
modern economic conditions could define their public identities
primarily through their patterns of consumption. Mandeville forced
his audience to confront the possibility that a conceptual environment
had developed in which notions of moral goodness, now degenerated
into mere codes of manners and politeness, are merely markers
distinguishing habits which easily could be altered or discarded when
they came into conflict with economic rationality.

Mandeville's interests always centered on the social dynamics of
what he repeatedly styled an "opulent, flourishing and warlike state,"
the polity created in Britain by the financial and military revolutions
at the end of the seventeenth century. Here, one's public role no

---

[21] John Brown, *Estimate of the Manners and Principles of the Times* (London, 1757), 1, p. 173.

longer had any necessarily official connection to the state administration; it could instead largely be constructed from the processes of economic opportunity. The desire of persons activated by self-liking to have their self-image shared by others, so he argued, could account for social cohesion in a commercial world of self-interested egoists, in a society whose habits and social hierarchies were primarily delineated by the mechanisms of fashion, public display and role distance. In this new setting, individuals *qua* individuals could achieve their social identities through the exchange of goods and ideas, practicing a secular ethos of manners "that will joyn worldly Prudence to Sensuality, and make it their chief Study to refine upon Pleasure" (II, 127). Mandeville claims, in other words, that, from the point of view of the dramatically altered intersubjective conditions which characterize commercial society, an enormous range of social actions should be understood without *any* reference to moral categories, but rather as starkly instrumental attempts to satisfy pride through the establishment of one's status. Echoing Mandeville's words, the popular moralist Erasmus Jones expressed regret that "in large and populous cities where obscure Men may hourly meet with fifty strangers, handsome Apparel is a main point ... and People where they are not known, are generally honoured according to the Clothes, and other accoutrements they have about them."[22]

Mandeville thus situated his audience as agents possessing a subjectivity at a considerable remove from any available contemporary account of the person in terms of which he may assent to society's norms as a unified, autonomous, self-reflecting member. He put it to his readers that the actual economy and polity in which they lived had insensibly given birth to a semi-autonomous region of civil society, a zone sustained by private fantasies and driven by future prospects of wealth. He extolled the fact that certain features of social power were radically unstable, and he aimed to show in some detail how emerging opportunities for the advancement of status could thereby be maximized. Social personality in Mandeville's vision became discontinuous with moral commitment; character was now an artifact crafted by role-players within contemporary forms of social exchange and inherited hierarchies of power, and had to remain so if commercial society was to survive and flourish. By highlighting the role of fantasy

[22] Erasmus Jones, *Luxury, Pride and Vanity the Bane of the British Nation* (London, 1736; reprinted 1750), p. 14. Compare *Fable*, I, pp. 127–128.

in modern social intercourse, Mandeville's account of social cohesion in commercial conditions struck at his readers' understanding of themselves and of the very moral foundations of society.[23] He provided an ethically subversive analysis of interest and economic action, understood as founded upon the power of hypocrites guiltlessly to meet as strangers, who each day assembled personae composed of promises and signs of display which signified the "character" of their possessors. *The Fable* described an emergent zone of human interaction notionally bereft of undivided personalities and populated by characters who threatened to dissolve and reassemble in their staged appearances before others. By identifying the "restless desire after Changes and Novelty" (II, 260) as the psychologically activating mechanism of commercial societies, Mandeville placed the issue of wealth creation within the enlarged and precarious context of markets for rapidly changing symbols of esteem, the demand for which ironically dominated the demand for articles of use. Unsurprisingly, Mandeville's thesis that social identity had come to depend upon the acquisition of things was most starkly expressed (and despised) by Rousseau, who lamented in *Emile* that "the introduction of the superfluous makes division of labour possible," and that "a society ... of commerce [consists in] the exchange of things, that of banks in [the] exchange of money," which quickly becomes "the true bond of society."[24]

The explicitly economic dimensions of this vision should not however be exaggerated. One must keep in mind that Mandeville gave remarkably little sustained attention to the articulation of any consistently held set of economic principles, and certainly none that are adequately captured by the retrospective application of the language of classical economics.[25] The overwhelming majority of readers never understood *The Fable* as a work whose primary significance derived from its economic doctrines. For them, the text was seen as one which pointed uncomfortably to the paradoxes Mandeville

---

[23] Compare J.G.A. Pocock, *The Machiavellian Moment: Florentine Political Thought and the Atlantic Republican Tradition* (Princeton University Press, 1975), pp. 465–6.

[24] Jean-Jacques Rousseau, *Emile*, trans. Allan Bloom (New York: Free Press, 1979), pp. 185 and 189.

[25] For the literature on this subject, primarily by historians of economic doctrine, see Goldsmith, *Private Vices, Public Benefits*, Chapter 5; Nathan Rosenberg, "Mandeville and Laissez-Faire," *Journal of the History of Ideas* 24 (1963), pp. 183–196; and Salim Rashid, "Mandeville's *Fable*: Laissez-Faire or Libertinism?," *Eighteenth-Century Studies* 18, 3 (1985), pp. 313–330.

insisted were unresolvable within prevailing conceptions of the moral responsibilities of wealth. *The Fable*'s discussion of wealth creation was scandalous not because of Mandeville's visionary purchase on the hidden laws of economic life, nor yet because of his satiric mockery of elite patterns of consumption,[26] but, rather, because he succeeded in placing before the moral imagination of his readers an unsettling vision of a prosperous, powerful and pleasure-filled dystopia, a necessarily desacralized society sustained, as he first put it, only by pride, avarice, prodigality, luxury, envy, folly and fickleness (1, 25).

Many of Mandeville's observations about wealth creation were conventional in the context of early eighteenth-century economic understanding, while at other times his claims could be confused, uninformed or simply unimaginative. As Sir James Steuart remarked of virtually all of his immediate Augustan contemporaries who wrote on the economy, Mandeville had almost no concern for – indeed, he hardly took any notice of – the processes of investment and savings.[27] Moreover, unlike Pufendorf or Locke before him, Charles Davenant amongst his contemporaries, or particularly the Scots like Hume, Steuart, Ferguson and Smith who wrote in *The Fable*'s wake, Mandeville showed no abiding interest in the role of property in the development of justice, morals and civilization. Mandeville's great and, to his immediate contemporaries, shocking insight that national prosperity depended substantially upon an enlarged availability of consumer goods, and the consequently enlarged, but, he thought, politically harmless social power of the *nouveaux riches* who could command them, was nevertheless yoked in *The Fable* to a wholesale disregard of the economic importance of the mobility of wealth between individuals and families. Mandeville's most striking assertions clearly depend on his assumption that "[a]ll Human Creatures have a restless Desire of mending their condition,"[28] and that in commercial societies, and by contrast with previous formations bound by codes of honor, money serves as a singularly significant index of an individual's ability to satisfy his passions (II, 348–349; 353). Yet at the same time, he thought that "all the trading part of the

[26] Jacob Viner, "Satire and Economics in the Augustan Age of Satire," in H.K. Miller, G. Rothstein and G.S. Rousseau (eds.), *The Augustan Milieu: Essays Presented to Louis A. Landa* (Oxford: Clarendon Press, 1970), pp. 77–101.

[27] Sir James Steuart, *Inquiry Into the Principles of Political Œconomy* (1767), ed. Andrew Skinner (Edinburgh: Olner and Boyd, 1966), 2 volumes, II, pp. 606–607.

[28] Mandeville, *Honour*, pp. 15–16.

people" are motivated by the want of unfair advantage (I, 61), seeking to conceal their costs,[29] and, moreover, often lying in order to turn a profit (I, 81–82). Mandeville accused his contemporaries of being imaginatively imprisoned by atavistic moral ideals. Still, he was quite capable of speaking in the voice of the vanishing age in whose demise he gloried. For example, Mandeville enthusiastically approved of the sumptuary law requiring the dead to be buried in wool instead of linen (I, 329), and defended the privileges of the Turkey Company's monopoly in the Near East, despite its mismanagement and declining business (I, 109). Even Mandeville's criticism of Dutch frugality could reasonably be taken as an example of his failure to understand the relationship between social discipline and national economic success. George Bluett noticed this immediately, pointing out that the example of Holland could be invoked against *The Fable's* thesis in order to demonstrate that virtue and interest were in fact consonant. "[I]f the Necessities and Poverty of the *Dutch* made the Practice of Frugality the *Interest*, and that the keeping up to that Policy, has raised them from Poverty, to the State of Wealth and Grandeur they now enjoy," Bluett inquired,

why is it not as much the Interest of those Kingdoms to do so, who have none of those Wants to provide against? If the *Dutch* in their present Condition are oblig'd to be more frugal than their Neighbours, from the vast Experience they have at Repairing their Dykes, the Weight of other Taxes, and the Scantiness of their Dominions; would not the same Frugality in their Neighbours, who have a greater Extent of Land, and no such Demands of Expense, keep them in a Condition still proportionably above them, and continue them still proportionably richer?[30]

Mandeville's most comprehensive economic argument rests upon the assertion that in commercial societies self-interest, driven by ineradicable human passions, is at once the "cause of earthly greatness" (II, 260) and consonant with social order because of its self-regulating properties. He first developed one facet of this argument in a wholly satirical mode, seeking to infuriate contemporary moralists by praising the illegal practices of thieves who provide work for locksmiths, drunkards who benefit brewers and contribute to the duty on malt, and highwaymen who spend more freely than the cautious citizens they prey upon (I, 86–87). Still, while divines like Law were suitably outraged by this defense of vice on the grounds of public

---

[29] Mandeville, *Free Thoughts*, p. 292.   [30] Bluett, *Enquiry*, pp. 48–49.

utility, the more economically educated of Mandeville's readers recognized that he had implied the absurdity that unproductive labor could in fact create wealth. "I have known an Overseer of the Poor in the Country," Bluett mockingly reported, "when a lusty Fellow has complain'd to him of his want of Work, employ him for a whole Day together in turning a Grindstone tho' nothing was all that while ground upon it. I believe it won't be said that the Parish was the richer for the Fellow's Labour."[31] Mandeville soon came to realize that in commending robbery and drunkenness as wealth-creating he had made a polemical mistake, and he was at pains in *The Fable*'s second volume to provide his audience with no opportunity to echo Bluett's effective mockery. But as with the filth in London streets produced by "the great Traffick and Opulency of that mighty City" (I, 11), and the butchered castrati who on that account sing so beautifully (II, 106), Mandeville's intention in raising these examples was not to suggest that all vice produced wealth, but to ask what inconveniences or outright damage may be the *necessary consequence* of opulence. This question Bluett, like most of *The Fable*'s immediate audience, either failed fully to understand or simply wished to elide.[32] Following Addison, and particularly Shaftesbury, Mandeville's critics were prepared to recognize rather than deny the importance of self-regarding interests, particularly "that passion ... having for its aim the possession of wealth ... [for] the public as well as private system is advanced by the industry which this affection excites." "But," Shaftesbury continued,

if it grows at length into a real passion, the injury and mischief it does the public is not greater than that which it creates to the person himself. Such a one is in reality a self-oppressor, and lies heavier on himself than he can ever do on mankind.[33]

Mandeville intended directly to challenge this attempt to moralize self-regard in the name of affluence. If some morally or materially pernicious effects necessarily accompany the causes of prosperity in commercial societies, then it is mcrc cant, he uncomfortably insisted, to claim that one favors the cause but despises the effect. In fact, as his criticism of the executions at Tyburn demonstrates, Mandeville neither praised all pernicious effects, nor claimed that all of these effects were necessary. "Should any of my Readers," he wrote,

---

[31] Bluett, *Enquiry*, p. 5.   [32] For example, see Bluett, *Enquiry*, p. 17.
[33] Shaftesbury, "An Inquiry Concerning Virtue and Merit," p. 326.

draw Conclusions *in infinitum* from my Assertions that Goods sunk or burnt are as beneficial ... as they had been well sold and put to proper Uses, I would count him a Caviller and not worth answering: Should it always Rain and the Sun never shine, the Fruits of the Earth would soon be rotten and destroy'd; and yet it is no Paradox to affirm, that, to have Grass or Corn, Rain is as necessary as the Sunshine. (i, 364)

Mandeville intended to emphasize the consequences of the point – essentially a moral one – that prosperity cannot possibly be caused by other-regarding virtues. As Cleomenes put it, mocking Shaftesbury, it is absurd to think that the barrister toils to secure the property of others, that the doctor works day and night to secure the health of his patients, or that the clergyman who holds several livings does so in order to minister to many souls (ii, 52). The primary economic conclusion Mandeville derived from this fundamentally ethical argument was this, that in commercial societies many vices were systemic features of heightened mediums of exchange, in the same way as are the "Hardships and Calamities" of dangerous commercial voyages:

When we are acquainted with ... and duly consider [the physical perils of the open sea] it is scarce possible to conceive a Tyrant so inhuman and void of Shame, that beholding things in the same View, he should extract such terrible services from the innocent Slaves; and at the same time dare to own, that he did it for no other Reason, than the Satisfaction a Man receives from having a Garment made of Scarlet or Crimson Cloth. But to what Height of Luxury must a Nation be arrived, where not only the King's Officers, but likewise his Guards, even the Private Soldiers should have such impudent Desires! (i, 337–338)

Mandeville never tired of repeating his fundamental point that suchlike narrow motives underlie the widest range of individual pursuits in commercial societies. The private soldier, the wealthy barrister and the grasping parson would eagerly perform prodigious feats of self-denial in the process of responding to their petty but unyielding desires for money and the ornaments of status money commanded. In so doing, they unknowingly (and uncaringly) create employment for others. In the minds of his contemporaries, *The Fable*'s analysis of these reciprocally dependent processes offered a direct challenge to the moral legitimacy of modern, opulent nations. So too did Mandeville's corollary claim that the mechanisms of commercial societies were best understood as natural artifacts of hidden, systemic social forces, properly a subject for philosophic inquiry, and a subject which promised to provide scientific foundations for social understanding. For just as physicians "write on Poisons" (I, 408) from a physiological perspective, so too

Philosophers, that dare extend their Thoughts beyond the narrow compass of what is immediately before them, look on the alternate Changes in the Civil Society no otherwise than they do on the risings and fallings of the Lungs; the latter of which are as much a Part of Respiration in the more perfect Animals as the first; so that the fickle Breath of never-stable Fortune is to the Body Politick, the same as floating Air is to a living Creature. (I, 149)

In ways which directly bore upon issues of economic and social policy, Mandeville developed the second facet of his thesis, that is, that in modern conditions, economic self-interest is a natural, progressive and self-regulating human propensity. Thus, on the local level, he argued that "as it is folly to set up trades that are not wanted, so what is next to it is to increase in any one trade the numbers beyond what are required ... This proportion as to numbers in every trade finds itself and is never better kept than when nobody meddles or interferes with it" (I, 299–300), while

[i]n the compound of all nations, the different degrees of men ought to bear a certain proportion to each other, as to numbers, in order to render the whole a well proportioned mixture. And ... this due proportion ... is never better attained to, or preserved than when nobody meddles with it. Hence we may learn how the shortsighted wisdom of perhaps well-meaning people may rob us of a felicity that would flow spontaneously from the nature of every large society if none were to divert or interrupt that stream. (II, 353)

These arguments, however, were almost invariably confined to issues bearing upon the domestic economy rather than on problems of international commerce, a subject about which Mandeville simply repeated the conventional view regarding the need for government to ensure a positive balance of trade, believing as he did that unregulated international exchange in goods would reduce employment (I, 248–249; 312–317). Even when discussing the domestic economy, in fact, Mandeville was far from consistent. For example, he emphasized the importance of unconstrained material ambition, while praising the regulation of trades, handicrafts and occupations in London as an example of the "dextrous management" of politicians (II, 321). Indeed, the types of organizations which most aroused Mandeville's interest in both volumes of *The Fable* and its supplement on "Honour" were neither financial nor productive institutions, but churches, sects and armies. The latter were not viewed by him as bodies which provide their members or the community at large with material resources for living, but as vehicles for the management of men through the manipulation of their pride.

Only two significant regions of economic activity, labor and luxury consumption, attracted Mandeville's sustained attention. In his "Vindication" of *The Fable* (1, 383–412), addressing the attacks of those seeking to censor the book, he suggested that the main reason for the work's sudden popularity may have been the long "Essay on Charity, and Charity Schools" (1, 253–322), which he had appended to the second printing of the original 1723 edition. There Mandeville criticized the charity schools as ineffectual in their expressed goal of disseminating morality, and as pernicious too, since they encouraged a weakening of the established hierarchies of power, obedience and knowledge upon which the British state rested. He argued that proponents of the schools in the Societies for the Reformation of Manners were nothing but smug hypocrites who supported the schools solely in order to indulge their appetite for praise. Contemporaries expressed outrage at the "Essay"'s brutal assertions that in free and prosperous nations the labor force must be kept poor and ignorant if its members are to be efficiently exploited in heavy, dirty and low-wage work; and that, in direct consequence, the lower orders could no longer be treated within the confines of an inherited morality of protection and obedience. It was a potentially disastrous, as well as hypocritical, mistake, Mandeville thought, to accept, let alone encourage, a paternalist view of the laboring poor as quasi-familial dependents of the social superiors charged with their governance. Laborers were little more than drones in a prosperous hive, creatures whose unrelieved drudgery was a necessary, and thus acceptable, requirement for continued prosperity.

Mandeville's conception of the laboring poor was hardly novel. He allied himself with contemporary economic writers, particularly merchants, who stressed the importance of the dynamics of consumption based on expansion of demand in the domestic market, and who realized that levels of employment, rather than stores of precious metals, held the key to national prosperity (1, 197).[34] Mandeville seemed fully to accept the opinion that rich countries would be pulled into a cycle of decline unless their goverments enforced low wages by

---

[34] On these writers see Jacob Viner, *Studies in the Theory of International Trade* (New York: Harper and Row, 1937), pp. 52–57, and 117–118, and William Letwin, *The Origins of Scientific Economics* (London: Methuen, 1963), pp. 59–60 and 198–201.

way of compelling the poor to industry (1, 286–287) – an already old-fashioned view of wealth creation which was attacked by Josiah Child, Charles Brewster, Nicholas Barbon, Dudley North, and John Cary before *The Fable* was published, and by Defoe amongst others soon after.[35] Even so implacable a foe of extravagance and licentiousness as Mandeville's enemy Bishop Berkeley flatly stated in *The Querist* that "the creating of wants is the likeliest way to produce industry in a people."[36] For unlike the elites to which his argument was directed, and the abstract "man" whose passions *The Fable* anatomized, Mandeville claimed in *The Fable*'s second edition of 1723 that the poor are "seldom powerfully influenced by pride and avarice" to exert themselves (1, 194 and 242), and that they would only work from "immediate necessity" (1, 192), usually preferring to remain idle in the most rudimentary conditions rather than work to improve their comforts. Bound by customary habits and natural sloth, laborers would attempt to support themselves in conditions of bare subsistence by downwardly adjusting their working hours to any rise in wages. "Every Body knows," he thought, "that there is a vast number of Journey-men Weavers, Tailors, Cloth-workers, and twenty other Handicrafts; who, if by four Days Labour in a Week they can maintain themselves, will hardly be persuaded to work the fifth" (1, 192). Low wages supplemented by ignorance would thus have a three-fold beneficial effect: individual employers would retain more money to meet their other costs, Britain would gain a competitive advantage for its relatively cheap finished products in the export trade, while enforced material desperation would insure a continuing supply of hands.

Now although the "Essay" on the charity schools was the most likely cause of *The Fable*'s prosecution and Mandeville's sudden rise to fame, none of its central arguments about the laboring poor, it should be noted, was seen to be of importance by Hutcheson, Butler, Hume, Rousseau or, as we shall see, Adam Smith.[37] Indeed, by the mid-

[35] See, amongst a large literature, Charles Wilson, "The Other Face of Mercantilism," in D.C. Coleman (ed.), *Revisions in Mercantilism* (London: Methuen, 1969), pp. 118–139, and Daniel Defoe, *A Plan of the English Commerce*, in J.R. McCulloch (ed.), *A Select Collection of Scarce and Valuable Tracts on Commerce* (London: Harrison, 1859), p. 109 and *passim*.

[36] See T.W. Hutchinson, "Berkeley's *Querist* and its Place in the Economic Thought of the Eighteenth Century," *British Journal for the Philosophy of Science* 4 (May 1953–February 1954), pp. 52–77.

[37] They did, however, receive the approval of Voltaire. See A. Owen Aldridge, "Mandeville and Voltaire," in Irwin Primer (ed.), *Mandeville Studies* (The Hague: Nijhoff, 1975), pp. 142–156.

eighteenth century the European discussion of work and workers began to be placed on a new conceptual footing as the intimate relationship between high wages, worker motivation and commercial prosperity began to be better understood.[38] And even in the immediate wake of the scandal initiated by the charity school "Essay," Bluett, among others, recognized that Mandeville's objections to the schools contradicted some of his own stated principles. There were obvious, indeed Mandevillian, reasons to think that able-bodied laborers wished to better themselves, and that governments exercising the intrusive powers Mandeville had advocated in order to discipline the poor would only damage the economy, in which "trades and Employments will take their natural Course where Profit directs them."[39]

As was the case with Butler's important attack upon *The Fable's* anatomy of self-love, Mandeville carefully responded to some of his critics of the 1720s by revising his original arguments, while never openly conceding in the process that the efforts of these critics held the slightest importance for him. Thus, solely from the text of *The Fable*, it is impossible to judge the degree to which Mandeville was impressed by the telling criticisms made against the "Essay" on charity schools. Yet it nevertheless remains the case that Mandeville neither repeated nor enlarged upon his first thoughts about labor after 1723, save to mock the supposedly bruised moral sensibilities of those who sought to proscribe his work. Moreover, in *The Fable's* second volume of 1728, not only did Mandeville dispense with any further discussion of the necessity of low wages or continue to denegrate the capacities of the poor, but he in fact looked to the natural proclivities of "none but Men of ordinary Capacity" as a critical source of economic progress. Contemplating the classical Epicurean (and Baconian) figure of a ship at sea, as Hume was later to do in an identical context,[40] Mandeville speculated about the processes by which such technical perfection could have been attained.

[38] See, for example, Edgar S. Furniss, *The Position of the Laborer in a System of Nationalism* (New York: Houghton Mifflin, 1920); A.W. Coates, "Changing Attitudes Toward Labour in the Mid-Eighteenth Century," *Economic History Review* 2nd series, 11, 1 (1958), pp. 35–51; Richard C. Wiles, "The Theory of Labour in Later English Mercantilism," *Economic History Review* 2nd series, 30, 1 (1968), pp. 113–126, and E.J. Hundert, "The Achievement Motive in Hume's Political Economy," *Journal of the History of Ideas* 35 (1974), pp. 139–143.

[39] Bluett, *Enquiry*, p. 181. See, too, William Hendley, *A Defence of the Charity Schools* (London, 1725), pp. 27–28.

[40] David Hume, *Dialogues Concerning Natural Religion*, ed. J.V. Price (Oxford University Press, 1976), p. 167.

There are many Sets of Hands in the Nation, that, not wanting proper Materials, would be able in less than half a Year to produce, fit out, and navigate a First-Rate [Man of War]: yet it is certain, that this Task would be impracticable, if it were not divided and subdivided in a great Variety of different Labours; and it is certain, that none of these Labours require any other, than working Men of ordinary Capacities. (II, 142)

Even in rudimentary societies,

if one will wholly apply himself to the making of Bows and Arrows, whilst another provides Food, a third builds Huts, a fourth makes Garments, and a fifth Utensils, they not only become more useful to one another, but the Callings and Employments themselves will in the same Number of Years receive much greater Improvements, than if all had been promiscuously follow'd by every one of the Five. (II, 284)

These examples served further to enhance the aggressively evolutionary perspective Mandeville had adopted by 1728. They further emphasize the point that "we often ascribe to the Excellency of Man's Genius ... what is in Reality owing to ... the experience of many Generations, all of them very little differing from one another in natural Parts and Sagacity" (II, 142), But in contrast to his earlier claim that "what we call Evil in this World ... is the ... solid Basis, the Life and Support of all Trades and Employments without Exception" (I, 369), in *The Fable*'s second volume Mandeville makes no reference at all to vice when discussing the division of labor. Indeed, without any moral comment, he simply treats material improvement as the necessary consequence of the unplanned development of specialized skills, a process so ubiquitous, as he later wrote in "Honour," that one could recognize its profound effects even in the organization of the Roman Church.[41]

This argument about the centrality of the division of labor Mandeville made specifically in support of an original sociological thesis, that is, that the progress of society depends upon increasing specialization, which in turn is the natural outgrowth of political stability. The entry in *The Fable*'s index of 1728, "Labour, The usefulness of dividing and subdividing it" (II, 335), directs the reader precisely to this point: "When once Men come to be govern'd by written Laws, all the rest comes on a-pace," since "[n]o number of Men, when once they enjoy Quiet, and no Man needs to his Neighbour, will be long without learning to divide and subdivide their Labour" (II, 283–284). An

---

[41] Mandeville, *Honour*, pp. 102–103.

intensified division of labor is at once the axial productive characteristic of economically advanced communities, Mandeville claimed, and a wholly natural concomitant of civilization itself. Moralists who drew their principles from the civic tradition's ideal of self-sufficiency saw in commercial specialization a threat to personal integrity and the power of the full citizen to command his landed dependents. Mandeville countered with the startling claims that civilized living and commercial opulence entailed the liberation of large numbers of persons from previous martial dependencies, encouraged social mobility because of the increase of monied wealth at the expense of landed power, and simultaneously brought forth *new* mutual dependencies fostered by the progress of the division of "Art into many Branches" (II, 284).

When he first addressed the pretensions of London moral reformers in the charity school "Essay," Mandeville embraced the conventional view that the consumer demand of the masses was and would continue to be economically insignificant, and that enforced subsistence living amongst the poor could therefore be regarded as an economically benign instrument of social discipline. But he abandoned this view by 1728 in the face of trenchant criticism, shifting his focus to the necessary connections between the development of the division of labor and the growth of civilization. There is good reason to think that Mandeville only provisionally adopted conventional presumptions about the laboring classes in the "Essay" on charity schools for the immediate polemical purpose of heaping scorn on the pretensions of his enemies, the London moral reformers. For even in *The Fable*'s first volume of 1723, Mandeville's primary economic insight was that wealth creation in commercial society depended upon the "emulation and continual striving to out-do one another." While he here mainly referred to the conspicuous consumption of monied elites, Mandeville clearly intended to encompass all persons throughout the social hierarchy, beginning with "the poorest Labourer's Wife." His main example is worth quoting in full:

The poorest Labourer's Wife in the Parish, who scorns to wear a strong wholesome Frize, as she might, will half starve herself and her Husband to purchase a second-hand Gown and Petticoat, that cannot do her half the Service; because forsooth, it is more genteel. The Weaver, the Shoemaker, the Tailor, the Barber, and every mean working Fellow, that can set up with little, has the Impudence with the first Money he gets, to Dress himself like a Tradesman of Substance: The ordinary Retailer in the clothing of his Wife, takes Pattern from his Neighbour, that deals in the same Commodity by Wholesale, and the Reason he gives for it is, that Twelve Years ago the other had no bigger a Shop than himself. The Druggist, Mercer, Draper, and other creditable Shopkeepers can find no difference between themselves and Merchants, and therefore dress and live like them. The Merchant's Lady, who cannot bear the Assurance of those Mechanics, flies for refuge to the other End of the Town, and scorns to follow any Fashion but what she takes from thence. This Haughtiness alarms the court, the Women of Quality are frighten'd to see Merchants Wives and Daughters dress'd like themselves: this Impudence of the City, they cry, is intolerable; Mantua-makers are sent for, and the contrivance of Fashions becomes all their Study, that they may have always new Modes ready to take up, as soon as those saucy Cits shall begin to imitate those in being. The same Emulation is continued through the several degrees of Quality to an incredible Expence, till at last the Prince's great Favourites and those of the first Rank of all, having nothing else left to outstrip some of their Inferiors, are forc'd to lay out vast Estates in pompous Equipages, magnificent Furniture, sumptuous Gardens and Princely Palaces.

To this Emulation and continual striving to out-do one another is owing, that after so many various Shiftings and Changings of Modes, in trumpting up new ones and renewing old ones, there is still a *plus ultra* left for the ingenious; it is this, or at least the consequence of it, that sets the Poor to Work, add Spurs to Industry, and encourages the skilful Artificer to search after further Improvements. (I, 129–130)

Some critics may have merely feigned outrage at Mandeville's hackneyed assertion in the "Essay" on charity schools that continued British prosperity depended upon the exploitation of the laboring poor. Yet most of *The Fable*'s first readers, and many others during the next generation, found this foundational claim about the crucial social significance of hyper-consumption and luxury spending both conceptually shocking and morally suspect. For if true, they sensed, the unbridled emulative propensities Mandeville described posed a threat to social stability. In such a society, Henry Fielding warned, in a virtual paraphrase of *The Fable*'s remarks, "while the Nobleman will emulate the Grandeur of a Prince and the Gentleman will aspire to the proper state of a Nobleman, the Tradesman steps from behind his Counter into the vacant place of the Gentleman. Nor doth the confusion end there: It reaches the very Dregs of the People, who aspire still to a degree beyond that which belongs to them."[42]

---

[42] Henry Fielding, *Enquiry into the ... Recent Causes of the ... Increase of Robbers*, in *Complete Works*, II, p. 783.

Seen as an excess every bit as fatal to individuals as to states, luxury was an established pejorative designator belonging both to the vocabularies of morals and politics during much of the early eighteenth century. The term retained its strong association in historical memory with the licentiousness, corruption and political enfeeblement of great states, most notably the Roman Republic.[43] Moreover, Mandeville's contemporaries had before their eyes two competing and exclusive models of modern economic history: the frugal Dutch as leaders in economic growth and the luxurious Spaniards (or most recently, the French) as exemplars of decadence accompanied by material decline. From the beginning of his literary career, Mandeville strove to subvert these defective notions about the association between inherited moral ideals and the requirements of economic advance by offering a competing account of the relationship of prosperity to social hierarchies of wealth and power in societies as diverse as republican Holland, absolutist France, and the limited monarchy of contemporary Britain. His model stressed that man was a consuming animal with boundless appetites to emulate the "Gayety and Fickleness" of the opulent, to follow the ephemeral conformity dictated by fashion and to seek social promotion through spending.

Mandeville made two important, linked claims about luxury consumption, each following from the historical thesis that if we "look back on old *Greece*, the *Roman* Empire, or the great Eastern Nations, that flourish'd before them, and we shall find, that Luxury and Politeness ever grew up together, and were never enjoy'd asunder" (II, 147). Here he developed his original discussion of modern consumption in *The Fable*'s Remark L (I, 107–123), drawing for the purpose on Bayle's observation that luxury enriches a nation through the promotion of avarice, the particular vice which encourages the manufacture and circulation of goods.[44] This argument had as its primary targets the moralizing arguments of writers like Addison, Boyer and Shaftes-

---

[43] Ellen Ross, "Mandeville, Melon and Voltaire: The Origins of the Luxury Controversy in France," *Studies on Voltaire and the Eighteenth Century* 155 (1976), pp. 1897–1912; John Sekora, *Luxury: The Concept in Western Thought, Eden to Smollett* (Baltimore: John Hopkins University Press, 1977), especially pp. 80–88, 113–115 and 138; André Morize, *L'Apologie du luxe au XVIIIe siècle et 'Le Mondaine' de Voltaire* (Geneva: Slatkine Reprint, 1970); and Hans Kortum, "Frugalité et luxe à travers la querelle des anciens et des modernes," *Studies on Voltaire and the Eighteenth Century* 56 (1987), pp. 705–775.

[44] Pierre Bayle, *Continuation des pensées divers*, in *Œuvres diverses de Pierre Bayle*, ed. Pierre Des Maizeaux (The Hague, 1717–1731), III, Section 124, p. 361, and Bayle, "Ajax, fils de Telamon B," in *Dictionnaire*.

bury, for whom the polished habits of the expanding urban elites they sought further to refine were a vital aspect of improvement and civilization. Leisured ways of polished intercourse, so they argued, were indispensable to an expanding society, in which tolerant sociability and broadened views are the necessary concomitants of material growth. Mandeville challenged these claims. He did so not by attempting to show them as strictly false, but by exposing to view what he argued was the essential psychological reality of opulent societies – that they were driven by excess rather than moderation, and characterized by extravagance masquerading as refinement. Not only did all "great societies" rest upon "increased wants," but the satisfaction of these wants and the consequent creation of others in their stead constitute the propulsive mechanism for change in the interdependent domains of fashion and morals. Since "our Liking or Disliking of things chiefly depends on Mode and Custom, and the Precepts and Example of our Betters and such whom one way or other we think to be Superior to us,"

In Morals there is no greater Certainty [than] . . . What Men have learned from their Infancy enslaves them, and the Force of Custom warps Nature, and at the same time imitates her in such a manner, that it is often difficult to know which of the two we are influenced by. (I, 330)

Mandeville did not simply give voice to the much-repeated Latin proverb that "fashion is more powerful than any tyrant." Nor, in pointing to an intimate connection between moral habits and prevailing tastes, did he wish merely to make satirical sport of philosophers like Locke, here in agreement with the main stream of British and continental Protestant casuistry, who regretted that "the greatest part" of mankind "govern themselves chiefly, if not solely, by the Law of Fashion" rather than "the unchangeable Rule of Right and Wrong, which the Law of God hath established."[45] Instead, Mandeville proposed a radical thesis, systematically elaborated in "A Search into the Nature of Society" (I, 323–370), that the history of the civilizing process offered conclusive evidence for thinking that moral reasoning itself was a species of fashion and, like habits of dress, a dependent feature of the search for esteem.

Mandeville's second significant point about luxury was that hyper-consumption should properly be understood as the direct conse-

---

[45] John Locke, *An Essay Concerning Human Understanding*, ed. Peter Niddich (Oxford: Clarendon Press, 1975), II.28.12.

quence of social processes. The conventional moral condemnation of supposedly superfluous material indulgence rested, he argued, upon a patent absurdity – a point neatly expressed in *The Fable*'s parable of small beer, repeated in *A Letter to Dion*,[46] where a community is supposed in which

the chief moral evil ... was Thirst, and to quench it, a Damnable Sin; yet they unanimously agreed, that Every one was born Thirsty more or less. Small Beer in Moderation was allow'd to All; and he was counted an Hypocrite, a Cynick, or a Madman, who pretended that One could live together without it; yet those who owned they loved it, and drank it to Excess, were counted Wicked. All this while the Beer itself was reckon'd a Blessing from Heaven, and there was no Harm in the use of it; all the Enormity lay in the Abuse, the Motive of the Heart, that made them drink it. He that took the least Drop of it to quench his Thirst, committed a heinous Crime, while others drank large Quantities without any Guilt, so they did it indifferently, and for no other Reason than to mend their Complexion. (I, 235)

Luxury, Mandeville sought to show, effectively captures the behavior of individuals possessed of the ability by virtue of their command of wealth to satisfy the desires they share with others. In commercial societies these desires are decisively shaped by newly liberated emulative propensities which may be (temporarily) satisfied through the acquisition of socially esteemed goods. If correct, Mandeville recognized, this understanding of consumption would immediately throw into question the semantic force of "luxury" as conventionally understood, a point which revolted Rousseau,[47] and one Diderot emphasized to readers of the *Encyclopédie* when he proposed "luxury" as the term best exemplifying the abuses to which words have commonly been put.[48] In conventional usage, Mandeville wrote, luxury is "that not immediately necessary to make Man subsist" (I, 107). "It increases Avarice and Rapine: And where they are reigning Vices, Offices of the greatest Trust are bought and sold; the Ministers that should serve the Publick ... corrupted, and the Countries every Moment in danger of being betray'd to the highest Bidders: And lastly, that it effeminates and enervates the people, by which the Nations become an easy Prey to the first Invaders" (I, 135). But, he added,

If you tell me, that Men may make use of all ... [supposedly luxurious] things with Moderation, and consequently that the Desire after them is no Vice,

---

[46] Mandeville, *A Letter to Dion*, pp. 25–26.
[47] Jean-Jacques Rousseau, *Discourse on the Origins of Inequality*, note i.
[48] Diderot, "Encyclopédie," in *Encyclopédie*, IV, pp. 635–636.

then I answer, that either no Degree of Luxury ought to be called a Vice, or that it is impossible to give a definition of Luxury, which Everybody will allow to be a just one ... [for] if once we depart from calling every thing Luxury that is not absolutely necessary to keep a Man alive, then there is no Luxury at all. (1, 108)

Indeed,

if we are to abate one Inch of this Severity [in the definition of luxury], I am afraid we shan't know where to stop. When People tell us they only desire to keep themselves sweet and clean, there is no understanding what they would be at; if they made use of these Words in their genuine proper literal Sense, they might soon be satisfy'd without much cost or trouble, if they did not want Water; But these two little Adjectives are so comprehensive, especially in the Dialect of some Ladies, that no body can guess how far they may be stretched. (1, 107)

Francis Hutcheson immediately recognized that Mandeville's primary intention was to displace the conventional meaning of luxury, as well as terms like intemperance and pride, in public discourse[49] – meanings which, for Hutcheson, were foundational moral concepts. Luxury, he said, was properly to be defined as

an excessive desire or use of the lowest pleasures as is consistent with discharging the offices of life ... Luxury ... lavishes out men's fortunes, and yet increases their keen desires, making them needy and craving. It must occasion the strongest temptations to desert their duty to their country, whenever it is inconsistent with pleasure: it must lead the citizens to betray their country, either to a tyrant at home, or to a foreign enemy ... With the luxurious generally everything is venal.[50]

In defending Shaftesbury, Hutcheson objected to Mandeville by insisting that any "man of good sense" would immediately recognize when a superfluity of consumption would be injurious to his health or fortune.[51] He perfectly expressed the ambivalent and, in Mandeville's view, essentially incoherent contemporary attitudes to prosperity that *The Fable* intended to expose. Mandeville's most insistent scorn was always reserved for those, like Shaftesbury and Hutcheson, who sought to moralize prosperity by claiming that excessive consumption, symbolizing a loss of independence and self-control, was nothing beyond the character defect of a socially insignificant minority within progressive and polished societies.

---

[49] Francis Hutcheson, *A Collection of Letters*, in *Collected Works*, pp. 146 and 386.
[50] Hutcheson, *A Short Introduction to Moral Philosophy* (Glasgow, 1747), in *Collected Works*, IV, p. 321. [51] Hutcheson, *A Collection of Letters*, p. 385.

Hutcheson focused on this point in order to refute Mandeville's main contention about the beneficial effects of vice, envisioning the common-sensical possibility that the development and expansion of commercial exchanges could be founded upon socially moderate and, in Hutcheson's view, virtuous behavior. He offered the counter-example of how the beer industry would be better supported by people who drank in moderation, and who therefore had a normal life expectancy, than the immoderate imbibers suggested by Mande-ville's parable, who ran the risk of dying young.[52] What this criticism missed or, more likely, what Hutcheson wished to elide, was Mande-ville's pointing out the absurdity of *any* strict definition of luxury, and thus of moderation, in which consumption above the level of subsis-tence could be considered an indulgence, and therefore vicious. Furthermore, Mandeville had already anticipated and roundly dis-missed the heart of Hutcheson's argument when he maintained that even a looser definition of luxury than the one inherited from classical and Christian ethics would offer no conceptual advantage in under-standing the moral implications of large populations living in societies characterized by rapidly increasing levels of consumption. A more lax and apparently reasonable standard of moderate behavior would serve merely to rescue rhetorical space for the hypocritical jeremiads of traditional strict moralists – precisely the persons from whom both Shaftesbury and Hutcheson wished to distance themselves.

Mandeville stuck fast to his initial paradox, first developed in "A Search Into the Nature of Society": the establishment of morality was conventional; and without a precise, socially agreed-upon limit between necessity and luxury, it would have been quite impossible to imagine the establishment of self-denial as the foundation of moral virtue. Although this standard could be shown to be philosophically empty, it was nevertheless a socially necessary device, since without its foundation in a putatively objective language of morals society could not safely regulate the passions of its members through the promotion of shame.

The Fable's analysis of luxury, then, follows from a consistent adherence by Mandeville to his initial rigoristic definition of morality as self-denial, which he then supported with arguments and often examples that paralleled Bayle's, as some of his initial opponents like Bluett recognized. But Mandeville approached the problem of the

---

[52] Hutcheson, *Reflections on Laughter*, pp. 144–156.

morality of hyper-consumption from a different perspective when considering the *public* effects of immoderate and vicious behavior. He pointed out another paradoxical and counter-intuitive disjunction between private pleasures and public policies in modern states. As with his argument about the unexpectedly self-regulating and publicly beneficial workings of hypocrisy – when, of course, this vice was considered from the perspective of the community as a whole rather than from the point of view of the individual actor – Mandeville sought to demonstrate that in commercial as opposed to antique and static societies two distinct sets of criteria were required in order to evaluate the propriety of actions. Mandeville took a thoroughly conventional line in stressing the dangers posed by indulgence to the fortunes of individuals. As he put it, "[i]t is certain that the fewer Desires a Man has and the less he covets, the more easy he is to himself; the more active he is to supply his own Wants, and the less he requires to be waited upon, the more he will be beloved and the less trouble he is in a Family" (I, 355). But he then added forthwith that the personal tragedies born of imprudent spending were of no concern to the public at large, since from the point of view of commercial prosperity it was only the aggregate gain from the mobility of goods and money that counted, and that the power of states themselves was markedly increased by the acceleration of commercial exchanges, regardless of the immediate fortunes of any given participant in them. For, "let us be Just," he said, and ask

what Benefit can these things be, or what earthly good can they do to promote the Wealth, the Glory and the worldly Greatness of Nations? It is the sensual Courtier that sets no Limits to his Luxury; the Fickle Strumpet that invents new fashions every Week; the haughty Duchess that in Equipage, Entertainments, and all her Behaviour would imitate a Princess ... It is these that are the Prey and proper Food of a full grown Leviathan; or in other words ... we stand in need of the Plagues and Monsters I named to have all the Variety of Labour perform'd ... in order to procure an honest Livelihood to the vast Multitudes ... that are required to make a large Society: And it is folly to imagine that Great and Wealthy Nations can subsist, and be at once Powerful and Polite without. (I, 355–356)

The mobility of modern property as exemplified by the explosion of the luxury trades, Mandeville contended, had effectively amplified natural emulative propensities. These could no longer be moralized, as both traditional moralists and the followers of Shaftesbury hoped, but now had to be managed by governing elites. Unlike the ascetics of economically rudimentary ancient republics, or the culturally and materially primitive dependents of predatory feudal warriors, a commercial public could, under conditions of modern opulence, be the direct if unintended beneficiaries of personally disastrous private indulgence. On the level of the polity, moreover, the intemperance of the great, and of those who could afford to emulate them, in no way threatened public security by draining the courage and fortitude of a patriotic citizenry. The military fortunes of commercial states no longer depended upon the supposed virtues of ancient republics, "public spiritedness to one's ruin, and the contempt of death to any extreme," as Mandeville put it when defending the Whig regime. These "romantick notions" are now "laugh'd out of countenance by those who best understand the world,"[53] for the recent victories against France, solidified by the Peace of Utrecht, had amply demonstrated that the power of modern states like Britain no longer depended upon the martial virtues of citizens, but on the capacities of their treasuries to arm and support a professional soldiery.

Recent domestic and European history thus provided Mandeville with conclusive evidence of a transformation of both morals and public priorities, in the process of which the arms-bearing citizen whose stable holdings provided the foundation for his martial independence and civic identity was relegated to the realm of nostalgic romance. He argued that the social dynamics of what was commonly decried as morally degenerate luxury consumption in fact revealed the most startling example of public benefits issuing from private vice.

Required by their recently unshackled emulative propensities to live within the parameters of Mandeville's animating paradox, commercial moderns had unintentionally traversed an unbridgeable gulf, separating them irrevocably from an antique or Christian ethic of private restraint. Like Hume, following Hutcheson, a number of critics sought to deny Mandeville's paradox, since it is, as Hume said, "little less than a contradiction in terms, to talk of a vice, which is in general beneficial to society."[54] Yet *The Fable*'s argument was nevertheless purveyed on the continent by Montesquieu's friend and John Law's secretary Jean-François Melon, then by Montesquieu himself in *The Spirit of the Laws*,[55] and triumphantly by Voltaire in *Le*

---

[53] Mandeville, *Free Thoughts*, p. 285.

[54] Hume "Of Refinement in the Arts," in *Essays Moral, Political and Literary* (Indianapolis: Liberty Press, 1985), p. 280.

[55] See Jean François Melon, *Essai politique sur le commerce* (Bordeaux, 1734; English trans., 1735), Chapter 9, and Montesquieu, *The Spirit of the Laws*, VII.1 and IX.8.

Mondain and the entry "Luxe" in the *Philosophical Dictionary*. By mid-century a critically important segment of his European audience had been convinced that in modern commercial conditions, as Hume himself said, classical moral "principles are too disinterested and too difficult to support, [and] it is requisite to govern men by other passions, and animate them with a spirit of avarice and industry, art and luxury."[56] *The Fable*'s account of a public sphere transformed by wealth, in which the arts and sciences flourished, rapidly became conventional within a large segment of Enlightenment Europe. The assumption was as pivotal in Voltaire's account of the ascendancy of French culture in *La Siècle de Louis XIV* as in Gibbon's praise of aristocratic civility under the Antonines in *The Decline and Fall of the Roman Empire*. After Mandeville, even a pious Christian like Doctor Johnson could offer a defense of luxury on moral grounds by comparing its effects on the industry of the poor with those slothful habits induced by charity.[57] Men had to be governed by, in Mandeville's idiom, "playing" their passions against each other. Or as Hume put it in the conclusion of his essay, "Of Refinement in the Arts," "[b]y banishing *vicious* luxury, without curing sloth and an indifference to others, you only diminish industry in the state, and add nothing to men's charity or their generosity. Let us, therefore, rest contented with asserting, that two opposite vices in a state may be more advantageous than either of them alone."[58]

HOMO ECONOMICA AND HER DOUBLE

If Mandeville's striking claims about the causal relationship of abundance to refinement proved a critical point of departure in the Enlightenment's attempt to comprehend commercial modernity, *The Fable*'s discussion of luxury consumption also had embedded within it a particularly disturbing, because less easily moralized, implication regarding the psychological foundations of economic activity. In satirically trading upon the classical and Christian conceptions of luxury as a self-indulgent diversion from the exercise both of public and private responsibilities, Mandeville highlighted the paradox that the pursuit of leisure, rather than disciplined attention to work and

---

56 Hume, "Of Commerce," *Essays*, p. 263.
57 James Boswell, *Life of Johnson*, ed. R.W. Chapman, revised by J.D. Fleeman (Oxford University Press, 1970), pp. 755–756 and 947–948.
58 Hume, "Of Refinement in the Arts," *Essays*, p. 250. The essay was originally entitled "Of Luxury."

duty, was the energizing force of contemporary prosperity. He denied, in the words preached by an Anglican divine in 1700, that "Industry, Temperance, and Frugality are most inexhaustible mines, and make the certainest, if not the most ample Returns to the Publick; whilst Luxury, Prodigality and Idleness are continually preying upon it, and dayly tending to enervate by Impoverishing it."[59] At the same time, *The Fable*'s ideal economic agent was the person whose voracious self-seeking produces materially beneficial effects in commercial societies. It is apparent that Mandeville's actor is primarily motivated not by considerations of rational economic choice, but by inconstancy and whimsy – by the frivolity of those wants whose satisfaction energizes the economy.

This celebration of perfidious desire as a signal source of economic advance followed from *The Fable*'s thoroughgoing attack upon frugality in Remark Q (1, 181–198). Here the promotion of "prudent Oeconomy, which some people call *Saving*," Mandeville understands in terms of what we now call the fallacy of composition. While an obvious course of action from the point of view of distressed individuals seeking to improve their family's meagre fortunes, frugal practices have ruinous consequences when understood as a principle meant to govern the economy as a whole (1, 182). And when thoroughly practiced, as by the Spartans or Dutch, Mandeville views prudence and thrift merely as consequences of impending poverty, when the "Necessaries of life [are] scarce, and consequently dear" (1, 183). For "[f]rugality is like Honesty, a mean starving Virtue, that is only fit for small Societies of good peaceable Men, who are contented to be poor so they may be easy; but in a large stirring Nation you may soon have enough of it." "Prodigality," by contrast, "has a thousand Inventions to keep People from sitting still, that Frugality would never think of; and as this must consume a prodigious Wealth, so Avarice again knows innumerable Tricks to rake it together, which Frugality would scorn to make use of" (1, 104–105).

In his early journalism in *The Female Tatler*, Mandeville had drawn a portrait of a wealthy merchant, Labourio, ever diligent "in getting a penny." Labourio explained to a friend who wondered why he would

59 Matthew Heynes, *A Sermon for the Reformation of Manners Preac'd in St. Paul's Church in Bedford at the Assizes there held March the 15th 1700* (London, 1701), pp. 7–8, quoted in M.M. Goldsmith, "Liberty, Luxury and the Pursuit of Happiness," in Anthony Pagden (ed.), *The Languages of Political Theory in Early-Modern Europe* (Cambridge University Press, 1987), pp. 225–251, p. 236.

rise at five in the morning and pore over his accounts all day, rather than enjoy a life of luxury, that parsimony was his pleasure, and that the accumulation of money itself, rather than the goods it commands, was his reward. "Some never think themselves happy but in the enjoyment of a thing," Mandeville has Labourio say, "whilst the happiness of others consists in the Pursuit only ... I am sure that I enjoy the same satisfaction in the keeping of money, that a Sovereign has in being possessed of a power which he doesn't care to exert."[60] Labourio's point, emphasized in a following number of the journal by Mandeville's Lucinda, is that since all action results from the attempt to satisfy desire, and since the strength of different passions varies amongst individuals, anybody "is happy who thinks himself so."[61] No behavioral style can be deemed superior to any other, save on the grounds of the satisfactions it brings. In commercial societies, satisfactions derived from the habit of gain rather than the demands of vanity could be seen to engender the small but significant virtues of thrift and punctuality, a view later adopted by Hume and then Smith.[62] By the time he published *The Fable*, however, Mandeville had abandoned this defense of frugality, however emotionally and socially plausible. Rather than a virtue, he relocated frugality in opulent nations within an altered psychological context, that of the indolent drone with a strong fear of shame who embraces this supposed virtue merely in order to escape contempt. By contrast, the active man with the same share of vanity would do anything rather than submit to frugality's restraints, "unless his avarice forc'd him to do it" (II, 113). In attempting to devalue both moderation and self-discipline as either moral or economic virtues, Mandeville's attack upon frugality immediately placed *The Fable* within contentious streams of ideological dispute.

As Tawney long ago pointed out, what we have come to identify as a vital feature of Weber's thesis about the development of capitalism – the ascription to different confessions of distinctive economic orientations – was by the late seventeenth century something not far from a

---

[60] *The Female Tatler*, No. 108 (misnumbered as 105), 13 March–15 March, 1710. Compare the discussion of this character in M.M. Goldsmith, "Mandeville and the Spirit of Capitalism," *Journal of British Studies* 17 (1977), pp. 63–68, and Goldsmith, *Private Vices, Public Benefits*, pp. 137–139.

[61] *The Female Tatler*, No. 112 (misnumbered as 109) 22 March–24 March, 1710.

[62] See, David Hume, "Of Interest," in *Essays*, pp. 300–301, and Adam Smith, *The Wealth of Nations*, III.iv.3.

platitude.[63] Among writers concerned with the contrasts between different post-Reformation European societies it was almost a common form of argument, as it was a standard feature occurring repeatedly in works of religious controversy. Routinely, the extravagance of Catholic ruling elites was contrasted with the indolence of their subjects on the one hand, and, on the other, to the disciplined attention paid by Protestants to the mundane economic opportunities afforded by daily life in reformed communities. The same link can be found, as we have seen, in Sir William Temple's account of the United Provinces, in which he repeats identical views of the De la Courts,[64] as well as in Petty's *Political Arithmetic*.[65] In England particularly, the explanation of economic superiority by resort to the habits promoted by Protestant churches merged with establishment Whig celebrations of trade, notably in the homilies of Addison's Sir Andrew Freeport in *The Spectator*. As Defoe attested,[66] such assumptions easily meshed with Dissenting self-assertion and anti-Catholic animus after the Revolution of 1688. Clearly aware of these ideologically charged associations, Mandeville offered an explicitly competing explanation of the modern history of economic advance. "I protest against Popery as much as ever *Luther* and *Calvin* did, or Queen *Elizabeth* herself," he said in "A Search Into the Nature of Society," "but I believe from my Heart, that the Reformation has scarce been more Instrumental in rend'ring the Kingdoms and States that have embraced it, flourishing beyond other Nations, than the silly and capricious Invention of Hoop'd and Quilted Petticoats" (1, 356).

The association of luxury with women's inconstancy and the social power of female desire was ancient. It served most potently as a standard resource in classical republican as well as Augustinian-inspired accounts of political decline, where "effeminacy" and the luxury it entailed were standardly considered integral features of moral and political corruption.[67] In this discourse, the term "virtue" itself, as Mandeville pointed out, derived from the Latin *vir* – the disciplined manliness which distinguished a genuine man.[68] At

---

[63] R.H. Tawney, *Religion and the Rise of Capitalism* (1926) (New York: Harcourt, Brace, 1954), especially pp. 8–9, and 171–172.

[64] *The True Interest and Political Maxims of the Republick of Holland*, Part I, Chapter 4.

[65] William Petty, *Political Arithmetic* (London, 1690), pp. 25–26.

[66] Daniel Defoe, *Enquiry into Occasional Conformity* (London, 1702), pp. 18–19.

[67] Hanna Fenichel Pitkin, *Fortune is a Woman: Gender and Politics in the Thought of Niccolo Machiavelli* (Berkeley: University of California Press, 1984).   [68] *Honour*, iii–iv.

Chartres, luxury appears as a woman carrying the comb and mirror of cupidity and self-love, while in many other medieval and Renaissance depictions she holds a scepter to mark her omnipotence and sexual domination over men, several of which depictions place beneath her name the subtitle: "The Power of Woman."[69] By the late seventeenth century, however, the argument *ad feminam* against luxury consumption had significantly intensified, notably amongst economic writers who observed a rising demand by women for imported items, which these writers saw as hurting the home economy by draining money from the country as well as fostering lax morals.[70] The words "commerce," "intercourse" and "conversation" typically came to be employed equally as terms for social and sexual exchange, while the analysis of desire in the literature regarding the economy exposed sexuality as a visibly threatening and unstable feature of the market's liberation of private instinct,[71] which Dudley North called the "exorbitant appetites of man," while using women as his main examples.[72] Women were often pictured as capricious beings entirely devoted to traffic, to sexual and social human intercourse, to the unreflective and unending activities of shopping, and especially to fashion, which incessantly urges trivial shifts in custom and appearance.

By the time Mandeville added his comments on the social significance of female luxury in *The Fable*'s Remark T (I, 225–238), women made up a significant proportion of owners of Bank of England stock and subscribers to government loans.[73] They commanded earnings of their own, had access to a greater proportion of rapidly rising metropolitan incomes, and had established a burgeoning market for goods dominated by their own consumer choices, particularly for fashion accessories which, by the turn of the century, formed a significant segment of international trade.[74] An observer of British society could not help but notice the profusion of manuals of decorum, like John Gay's *Implements Proper for Female Walkers* (1716), specifically

---

[69] Sekora, *Luxury*, pp. 44–45.

[70] Joan Thirsk, *Economic Policy and Projects* (Oxford: Clarendon Press, 1978). p. 134.

[71] See J.G.A. Pocock, *The Machiavellian Moment*, pp. 452–453, and Pocock, "The Mobility of Property and the Rise of Eighteenth-Century Sociology," in *Virtue, Commerce and History* (Cambridge University Press, 1985), p. 114.

[72] Dudley North, *Discourses on Trade*, pp. 14–15.

[73] Dickson, *The Financial Revolution*, p. 256.

[74] Neil McKendrick, John Brewer and J.H. Plumb (eds.), *The Birth of a Consumer Society* (London: Hutchinson, 1983), Chapter 2, especially p. 23.

addressed to women with recently acquired disposable incomes. Both these "ladies" and their serving maids, Defoe observed in a pamphlet that went through at least five editions in 1725 alone, were thought habitually to exhibit in their costumes "an excess of pride and extravagance,"[75] a common literary observation which Mandeville noted in *The Fable* (I; 115; 117; 122) and Hogarth made part of eighteenth-century popular imagery. The heroine of Richardson's *Pamela* (1740), although the humble personal maid to a lady of the gentry, found that by assiduous application of the social niceties – dress, deportment, conversation – she was able to achieve her ambition of marrying into the family of her late mistress. Pamela's impenetrable virtue was not so attractive to the rakish Mr. B. as was her acceptability gained through the heightening of her natural virtues by applied intelligence. Clothes, Richardson knew, were the visible emblems of social standing in a society where fashions were no longer dictated at court, but were increasingly manipulated by industries catering to monied social ambitions. When Pamela dressed in her home-spun gown and petticoat with a plain muslin tucker, instead of the cast-off fine silk gown and lace which she had been given from her mistress's wardrobe, Mr. B. was literally unable to recognize his mother's servant, so accustomed was he to seeing her in clothes befitting a newly acquired gentility – a recurring theme in eighteenth-century novels and plays, where potential suitors mistake the mistress for the maid dressing up in fancy costume.

Thus feminized, attendance to fashion easily conveyed an image of masculine corruption, as in Fielding's portrait of the decadent Bellarmine in *Joseph Andrews*. Bishop Berkeley thought that the luxurious desires of "women of fashion … enslave[d] men to their private passions,"[76] while William Law, Mandeville's persistent adversary, claimed that "fictions of reason" and "fictions of behaviour" were leading characteristics of contemporary society. What is more extravagant, he asked,[77]

than to suppose a man racking his brains, and studying night and day how to fly? – wandering from his own house and home, wearying himself with climbing in every ascent, cringing and courting everybody he meets to lift him from the ground, bruising himself with continual falls and at last breaking his neck.

---

[75] Daniel Defoe, *Everybody's Business is Nobody's Business* (1725), in *Works* (London: Bohn's Classics, 1870), II, p. 504.   [76] Berkeley, *The Querist*, pp. 20 and 308–309.
[77] William Law, *A Serious Call to A Devout and Holy Life* (London, 1729), p. 119.

Such were the deplorable effects of a public sphere dominated by feminine whimsy, a zone in which, Law observed to his horror, women might buy "two hundred suits of clothes" in ten years.[78] The pursuit of wealth itself was hardly immune to these associations. When seen to be the province of sober mercantile interests, commerce, viewed as a source of national power, posed little ideological threat to established conceptions of social order. But when conceived as driven by fashion industries catering primarily to female tastes and women's liberated incomes, commercial exchange could appear radically transfigured. Trade was "a mystery, which will never be completely discovered or understood," Defoe wrote in his *Review* of 1706. "[I]t suffers convulsive fits, hysterical disorders, and most unaccountable emotions – sometimes it is acted by the evil spirit of general vogue; tomorrow it suffers violence from the storms and vapours of human fancy – a sort of lunacy in trade attends all its circumstances, and no man can give a rational account of it."[79] A generation later, in a work modelled on Defoe's *Compleat English Tradesman*, commerce was simply assumed to require "a fruitful Fancy, to invent new Whims, to please the Changeable Foibles of the Ladies," habits of capricious consumption which had penetrated the entire social body.

No man is ignorant that a Taylor is the Person that makes our Cloathes; to some he not only makes their Dress, but, in some measure, may be said to make themselves. There are Numbers of Beings in and about the Metropolis who have no other identical Existence than that what the Taylor, Milliner and Periwig-Maker bestow upon them. Strip them of these Distinctions, and they are a quite different Species of Beings; have no more Relation to their dressed selves, than they have to the Great Mogul, and are as insignificant in Society as Punch, deprived of his moving Wires, and hung up upon a Peg.[80]

Even Montesquieu, whose *Persian Letters* was one of the century's most prominent declarations of female rationality and moral insight,[81] took care in that work, and again in *The Spirit of the Laws*, to reassure his audience that while emulation and luxury consumption, powerfully promoted by women, were amongst the most effective spurs to prosperity, these arts of civilization in no way "make men effeminate,"[82] a claim John Brown forcefully denied in his famous *Estimate* of

---

[78] William Law, *A Serious Call*, p. 69.   [79] Daniel Defoe, *The Review* No. 3 (1706), p. 503.

[80] Richard Campbell, *The London Tradesman* (London, 1747), p. 191.

[81] E.J. Hundert, "Sexual Politics and the Allegory of Identity in Montesquieu's *Persian Letters*," *The Eighteenth Century: Theory and Society* 31, 2 (1990), pp. 99–113.

[82] Montesquieu, *The Persian Letters*, Letter CVI. See, too, *The Spirit of the Laws*, VII.1 and XIX.8.

1757. Condillac, perhaps alluding to *The Fable*, saw in the faculty of the imagination – "a bee that culls its treasure from the finest blooms of a flower bed" – the feminine principle lurking behind the confusions wrought by the liberation of fancy.

It is a flirtatious woman whose only desire is to please, and who draws on her fancy rather more than on her reason. Ever obliging, she adapts herself to our tastes, passions weaknesses. One she attracts and persuades by her saucy flirting manners, the other she surprises and astonishes by her grand and noble ways ... Although imagination changes everything it touches, it often succeeds when its meaning is merely trying to please.[83]

Mandeville's "petticoat" thesis achieves its full import when situated within these ideological contexts. In Britain particularly, Protestant, especially "vulgar Whig," associations of commerce with liberty,[84] were fed by complementary misogynist fears that were themselves exacerbated in the early eighteenth century by the explosion of the European luxury trades. In reducing to self-serving cant the attempt to moralize economic expansion by associating it with the frugal virtues of pious, independent citizens, Mandeville, while insisting that "Religion is one thing and Trade is another" (1, 336), forced his readers to confront the sheer power of their now unadorned avarice. As he put it, "nothing could make amends for the Detriment Trade would sustain, if all those of that Sex, who enjoy the happy State of Matrimony, should act and behave themselves as a sober wise Man could wish them" (1, 356). Indeed,

a considerable Portion of what the Prosperity of *London* and Trade in general ... and all the worldly Interest of the Nation consists in, depends entirely on the Deceit and vile Strategems of Women; and that Humility, Content, Meekness, Obedience to reasonable Husbands, Frugality, and all the Virtues together, if they were possess'd of them in the most eminent Degree, could not possibly be a thousandth Part so serviceable, to make an opulent, powerful, and what we call a flourishing Kingdom, than their most hateful Qualities. (1, 228)

Following upon this argument, Mandeville then transformed female desire from a localized force driving recent economic advance into a

---

[83] Condillac, "Where the Imagination Gets the Embellishments it Gives to Truth," in *Philosophical Writings of Etienne Bonnot, Abbé de Condillac*, trans. Franklin Philip (Hillsdale, New Jersey: Lawrence Erlbaum Associates, 1987), II, pp. 478–479.

[84] Duncan Forbes, "Sceptical Whiggism, Commerce and Liberty," in A.S. Skinner and T. Wilson (eds.), *Essays on Adam Smith* (Oxford: Clarendon Press, 1976), pp. 179–202.

general principle of social explanation. His acid observation that a great society depends upon "the abominable improvement of Female Luxury" (I, 356) was meant to and succeeded in challenging one of his audience's deepest assumptions about the moral integrity of its own aspirations. Luxury, as one of the characters in *The Tryal of the Lady Allurea Luxury* bemoaned, "is the Author of all the Books that have been published these last fifty Years in Favour of ... Gaming, Atheism, and every Kind of Vice, public as well as private." Indeed, "[s]he wrote the Fable of the Bees, and published it under the Name of Mandeville."[85] Mandeville endorsed precisely the behavior which horrified Law, observing that women, "when they have half a Score Suits of Clothes, Two or Three of them not the worse for wearing, will think it a sufficient Plea for new Ones, if they can say that they have never seen a Gown or Petticoat, but what they have been often seen in, and are known by" (I, 226). He took information of this kind as evidence for the provocative thesis "that the worst of Women and most profligate of the Sex did contribute to the Consumption of Superfluities, as well as the Necessaries of Life, and consequently were Beneficial to ... peaceable Drudges, that ... have no worse design than an honest Livelihood." Indeed, "the number of Hands employ'd to gratify the Fickleness and Luxury of Women" is nothing short of "prodigious" (I, 225–226). After incorporating these passages into his own defense of luxury, Helvétius nicely caught one of Mandeville's primary implications when he attributed to the euphemistically titled "femmes Galantes" a primary role in the promotion of public welfare.[86]

The Fable's ironic arguments about the liberating economic effects of female desire derived from the established libertine literary genre within which Mandeville first began to publish. In the so-called "Querelle des Femmes" of the previous century, paradoxical elaborations of women's supposed failings had as their intended purpose the satirical exploitation of conventional misogynist sentiments in order to offer a critique of institutions like marriage, coupled with a defense of women's abilities. Many were founded upon a materialist assumption that social expressions of sexuality were historically

[85] Anon., *The Tryal of the Lady Allurea Luxury* (London, 1757), pp. 40 and 52, quoted in James Raven, *Judging New Wealth: Popular Publishing and Responses to Commerce in England, 1750–1800* (Oxford: Clarendon Press, 1992), p. 173.   [86] Helvétius, *De L'Esprit*, Discourse II, 15.

conditioned phenomena.[87] In *The Virgin Unmask'd* (1709), as well as in his articles in *The Female Tatler* during the two following years, Mandeville exploited these conventions by speaking through female personae – one of whom, Lucinda, is "a student of medicine"[88] – in order to expose as exploitative contemporary prejudices against women. "The Men like wary Conquerors," one of his women says, "keep us Ignorant, because they are afraid of us, and that they may the easier maintain their Dominion over us, they Compliment us into Idleness, pretending those P[r]esants to be the Tokens of their Affection, which in reality are the Consequences of their Tyranny."[89] Mandeville sought to show how female avarice, inconstancy and ambition, now "at their height" as he put it,[90] were socially generated "vices" of opulent living rather than natural artifacts of femininity. He situated his main characters, like Mrs. Crackenthorpe in *The Female Tatler*, "the Lady who knows everything," as persons cognitively empowered by their sexually constituted social inferiority to voice pertinent truths to which men were blind. Lucinda brushes aside all moralized accounts of social intercourse by baldly insisting that money is "the only thing that standing by itself has any signification, to which all the vertues and good qualities are meer cyphers, that are never to be used but to advance the figure,"[91] a point whose informing principle regarding the illusions fostered by commercial life Fulvia articulated in *The Fable*, insisting that "no body can please my Eye that affronts my Understanding" (II, 33).

While Mandeville had no interest in arguing that women should have equal political rights, he thought the conventional view that women are more lustful than men because of a defect in their constitution – a view which he would have found not only in contemporary moralizing, but clearly asserted by Bayle[92] – to be physiologically absurd. "There is no Reason to imagine," as he said in

---

[87] Rosalie L. Colie, *Paradoxia Epidemica: The Renaissance Tradition of Paradox* (Princeton University Press, 1966), pp. 53–60 and 102–107. See, too, Gordon S. Vichert, "Bernard Mandeville's *The Virgin Unmask'd*,," in Irwin Primer (ed.), *Mandeville Studies* (The Hague: Nijhoff, 1975), pp. 1–10, M.M. Goldsmith, "'The Treacherous Arts of Mankind': Bernard Mandeville and Female Virtue," in M.M. Goldsmith and Thomas A. Horne (eds.), *The Politics of Fallen Man* (Exeter: Imprint Academic, 1986), pp. 93–114, and Carol J. Gibson, "Bernard Mandeville: The Importance of Women in the Development of Civil Societies," MA thesis, University of British Columbia, 1989.   [88] *The Virgin Unmask'd*, p. 123.
[89] *The Female Tatler* No. 88 (1 February 1710), p. 68.   [90] *The Virgin Unmask'd*, pp. 3–4.
[91] *The Virgin Unmask'd*, pp. 58–59.
[92] Pierre Bayle, *Pensées diverses sur la comète*, 2 volumes ed. A. Prat (Paris: Droz, 1939), II, pp. 79–80 and 82.

The Fable, "that Nature should have been more neglectful of them . . . and not have taken the same Care of them in the Formation of the Brain, as to the Nicety of the Structure, and superior Accuracy in the Fabrick, which is so visible in the rest of their Frame" (II, 173). Mandeville also found derisory the attempt by followers of Shaftesbury to moralize the supposed constitutional opposition between the sexes into a higher form of cosmic harmony, presenting society as an ordered moral whole, only apparently composed, as in Addison and Steele, of discordant parts. It was nothing but self-delusion to believe with Pope that

> Each loves itself, but not itself alone,
> Each sex desires alike, till two are one.
> Nor ends the pleasure with the fierce embrace;
> They love themselves, a third time, in their race.[93]

For Mandeville, conflict and contrivance, dissimulation and deception, are elemental and necessary features of polished social life. In sexual relations particularly, self-love never finds "the private in the public good," as Pope would have it. Rather, women, less attractive "naked and unenhanced" in the state of nature than men, quickly discover that they are able to augment their beauty by the use of artifice and ornament.[94] Since all human beings strive to emulate those whom they feel are superior, women are driven to dress above their stations and enthusiastically embrace the world of fashion as they compete with one another for men's attention (II, 123–125). Women have more pride than men, and efficiently exploit it, not because of their natures, but from an education which, especially amongst the higher ranks, at once puts a premium on virginity and coquettishness.[95] Women thus have a powerful, historically constituted interest in perfecting the arts of flattery, especially in the cultivation of devices linking sexual attraction with modesty (I, 63–69), and unnaturally maintaining their virginity at the expense of their mental health (I, 46). Engendered by the sexual division of labor, enhanced female pride and the need for the attentions of men combine to produce in modern conditions an almost insatiable desire for fashionable goods amongst women of all ranks.

Once unmasked, the "modesty" of virgins can properly be understood as "the Result of Custom and Education . . . the Lessons of it,

---

[93] Alexander Pope, *An Essay on Man*, Epistle III, lines 121–124.
[94] Mandeville, *The Virgin Unmask'd*, pp. 10–12. [95] *The Virgin Unmask'd*, p. 27.

like those of *Grammar*, are taught us long before we have occasion for, or understand the Usefulness of them" (1, 69; 72). Conversely, while "Men may take greater Liberty, because in them the Appetite is more violent and ungovernable" (1, 74–75), women, as bearers of children, are more in need of "good breeding" and the arts of dissimulation to achieve their socially specified ends. So while both sexes cultivate "politeness" to enhance, rather than abridge, their sensual pleasures (1, 73), the sexual marketplace mediated by modern habits of sociability, Mandeville argued, provides an occasion to reflect on market mechanisms themselves.

In *A Modest Defence of Publick Stews*, published shortly after the charge against *The Fable*'s publisher, and elaborating upon his comments on the function of prostitution in Remark H (1, 94–100),[96] Mandeville offered his fullest technical account of how vice may lead to public benefit. He proposed the establishment of public houses of prostitution in London and market towns, above all to allay male sexual desire and to reduce overall whoring. Mandeville would have the licensed public stews maintain healthy women, who would attract men, even without penalties designed to keep them away from other prostitutes, and by so doing protect respectable ladies from male lust. "As there is constantly in the nation a certain number of young men, whose passions are too strong to brook any opposition, our business is to contrive a method how they may be gratified, with as little expense of female virtue as possible."[97] But when his project is first launched, Mandeville expects a run upon the stews, which would involve too much neglect of private whoring, "the only nursery for our courtezans," since "the whole body of our incontinent youth, like a standing army, being employ'd in constant action, there cannot well be spar'd a sufficient detachment to raise the necessary recruits."[98] Thus, while it is in the public interest to discourage private prostitution, the demands of the market require that the ranks of privately debauched women be permitted at a level acceptable for continued recruitment into public houses.

Anticipating criticism, Mandeville then argued that even if the run on the stews should not be remedied by supplies of young women from

---

[96] Bernard Mandeville, *A Modest Defence of Publick Stews: Or an Essay upon Whoring as it is now Practis'd in these Kingdoms*, Written by a Layman (London, 1724). See too Richard I. Cook, "The Great 'Leviathan of Lechery': Mandeville's *Modest Defence of Public Stews* (1724)," in Irwin Primer (ed.), *Mandeville Studies* (The Hague: Nijhoff, 1975), pp. 22–33.
[97] Mandeville, *Publick Stews*, pp. 63–64.　　　[98] Mandeville, *Publick Stews*, p. 64.

private employment, the worst that would happen would be "a gradual relapse into our former state of private whoring; and this no farther than is just necessary to recruit the stews and thereby make them retrieve their former character." The debauching of more numbers of women than are strictly necessary to allow the stews to satisfy demand will make these public houses popular, thereby curtailing private whoring which, in consequence, "must be reduced so low that there will remain just a sufficient quantity to supply the stews; which is as low as in the nature of the thing is possible." While whoring would be diminished to the lowest level possible, ample scope for male sexual drives outside of marriage would nevertheless be accommodated. The mechanism of supply and demand alone would thus work to effect maximum public benefit or, as Mandeville says of his proposal, it "necessarily executes itself."[99]

Mandeville's wry but wholly unsatirical scheme for the licensing of prostitutes followed from and was meant to supplement his initial aim of exploiting the anxiety of his readers about the intrusion of vicious desire into the heart of prosperity. In the essay on *Publick Stews* he deliberately invoked culturally threatening images of unbridled male lust and the morally undecorated acceptance of its consequences. In *The Fable* he employed images of feminine instability, where fashion reigns and even merchants are imagined as so overcome by luxury that one might expect them to "walk along the street in petticoats" (I, 118). Mandeville combined an aggressive insistence that commercial modernity heavily depended upon female desire – upon both the "fickle strumpet" and the "haughty Dutchess" (I, 355), whose "Fickleness and Luxury" employ a "prodigious number of Hands" (I, 226) – with the unsettling observation that the technical operations of the market could be seen to govern even the most intimate aspects of civilized living. In so doing, he achieved some of the most disturbingly paradoxical of his purposes: to show first, that modern prosperity not only depended upon the emancipation of persons from their former political dependencies, but, equally important, upon the liberation of their self-regarding wants; and second, to show that the desires of these persons were rooted in the most elemental of passions, whose capricious expressions, while governable, were nevertheless the necessarily defining features of commercial society's occluded moral life. After Mandeville, particularly after the incorporation of *The Fable*'s

---

[99] Mandeville, *Publick Stews*, pp. 64–65.

primary arguments about luxury consumption into the heart of Enlightenment public discourse, any systematic defense of commercial society's moral legitimacy remained vulnerable to a Mandevillian critique of the substructure of viciousness and sublimated sexual license upon which it rested. This problem was nowhere more importantly confronted than in the work of Adam Smith.

CHAPTER 5

Imposing closure – Adam Smith's problem

At the time of his death in 1790, Adam Smith, the former professor of Moral Philosophy at the University of Glasgow, had begun to achieve international prominence as the author of *An Inquiry into the Nature and Causes of the Wealth of Nations* (1776). In this masterpiece, Mandeville's name appears only once in a critical aside about foreign trade, and Smith's frequent oblique allusions to *The Fable* would have been apparent only to those colleagues together with whom Smith confronted Mandeville's challenge to the moral legitimacy of commercial society.[1] When considering Smith's deliberate effacement of *The Fable*'s importance for his analysis of commercial modernity – a characteristic reticence, evident with regard to almost all of his other intellectual debts – it is tempting to assume that he was simply following in the footsteps of Condillac and Helvétius, who plausibly suspected that an open acknowledgement of Mandeville would prevent their own work from receiving a proper hearing. Marx, probably unaware that Dugald Stewart, Smith's former pupil and

---

[1] Amongst the considerable recent literature revising our understanding of Smith I have profited particularly from Donald Winch, *Adam Smith's Politics: An Essay in Historiographic Revisionism* (Cambridge University Press, 1978); Winch, "Adam Smith: Scottish Moral Philosopher as Political Economist," *Historical Journal* 35, 1 (1992), pp. 91–113; Istvan Hont and Michael Ignatieff, "Needs and Justice in the Wealth of Nations," in Hont and Ignatieff (eds.), *Wealth and Virtue: The Shaping of Political Economy in the Scottish Enlightenment* (Cambridge University Press, 1983), pp. 1–44; D.D. Raphael, "The Impartial Spectator," in A.S. Skinner and Thomas Wilson (eds.), *Essays on Adam Smith* (Oxford: Clarendon Press, 1975), pp. 82–99; Ralph Lindgren, *The Social Philosophy of Adam Smith* (The Hague: Nijhoff, 1973); Douglas Long, "Adam Smith's 'Two Cities,'" *Studies in Political Thought* 1, 1 (1992), pp. 43–60; Harvey Mitchell, "The Mysterious Veil of Self-Delusion in Adam Smith's *Theory of Moral Sentiments*," *Eighteenth-Century Studies* 20 (1987), pp. 405–421; Lucio Colletti, "Mandeville, Rousseau and Smith," in *From Rousseau to Lenin: Studies in Ideology and Society*, trans. John Merrington and Judith White (London: New Left Books, 1972), pp. 195–218, and the introductions to the Glasgow editions of Adam Smith, *The Theory of Moral Sentiments*, ed. D.D. Raphael and A.L. MacPhie (Oxford University Press, 1976), and *An Inquiry Into the Nature and Causes of the Wealth of Nations*, ed. A.S. Skinner, W.B. Todd and R.H. Campbell (Oxford University Press, 1976).

successor at Glasgow, had already revealed these connections,[2] seems to have held this view, noting with some relish in his discussion of the division of labor in *Capital* that

[t]he famous passage [on the division of labor in Book 1.i of *The Wealth of Nations*] ... which begins with the words, "Observe the accommodation of the most common artificer or day-labourer in a civilised and thriving country," etc., and then proceeds to depict what an enormous number and variety of industries contribute to the satisfaction of the needs of the ordinary worker, is copied almost word for word from the "Remarks" added by B. de Mandeville to his *Fable of the Bees, or Private Vices, Public Benefits*.[3]

Marx might well have added that Smith's appropriation of *The Fable*'s account of the division of labor, now fully documented by Smith's modern editors,[4] enabled him to argue with Mandeville against traditional-minded civic moralists, as well as his Scots contemporaries like Ferguson and Kames, who lamented the loss of the undivided personality which they believed had characterized the citizens of the ancient republics. Like Mandeville, Smith thought that only in "barbarous" societies could an individual be at once a producer and a "statesman, a judge, a warrior,"[5] while in the concluding Book of *The Wealth of Nations* he sought to demonstrate that the disintegration of the undivided personality was indissolubly wedded to the most dynamic features of commercial society, particularly its capacity adequately to provide for its poorest members.

It is important to remember that Smith began his literary career with a 1755 attack upon Rousseau in *The Edinburgh Review*, where he praises many of the insights of Mandeville's science of man into commercial society, while criticizing the "philosophical chemistry" and "rhetoric" by virtue of which "the principles and ideas of the profligate Mandeville seem in [Rousseau] to have all the purity and sublimity of the morals of Plato."[6] For Smith, confronting Rousseau's

---

[2] Dugald Stewart, *Account of the Life and Writings of Adam Smith, LL D.* (1794), in Adam Smith *Essays on Philosophical Subjects*, ed. I.S. Ross and J.C. Bryce (Indianapolis: Liberty Press, 1982), pp. 269–351, reported that Smith's account of the division of labor was derived from Mandeville's. In his *Lectures on Jurisprudence*, ed. R.L. Meek, D.D. Raphael and P.G. Stein (Indianapolis: Liberty Classics, 1982), VI.27, Smith uses Mandeville's ship example for the division of labor without attribution, while at VI.169 he criticizes Mandeville's views on foreign trade. See too Ronald L. Meek and Andrew S. Skinner, "The Development of Adam Smith's Ideas on the Division of Labour," *Economic Journal* 83 (1973), pp. 1094–1116.
[3] Karl Marx, *Capital*, I, p. 354 n.2.   [4] See the notes to *The Wealth of Nations*, I.i–2.
[5] *The Wealth of Nations*, v.i.a.1–20.
[6] Adam Smith, *A Letter to the Authors of the Edinburgh Review*, in *Essays on Philosophical Subjects*, ed. W.P.D. Wightman and J.C. Bryce (Indianapolis: Liberty Classics, 1982), p. 251.

picture of the development of civility and commerce as the last phase of a history of moral decline was the necessary preliminary to his qualified endorsement of competitive individualism in *The Theory of Moral Sentiments* (1759). Discussed after a preliminary account of Epicurus' morals, Mandeville is the only contemporary thinker aside from his greatly esteemed teacher Hutcheson that Smith considered at length.[7] Moreover, Smith ended his career with the sixth, 1790, edition of his treatise on morals, adding an "entirely new" treatment of the character of virtue,[8] which complemented his original consideration of the implications of Mandeville's "licentious system ... which once made so much noise in the world."[9] Smith's silence in *The Wealth of Nations* about his debt to Mandeville was thus not a sign of his rejection of the entirety of Mandeville's arguments about human motivations, or the bold assertion in *The Fable* that commercial society was paradoxical in the crucial sense that private vice and public benefits were indissolubly connected. On the contrary, following Mandeville, and then Hume's critical elaboration of Mandeville's argument, Smith claimed in the *The Theory of Moral Sentiments* that it was incontestable that self-interest is one among the very few passions that any genuinely scientifically committed investigator of morals could simply assume as the basis for action. In *The Wealth of Nations*, paraphrasing Cleomenes' remarks on "[t]he restless Industry of Man to supply his Wants, and his constant endeavours to meliorate his Condition" (II, 128), Smith asserted that "the desire of bettering our condition comes with us from the womb."[10] It was this outright acceptance of the heart of Mandeville's account of self-interest that led Smith to claim that howsoever "destructive" Mandeville's licentious system may appear due to *The Fable*'s "air of truth and probability which is very apt to impose upon the unskilful,"[11] the book's message "in some respects borders upon the truth."[12]

In contrast to virtually all of *The Fable*'s previous critics, most notably Hutcheson, Smith was never deeply concerned with the tangible licentiousness of Mandeville's conclusions. While, following

---

[7] *The Theory of Moral Sentiments*, VII.ii.4, "Of Licentious Systems." As the editors point out, in the first five editions of *The Theory of Moral Sentiments* Mandeville's name was coupled with La Rochefoucauld's, but Smith's actual exposition and criticism of "licentious systems" of ethics in this chapter were always confined to Mandeville's work.

[8] *The Theory of Moral Sentiments*, VI.   [9] *The Theory of Moral Sentiments*, VII.ii.4.3.

[10] *The Wealth of Nations*, II.iii.   [11] *The Theory of Moral Sentiments*, VII.ii.4.6.

[12] *The Theory of Moral Sentiments*, VII.ii.4.14.

Hume, he repeated Hutcheson's jibe that "some popular aescetic doctrines ... were the real foundations of this licentious system,"[13] Smith devoted almost no space in *The Theory of Moral Sentiments* to consider Mandeville's chosen examples of beneficent vice; did not, for he accepted as obvious the gist of *The Fable*'s maxim concerning the systematic connection between private vice and public benefit.[14] In fact, much of Smith's wider project follows from his attempt to confront head on the paradox Mandeville successfully advanced in his discussion of the unintended consequences of wholly self-regarding action. To this end, he incorporated as a principle in his own account of social history in *The Wealth of Nations* the discomforting fact that certain material and even political benefits (like the expansion of liberty) could not have been attained without accompanying disadvantages. Mandeville's argument from unintended consequences in this way inserted an irreducibly ironic dimension into Smith's discussion of human motivation. It provided him with a perspective eminently suited to the task of analyzing the impersonal and anonymous relationships that characterized commercial society. This was precisely Mandeville's point about the social consequences of the modern metropolis, understood as a commercial hub, and characterized by hidden and largely informal, rather than the direct dependencies of its feudal predecessor (1, 128); and it was just this point that Smith paraphrased without attribution, noting that the effect of "dress and equipage" on the opinions of others is the most potent of the "illusions of vanity" in great cities, where "obscure strangers ... most frequently attempt to practise it."[15]

Following Mandeville, Smith remarked on the utter moral vacuity of the "enormous and operose machines contrived to produce a few trifling conveniences" for the rich man, so that he may win the approval and admiration of his fellows, "but [which] leave him always as much, and sometimes more exposed than before, to anxiety, to fear, and to sorrow; to diseases, to danger, and to death."[16] Yet, he continued, breaking entirely with the Stoic critique of deception, whose most trenchant modern version he found in Rousseau,

it is well that nature imposes upon us in this manner. It is this deception which rouses and keeps in continual motion the industry of mankind. It is this

---

[13] *The Theory of Moral Sentiments*, VII.ii.4.3.   [14] *The Theory of Moral Sentiments*, VII.4.14.
[15] *The Theory of Moral Sentiments*, V.1.
[16] *The Theory of Moral Sentiments*, IV.i.8. Compare Mandeville's discussion of the "operose Contrivances" of the luxury trades in *Fable* I, 119.

which first prompted them to cultivate the ground, to build houses, to found cities and commonwealths, and to invent and improve all the sciences and arts ... which have entirely changed the whole face of the globe ... The rich ... consume little more than the poor, and in spite of their natural selfishness and rapacity, though they mean only their own conveniency, though the sole end which they propose from the labours of thousands whom they employ, be the gratification of their own vain and insatiable desires, they divide with the poor the produce of all their improvements. They are led by an invisible hand ... and thus without intending it, without knowing it, advance the interest of society, and afford means to the multiplication of the species.[17]

In accepting this profoundly disturbing moral reality, Smith placed himself on Mandeville's side of the dispute between strict Christian or classical ethics and the modern habits of civility which Rousseau had most influentially characterized as degraded. Yet he wished at the same time to resist the wider licentious implications of Mandeville's line of reasoning. Smith sought to show that while wealth and status are, as Mandeville argued, attributes which commonly receive respect and admiration, and serve as materially useful spurs to social action, unlike wisdom and virtue they do not merit our praise.[18] This Mandevillian context of Smith's attempt to provide stable moral principles with which to evaluate self-seeking in *The Theory of Moral Sentiments* and then in *The Wealth of Nations* is a consistent and prominent feature of his overall enterprise.

Smith strove to articulate a philosophical position related to Hume's naturalistic account of the development of morals and justice, but free of its starker utilitarian conclusions, and their obvious Mandevillian overtones. He accepted Hutcheson's conception of sympathy as the uniquely human capacity which enables moral judgement, but expressly differed from Hutcheson's view that, as he put it, self-love could not "be in any case a motive of virtuous action." Smith denied as contrary to our make-up, and therefore morally implausible, Hutcheson's claim that if any apparently benevolent action was motivated even by "a regard to the pleasure of self-approbation, to the comfortable applause of our own conscience," its merit was diminished or even extinguished.[19] In its place, he developed a line of argument first fully articulated by Butler, resting on the claim that a prudential regard for one's personal affairs could be a

---

[17] *The Theory of Moral Sentiments*, IV.i.10. See too, for an almost identical formulation, *The Wealth of Nations* IV.ii.9.   [18] *The Theory of Moral Sentiments*, I.iii.3.
[19] *The Theory of Moral Sentiments*, VII.ii.3.13.

virtue, and that it was possible to distinguish this virtue from what Mandeville insisted was unalloyed selfishness and therefore vice. Smith argues that the entire range of our actions, irrespective of whether we be prudent men, men of propriety, deeply benevolent or fully just, stems from a wide range of often mixed motives, and that this is most importantly true for virtuous action. These motives certainly include self-interest or, to use Mandeville's term, self-liking. But as opposed to Mandeville, motives of this kind are neither strictly anti-social nor perverse in Smith's account; rather, they are entirely natural, since "[e]very man, as the Stoics used to say, is first and principally recommended to his own care,"

and every man is certainly, in every respect, fitter and abler to take care of himself than of any other person. Every man feels his own pleasures and his own pains more sensibly than those of other people.[20]

Indeed, "self-command," the Stoic principle signifying the controlled, masculine properties of the citizen independent of fortune, and perhaps the most important element in virtuous behavior as Smith understands it,[21] presupposes self-love as a natural, ever-present property of human constitutions. For even "the most perfect knowledge of those rules [of prudence, justice and benevolence] will not alone enable [a man] to act in this manner: his own passions are very apt to mislead him ... The most perfect knowledge, if it is not supported by the most perfect self-command, will not always enable him to do his duty."[22] It is this disciplined ability, even more than "perfect knowledge" of one's duty, that enables this duty to be performed by men as we now often find them – self-regarding individuals involved in the self-interested negotiations which necessarily define commercial society. Smith's main, and strongly anti-Mandevillian, point is to emphasize that while, as he famously put it in *The Wealth of Nations*,[23] we may have no need of the benevolence of the butcher or baker when we appeal to his self-interest in selling us the goods he purveys for our dinner, we nevertheless retain the capacity, which can be improved if not perfected, to understand and morally evaluate his behavior. Smith's purpose was to argue, against Mandeville, that men exhibit the whole range of combinations of self-love and sympathy suited for engaging in a wide spectrum of possible

---

[20] *The Theory of Moral Sentiments*, vi.ii.i.i. [21] *The Theory of Moral Sentiments*, vii.iii.11.
[22] *The Theory of Moral Sentiments*, vi.ii.3.6. [23] *The Wealth of Nations*, i.ii.

forms of civil life, the pre-eminent philosophical historian of whose morals and manners Smith aspired to become. The primary object of his theory of morals is to show how self-interest, *mitigated* by sympathy and self-command, can result in prudent and sometimes beneficent actions, even, again against Mandeville, in the inescapably utility-maximizing exchange relationships of contemporary commercial societies.

Smith's understanding of social advance mirrors *The Fable*'s account of the communal function of pride. It relies heavily on vanity and competition for status to explain the workings of ambition, which always threatens to corrupt our moral sentiments by encouraging the mass of men to "worship" the rich and great, while neglecting the deserving poor.[24] Following Mandeville, he assumes that in modern conditions, "an acquisition of fortune is the means by which the greater part of men propose and wish to better their condition."[25] At the same time, Smith argued with Hume, and *pace* Mandeville, that deference and hierarchy are "natural" features of social life, providing a bedrock of stability even in highly mobile commercial societies.[26] Smith thought that the material aspirations of the great and powerful were nothing more than vain illusions, as the King of Epirus was long ago told by his favorite.[27] So in *The Wealth of Nations* he ridicules the claims of merchants to be seeking the public good, and the great lords of the late middle ages for destroying their own dominions by the scramble for baubles and trinkets, "fitter to be the play-things of children than the serious pursuits of men."[28] Smith's main objections to Mandeville lay in a different and, in his view, more fundamental realm. The main error in *The Fable*, he thought, was Mandeville's neglect of certain fundamental human capacities and the social practices built upon them. The most important of these practices, derived from our capacity for sympathy, is our distinguishing between desiring praise, for Mandeville the primary object of pride, and being praiseworthy, a category Smith thought fatally absent from Mandeville's moral theory, since

this desire of the approbation, and this aversion to the disapprobation of his brethren, would not alone have rendered [man] fit for that society for which he was made. Nature, accordingly, has endowed him, not only with a desire

---

[24] *The Theory of Moral Sentiments*, i.iii.3.   [25] *The Wealth of Nations*, ii.iii.
[26] *The Theory of Moral Sentiments*, iii.2–3 and vi.2.1.
[27] *The Theory of Moral Sentiments*, iii.3.31.   [28] *The Wealth of Nations*, iii, Book iv.

of being approved of, but of a desire of being what ought to be approved of; or of being what he himself approves of in other men. The first desire could only have made him wish to appear to be fit for society. The second was necessary in order to inspire him with the real love of virtue, and with the real abhorrence of vice. In every well-formed mind this second desire seems the strongest of the two. It is only the weakest and most superficial of mankind who can be much delighted with that praise which they themselves know to be altogether unmerited ... This self-approbation, if not the only, is at least the principal object, about which he can or ought to be anxious. The love of it is the love of virtue.[29]

Smith, in other words, regarded Mandeville's attempt to answer Butler's critique through the introduction of "self-liking" as a failure, and he thought that this failure vitiated *The Fable*'s primary moral argument because Mandeville was unable, even in *The Fable*'s second volume – which Smith studied with care – to provide a way adequately to explain the stark empirical fact that human beings quite regularly experience benevolent impulses, act upon them and, moreover, wish to be praised for these actions rather than their counterfeits.[30] In essence, Smith found that Mandeville failed to address what Butler had called the faculty of conscience. Just as he could not account for other-regarding feelings, in Smith's view Mandeville was blind to the transparent psychological reality that most men do in fact find themselves reflecting upon their desires and actions, and that these reflections quite regularly result in self-criticism, condemnation and feelings of guilt; result in these even where one's immoral desires are unknown to others, successfully gratified and then rewarded with praise.

In the course of his argument, Smith echoes Butler's remarks about the authority of conscience, "given us," he says, "for the direction of our conduct in this life." Our moral faculties "carry along with them the most evident badges of this authority, which strongly imply that they were set up within us to be the supreme arbiters of all our actions, to superintend all our senses, passions, and appetites, and to judge how far each of them was either to be indulged or restrained." These faculties, moreover, "judge [and] bestow censure or applause upon all the other principles of our nature."[31] Smith, however, sought to remedy what he took to be the deficiencies in Butler's (and Hutche-

---

[29] *The Theory of Moral Sentiments*, III.2.7–8.
[30] *The Theory of Moral Sentiments*, VI.1. See, too, *The Wealth of Nations*, Introduction, pp. 5–9.
[31] *The Theory of Moral Sentiments*, III.5.5–6.

son's) argument by providing the faculty of conscience with firm intersubjective foundations, introducing the figure of "the impartial spectator" to explain the source and the nature of a person's capacity to judge his own actions and properly evaluate his duties. Conscience, in this revision of Butler's view, emerges as the product of our relations with our fellows. As spectators we not only find ourselves judged by others, as we judge them, but "[w]e suppose ourselves the spectators of our own behaviour, and endeavour to imagine what effect it would, in this light, produce upon us." For "[t]his is the only looking-glass by which we can, in some measure, with the eyes of other people, scrutinize the propriety of our own conduct."[32]

Though conscience reflects the feelings of other spectators, Smith contends that it is nevertheless potentially free from partiality to oneself. Nor does conscience merely mirror public opinion, in Mandeville's account the supreme arbiter of our performances and the audience whose praise we require. For unlike the real spectator who seeks applause, Smith's imagined spectator is governed by an innate, wholly natural, desire for praiseworthiness, achieved by the man of self-command.[33] For Smith then, as against Mandeville, the theatricality of society, its morally threatening quality as a "masquerade,"[34] has been tamed. The impartial spectator is meant to offer a transcendent ideal of performance, contrasting the "indulgent and partial spectator" of *The Fable* to the Addisonian "indifferent and impartial spectator" of the *Theory of Moral Sentiments*. In Smith's view, we develop our conscience as members of an audience, training ourselves to meet the expectations of this audience of which we are a part. The impartial spectator, whose sensitivities are most often awakened by the presence of the real (outer) spectator, first reviews the responses of his audience – society – and then is able to judge its applause as either genuine or feigned. Spectatorship thus embodies the capacity for sympathy and independent judgement that enables men to adopt the perspective of impartiality, since natural sympathy is not a criterion but a capacity for our moral conduct. Again echoing Butler, but now in the less than naturalistic mode of which Hume disapproved, Smith concludes that since the commands of conscience – of the impartial spectator – "were plainly intended to be the governing principles of human nature, the rules which they prescribe are to be regarded as

---

[32] *The Theory of Moral Sentiments*, iii.i.5.   [33] *The Theory of Moral Sentiments*, iii.2.32.
[34] *The Theory of Moral Sentiments*, vii.ii.4.10.

the commands and laws of the Deity, promulgated by those vice-gerents which he has thus set up within us.''[35]

Smith, then, argued that the capacity for sympathy embodied in conscience is a condition which enables our continuing desire to evaluate our goals and wishes themselves as desirable or undesirable in the light of those moral concepts embedded in our constitutions and potentially brought to light in our interaction with others. Most importantly, as against Mandeville, he sought to show that a commitment to these ethical foundations in no way impedes a genuinely perspicuous account of commercial modernity. For once he established these principles, Smith employed them directly to confront the puzzle that while men, above all the animals, have continuing need of the assistance of their fellows, it is nevertheless vain to expect it to flow from their benevolence alone. In commercial society, sympathy, while active, was at its weakest. Here Smith developed Hume's (Mandevillian) argument about the self-interest and limited generosity which ironically fit men for social life.[36] Equally as important, he followed the line of reasoning that both he and Hume found laid out in its cynical and licentious form in *The Fable*, particularly Mandeville's 1728 elaboration of the paradoxical relationship between private vices and public benefits. "To expect," as Mandeville put it,

that others should serve us for nothing, is unreasonable; therefore all Commerce, that Men can have together, must be a continual bartering of one thing for another. The Seller, who transfers the Property of a Thing, has his own Interest as much at Heart as the Buyer, who purchases that Property; and if you want or like a thing, the Owner of it ... will never part with it, but for a Consideration, which he likes better, than he does the thing you want. Which way shall I persuade a Man to serve me, when the Service, I can repay him in, is such as he does not want to care for? No Body, who is at Peace, and has no Contention with any of the Society, will do anything for a Lawyer; and a Physician can purchase nothing of a Man, whose whole Family is in perfect Health. Money obviates and takes away all those Difficulties, by being an acceptable Reward for all the Services Men can do one another. (II, 349)

Smith used the same example, and for the same purpose, as had Mandeville in 1728 (II, 284) when he pointed out that even in a tribe of hunters or shepherds the man who is most dextrous at fashioning bows and arrows frequently exchanges these for cattle and venison,

---

[35] *The Theory of Moral Sentiments*, III.5.6.   [36] Hume, *Treatise*, III.ii.1–2.

"from a regard to his own interest, [and] therefore, the making of bows and arrows grows to be his chief business."[37] In agreement with Mandeville, Smith accepted the benefits associated with the desire to better one's condition by pursuing objects of vanity, the "few trifling conveniences" of material possessions[38] which men in commercial societies seek in order to win the approval of others.[39]

Smith thus refused to deny that when self-interest was connected with regard for public utility in judging social institutions, "selfish systems" like Mandeville's had an "appearance of probability."[40] But again, very much in the vein of Butler, he attacked Mandeville's argument (as he had criticized Hume's[41]) that self-interest was the primary human motive. Smith believed that he had established that his enlarged theory of sympathy, embodied in the notional person of the impartial spectator, had greater explanatory power because it was considerably more comprehensive in its ability to account for the widest range of actual human actions. Public utility might be the outcome of *any* well-functioning moral or economic system. Indeed, as Mandeville implied and Hume directly argued,

Society may subsist among different men, as among different merchants, from a sense of utility, without any mutual love or affection; and though no man in it should owe any obligation, or be bound in gratitude to any other, it may still be upheld by a mercenary exchange of good offices according to an agreed valuation.[42]

But the strict invocation of utility as the source of justice, and thus the rules governing social and commercial exchange was still, so Smith insisted, an inadequate explanation of how actual social outcomes were produced, since it neglected entirely to account for the self-awareness of social actors in their mutual engagements. Indeed, Smith thought that if, *per impossibile*, the Mandeville–Hume account of the utility of justice and morals were true, it would follow, contrary to all experience, that

Men, though sympathetic, feel . . . little for another, with whom they have no particular connection, in comparison with what they feel for themselves . . . they have it so much in their power to hurt him, and may have so many temptations to do so, that if this principle did not stand up within them in his

---

[37] *The Wealth of Nations*, i.ii. [38] *The Theory of Moral Sentiments*, iv.i.6–10.
[39] *The Theory of Moral Sentiments*, i.iii.2. [40] *The Theory of Moral Sentiments*, vii.iii.1.2.
[41] *The Theory of Moral Sentiments*, iv.i–ii. [42] *The Theory of Moral Sentiments*, ii.ii.3.2.

defence . . . they would, like wild beasts, be at all times ready to fly upon him; and a man would enter an assembly of men as he enters a den of lions.[43]

Convinced that he had defeated Mandeville's fundamental claim that opulence necessarily rested only upon competitive viciousness, Smith was then free to pay particular attention in the last edition of *The Theory of Moral Sentiments* to the Mandevillian temptations of short-sighted vanity and avarice which, particularly in commercial society, lead to "the corruption of our moral sentiments."[44] He recognized that

[i]t is from our disposition to admire, and consequently to imitate, the rich and the great, that they are enabled to set, or to lead what is called the fashion. Their dress is the fashionable dress; the language of their conversation, the fashionable style; their air and deportment, the fashionable behaviour. Even their vices and follies are fashionable; and the greater part of men are proud to imitate and resemble them in the very qualities which dishonour and degrade them. Vain men often give themselves airs of fashionable profligacy, which, in their hearts, they do not approve of, and of which, perhaps, they are really not guilty. They desire to be praised for what they themselves do not think praise-worthy, and are ashamed of unfashionable virtues which they sometimes practise in secret, and for which they have secretly some degree of real veneration. They are hypocrites of wealth and greatness, as well as of religion and virtue.[45]

Smith agreed with Mandeville (and Rousseau), not only that the pressures of the market encourage an endless search for novelty, but also that the effect of fashion on the opinions of others is the most potent of "the illusions of vanity" which infect commercial society. The rise of commerce could be seen to depend in the first instance upon perfidy and whimsy, since "merchants and artificers . . . in pursuit of their own pedlar principle of turning a penny" were quick to turn their self-regarding attention to the childishly vain desires of the great lords.[46] Yet Smith makes his most telling point about the tyranny of fashion when he adamantly denies the most morally unsettling features of Mandeville's "petticoat" thesis – epitomized in the High Enlightenment by Rousseau's association of commercial modernity's decadence with "the disorder of women."[47] Although regimes of style rather than substance characterize the feminine

---

[43] *The Theory of Moral Sentiments*, II.ii.3.4.   [44] *The Theory of Moral Sentiments*, I.iii.3 and VI.i.

[45] *The Theory of Moral Sentiments*, I.iii.3.7.   [46] *The Wealth of Nations*, III.iv.17.

[47] Rousseau, *Letter to M. d'Alembert on the Theatre*, p. 109. See, too, *Emile*, pp. 358–359, 369 and 397 on how easily women lead men into dissipation, frivolity, inconstancy and corruption.

domains of "gaiety,"[48] of trinkets and baubles, of "dress and equipage" where one can expect "an entire revolution" every five or six years, and "extends itself to whatever is in any respect the object of taste," Smith insists, for all that, that fashion is considerably less important and volatile in the province of morals.[49] "The different manners which custom teaches us to approve of in the different professions and states of life, do not concern things of greatest importance," since "the sentiments of moral approbation and disapprobation, are founded on the strongest and most vigorous passions of human nature; and though they may be somewhat warpt, cannot be entirely perverted."[50] These undistorted sentiments are, so he argues, most often and strongly felt by the man of regular and orderly virtue, the man of disciplined self-command who, as he said of himself, even struggles against crying at the theatre, lest "any spectators . . . should regard it as effeminacy and weakness."[51]

Smith claimed in his lectures on jurisprudence that morals could only be collapsed into fashion, as Mandeville attempted to do, by failing to distinguish healthy, functioning societies from those degenerated by effeminacy and the corruption of women's morals.[52] By contrast, "temperance and chastity," so derided by Mandeville, Smith remarked,[53] characterize the prudent as well as the virtuous man, whose discipline and "exact decorums which ought to be observed in the conversation of the two sexes"[54] enable him properly to evaluate effeminate trivialities, like the unproductive labor of "buffoons, players, musicians, opera-singers, opera-dancers."[55] Generosity itself was "the virtue of a man," he of self-command and the ability to "sacrifice some great and important interest of our own to an equal interest of a friend or superior."[56] As Smith describes it, the character of the virtuous man embodies even in commercial societies a trace of that "proper manhood and firmness" which once permitted "any American savage who, upon being taken prisoner by some hostile tribe, refuses to kill himself," but rather "places his glory in supporting [the] torments [inflicted upon him] with manhood."[57]

---

[48] *The Theory of Moral Sentiments*, I.ii.1.2.
[49] Compare, Hume, *Treatise*, III,ii.1–2, and III,iii,1.
[50] *The Theory of Moral Sentiments*, v.ii.1.   [51] *The Theory of Moral Sentiments*, I.iii.1.9.
[52] *Lectures on Jurisprudence*, A.iii.10–16.   [53] *The Theory of Moral Sentiments*, VII.ii.4.11.
[54] *The Theory of Moral Sentiments*, VII.iv.21.   [55] *The Wealth of Nations*, I.4.
[56] *The Theory of Moral Sentiments*, IV.ii.10. Compare Shaftesbury, "An Inquiry Concerning Virtue and Merit," in *Characteristics*, I, p. 325.
[57] *The Theory of Moral Sentiments*, VII.ii.1.34.

Preserving manly virtues in the face of the trivial effeminacies inherent in societies shaped by heightened forms of commercial exchange as Mandeville had argued, was, for Smith, anything but a trivial matter. For even in the most modern polities like Britain, where the division of labor had reduced warfare to a specialized activity, the manly martial virtues had to be kept alive. While discussing the education of the common people in *The Wealth of Nations*, Smith wrote that "[e]ven though the martial spirit of the people were of no use towards the defence of society,"

> yet to prevent that sort of mental mutilation, deformity and wretchedness, which cowardice necessarily involves in it, from spreading themselves through the great body of the people, would still deserve the most serious attention of government; in the same manner as it would deserve its most serious attention to prevent a leprosy or any other loathsome and offensive disease, though neither mortal not dangerous, from spreading among them; though, perhaps, no other publick good might result from such attention besides the prevention of so great a publick evil.[58]

Precisely because he was secure that he had established a firm moral foundation for commercial society in the workings of sympathy, a foundation which accepted Mandeville's primary insights but was at the same time immune to *The Fable*'s charge of immoralism, Smith could critically appraise what Mandeville termed "the cause of earthly greatness" (II, 260). In what Smith called the "economy of greatness," he recognized that the rich tend merely to pursue the "gratification of their own vain and insatiable desires," and often "ruin themselves by laying out money on trinkets of frivolous utility."[59] Yet if, in commercial society, the fully integrated life of the virtuous classical citizen was no longer possible, there nevertheless remained "two different roads, [one of wisdom and virtue, the other of wealth and greatness] equally leading to the attainment [of] the respect and admiration" of others.[60] Despite the regrettable fact that most people admire and worship the second, frivolous, path, and even though men whose illusions of vanity are fed by economic opportunity and rewarded by the praise of "the great mob of mankind,"[61] the

---

[58] *The Wealth of Nations*, v.i.f.60.
[59] *The Theory of Moral Sentiments*, IV.i.6. Compare, Lawrence Dickey, "Historicizing the 'Adam Smith Problem': Conceptual, Historiographical and Textual Issues," *Journal of Modern History* 58 (September 1986), pp. 579–609.   [60] *The Theory of Moral Sentiments*, III.3.2–4.
[61] *The Theory of Moral Sentiments*, vII.3.37.

frugal and prudent man, the man whose actions are disciplined by his self-command, continues to deserve our admiration and respect.

In the steadiness of his industry and frugality, in his steady sacrificing the ease and enjoyment of the present moment for the probable expectation of the still greater ease and enjoyment of a more distant but more lasting period of time, the prudent man is always both supported and rewarded by the entire approbation of the impartial spectator, and the representative of the impartial spectator, the man within the breast.[62]

Smith understood that a profound change had occurred, largely during his own lifetime, in his contemporaries' consciousness of their social identities. He recognized that Mandeville's *Fable* was a crucial document in this transformation, one which marked the appearance during the eighteenth century of a mode of social apprehension that we might call, adopting contemporary usage, the competitive sub-lime. In this mode, no act sprung from disinterested motives, all human relationships were contaminated by self-love, and the extra-ordinary material progress of modern polities was the unintended consequence of egoism. Intensely disturbed by this vision, Smith sought to correct what he thought were its "wholly pernicious" conclusions, most powerfully articulated by Mandeville, and to reduce the anxieties generated by Mandeville's "system ... [which] could never have occasioned so general an alarm ... had it not in some respects bordered upon the truth."[63] Mandeville was thus a privileged object of Smith's enterprise and a starting point of his theoretical labors. When he argued that self-governing market relations directly expressed the natural order, Smith understood that this thesis was, and could immediately be seen as, a variant of Mandeville's. He also understood that if his own account of the market was to be ethically persuasive, it would have to entail a morally informed, and thus strongly anti-Mandevillian, analysis of its workings.

Smith was confident that his expansion of the notion of sympathy in the theory of the impartial spectator provided the firmest possible grounds to argue, against Mandeville, that commercial society could not plausibly be understood simply as issuing from and dependent upon the promotion of vice. Thus, in *The Wealth of Nations*, he could concentrate upon the workings of self-interest as the primary propul-sive mechanism of commerce, while yet maintaining the stance of a

---

[62] *The Theory of Moral Sentiments*, VI.i.11. See, too, VI.1.12–13.
[63] *The Theory of Moral Sentiments*, VII.ii.4.14.

moralist whose office was not to celebrate what he analyzed, but to alert the public to the threats posed by modern manners to the living of the moral life. This he did in Book v of his masterpiece, and then again in the final edition of *The Theory of Moral Sentiments*. Smith, however, could not guard against the unintended consequences of his own achievement. The most important of these were already strongly suggested in the oft-quoted anecdote about Smith published by *The Times* of London on 16 August 1790, a few weeks after his death. Smith was said to have embraced entirely the position of merchants in his lectures, and "converted the chair of Moral Philosophy into a professorship of trade and finance." The anonymous author of these remarks had merely confirmed the practice, common by the end of the eighteenth century, of reading *The Wealth of Nations* along the grid provided by Mandeville's *Fable*, thus effectively marginalizing Smith's moral philosophy and divorcing his "political economy" from his history of manners. Gibbon, Smith's acquaintance and a critic of Mandeville in his autobiography, voiced a similar view when he regretted that Smith "proves, perhaps too severely, that the most salutary effects have flowed from the meanest and most selfish causes."[64] The process of reading Smith as if he spoke as a Mandevillian was virtually complete by the early nineteenth century, as his identity had been transformed from that of an inheritor of the wider moral and civil projects of Hutcheson and Hume, and the traditions of natural jurisprudence in which his other Scots colleagues worked, into the founder of a science of political economy meant to address the problems of modern industry. Hegel put it well in 1821: Smith, he wrote, had established "one of the sciences which have arisen out of the conditions of the modern world,"[65] in which civil society is shown to be "a battlefield where everyone's private interest meets everyone else's."[66] Seen in this light, Smith's resort to public education and a militia to remedy the deformities brought on by commerce in the last Book of *The Wealth of Nations* must have seemed at best utopian and at worst pathetic or unbelievable to his industrial readers.

A related issue beats at the heart of the so-called *Adam Smith Problem*, first formulated in the mid-nineteenth century, and coming into full

---

[64] Edward Gibbon, *The History of the Decline and Fall of the Roman Empire*, ed. J.B. Bury, 7 volumes (London: Methuer, 1912), 6th edition, VII, p. 298, n. 104.
[65] G.W.F. Hegel, *The Philosophy of Right*, ed. T. M. Knox (Oxford: Clarendon Press, 1952), p. 126.   [66] Hegel, *The Philosophy of Right*, p. 189.

flower in Germany during the late 1890s – interestingly enough shortly before the appearance of the first new edition of *The Fable* published in the twentieth century.[67] The claim by a raft of distinguished German scholars that Smith held two incompatible views, one based upon sympathy in *The Theory of Moral Sentiments*, and the other on the selfishness that informed *The Wealth of Nations*, did not, as Smith's modern editors maintain, issue from mere "ignorance and misunderstanding."[68] Rather, it arose from the by-then established disembedding of Smith's analysis of commercial society, now called capitalism, from his wider and immediate moral and historical concerns. The problem revolves around Smith's effort to integrate a morally informed, yet naturalistic, statement of social relations of the kind first achieved by Mandeville, with an ethically enriched, yet socially realistic, understanding of competitive individualism which Mandeville argued was impossible within the context of a value-neutral language of explanation. In *The Wealth of Nations*, Smith expressly concentrated on the emergence of commercial society. He subsumed the passions promoting the need for recognition under the category of the pursuit of economic advantage, which, in turn, he understood as the unique vehicle through which the universal desire for approbation would be satisfied. All non-economic drives could then be translated for the purposes of analysis into economic ones, since in commercial societies marks of wealth were converted without prompting or intervention into objects generating esteem.[69] The individual's unending struggle to better his condition at once directly served his need for recognition, and had the unintended consequence of promoting the interests of society as a whole. Once removed from the context of moral argument within which these arguments emerged, it was but a short step to understand Smith's primary domain of interest as "the economy," a realm analytically indepen-

---

[67] August Onken, "Das Adam Smith-Problem," *Zeitschrift für Socialwissenschaft*, ed. Julius Wolf, I. (Berlin, 1898), pp. 25–33, 101–108, and 276–287, and Richard Zeyss, *Adam Smith und der Eigennutz* (Tübingen: Laupp, 1889). See *Mandevilles Bienenfabel*, ed. Otto Bobertag (Munich: Georg Müller, 1914). See too the editors' introduction to *The Theory of Moral Sentiments*, pp. 20–25; Thomas Wilson, "Sympathy and Self-Interest," in *The Market and the State*, ed. Thomas Wilson and Andrew Skinner (Oxford University Press, 1976), pp. 73–99, and Thomas Sowell, "Adam Smith in Theory and Practice," in *Adam Smith and Modern Political Economy*, ed. Gerald D. O' Driscoll, Jr. (Ames, Iowa: Iowa State University Press, 1979), pp. 3–18.

[68] *The Theory of Moral Sentiments*, p. 20.

[69] On this point see Albert O. Hirschman, *The Passions and the Interests: Political Arguments for Capitalism Before Its Triumph* (Princeton University Press, 1977), pp. 100–113.

dent of non-economic desires, and dependent for its theoretical power on the obliteration of a moral vocabulary as a suitable instrument for its description and understanding. This was precisely Mandeville's point about the methodological requirements of any systematic understanding of commercial society. And it is these very requirements which have made the moral philosophy Smith attempted to integrate into a scientific account of commercial society so problematic, both for his immediate and subsequent audiences.

While Smith adopted most of Mandeville's methodological criteria regarding the protocols appropriate for a scientific study of society, he nevertheless sought to deny their moral implications. But, in the process, Smith appeared to his various audiences to have dramatically reduced the ethical space to which an individual could possibly withdraw in order to judge the actions of others, or morally to regulate his own behavior in the face of the deceptive moral practices which, as Mandeville so convincingly argued, were required of market actors in their strategies for social promotion. While discussing Smith's attempt to confront the ethical problems posed by *The Fable* to the understanding of capitalism, Joan Robinson, one of the most eminent economists of the post-war generation, claimed that Mandeville "has never been answered."[70] In so doing, she provided a sign more telling than she perhaps knew of the power of Mandeville's argument as it inaugurated in Western consciousness a new paradigm for the language in which social life might be comprehended.

[70] Joan Robinson, *Economic Philosophy* (Chicago: Aldine, 1963), p. 19.

Epilogue: The Fable's modern fate

In 1833, upon attaining his majority, Robert Browning's father presented his son with a copy of the 1795 edition of *The Fable of the Bees*. The younger Browning seems to have read at least part of Mandeville's work, but showed no evidence of this until 1887, when he published "With Bernard De Mandeville," a poem of 321 iambic pentameter lines in 11 sections, in a book of poems on persons eminent in their day.[1] (A contemporary remarked that many of these people were "names to be reached for in a biographical dictionary."[2]) When Browning returned to *The Fable* at the age of seventy-five, he concentrated almost entirely on "The Vindication of the Book," paraphrasing some of Mandeville's sentences as he wrote. He aims in the poem to answer what he understood to be the pessimism of Carlyle, who offended the poet's unwavering belief that God used evil to produce virtue in men's souls. Mandeville, Browning thought, knew long ago what Carlyle was unable to see, that

> as with body so deals law with soul
> That's stung to strength through weakness, strives for good
> Through evil – earth its race-ground, heaven its goal.[3]

One of Mandeville's few readers who completely failed to grasp any feature of his satire, Browning read *The Fable* as a theodicy. He took Mandeville's purpose to be a strict defense of human virtue that was entirely compatible with the doctrine of original sin, a belief without which Browning's own faith in the possibility of redemption would lapse into incoherence. Praising Mandeville's bright humor and sound practical sense, Browning then invoked "sage Mandeville" to

[1] Robert Browning, *Parleyings With Certain People of Importance in Their Day* (London: Smith, Elster, 1887).
[2] From the anonymous review of *Parleyings* in *The Westminster Review* 128 (April 1887), p. 132.
[3] "With Bernard de Mandeville," III, lines 1–3.

confute for me
This parlous friend who captures or set free
Thunderbolts at his pleasure, yet would draw
Back, panic-stricken by some puny straw
Thy gold-rimmed amber-headed cane had whisked
Out of his pathway if the object risked
Encounter, 'scaped thy kick from buckled shoe!
As when folks heard thee in old days pooh-pooh
Addison's tye-wig preachment, grant this friend –
(Whose groan I hear, with guffaugh at the end
Disposing of mock-melancholy) – grant
His bilious mood one potion, ministrant
Of homely wisdom, healthy wit! For, hear!
"With power and will, let preference appear"
By intervention ever and eye, help good
When evil's mastery is understood
In some plain outrage, and triumphant wrong
Tramples weak right to nothingness: nay, long
'Ere such sad consumation bring despair
To right's adherent's, ah, what help it were
If wrong lay strangles in the birth – each head
Of the hatched monster promptly crushed, instead
Of spared to gather venom! We require
No great experience that the inch-long worm,
Free of our heel, would grow to vomit fire,
And one day plague the world in dragon form.
So should wrong merely peep abroad to meet
Wrong's due quietus, leave our world's way safe
For honest walking.[4]

Though a curiosity, Browning's poem nevertheless illustrates the degree to which Mandeville had become a barely remembered figure during much of the nineteenth century.[5] Unconcerned with questions of suffrage and representation, or any other political issue that even remotely bore upon the struggles of post-revolutionary Europe, *The Fable* was equally innocent of any conception of class conflict or notions of social progress which encompassed the economic transfor-

---

[4] With Bernard de Mandeville, iv.
[5] I am indebted to the only satisfying treatment of Mandeville's posthumous reputation, Dario Castiglione's "Excess, Frugality and the Spirit of Capitalism: Readings of Mandeville on Commercial Society," in Joseph Melling and Jonathan Barry (eds.), *Culture in History: Production, Consumption and Values in Historical Perspective* (University of Exeter Press, 1992), pp. 155–179. See too E.J. Hundert, "Bernard Mandeville and the Rhetoric of Social Science," *Journal of the History of the Behavioral Sciences* 22 (1986), pp. 311–320.

mations wrought by industrial production. Moreover, by the time *The Wealth of Nations* had been canonized in the 1820s by Malthus, Say and Ricardo as the foundational text of the modern science of political economy, Mandeville's animating paradox, that vice was essential to modern progress, and its corollary paradox, that the practice of moderation would destroy economic motivations, had effectively been domesticated through dilution into unthreatening axioms of common sense. Modern society's development could conventionally be explained, after the fashion of Hutcheson, Hume and above all Smith, in terms of the calm passions and moderate satisfactions that supported commercial institutions. Transformed into self-interest, and tautologically presumed to be the source of any and every action, Mandevillian self-love was smoothly transformed, and so marginalized, into the innocently universal desire to better one's condition. Far from being crude and unbridled, interest – appropriately moderated by conscience, education and the Christian religion – could instead be conceived as a necessary ingredient of those social negotiatons whose outcome crucially included individual decency and publicly supported morality. Equally important, Mandeville's nineteenth-century successors confronted a paradox at a great remove from the one presented by *The Fable* to eighteenth-century audiences. Rather than being concerned with the ironic moral disjunction between vice and benefits, intellectuals reflecting upon the repeated bouts of economic downturn and scarcity during the first half of the nineteenth century were consumed by the appalling possibility that the recent explosion of machine industry entailed both a hitherto unimagined power of wealth creation, and an ungovernable expansion of poverty – a problem totally alien to Mandeville's enterprise.

Mandeville's eclipse was never total, however, nor did it immediately follow Smith's unintended triumph, as might be suggested by Jean-Baptiste Say's *Treatise on Political Economy* (1803), where the pre-eminent classical economist on the function of demand addressed the importance of luxury consumption, and discussed the views of Lucretius, Franklin, Steuart, Montesquieu, Voltaire and Smith, while nowhere mentioning Mandeville.[6] For example, in a note to the

---

[6] Jean-Baptiste Say, *A Treatise on Political Economy*, trans. C.R. Prinseps (Philadelphia: Lippincott, 1857), Book III, "Of the Consumption of Wealth," Chapter 5, "Of Individual Consumption – Its Motives and Effects," pp. 401–411.

1818 appendix of *The Essay on Population*, Malthus argued that the poor could not claim the right to support since such a putative right would be impossible to implement. The parson here addressed the paradox that while it was just and beneficial to renounce superfluous consumption in order to gratify the immediate needs of the poor, generalizing this behavior into a moral principle would not result in a more equitable distribution of goods, but would instead reduce mankind to universal poverty. Malthus echoed Smith in claiming that benevolence could only be effective in a state of "perfect knowledge" unavailable to men. But God, in making self-love a stronger passion, had providentially benefited humanity, since "by this wise provision the most ignorant are led to promote the general happiness, an end which they would have totally failed to attain, if the moving principle of their conduct had been benevolence." Malthus, who could still reasonably assume that his audience was familiar with *The Fable*, then quickly sought to sever his own theodicy from any association with Mandeville's "system of morals," which was, as he put it, "absolutely false, and directly contrary to the just definition of virtue."[7]

Related anxieties about being associated with Mandeville's taint seem to have have lasted into the 1830s, when educated persons from the older generation, like Browning's father, still viewed *The Fable* as an important book, and Richard Whately, the successor to Nassau Senior as Drummond Professor of Political Economy at Oxford, included a discussion of *The Fable* in his lectures.[8] For many, however, the name of Mandeville might by this time just as easily have been linked with the medieval traveller Sir John Mandeville, or the eponymous hero of William Godwin's *Mandeville*, a dystopic novel of bigotry, religious war and unrequited love during the seventeenth century.[9] Perhaps the most interesting example of a residual concern with *The Fable* was produced by Sir James Mackintosh, barrister, judge and historian, who was renowned as the author of *Vindicae Gallicae* (1791), a polemical critique of Burke's *Reflections on the Revolution in France* (1790), and the most effective radical Whig defense of the French Revolution. Mackintosh recanted his former principles

---

[7] T.R. Malthus, *An Essay on the Principle of Population* (London: Murray, 1826), II, p. 454.
[8] Richard Whately, *Introductory Lectures on Political Economy: Being Part of a Course Delivered in Easter Term, 1831* (London: Fellowes, 1832), Lecture 2.
[9] William Godwin, *Mandeville: A Tale of the Seventeenth Century in England* (Edinburgh: Constable, 1817).

and friendships in a famous lecture series at Lincoln's Inn in 1799, The Law of Nature and Nations, in which he supported Burke while attacking Godwin's radicalism. He claimed that his revised opinions were sustained by universal human feelings of right and wrong, by a moral sense expressed in sentiments like friendship, whose necessity and immutability were enforced by a divine authority. Mackintosh wished to distinguish the question of the psychological development of the moral sense from that of the criteria of morality, a distinction essential for his larger philosophical project of reconciling the necessary universality of the dictates of conscience with its considerably varied historical progress in different communities. In his *Dissertation on the Progress of Ethical Philosophy, Chiefly during the 17th and 18th Centuries* (1830),[10] an anti-utilitarian tract inspired, as William Whewell observed in a Preface added in 1836, by Butler's discussion of self-love, Mackintosh enlarged upon the issue. In the course of arguing that the path of virtue consists in "following nature," and that self-interest is not the basic motive of all rational action, he pointedly dismissed Mandeville as "the buffoon and sophister of the ale-house," whose writing was "occasioned by the doctrines of Hobbes."[11] One of Mackintosh's essays in this book was intended for the introductory volume of the eighth, 1842, edition of *The Encyclopaedia Britannica*, in which he argued, again contra Mandeville, that the foundation of man's moral sense resided in several social instincts which consisted in "a feeling of love (& sympathy) or benevolence."[12]

Mackintosh's book elicited two of the last noteworthy, if brief, considerations of *The Fable* during the first half of the nineteenth century. In 1835 James Mill published *A Fragment on Mackintosh*, a scathing attack on the sentimental moral philosophy of Mackintosh's *Dissertation*. Mill knew that Bentham's principle of the artificial identification of interests – which the legislator would solve by identifying the interest of the individual with the interest of the community – had important affinities with arguments in Helvétius, which had been criticized by Mackintosh in the *Fragment* as "the low and loose moralist of the vain, the selfish and the sensual." Like Mackintosh, Mill also recognized that some of these arguments had

---

[10] Sir James Mackintosh, *Dissertation on the Progress of Ethical Philosophy* (Edinburgh: Black, 1862), 3rd edition, Preface by William Whewell.
[11] *Dissertation on the Progress of Ethical Philosophy*, p. 87.
[12] *Encyclopaedia Britannica*, "Dissertation Second" (London, 1842), I, p. 323.

their source in Mandeville, whom Bentham had praised in the chapter "Motives" in his *Introduction to the Principles of Morals and Legislation* (1800). It was thus important for Mill to support Mandeville against Mackintosh, not only because it gave him an opportunity to expose what he regarded as the cant that often passed for contemporary moral argument, but also because in so doing he would be defending the foundational principles of utilitarianism. For Mill, *The Fable*'s

propositions were part of the theological morality of Mandeville's time, not altogether renounced in our own ... the wonder is not much that the sentimental talk which philosophers of the Sir Jamesical cast hold about human nature, should appear deceitful, and to deserve the exposure Mandeville bestowed upon it.[13]

Given his temperament, it is unsurprising that Mill was deaf to Mandeville's satirical voice. He found "no mirth" whatsoever in *The Fable*, "the gravest thing for a satire that was ever written,"[14] and thought that Mandeville himself believed that all indulgence is vicious and that without self-denial there could be no virtue. Yet Mill was perhaps the last writer of his generation to appreciate *The Fable*'s historical significance. He understood that Mandeville differed significantly from Hobbes, that he "had a pride in rousing men to opposition, by running directly counter to their habitual modes of thinking," and that *The Fable*'s primary object in morally degrading the things commonly taken to be benefits "is to expose the *mummery* of the world, and the affectations of those who laid traps for praise by singing eulogisms on the dignity of human nature."[15]

Unbeknownst to Mill or his audience, Darwin read Mackintosh's essay late in 1838, two years after he had returned from his voyage on *The Beagle*, and at the same time that he began to study Malthus, whose invocation of nature's indifference to human wishes the young naturalist found profoundly disturbing. In 1839 Darwin, who knew Mackintosh and was related to him through marriage, wrote *On the Moral Sense*, a ten-page manuscript commentary on Mackintosh's *Dissertation* from the point of view of a naturalist.[16] Darwin hoped that Mackintosh's argument, which he thought failed entirely to explain

---

[13] *A Fragment on Mackintosh* (London: Longman, 1870), pp. 62–63.
[14] *A Fragment on Mackintosh*, p. 58.   [15] *A Fragment on Mackintosh*, pp. 57–58 and 59–60.
[16] See Edward Manier, *The Young Darwin and His Cultural Circle* (Dordrecht and Boston: Reidel, 1978), pp. 141–146 and 163–164.

why acting upon the moral sense would increase the happiness of the species, still could be adapted to demonstrate that Darwin's own system was not selfish in the vein of Malthus and Mandeville. Darwin proceeded to discuss men as the last in a series of animals in which many specialized instincts were least influential, but a species in which the conjugal and social instincts, the "feeling of love (& sympathy) or benevolence," nevertheless remained, since moral action could be seen as a special case of adaptive behavior. Man had evolved into an ethical animal, Darwin speculated, one who recognized that he ought to act in certain ways or accept certain types of authoritative direction, even when his own passions and appetites powerfully induced him to forgo his duty. Accordingly, so Darwin argued, feelings of love, benevolence and sympathy could be understood as constituent features of basic human social instincts which encouraged "the protection of others," and thereby had survival value for the species. Benevolence, Darwin concluded – again trying to resist the Malthusian and Mandevillian implications he detected in his own thinking – would therefore have some advantage in the struggle for existence.

After Mill and Darwin, neither the efficacy of utilitarianism nor what Carlyle had called the dismal science of Malthusian political economy could usefully be debated in terms which drew upon *The Fable*, whose primary objects of inquiry were seen to have no relevance to the moral and political dilemmas occasioned by industrial production after the 1840s. Indeed, by 1850, Mandeville's name had largely been expunged from the active vocabulary of most members of the educated public, while no new edition of *The Fable* was published during the nineteenth century in any European language after 1818. The century's last extended consideration of *The Fable*, contained in Leslie Stephen's *History of English Thought in the Eighteenth Century* (1876),[17] testifies to Mandeville's nineteenth-century marginality, although Stephen's essay in many ways remains one of the most perceptive short treatments of his work. Stephen recognized the importance of the "petticoat" thesis for *The Fable*'s larger purposes. Attentive to paradox and satire, he also understood how Mandeville's moral arguments depended for much of their force upon a strict

---

[17] Sir Leslie Stephen, *History of English Thought in the Eighteenth Century* (New York: Harcourt, Brace & World, 1962), 2 volumes, I, especially pp. 28–35. See too Stephen, "Mandeville's 'Fable of the Bees,'" Chapter 7 of *Essays on Freethinking and Plainspeaking* (1873) (London: Smith, Elder, 1907).

acceptance of Augustinian theology. Stephen appreciated the power of William Law's critique of *The Fable* and he was equally attentive to the significance for Mandeville of figuring society as a "masquerade." Moreover, Stephen was aware of the importance of conjectural history for Mandeville's enterprise, realizing as well that *The Fable's* speculations about language origins were a central feature of Mandeville's work. Perhaps most insightfully, Stephen understood that, unlike Shaftesbury, Mandeville approached his project as a "man of science," and in a fashion that, ironically, reminded Stephen of Darwin's. "[B]y attempting to resolve all virtue into selfishness," Mandeville, Stephen said, "stimulated the efforts towards a scientific explanation of the phenomena."[18]

Yet Stephen saw no important connections between Mandeville and the work of Butler, Hutcheson and Hume, or writers on the continent during the eighteenth century; nor did he think that *The Fable* was a significant point of departure for Smith, even in *The Theory of Moral Sentiments*, which Stephen discussed without mentioning Mandeville's name. For despite his deep appreciation of many of *The Fable's* previously neglected aspects, and a deft understanding of the seriousness of the issues it raised, Stephen nevertheless viewed Mandeville as a severely limited figure, one who deserved be offered up to his readers in a largely dismissive vein. "Mandeville is said to have been in the habit of frequenting coffee-houses, and amusing his patrons by ribald conversations," Stephen wrote at the start of his discussion.

The tone of his writings harmonises with this account of his personal habits. He is a cynical and prurient writer, who seems to shrink from no jest, however scurrilous, and from no paradox however grotesque, which is calculated to serve the purpose, of diverting his readers – readers, it may be added, not very scrupulous in their tastes . . . Mandeville shares Swift's contempt for the human race; but his contempt, instead of urging him to the borders of madness, merely finds vent in a horse-laugh. He despises himself as well as his neighbours, and is content to be despicable. He is a scoffer, not a misanthrope. You are all Yahoos, he seems to say, and I am a Yahoo; and so – let us eat, drink and be merry.[19]

During the late Victorian twilight, Christian moralists like Butler – whose work was brought out in two well-received editions, one by

[18] *History of English Thought in the Eighteenth Century*, p. 35.
[19] *History of English Thought in the Eighteenth Century*, p. 28.

former Prime Minister Gladstone in 1897,[20] the other under the auspices of the English Theological Library three years later[21] – were thought more worthy of serious attention than the prurient cynic of the Augustan coffee-house.

This attitude of dismissal sustained by neglect began to be transformed almost beyond recognition during the next generation, most importantly with the publication in 1924 by the Clarendon Press of F.B. Kaye's edition of *The Fable*, a text unlikely ever to be superseded.[22] Kaye, an American literary historian, brought a wide and informed comparative perspective to his meticulous scholarship. More than Stephen, he appreciated *The Fable*'s eighteenth-century importance, as well as of many of the central philosophical problems that Mandeville had addressed.[23] Kaye's edition set the course of Mandeville studies in the twentieth century. He offered a superbly annotated text which proved suitable for re-incorporation into the Augustan literary canon,[24] and a guide to Mandeville's sources from which every subsequent study of *The Fable* would be obliged to begin. Most importantly, in his extended commentary Kaye suggested a wider context than was previously available for the understanding of Mandeville's work.[25] Mandeville was not merely a satirist with a significant philosophical agenda: *The Fable*, he argued, was a crucial text for understanding the conflict between mercantilism and *laissez-faire*. In this way, Kaye was instrumental in placing Mandeville in the history of economic doctrines and inserting *The Fable* within the ambit of contemporary controversies concerning the nature of capitalism.

One of these disputes flourished in German and Austrian academic circles during the first two decades of the twentieth century, in the midst of which the 1914 German edition of *The Fable* appeared. While Mandeville had already begun to attract some scholarly interest in

---

[20] *The Works of Joseph Butler*, ed. The Honorable W.E. Gladstone (Oxford: Clarendon Press, 1897). [21] *The Works of Joseph Butler*, ed. J.H. Bernard (London: Macmillan, 1900).

[22] Bernard Mandeville, *The Fable of the Bees: Or, Private Vices, Publick Benefits*. With a Commentary Critical, Historical, and Explanatory by F.B. Kaye (Oxford: Clarendon Press, 1924).

[23] See too F.B. Kaye, "The Influence of Bernard Mandeville," *Studies in Philology* 19 (1922), pp. 83–108, and Kaye, "Mandeville and the Origin of Language," *Modern Language Notes* 34 (1924), pp. 136–142.

[24] See, most notably, Martin Price, *To the Palace of Wisdom: Studies in Order and Energy from Dryden to Blake* (Garden City, New York: Doubleday, 1964).

[25] *The Fable of the Bees*, pp. xxxviii–cxiii.

Germany at the turn of the century,[26] Simmel, Sombart, Troeltsch and Weber, the major participants in a debate about how to distinguish "the spirit of capitalism" at the level of motivation from mere greed, had little knowledge of or interest in *The Fable*.[27] But a number of these writers, especially Simmel who disagreed with Weber about the significance of a secularized asceticism for the development of capitalism, emphasized, like Mandeville, the social force of sheer avarice unconstrained by custom in nascent capitalist societies, and the psychologically transformative power of wealth computed solely in monetary terms. In his discussion of "the style of life" in such societies, Simmel concentrated upon the peculiar habits intrinsic to the social interactions shaped by finance capital. He put his argument in terms the Augustans would have found familiar: "it is not necessary to be a gentleman in order to obtain credit, but rather that whoever demands credit is a gentleman." Simmel proceeded to describe such persons in a distinctly Mandevillian mode. "These products of urban existence," he wrote, "form a major contingent of that type of insecure personality which can hardly be pinned down and 'placed' because their mobility and their versatility saves them from committing themselves, as it were, in any situation."[28] Indeed, in Simmel's view, modern financial institutions were "the nurseries of cynicism," since

the more money becomes the sole centre of interest, the more one discovers that honour and conviction, talent and virtue, beauty and salvation of the souls, are exchanged against money and so the more a mocking and frivolous attitude will develop in relation to these higher values that are for sale for the same kind of value as groceries, and that also command a "market price."[29]

---

[26] See Paul Sackmann, *Bernard de Mandeville und die Bienenfabel-Controverse* (Leipzig: Mohr, 1897) and Albert Schatz, "Bernard Mandeville: Contribution à l'étude des origines du libéralisme économique," *Vierteljahrschrift für Social und Wirtschaftsgeschichte* (1903), pp. 434–488. A reprint of the 1818 German edition of *The Fable* was published in Heidelberg in 1891.

[27] Lujo Brentano, *Der Wirtschaftende Mensch in der Geschichte* (Leipzig: Meiner, 1913); Georg Simmel, *Philosophie des Geldes* (Leipzig: Dunker & Humblot 1900); translated as *The Philosophy of Money*, by Tom Bottomore and David Frisby (London: Routledge, 1990) Werner Sombart, *Der Moderne Capitalismus*, 2 volumes (Leipzig: Dunker and Humblot, 1902); Ernst Troeltsch, *Die Bedeutung des Protestantismus für die Enststehung der Modernen Welt* (Berlin: Oldenberg, 1906), and Max Weber, "Die Protestantische Ethik und der 'Geist' des Kapitalismus," *Archiv für Sozialwissenschaft und Sozialpolitik* 20 (1905), pp. 1–54. For the context of this debate see Gordon Marshall, *In Search of the Spirit of Capitalism: An Essay on Max Weber's Protestant Ethic Thesis* (New York: Columbia University Press, 1982), pp. 17–40.

[28] Georg Simmel, *The Philosophy of Money*, trans. Tom Bottomore and David Frisby (London: Routledge, 1990), 2nd edition, pp. 480 and 473.   [29] *The Philosophy of Money*, p. 256.

Although not translated immediately, the works of Simmel and his colleagues were nevertheless generously reviewed in *The American Journal of Sociology*, the flagship publication of a recently established profession, edited by Albion Small who had studied in Berlin and was particularly enthusiastic about Simmel's views. These works were given further prominence by leading social scientists, most notably Talcott Parsons.[30] By 1924, Kaye was able to situate *The Fable* in the context of what had become – especially after the Bolshevik Revolution – an international concern with the essence of capitalism. Ignoring the German debate, he argued that Mandeville's work prefigured the then most prominent American analysis of capitalist social habits, Thorstein Veblen's *Theory of the Leisure Class* (1899), in which the term "conspicuous consumption" figured prominently in a devastating picture of the irrationalities attendant upon modern forms of wealth. Reminding his readers that "esteem is awarded on evidence," Veblen pointed to the display of luxury items in capitalist societies as a primary device for winning respect. Kaye privately suggested a relationship between Mandeville and Veblen to Arthur O. Lovejoy, the most eminent intellectual historian of his era. Lovejoy responded in a letter, which Kaye printed in his edition of *The Fable*.

Nearly all of the fundamental ideas of Mr. Thorstein Veblen's *Theory of the Leisure Class* – regarded, when it appeared, as a very original contribution to economic theory and social psychology – may be found in Mandeville's *Remark M*, and elsewhere in his prose appendices to *The Fable*.[31]

Members of the generation which came to maturity after 1918 were more anxiously concerned than their nineteenth-century predecessors with the dynamics of consumption, and with the stimulation of consumer demand, especially after the Great Crash. For a number of them and their successors, one of the striking features of Kaye's edition of *The Fable* was, as Lovejoy agreed, Mandeville's prescient modernity. This point was nowhere more famously (and self-servingly) asserted than in *The General Theory of Employment*. Here Keynes improbably pictured Mandeville as a member of the "brave army of heretics" who resisted the logic of unfettered *laissez-faire*, and who formulated an early version of his own doctrine of underconsump-

---

[30] Talcott Parsons, "'Capitalism' in Recent German Literature: Sombart and Weber," *The Journal of Political Economy* 36 (1928), pp. 641–661.
[31] *The Fable of the Bees*, p. 452. Lovejoy later elaborated upon the relationship between Mandeville and Veblen in *Reflections of Human Nature*, pp. 208–215.

tion.[32] If, during the nineteenth century, Mandeville's meaning had been effectively reduced to the prurience of his famous paradox, in the twentieth *The Fable* came to represent for some prominent social scientists a template, from which one could read off a variety of doctrinal messages according to interest and taste. Rationally reconstructed with the aid of hindsight, *The Fable*, completely disregarded by St.-Simon, Comte, Durkheim and Weber, and only passingly attended to by Marx, could now be viewed as a forerunner of modern sociology. Robert Merton gave this idea considerable support when he saw in *The Fable* the first articulation of the doctrine of unintended consequences, an achievement for which Mandeville is often credited in histories of the social sciences.[33] As well, it was often suggested that Mandeville first formulated the idea of *homo economicus*, a discovery for which *The Fable* was praised in major works on economic doctrine by, among others, James Bonnar, Edwin Cannan, J.R. McCulloch, Joseph Schumpter and, as we have mentioned, Joan Robinson.[34] It was a discovery, moreover, for which Mandeville was roundly condemned, both by Catholic critics of economic liberalism,[35] and by the neo-Marxists Max Horkheimer and Theodore Adorno, who asserted with characteristic confidence that *The Fable*'s anatomy of egoism established Mandeville, along with Machiavelli and Hobbes, as one of the major writers "of the bourgeois dawn."[36] Furthermore, in the light of Kaye's commentary, *The Fable*'s approach to self-interested individualism also appeared in a philosophically interesting light, as a significant endorsement of utilitarianism, whose confrontation with rigorism, as Kaye suggested, provided an occasion to re-evaluate the claims of non-consequentialist moral philosophies.[37] During the last generation, Mandeville was declared to be a

---

[32] J.M. Keynes, *The General Theory of Employement* (London: Macmillan, 1936), XXIII.vii.

[33] Robert Merton, "The Unanticipated Consequences of Purposive Social Action," *American Sociological Review* 1 (1936), pp. 894–904. See too Louis Schneider, "Mandeville as a Forerunner of Modern Sociology," *Journal of the History of the Behavioral Sciences* 6 (1970), pp. 219–230, and Jon Elster, *Logic and Society* (New York: Wiley, 1978), pp. 106–108.

[34] See Harry Landreth, "The Economic Thought of Bernard Mandeville," *History of Political Economy* 7, 2 (1975), pp. 193–208 for a review of this literature.

[35] J. Lecler, "Liberalisme économique et libre pensée au XVIIIᵉ siècle: Mandeville et *La Fable des abeilles*," *Etudes* 230 (1937), pp. 624–645.

[36] Max Horkheimer and Theodore Adorno, *The Dialectic of Enlightenment*, trans. John Cumming (New York: Seabury Press, 1972), p. 90.

[37] See, for example, Sterling L. Lamprecht, "The Fable of the Bees," *The Journal of Philosophy* 23, 21 (1926), pp. 561–579, published in the wake of Kaye's edition and, most usefully, M.J. McTaggart, "Mandeville: Cynic or Fool"," *Philosophical Quarterly* 16 (1966), pp. 221–233.

"master-mind" by Friedrich von Hayek in a much-publicized lecture. He was a thinker who "asked the right question" – that is, whether rational social planning was possible. As Hayek saw it, part of Mandeville's genius consisted in his answering this question with a resounding "no." And while he didn't fully grasp his own discovery, Mandeville, so Hayek argued, "developed all of the classical paradigmata of the spontaneous growth of orderly social structure." He was the first in a great line of theorists to consider society solely from Hayek's own individualist and evolutionary perspective, in which persons, freely following their inclinations, inadvertently establish the most efficient social institutions.[38]

The Fable's passage from delinquent fame, through obscurity to, more recently, respectful appreciation, no doubt reveals more about the concerns of his subsequent readers than it does about Mandeville's own. And it is perhaps unlikely that Mandeville himself would have been terribly surprised that an unintended consequence of the intensified modern academic division of labor would result in the production of many contemporary "Mandevilles," a number of whom stand at some remove both from his own purposes and from the achievements which his Enlightenment contemporaries reluctantly granted to *The Fable*. But it can hardly be doubted that Mandeville would have derived the greatest satisfaction, if not perverse delight, from a more pervasive historical irony. Outside those precincts of the academy where Mandeville's work is now studied – and sometimes within them as well – persons for whom the affluence of advanced societies is soiled by their diminished moral legacy, and for whom nothing so clearly fails morally as commercial success, tend to repeat in their criticisms of capitalism the very arguments about vicious self-regard, barely concealed greed and cunning deception brought to the heart of eighteenth-century public consciousness by the first thoroughgoing defender of commercial modernity, in a book they are unlikely to read, written by an author whose name they may very well have never heard.

---

[38] F.A. Hayek, "Dr. Bernard Mandeville," *Proceedings of the British Academy* 52 (1966), pp. 125–141.

Bibliography

WORKS BY BERNARD MANDEVILLE: ORIGINAL EDITIONS, TRANSLATIONS AND RECENT REPRINTS

"In authorem de usu interno cantharidum scribentem." In *Titus cantharidum in medicina usus internus*, by Joannem Groenevelt, MD 2nd edition, London, 1703; 3rd edition, London, 1706. "Upon the Author, Treating of the Internal Use of *Cantharides*." In *A Treatise of the Safe, Internal Use of Cantharides in the Practice of Physick*, by John Greenfield. Translated by John Marten. London, 1706.

Bernardi a Mandeville, de medicina oratoria scholastica. Rotterdam: Regneri Leers, 1685.

British Journal, 36–7 (27 April–4 May 1725).

Disputatio medica inauguralis de Chylosi vitiata. Leiden: Abraham Elzevier, 1691.

Disputatio philosophica de brutorum operationibus. Leiden: Abraham Elzevier, 1689.

An Enquiry into the Causes of the Frequent Executions at Tyburn: And a Proposal for some Regulations concerning Felons in Prison, and the Good Effects to be Expected from them, by B. Mandeville, MD London: J. Roberts, 1725 (revised version of articles in *British Journal* 128–33 [27 February–3 April 1725]). Introduction by Malvin R. Zirker, Jr., Augustan Reprint Society, Publication No. 105, Los Angeles: William Andrews Clark Memorial Library, 1964.

An Enquiry into the Origin of Honour, and the Usefulness of Christianity in War, by "*the Author of the Fable of the Bees*." London: J. Brotherton, 1732. Reprinted, with introduction by M.M. Goldsmith. London: Cass Reprint, 1971.

La Fable des abeilles, ou les fripons devenus honnêtes gens, avec le commentaire, où l'on prouve que les vices des particuliers tendent à l'avantage du public, traduit de l'anglais sur la sixième edition. 4 volumes. Translated by J. Van Effen. London?, 1740; another translation by J. Bertrand, 4 volumes. London?: Aux Depens de la Compagnie, 1750.

The Fable of the Bees: Or, Private Vices, Publick Benefits. With a Commentary Critical, Historical and Explanatory. Edited by F.B. Kaye. 2 volumes. Oxford: Clarendon Press, 1924.

The Fable of the Bees: Or, Private Vices, Publick Benefits. London: J. Roberts, 1714 (two editions); 2nd edition, Edmund Parker, 1723; 3rd edition, J. Tonson, 1724; 4th edition, 1725; 5th edition, 1728; 6th edition, 1729; 1732.

The Fable of the Bees: Part II, 'by the Author of the First'. London: J. Roberts, 1730; 2nd edition, 1733.

The Female Tatler, by "a Society of Ladies." London: A. Baldwin, 1709–1710. Mandeville wrote thirty-two issues signed 'Lucinda' and 'Artesia' between No. 52 (4 November 1709) and No. 111 (31 March 1710).

Free Thoughts on Religion, the Church and National Happiness, by B.M. London: T. Jauncy, J. Roberts, 1720; reissued, T. Warner, 1721; reissued, "by the Author of the Fable of the Bees," J. Brotherton, 1723. 2nd edition, enlarged, by B.M., 1729.

The Grumbling Hive: Or Knaves Turn'd Honest. London: Sam Ballard, A. Baldwin, 1705.

A Letter to Dion, Occasion'd by his Book call'd Alciphron, or The Minute Philosopher, by "the Author of the Fable of the Bees." London: J. Roberts, 1732. Introduction by Jacob Viner. Augustan Reprint Society Publication No. 41, Los Angeles, 1953.

Mandevilles Bienenfabel. Edited by Otto Bobertag. Munich: Georg Muller, 1914.

The Mischiefs that Ought Justly to be Apprehended from a Whig-Government. London, J. Roberts, 1714. Introduction by H.T. Dickinson. Augustan Reprint Society, Publication No. 174, Los Angeles: William Andrews Clark Memorial Library Reprint, 1975.

A Modest Defence of Publick Stews: Or, an Essay upon Whoring as it is Now Practis'd in these Kingdoms, "Written by a Layman." London: A. Moore, 1724; another edition, *A Modest Defence ... Answer'd*. A. Bussy, 1725. Reprint of 1st edition, introduction by Richard I. Cook. Augustan Reprint Society Publication No. 162, Los Angeles, 1973.

The Pamphleteers: A Satyr. London, 1703.

Pensées libres sur la religion, l'eglise, le gouvernement et le bonheur de la nation. 2 volumes. Translated by J. Van Effen. Amsterdam, 1724.

Schrevelius, Reverend C. (pseud.) *A Sermon Preach'd at Colchester, to the Dutch Congregation*. Translated by B.M., MD. London, 1708.

St. James's Journal, 20 April, 11 May 1723.

Some Fables after the Easie and Familiar Method of Monsieur de la Fontaine, London: (Richard Wellington), 1703; enlarged edition, *Aesop Dress'd: Or a Collection of Fables Writ in Familiar Verse, by B. Mandeville, MD* London: (Richard Wellington), 1704, including ten added fables. Introduction by John S. Shea. Augustan Reprint Society Publication No. 120, Los Angeles, 1966.

A Treatise of the Hypocondriack and Hysterick Passions, Vulgarly Call'd the Hypo in Men and Vapours in Women, by B. de Mandeville, MD London: the Author, D. Leach, W. Taylor, John Woodward, 1711; 1715; reissued as *A*

Treatise of the Hypocondriack and Hysterick Diseases. 2nd edition enlarged, 1730; reissued 3rd edition, 1730. Reprint of 2nd edition, introduction by Stephen H. Good. Delmar, New York: Scholars' Facsimiles, 1976.

Typhon: Or The Wars Between the Gods and Giants: A Burlesque Poem in Imitation of the Comical Mons. Scarron. London: J. Pero, S. Illidge, J. Nutt, 1704.

The Virgin Unmask'd: Or Female Dialogues betwixt an Elderly Maiden Lady and her Niece on Several Diverting Discourses on Love, Marriage, Memoirs and Morals & of the Times. London: J. Morphew, J. Woodward, 1709; *The Virgin Unmask'd by Bernard Mandeville.* 2nd edition. London, G. Strahan, W. Meers, J. Stagg, 1724; reissued, London: A. Bettesworth, C. Hitch, 1731. Introduction by Stephen H. Good, Delmar, New York: Scholars' Facsimiles, 1975.

Wishes to a Godson, with other Miscellany Poems. London: J. Baker, 1712.

OTHER PRIMARY SOURCES

Abbadie, Jacques. *The Art of Knowing Oneself: Or, An Inquiry into the Sources of Morality.* Oxford, 1695.

Addison, Joseph and Steele, Richard. *The Spectator.* Edited by Donald F. Bond. 5 volumes. Oxford University Press, 1965.

Bacon, Francis. *Of the Proficience and Advancement of Learning.* In *The Works of Francis Bacon*, volume III. Edited by J. Spedding, R.L. Ellis and D.D. Heath. London: Longman, reprint 1963.

Baglivi, Giorgio. *The Practice of Physic.* 2nd edition. London, 1696 and 1704. Reprint, London, 1723.

Balguy, John. *The Foundation of Moral Goodness: Or a Further Inquiry into the Original or our Ideas of Virtue, in two Parts.* London, 1728–1729.

Barbeyrac, Jean. "An Historical and Critical Account of the Science of Morality and the Progress it has made in the World from the earliest times down to the Publication of this Work." In *Samuel Pufendorf, The Law of Nature and Nations.* Edited by Edmund Carew. 5th edition. London, 1749.

Bauzée, Nicolas. "Langue (Gramm.)." In *Encyclopédie, ou Dictionnaire raisonée des sciences, des arts et des métiers, par une société de gens de lettres.* Edited by Denis Diderot and Jean D'Alembert. Volume IX, pp. 249–266. Elmsford, New York: Pergamon Reprint, 1984.

Bayle, Pierre. *Continuation des pensées divers.* In *Œuvres diverses de Pierre Bayle.* Edited by Pierre Des Maiseaux. 4 volumes. The Hague, 1717–1731.

Dictionaire, historique et critique. 3 volumes. Rotterdam, 1702.

The Dictionary Historical and Critical of Mr. Peter Bayle. The Second Edition. London, 1702; 3rd edition, *To Which is Prefaced The Life of the Author, Revised, Corrected and Enlarged, by Mr. Des Maiseaux, Fellow of the Royal Society.* London, 1734.

Miscellaneous Reflections on the Comet. London, 1708.

Nouvelles de la République des Lettres. 1686.

Pensées diverses sur la comète. 2 volumes. Edited by A. Prat. Paris: Droz, 1939.

Bentham, Jeremy. *Introduction to the Principles of Morals and Legislation.* (1800) Edited by J.H. Burns and H.L.A. Hart. London: Athlone Press, 1970.

Bentley, Richard. *A Confutation of Atheism from the Origin and Frame of the World.* London, 1697.

The Folly and Unreasonableness of Atheism, demonstrated from the Advantage and Pleasure of a Religious Life, the Faculties of Human Souls, the Structure of Animate Bodies, and the Origin and Frame of the World.* London, 1692. Reprint, Glasgow, 1813.

The Folly of Atheism and (what is now called) Deism. London, 1693.

Berkeley, George. *Alciphron, ou le petit philosophe; en sept dialogues: contenant une apologie de la religion chrétienne contre ceux qu'on nomme esprit-forts.* Translated by E. de Joncourt. Paris: Rolin, 1734.

Alciphron: Or the Minute Philosopher; Containing and Apology for the Christian Religion against those who are called Free Thinkers. 2nd edition. 2 volumes. London, 1732.

Bibliothèque britannique, ou histoire des ouvrages des savans de la Grande Bretagne. Paris, 1733.

Bernier, François. *Abrégé de la philosophie de M. Gassendi.* Lyons, 1684.

Betterton, Thomas. *The History of the English Stage.* London, 1741.

Blackmore, Sir Richard. *Creation: A Philosophical Poem. . . .* London, 1712.

Prince Arthur. In *Critical Essays of the Seventeenth Century.* Edited by J.E. Springarn. Oxford University Press, 1909.

Blair, Hugh. "The Rise and Progress of Language." In *Lectures on Rhetoric and Belles Lettres.* 4th edition, pp. 122–148. London: Strahan and Cadell, 1790.

Bluett (or Blewitt), George. *An Enquiry Whether a General Practice of Virtue Tends to the Wealth or Poverty, Benefit or Disadvantage of a People?* London, 1725.

Boswell, James. *Life of Johnson.* Edited by R.W. Chapman, revised by J.D. Fleeman. Oxford: Oxford University Press, 1970.

Boyer, Abel. *Characters of the Virtues and Vices of the Age.* London, 1695.

Choice Letters of Gallantry and Friendship. London, 1701.

The English Theophrastus: Or the Manners of the Age. London, 1702.

Letters of Wit, Politicks and Morality. London, 1701.

Brittania Languens. (Anon.) London, 1680. In *Early English Tracts on Commerce.* Edited by J.R. McCulloch. Cambridge: Economic History Society, 1952.

Brown, John. *Essays on the Characteristics of the Earl of Shaftesbury.* (1751) New York: Garland Reprint, 1970.

An Estimate of the Manners and Principles of the Times. 1757.

Estimate of the Virtues and Vices of the Age. London, 1757.

Honour, a Poem. London, 1753.

Browning, Robert. *Parleyings with Certain People of Importance in Their Day.* London: Smith, Elster, 1887.

Burnett, Gilbert. *Lettters between the late Mr. Gilbert Burnet, and Mr. Hutchinson, Concerning the True Foundation of Virtue.* London, 1735.

Butler, Joseph. *The Works of Joseph Butler*. 2 volumes. Edited by J.H. Bernard. London: Macmillan, 1900.

The Works of Joseph Butler. Edited by the Hon. W.E. Gladstone. Oxford: Clarendon Press, 1897.

Campbell, Archibald. *Arete-logia: Or an Enquiry into the Original of Moral Virtue*. Westminster, 1728.

An Enquiry into the Original of Moral Virtue. Edinburgh, 1733.

Campbell, Richard. *The London Tradesman*. London, 1747.

Cervantes, Miguel de. *Don Quixote*. Translated by J.M. Cohen. Hammondsworth: Penguin, 1958.

Chamfort (Sebastian Roch Nicholas). *Maximes et pensées*. Edited by Claude Roy. Paris: Union Générale d'Editions, 1963.

The Character of the Times Delineated. (Anon.) London, 1732.

Charleton, Walter. *Natural History of the Passions*. 2nd edition. London, 1674; 2nd edition, London, 1701.

Physiologia Epicuro-Gassendo-Charltoniana. London, 1654.

Three Anatomic Lectures. London, 1683.

The Cheating Age Found Out: When Knaves Were Most in Fashion. (Anon.) London, 1705.

Cicero, Marcus Tullius. *De inventione*. Translated by H.M. Hubbel. Loeb Classical Library. Cambridge, Massachusetts: Harvard University Press, 1949.

De oratore. Translated by E.W. Sutton. Loeb Classical Library. Cambridge, Massachusetts: Harvard University Press, 1942.

Clarke, John. *The Foundation of Morality in Theory and Practice Considered*. London, 1726.

Collier, Jeremy. *A Short View of the Immorality and Profaneness of the English Stage*. London, 1698.

Condillac, Abbé de (Etienne Bonnot). *Essai sur l'origine des connaissances humaine*. Edited by Georges Le Roy. In *Œuvres philosophiques de Condillac*. Paris: PUF, 1947.

An Essay on the Origin of Human Knowledge: Being a Supplement to Mr. Locke's Essay. Translated by Thomas Nugent. London, 1756.

"Where the Imagination Gets the Embellishments it Gives to Truth." In *Philosophical Writings of Etienne Bonnot, Abbé de Condillac*. Volume II, pp. 478–479. Translated by Franklin Philip. Hillsdale, New Jersey, Lawrence Erlbaum Associates, 1987.

Creech, Thomas. *Lucretius his Six Books of Epicurean Philosophy: And Manilus his Five Books*. London, 1700.

Defoe, Daniel. *Enquiry into Occasional Conformity*. London, 1702.

Everybody's Business is Nobody's Business. In *Works*. London: Bohn's Classics, 1870.

A Plan of the English Commerce. In *A Select Collection of Scarce and Valuable Tracts on Commerce*. Edited by J.R. McCulloch. London: Harrison, 1859.

The Review, No. 3. London, 1706.

De la Court, Johan and Pieter. *Consideration van staat ofte politieke weegschaal.* Amsterdam, 1661.
Politieke discousen handelende in ses onderscheicle booken. Amsterdam, 1662.
The True Interest and Political Maxims of the Republic of Holland and West Friesland. London, 1702.
Dennis, John. *A Large Account of the Taste in Poetry.* (London, 1702) Edited by Edward Niles Hooker. In *The Critical Works of John Dennis.* Baltimore: John Hopkins University Press, 1939.
Vice and Luxury Publick Mischiefs: Or Remarks on a book Intitled, The Fable of the Bees or, Private Vices Publick Benefits. London, 1724.
Descartes, René. *Passions of the Soul.* In *Philosophical Works.* Edited by E.S. Haldane and G.R.T. Ross. Volume I, pp. 329–428. Cambridge University Press, 1931.
des Cousture, Baron. *La Morale d'Epicure.* Paris, 1685.
De Witt, John (?) *Fables, Moral and Political, With Large Explications. Translated from the Dutch.* In Two Volumes. London, 1703.
Diderot, Denis. "L'Ame des bêtes." In *Encyclopédie, our Dictionnaire raisonée des sciences, des arts et des métiers, par une société de gens de lettres.* Edited by Denis Diderot and Jean D'Alembert. Volume I, pp. 343–353. Elmsford, New York: Pergamon Reprint, 1984.
"Epicurus." In *Encyclopédie, ou Dictionnaire raisonée des sciences, des arts et des métiers, par une société de gens de lettres.* Edited by Denis Diderot and Jean D'Alembert. Volume V, pp. 783–785. Elmsford, New York: Pergamon Reprint, 1984.
Œuvres complètes. Edited by J. Assézat. Paris: Garnier, 1875–1877.
Rameau's Nephew. Translated by L.W. Tancock. London: Penguin, 1966.
Digby, John. *Epicurus's Morals, Translated from the Greek by John Digby, Esq. with Comments and Reflections Taken out of Several Authors.* London, 1712.
Du Bos, Jean-Baptiste. *Réflexions critiques sur la poésie et sur peinture.* Paris, 1719. Translated by Thomas Nugent, *Critical Reflections on Poetry and Painting.* London, 1748.
Duclos, Charles. "Declamation des anciens." In *Encyclopédie, ou Dictionnaire raisonnée des sciences, des arts et des métiers, par une société de gens de lettres.* Edited by Denis Diderot and Jean D'Alembert. Volume XIV, pp. 686–691. Elmsford, New York: Pergamon Reprint, 1984.
du Rondel, Jacques. *La Vie d'Epicure.* Amsterdam and Paris, 1679 and 1693.
England's Greatest Happiness. (Anon.) London, 1677. In *Early English Tracts on Commerce.* Edited by J.R. McCulloch. Cambridge: Economic History Society, 1952.
Epictetus. *Encheiridion.* 2 volumes. Translated by W.A. Oldfather. London: Heinemann, 1946.
Epicurus. *Epistula.* In *Epicurus, the Extant Remains.* Translated by Cyril Bailey. Oxford: Clarendon Press, 1926.
Esprit, Jacques. *Discourses on the Deceitfulness of Humane Virtues.* Translated by William Beauvoir. London, 1706.

The Falsehood of Human Virtue. London, 1691.

Ferguson, Adam. *An Essay on the History of Civil Society 1767*. Edited by Duncan Forbes. Edinburgh University Press, 1966.

Fiddes, Richard. *A General Treatise of Morality*. London, 1724.

Fielding, Henry. *Amelia*. Edited by David Blewitt. Harmondsworth: Penguin, 1987.

    Champion. In *Complete Works of Henry Fielding*. Edited by W.E. Henley. Volume xv. London: Heinemann, 1903.

    "An Essay on the Knowledge and of the Characters of Men." In *Complete Works of Henry Fielding*. Edited by W.E. Henley. Volume xi, pp. 173–216. London: Heinemann, 1903.

    The History of the Adventures of Joseph Andrews and his Friend Mr. Abraham Adams. Written in Imitation of the Manner of Cervantes, Author of Don Quixote. Edited by Martin C. Battestin. Boston: Houghton Mifflin, 1961.

    The History of Tom Jones, a Foundling. Edited by Sheridan Baker. New York: W.W. Norton, 1973.

    Enquiry Into the . . . Recent Causes . . . of the Increase in Robbers. (1751). New York: AMS Press Reprint, 1975.

    The Masquerade (1728). In *"The Female Husband" and Other Writings*. Edited by Claude E. Jones. Liverpool University Press, 1960.

    Miscellanies. In *Complete Works of Henry Fielding*. Edited by W.E. Henley. Volume xii. London: Heinemann, 1903.

Fontenelle, *Pluralité des Mondes* (1686).

Franklin, Benjamin. *Autobiography*. In *Works*. Edited by J. Bigelow. New York: Putnam, 1904.

Garrick, David. *An Essay on Acting*. London, 1744. In *Actors on Acting*. Edited by Toby Cole and Helen C. Chinoy. New York: Crown, 1954.

Gassendi, Pierre. "Fifth Set of Objections." In René Descartes, *Philosophical Works*. Edited by E.S. Holdane and G.R.T. Ross. Volume ii, pp. 135–203. Cambridge University Press, 1931.

    Three Discourses of Happiness, Virtue and Liberty: Collected from the works of the Learn'd Gassendi, By Monsieur Bernier. Translated out of the French. London, 1699.

Gay, John. "The Degenerate Bees." In *The Fables of John Gay*. Edited by E. Wright. Fable x, pp. 253–256. London: Warne, 1889.

Gibbon, Edward. *The History of the Decline and Fall of the Roman Empire*. Edited by J.B. Bury. 7 volumes. London: Methuen, 1912.

Gibson, Edmund. *Pastoral Letter to the People of His Diocese*. London, 1726.

Godwin, William. *Mandeville: A Tale of the Seventeenth Century in England*. London: Constable, 1817.

Hegel, G.W.F. *The Philosophy of Right*. Edited by T.M. Knox. Oxford: Clarendon Press, 1952.

Helvétius, Adrien Claude. *De L'Esprit*. Paris, 1757.

Hendley, William. *A Defence of the Charity Schools*. London, 1725.

(Hervey, John). *Some Remarks on the Minute Philosopher in a Letter from a Country Clergyman to his Friend in London*. London, 1732.

Heynes, Matthew. *A Sermon for the Reformation of Manners Preac'd in St. Paul's Church in Bedford at the Assizes there held March the 15th 1700*. London, 1701.
Hobbes, Thomas. *Leviathan*. Edited by C.B. Macpherson. Harmondsworth: Penguin, 1968.
Hogarth, William. *The Analysis of Beauty*. London, 1753.
Home, Henry, Lord Kames. *Elements of Criticism*. 6th edition. Edinburgh, 1795.
Hume, David. *Dialogues Concerning Natural Religion*. Edited by J.V. Price. Oxford University Press, 1976.
   Enquiry Concerning the Principles of Morals. Edited by L.A. Selby-Bigge. Oxford University Press, 1902.
   Essays Moral, Political and Literary. Indianapolis: Liberty Press, 1985.
   Letters of David Hume. Edited by J.Y.T. Greig. Oxford: Clarendon Press, 1932.
   A Treatise of Human Nature. Edited by L.A. Selby-Bigge. Oxford: Clarendon Press, 1955.
Hutcheson, Francis. *Collected Works*. Edited by Bernhard Fabian. 7 volumes. Hildesheim: Olms Reprint, 1971.
   Essay on the Nature and Conduct of the Passions and Affections. Glasgow, 1728.
   Reflections on Laughter and Remarks on the Fable of the Bees. Glasgow, 1750.
   A Short Introduction to Moral Philosophy. Glasgow, 1747.
Jones, Erasmus. *Luxury, Pride and Vanity the Bane of the British Nation*. London, 1736; reprinted 1750.
Joucourt, Chevalier du. "Langage." In *Encyclopédie, ou Dictionnaire raisonnée des sciences, des arts et des métiers, par une société de gens de lettres*. Edited by Denis Diderot and Jean D'Alembert. Volume IX, pp. 245–247. Elmsford, New York: Pergamon Reprint, 1984.
Kant, Immanuel. *Anthropologie in pragmatischer Hinsicht*. 6th edition. Edited by W. Weischedal. Wiesbaden: Insel-Verlag, 1956–1964.
   Anthropology From a Pragmatic Point of View. Translated by Mary J. Gregor. The Hague: Nijhoff, 1974.
   The Critique of Practical Reason. Translated by T.K. Abbott. London: Longman, 1909.
   Idea for a Universal History from a Cosmopolitan Point of View. In *Kant on History*. Translated and edited by Lewis White Beck. Indianapolis: Bobbs–Merrill, 1963.
   "What is Enlightenment." In *Kant's Political Writings*. Edited by Hans Reiss, pp. 54–60. Cambridge University Press, 1976.
Laertius, Diogenes. *The Lives of the Philosophers*. Translated by R.D. Hicks. London: Heinemann, 1925.
La Mothe le Vayer, François. *Cinq dialogues*. Mons, 1671.
   The Great Prerogative of Private Life: By Way of a Dialogue. London, 1678.
La Rochefoucauld. *Maxims*. Translated by Leonard Tannock, Harmondsworth: Penguin, 1959.
Law, William. *The Absolute Unlawfulness of Stage-Entertainment Fully Demonstrated*. London, 1726.

Remarks on a Late Book, Entitled the Fable of the Bees, or Private Vices Publick Benefits. In a Letter to the Author: To Which is Added, A Postscript, Containing an Observation or Two upon Mr. Bayle. London, 1724.

A Serious Call to a Devout and Holy Life. London, 1729.

Lebrun, Charles. *A Method to Learn to Design the Passions.* (1734) Los Angeles: William Andrew Clark Memorial Library Publication 200–201, 198X.

Le Clerc, Jean. *Sentiments de quelque theologiens hollandais sur l'histoire critique du Vieux Testament.* Amsterdam, 1685.

Leibniz, Gottfried Wilhelm von. *New Essays on Human Understanding.* Translated by Jonathan Bennett and Peter Remnant. Cambridge University Press, 1981.

Locke, John. *An Essay Concerning Human Understanding.* Edited by Peter Niddich. Oxford: Clarendon Press, 1975.

Lucretius, Carus Titus. *De rerum novarum.* Translated by W.E. Leonard. New York: Dutton, 1957.

Machiavelli, Niccolo. *The Discourses.* Translated by L. Walter. Edited by Bernard Crick. Harmondsworth: Penguin, 1970.

Mackintosh, Sir James. *Dissertation on the Progress of Ethical Philosophy.* 3rd edition. Preface by William Whewell. Edinburgh: Black, 1862.

Malebranche, Nicolas. *Entretiens sur la métaphysique et sur la religion suivre des entretiens sur la mort.* (1688) 2 volumes. Edited by Armand Cuviller. Paris: Vrin, 1945–1947.

Malthus, T.R. *An Essay on the Principle of Population.* 6th edition. London: Murray, 1826.

Melon, Jean-François. *Essai politique sur le commerce.* Bordeaux, 1734; English translation, 1735.

Mémoires pour l'histoire des sciences et des beaux-arts (Mémoires de Trévoux) Geneva: Slatkine Reprint, 1969.

Mill, John Stuart. "Bentham." In *Essays on Politics and Culture.* Edited by Gertrude Himmelfarb, pp. 77–120. New York: Anchor, 1963.

Misson, Henri de Valbourg. *Mémoires et observations faites par un voyage en Angleterre.* The Hague, 1698.

Montesquieu, Baron de (Jean de Secondat). *Œuvres complètes.* Edited by Daniel Oster. Paris: Seuil, 1964.

The Spirit of the Laws. Translated by A.M. Cohen, B.C. Miller and H.S. Stone. Cambridge University Press, 1989.

Neville, Henry. *Plato Redivivus.* Edited by Caroline Robbins. In *Two English Republican Tracts.* Cambridge University Press, 1969.

Nicole, Pierre. *Essais de morale.* Amsterdam: D. Elzevier, 1672–1677; Paris, 1675.

Moral Essayes: Contain'd in Several Treatises on Many Important Duties. London, 1696.

Traité de l'âme des bêtes. Paris, 1737.

Traité de la comédie. (1667) Edited by Georges Couton. Paris: Société D'Edition "Les Belles Lettres," 1961.

Visionaires. Letter VIII. In *Les Imaginaires et visionaires.* Cologne, 1683.

North, Sir Dudley. *Discourses on Trade.* London, 1690.

Pascal, Blaise. *Pensées.* Edited by A.J. Krailsheimer. Harmondsworth: Penguin, 1966.

Réflections sur la géométrie en général. De l'esprit de géométrique et de l'art de persuader. In *Œuvres complètes.* Edited by Jean Mesnard. Paris: Gallimard, 1954.

Petty, William. *Political Arithmetic.* London, 1690.

Phillips, E. *An Appeal to Common Sense: Or, Some Considerations Offer'd to Restore Publick Credit: As Also the Means of Reviving It.* London, 1720.

Philpot, Stephen. *Polite Education.* London, 1759.

Pluquet, Adrien. *De la sociabilité.* 2 volumes. Paris, 1767.

Plutarch. "The Life of Cleomenes." In *Plutarch's Lives.* Translated by Thomas Creech. London, 1685.

Pollexfen, John. *A Discourse on Trade, Coyne, and Paper Credit.* London, 1697.

Pope, Alexander. *An Essay on Man.* Edited by Maynard Mack. London: Methuen, 1950.

First Epistle of the Second Book of Horace. London, 1732.

"Project for the Advancement of the Stage." In *Peri Bathous.* London, 1728.

Purshall, G. *Essay on the Mechanical Fabric of the Universe.* London, 1708.

Quintillian, Marcus Fabius. *Institutio oratoria.* Edited by M.E. Butler. 4 volumes. London: Heinemann, 1920–1922.

Review of Robert Browning, *Parleyings with Certain People of Importance in Their Day.* (Anon.) In *The Westminster Review* 128 April 1880: 132.

Robinson, Nicholas. *The Christian Philosopher.* London, 1741.

Rousseau, Jean-Jacques. *The Confessions.* Translated by J.M. Cohen. Harmondsworth: Penguin, 1954.

"Contre l'opinion de Mandeville." In *Œuvres complètes.* Volume III. Edited by Jean Fabre. Paris: Seuil, 1967.

Discours sur l'origine et les fondements d'inégalité parmi les hommes. Edited by Jean Starobinski. Paris: Gallimard, 1964.

Discourse on the Origin and Foundations of Inequality. Translated by Roger D. Masters. New York: St. Martin's Press, 1964.

Discourse on the Sciences and Arts. Translated by Roger D. Masters. New York: St. Martin's Press, 1964.

Emile. Translated by Allan Bloom. New York: Free Press, 1979.

Essai sur l'origine des langues. Edited by Charles Porset. Bordeaux: Ducros, 1970.

Letter to Bordes. In *Œuvres complètes.* Volume II. Paris: Gallimard, 1964.

Narcisse, ou l'amant de lui-même. In *Œuvres complètes.* Edited by Jean Starobinski. Volume II. Paris: Gallimard, 1964.

Politics and the Arts: Letter to M. D'Alembert on the Theater. Translated by Allan Bloom. Glencoe: The Free Press, 1960.

Saint-Evrémond, Seigneur Charles de (Saint Deris de Marguetel). *Works of*

M. de St. Evrémond made English from the French Original. 3 volumes. Edited by Pierre Des Maiseaux. London, 1728.

Saint-Pierre. *Ouvrage de morales et de politique.* Rotterdam, 1734–1741.

Say, Jean-Baptiste. *A Treatise on Political Economy.* Translated by C.R. Prinseps. Philadelphia: Lippincott, 1857.

Shaftesbury, Third Earl of (Anthony Ashley Cooper). *Characteristics of Men, Manners, Opinions, Times, etc.* 2 volumes. Edited by John M. Robertson. London: Richards, 1900.

    Essai sur la merité et la vertu. Translated by Denis Diderot. In *Œuvres complètes.* Volume 1. Edited by J. Assézat. Paris: Garnier, 1874–1876.

    A Notion on the Historical Draught of the Judgement of Hercules. London, 1732. In *Shaftesbury's Second Characteristics.* Edited by Benjamin Road Cambridge University Press, 1914.

Sidney, Algernon. *Discourses on Government.* London, 1751.

Simon, Richard. *Histoire critique du Vieux Testament.* Amsterdam, 1678.

Skelton, Philip. *Ophiomaches, or Deism Revealed.* London, 1748.

Smith, Adam. *An Inquiry into the Nature and Causes of the Wealth of Nations.* 2 volumes. Edited by A.S. Skinner, W.B. Todd and R.H. Campbell. Oxford University Press, 1976.

    Lectures on Jurisprudence. Edited by R.L. Meek, D.D. Raphael and P.G. Stein. Indianapolis: Liberty Press, 1982.

    "Letter to the Edinburgh Review." In *Essays on Philosophical Subjects,* Edited by W.P.D. Wightman and J.C. Bryce. Oxford University Press, 1980.

    The Theory of Moral Sentiments. Edited by D.D. Raphael and A.L. Macfie. Oxford University Press, 1976.

Sorberius, Samuel. "De vita e moribus Petri Gassendi." In Pierre Gassendi (ed.), *Syntagma philosophiae Epicuri.* Amsterdam, 1684.

Sorbière, Samuel. *Avis a un jeune médecin sur la manière dont il se doit coporter en la practique de la médecine.* Lyons, 1672.

    A Voyage to England. (1664) London, 1702.

Spratt, Thomas. *The History of the Royal Society.* London, 1667. Edited by Jackson I. Cope and Harold W. Jones. St. Louis: Washington University Press Reprint, 1958.

    Observations on M. de Sorbière's Voyage. London, 1665.

Springarn, J.E. *Critical Essays of the Seventeenth Century.* Oxford University Press, 1909.

Stanley, Thomas. "The Doctrine of Epicurus." In *The History of Philosophy.* London, 1660.

Steele, Richard. *The Tatler.* London, 1709–1712.

Steuart, Sir James. *Inquiry into the Principles of Political Œconomy.* (1767). 2 volumes. Edited by Andrew Skinner. Edinburgh: Olner and Boyd, 1966.

Stewart, Dugald. *Account of the Life and Writings of Adam Smith, LL D.* (1794). In Adam Smith, *Essays on Philosophical Subjects.* Edited by I.S. Ross and J.C. Bryce. Indianapolis: Liberty Press, 1982.

Swift, Jonathan. *The Battle of the Books*. In *Prose Works*. Volume I. Edited by
H. Davis. Oxford University Press, 1939.

Temple, Sir William. *Observations upon the United Provinces of the Netherlands*.
5th edition. Edited by G.N. Clark. Cambridge University Press, 1932.

Therold, John. *A Short Examination of the Nations Advanc'd in a (Late) Book,
intitled, The Fable of the Bees or Private Vices, Publick Benefits*. London, 1726.

Tindal, Matthew. *A Defence of our Happy Establishment; and the Administration
Vindicated*. London, 1722.

Turgot, Anne Robert Jacques. "Etymologie." In *Encyclopédie, ou Dictionnaire
raisonnée des sciences, des arts et des métiers, par une société de gens de lettres*.
Edited by Denis Diderot and Jean D'Alembert. Volume XVI, pp. 98–
111. Elmsford, New York: Pergamon Reprint, 1984.

Reflections sur les langues. In *Œuvres de Turgot*. Edited by Eugène Daire and
Hyppolyte Dussard. Volume II. Paris: Guillaumin, 1844.

Voltaire, François M. Arouet de. *Correspondence*. Volume XXII. Edited by
Theodore Besterman. Banbury: Voltaire Foundation, 1972.

Dictionnaire philosophique. Preface by René Pomeau. Paris: Garnier–Flam-
marion, 1964.

"Envie." In *Questions sur l'Encyclopédie*. In *Œuvres complètes de Voltaire*.
Edited by Louis Moland. Volume II, pp. 537–538. Paris: Garnier, 1878.

Lettres philosophiques. Paris, 1733.

Traité de métaphysique. Edited by H. Temple Patterson. Manchester
University Press, 1937.

Voyages et aventures de Jacques Massé. (Anon., dated. 1710 on title page.)

Warburton, William. *Dissertations sur l'unions de la religion, de la morale, et de la
politique*. 2 volumes. Translated by Etienne Silhouette. London?, 1742.

The Divine Legation of Moses. (1738 and 1741) London: Cadell and Davies,
1811.

Essai sur les hieroglyphes des Egyptiens. 2 volumes. Translated by Leonard de
Malpines. Paris, 1744.

"A Supplement to the Translator's Preface, Communicated by a Learned
Writer, Well-Known to the Literary World." In Miguel de Cervantes,
Don Quixote. Translated by Henry Jarvis. London, 1742.

Ward, Ned. *The Character of a Covetous Citizen: Or a Ready Way to Get Riches*.
London, 1702.

The Miracles Performed by Money. London, 1695.

To That Celebrated Ideal Mamon. London, 1709.

Warder, J. *The True Amazons: Or the Monarchy of the Bees*. London, 1712.

Whately, Richard. *Introductory Lectures on Political Economy: Being Part of a
Course Delivered in Easter Term, 1831*. London: Fellowes, 1832.

Willis, Thomas. *Two Discourses Concerning the Soul of Brutes*. Edited by S.
Diamond. Translated by S. Pordage. London, 1683. Gainsville: Scholars' Facsimiles, 1971.

Wordsworth, William. *The Prelude*. Edited by J.C. Maxwell. Harmondsworth: Penguin, 1971.

SECONDARY SOURCES

Aarsleff, Hans. "Leibniz and Locke on Language in the Eighteenth Century and the Debate in the Berlin Academy Before Herder." In *From Locke to Saussure*, pp. 42–83 and 146–209. Minneapolis: University of Minnesota Press, 1982.

Agnew, Jean-Christophe. *Worlds Apart: The Market and the Theatre in Anglo-American Thought, 1550–1750*. Cambridge University Press, 1986.

Aldridge, A. Owen. "Mandeville and Voltaire." In *Mandeville Studies*. Edited by Irwin Primer, pp. 142–156. The Hague: Nijhoff, 1975.

Appleby, Joyce Oldham. *Economic Thought and Ideology in Seventeenth-Century England*. Princeton University Press, 1978.

Baczko, Bronislaw. "La Cité et ses langues." In *Rousseau After 200 Years*. Edited by R.A. Leigh, pp. 87–108. Cambridge University Press, 1982.

Barish, Jonah. *The Anti-Theatrical Prejudice*. Berkeley: University of California Press, 1981.

Bellamy, Richard. "'Da Metafisio a Mercatante': Antonio Genovese and the Development of a New Language of Commerce in Eighteenth-Century Naples." In *The Languages of Political Theory in Early Modern Europe*. Edited by Anthony Pagden. Cambridge University Press, 1987.

Berman, David. *A History of Atheism in Britain*. London: Croom Helm, 1988.

Blom, H.W. "Political Science in the Golden Age: Criticism, History and Theory in Dutch Seventeenth-Century Political Thought." *Netherlands Journal of Sociology*, 15 (1979): 47–71.

Brentano, Lujo. *Der Wirtschaftende Mensch in der Geschichte*. Leipzig: Meiner, 1913.

Brewer, John. *The Sinews of Power*. New York: Alfred Knopf, 1989.

Brown, Theodore M. "From Mechanism to Vitalism in Eighteenth-Century Physiology." *Journal of the History of Biology* 7, 2 (1974): 179–216.

Browning, Reed. *The Political and Constitutional Ideas of the Court Whigs*. Baton Rouge: Louisiana State University Press, 1983.

Burton, A.P. "Cervantes the Man Seen through English Eyes in the Seventeenth and Eighteenth Centuries." *Bulletin of Hispanic Studies* 45 (1968): 1–15.

Burtt, Shelly. *Virtue Transformed: Political Argument in England, 1688–1740*. Cambridge University Press, 1992.

Carrive, Paulette. *Bernard Mandeville: Passions, vices, vertus*. Paris: Vrin, 1980.
La Philosophie des passions chez Bernard Mandeville. 2 volumes. Paris: Didier Erudition, 1983.

Castiglione, Dario. "Excess, Frugality and the Spirit of Capitalism: Readings of Mandeville on Commercial Society." In *Culture in History: Production, Consumption and Values in Historical Perspective*. Edited by Joseph Melling and Jonathan Barry, pp. 155–179. University of Exeter Press, 1992.
"Mandeville Moralized." *Annali della Fondazione Luigi Einaudi* 17 (1983): 239–290.

Castle, Terry. *Masquerade and Civilization.* Stanford University Press, 1986.

Chaisson, Elias J. "Bernard Mandeville: A Reappraisal." *Philological Quarterly* 49 (1970): 489–519.

Chalk, Alfred F. "Mandeville's Fable of the Bees: A Reappraisal." *Southern Economic Journal* 33 (1966): 1–16.

Charlanne, L. *L'Influence française en Angleterre au XVIIe siècle.* Paris, 1906.

Charleton, D.G. "J.B. Du Bos and Eighteenth-Century Sensibility." In *Studies on Voltaire and the Eighteenth Century* 266 (1990): 151–162.

Christiaans, P.A. "De Mandeville." *Jaarboek Centraal Bureau voor Genealogie* 33 (1979): 118–125.

Clark, J.C.D. *English Society, 1688–1832.* Cambridge University Press, 1985.

Coates, A.W. "Changing Attitudes Toward Labour in the Mid-Eighteenth Century." *Economic History Review* 2nd series, 11, 1 (1958): 35–51.

Coleman, John. "Bernard Mandeville and the Reality of Virtue." *Philosophy* 47 (1972): 125–139.

Colie, Rosalie L. *Paradoxia Epidemica: The Renaissance Tradition of Paradox.* Princeton University Press, 1966.

Collins, R. A. "Private Vices, Public Benefits: Dr. Mandeville and the Body Politic." D. Phil. thesis, Oxford University, 1988.

Colletti, Lucio. "Mandeville, Rousseau and Smith." In *From Rousseau to Lenin. Studies in Ideology and Society,* pp. 195–218. Translated by John Merrington and Judith White. London: New Left Books, 1972.

Cook, Richard I. *Bernard Mandeville.* New York: Twayne Publishers, 1974. "The Great Leviathan of Lechery: Mandeville's *Modest Defence of Public Stews* (1724)." In *Mandeville Studies.* Edited by Irwin Primer, pp. 22–33. The Hague: Nijhoff, 1975.

Corman, Brian. "Congreve, Fielding and the Rise of Some Novels." In *British Theatre and the Other Arts, 1600–1800.* Edited by Shirley Strum Kenny, pp. 257–270. Washington: Folger Shakespeare Library, 1984.

Crowley, J.E. *This Sheba, Self: The Conceptualization of Economic Life in Eighteenth-Century America.* Baltimore: John Hopkins University Press. 1974.

Curtin, Michael. "A Question of Manners: Status and Gender in Etiquette and Courtesy." *The Journal of Modern History* 57 (September 1985): 395–423.

Curtius, Ernst Robert. *European Literature and the Latin Middle Ages.* Translated by Willard R. Trask. London: Routledge and Keegan Paul, 1953.

Daniel, Stephen H. "Political and Philosophical Uses of Fables in Eighteenth-Century England." *The Eighteenth Century* 28, 2 (1982): 151–171.

Davie, George. "Berkeley, Hume and the Central Problem of Scottish Philosophy." In *McGill Hume Studies.* Edited by Nicholas Capaldi, David Fate Norton and Wade Robson, pp. 43–62. San Diego: Austin Hill Press, 1979.

Dekker, Rudolf. "'Private Vices, Public Virtues Revisited: The Dutch Background of Bernard Mandeville." *History of European Ideas* 14, 4 (1992): 481–498.

Derrida, Jacques. "Genesis and Structure of the *Essay on the Origin of Languages.*" In *Of Grammatology.* Translated by Gayatri Chakravorty Spivak, pp. 165–268. Baltimore: Johns Hopkins University Press, 1976.

Desfond, Hélène. "Tyburn chez Mandeville et Fielding, ou le corps exemplaire du pendu." In *Le Corps et l'âme en Grand-Bretagne au XVIIIe siècle.* Edited by Paul-Gabriel Boucé and Suzi Halimi, pp. 61–70. Paris: Sorbonne, 1985.

Dickey, Laurence. "Historicizing the 'Adam Smith Problem': Conceptual, Historiographical and Textual Issues." *Journal of Modern History* 58 (1986): 579–609.

"Pride, Hypocrisy and Civility in Mandeville's Social and Historical Theory." *Critical Review* 4, 3 (Summer 1990): 387–431.

Dickinson, H.T. "Bernard Mandeville: An Independent Whig." *Studies on Voltaire and the Eighteenth Century* 151 (1976): 559–570.

"The Politics of Bernard Mandeville." In *Mandeville Studies.* Edited by Irwin Primer, pp. 80–97. The Hague: Nijhoff, 1975.

Dickson, P.G.M. *The Financial Revolution in England: A Study in the Development of Public Credit.* London: Macmillan, 1967.

Didier, J. *Montesquieu et la tradition politique anglaise en France.* Paris, 1909.

Duchet, Michèle. *Anthropologie et histoire au siècle des lumières.* Paris: Maspero, 1971.

Duchet, Michèle and Launay, Michel. "Sychronie et diachronie: l'essai sur l'origine des langues et le second *Discours.*" *Revue Internationale de Philosophie* 21 (1967): 421–442.

Dumont, Louis. *From Mandeville to Marx. The Genesis and Triumph of Economic Ideology.* Chicago University Press, 1977.

Duncan-Jones, Austin. *Butler's Moral Philosophy.* Harmondsworth: Penguin, 1952.

Elias, Norbert. *The Court Society.* Oxford: Blackwell, 1983.

Ellison, Charles E. "Rousseau and the Modern City: The Politics of Speech and Dress." *Political Theory* 13, 4 (November 1985): 497–534.

Elster, Jon. *Logic and Society.* New York: Wiley, 1978.

Fabian, Bernhard. "The Reception of Bernard Mandeville in Eighteenth-Century Germany." *Studies on Voltaire and the Eighteenth Century* 15, 2 (1976): 693–722.

Forbes, Duncan. *Hume's Philosophical Politics.* Cambridge University Press, 1975.

"Sceptical Whiggism, Commerce and Liberty." In *Essays on Adam Smith.* Edited by A.S. Skinner and T. Wilson, pp. 179–202. Oxford: Clarendon Press, 1976.

Formigiari, Lia. *Linguistica e anthropologia nel secundo settecento.* Messina: Editrice La Libra, 1972.

Foster, M. *Lectures on the History of Physiology.* Cambridge University Press, 1901.

Foxon, D.F. "Libertine Literature in England, 1660–1745." *Book Collector* 12 (1963): 21–36, 159–177 and 294–307.

France, Peter. *Politeness and Its Discontents*. Cambridge: Cambridge University Press, 1992.

Frank, R.G. "Thomas Willis and His Circle: Brain and Mind in Seventeenth-Century Medicine." In G.S. Rousseau (ed.), *The Longings of Psyche: Mind and Brain in Enlightenment Thought*, pp. 104–146. Berkeley: University of California Press, 1990.

Frayling, Christopher, and Wolter, Robert. "From the Orang-Utan to the Vampire: Towards an Anthropology of Rousseau." In *Rousseau After Two Hundred Years*. Edited by R.A. Leigh, pp. 109–32. Cambridge University Press, 1982.

Furniss, Edgar S. *The Position of the Laborer in a System of Nationalism*. New York: Houghton Mifflin, 1920.

Gibson, Carol J. "Bernard Mandeville: The Importance of Women in the Development of Civil Societies." M.A. thesis, University of British Columbia, 1989.

Glock, J. *Die Symbolic der Bienen*. Heidelberg: Groos, 1897.

Goldberg, Homer. *The Art of Joseph Andrews*. Chicago University Press, 1969.

Goldsmith, M.M. "Bernard Mandeville and the Spirit of Capitalism." *Journal of British Studies* 17 (1977): 63–81.

"Liberty, Luxury and the Pursuit of Happiness." In *The Languages of Political Theory in Early-Modern Europe*. Edited by Anthony Pagden, pp. 225–251. Cambridge University Press, 1987.

Private Vices, Public Benefits: Bernard Mandeville's Social and Political Thought. Cambridge University Press, 1985.

"Public Virtue and Private Vices: Bernard Mandeville and English Political Ideologies in the Early Eighteenth Century." *Eighteenth-Century Studies* 9 (1976): 477–510.

"Regulating Anew the Moral and Political Sentiments of Mankind: Bernard Mandeville and the Scottish Enlightenment." *Journal of the History of Ideas* 49, 4 (1988): 587–606.

"'The Treacherous Arts of Mankind': Bernard Mandeville and Female Virtue." In *The Politics of Fallen Man*. Edited by M.M. Goldsmith and Thomas A. Horne, pp. 93–114. Exeter: Imprint Academic, 1986.

Greenleaf, Ralph. *Order, Empiricism and Politics*. Oxford University Press, 1964.

Grégoire, F. *Bernard de Mandeville et La "Fable des abeilles."* Nancy: Georges Thomas, 1947.

Griswald, Charles L. Jr. "Rhetoric and Ethics: Adam Smith on Theorizing the Moral Sentiments." *Philosophy and Rhetoric* 24, 3 (1991): 213–237.

Gunn, J.A.W. "Mandeville: Poverty, Luxury and the Whig Theory of Government." In *Beyond Liberty and Property: The Process of Self-Recognition in Eighteenth-Century Political Thought*, pp. 96–109. Kingston: McGill–Queens University Press, 1983.

"Mandeville and Wither: Individualism and the Workings of Providence." In *Mandeville Studies*. Edited by Irwin Primer, pp. 98–118. The Hague: Nijhoff, 1975.

Politics and the Public Interest in the Seventeenth Century. London: Routledge, 1969.

Habermas, Jurgen. *The Structural Transformation of the Public Sphere*. Translated by Thomas Burger and Frederick Lawrence. Cambridge, Massachusetts: MIT Press, 1989.

Hacking, Ian. *Why Does Language Matter to Philosophy?* Cambridge University Press, 1975.

Haitsma Mulier, E.O.G. "The Language of Seventeenth-Century Republicanism in the United Provinces: Dutch or European?" In *The Languages of Political Theory in Early Modern Europe*. Edited by Anthony Pagden. Cambridge University Press, 1987.

The Myth of Venice and Dutch Republican Thought in the Seventeenth Century. Assen: Van Goram, 1980.

Halsband, Robert. "Stage Drama as a Source for Pictorial and Plastic Art." In *British Theatre and the Other Arts, 1600–1800*. Edited by Shirley Strum Kenny, pp. 149–170, 155. Washington: Folger Shakespeare Library, 1984.

Harrison, Bernard. *Henry Fielding's Tom Jones*. London: Sussex University Press, 1975.

Harth, Philip. "The Satiric Purpose of the Fable of the Bees." *Eighteenth-Century Studies* 2 (1969): 321–340.

Hayek, F.A. "Dr. Bernard Mandeville." *Proceedings of the British Academy* 52 (1966): 125–141.

Heckscher, Eli F. *Mercantilism*. 2 volumes. Translated by Mendel Shapiro. London: Allen and Unwin, 1955.

Hirschman, Albert. *The Passions and the Interests: Political Arguments for Capitalism Before Its Triumph*. Princeton University Press, 1977.

Hobson, Marion. *The Object of Art: The Theory of Illusion in Eighteenth-Century France*. Cambridge University Press, 1982.

Hont, Istvan and Ignatieff, Michael. "Needs and Justice in the Wealth of Nations." In *Wealth and Virtue: The Shaping of Political Economy in the Scottish Enlightenment*. Edited by Istvan Hont and Michael Ignatieff, pp. 1–44. Cambridge University Press, 1983.

Hopkins, Robert H. "The Cant of Social Compromise: Some Observations on Mandeville's Satire." In *Mandeville Studies*. Edited by Irwin Primer, pp. 168–192. The Hague: Nijhoff, 1975.

Horkheimer, Max and Adorno, Theodore *The Dialectic of Enlightenment*. Translated by John Cumming. New York: Seabury Press, 1972.

Horne, Thomas. "Envy in Commercial Society." *Political Theory* 9, 4 (1981): 551–569.

The Social Thought of Bernard Mandeville: Virtue and Commerce in Early Eighteenth-Century England. New York: Columbia University Press, 1978.

Howell, Wilber Samuel. *Eighteenth-Century British Logic and Rhetoric*. Princeton University Press, 1971.

Hughes, Leo. *The Drama's Patrons: A Study of the Eighteenth-Century London Audience*. Austin: University of Texas Press, 1971.

Huizinga, Johan. *Homo Ludens*. London: Routledge and Keegan Paul, 1949.

Hundert, E.J. "The Achievement Motive in Hume's Political Economy." *Journal of the History of Ideas*. 35 (1974): 139–143.

"Augustine and the Sources of the Divided Self." *Political Theory* 20, 1 (1992): 86–104.

"Bernard Mandeville and the Rhetoric of Social Science." *Journal of the History of the Behavioral Sciences* 22 (1986): 311–320.

"A Satire of Self-Disclosure: From Hegel through Rameau to the Augustans." *Journal of the History of Ideas* 47, 2 (1986): 235–248.

"Sexual Politics and the Allegory of Identity in Montesquieu's *Persian Letters*." *The Eighteenth Century: Theory and Society* 31, 2 (1990): 99–113.

Hundert, E.J. and Nelles, Paul. "Liberty and Theatrical Space in Montesquieu's Political Theory: The Poetics of Public Life in *The Persian Letters*." *Political Theory* 17, 2 (May 1989): 223–246.

Hutchinson, T.W. "Berkeley's *Querist* and its Place in the Economic Thought of the Eighteenth Century." *British Journal for the Philosophy of Science* 4 (May 1953–February 1954): 52–77.

Jack, Malcolm. "One State of Nature: Mandeville and Rousseau." *Journal of the History of Ideas* 39 (1978): 119–124.

"Progress and Corruption in the Eighteenth Century: Mandeville's 'Private Vices, Public Benefits.'" *Journal of the History of Ideas* 37 (1976): 369–376.

"Religion and Ethics in Mandeville." In *Mandeville Studies*. Edited by Irwin Primer, pp. 34–42. The Hague: Nijhoff, 1975.

James, E.D. "Faith, Sincerity and Morality: Mandeville and Bayle." In *Mandeville Studies*. Edited by Irwin Primer, pp. 43–65. The Hague: Nijhoff, 1975.

Pierre Nicole, Jansenist and Humanist. The Hague: Nijhoff, 1972.

Jones, E.L. "The Fashion Manipulators: Consumer Tastes and British Industries, 1660–1800." In *Business Enterprise and Economic Change*. Edited by L.P. Cain and P.J. Uselding, pp. 198–226. Athens, Ohio: Ohio University Press, 1973.

Jones, Peter. *Hume's Sentiments: Their Ciceronian and French Context*. Edinburgh University Press, 1982.

Juliard, Pierre. *Philosophies of Language in the Eighteenth Century*. The Hague: Nijhoff, 1970.

Kargon, Robert. *Atomism in England from Harriot to Newton*. Oxford: Clarendon Press, 1966.

Kaye, F.B. "Mandeville on the Origin of Language." *Modern Language Notes* 39 (1922): 136–142.

"The Influence of Bernard Mandeville." *Studies in Philology* 19 (1922): 83–108.

"The Writings of Bernard Mandeville." *Journal of English and Germanic Philology* 20 (1921): 419–467.

Keohane, Nannerl. *Philosophy and the State in France*. Princeton University Press, 1980.

Keynes, John Maynard. *The General Theory of Employment, Interest and Money.* New York: Harcourt, Brace, 1935.

Klein, Lawrence. "Liberty, Manners and Politeness in Early Eighteenth-Century England." *Historical Journal* 32, 3 (1989): 583–605.

"The Third Earl of Shaftesbury and the Progress of Politeness." *Eighteenth-Century Studies* 18, 2 (Winter 1984/5): 186–214.

Kortum, Hans. "Frugalité et luxe à travers la querelle des anciens et des moderns." *Studies on Voltaire and the Eighteenth Century* 56 (1987): 705–775.

Kossmann, E. H. *Politieke Theorie in het zeventiende-eeuwse Nederland.* Amsterdam: North Holland, 1960.

Kramnick, Isaac. *Bolingbroke and his Circle: The Politics of Nostalgia in the Age of Walpole.* Cambridge, Massachusetts: Harvard University Press, 1968.

Kroll, Richard W.F. *The Material World: Literary Culture in the Restoration and Early Eighteenth Century.* Baltimore: Johns Hopkins University Press, 1991.

Kuehner, Paul. *Theories on the Origin and Formation of Language in Eighteenth-Century France.* Philadelphia: University of Pennsylvania Press, 1944.

Labrousse, Elizabeth. *Pierre Bayle.* 2 volumes. The Hague: Nijhoff, 1964.

Lafond, Jean. "Mandeville et La Rochefoucauld, ou des avatars de l'augustinisme." In *Gestaltung–Umgestaltung: Beiträge zur Geschichte des romanischen Literaturen.* Edited by Bernhard König and Jutta Lietz, pp. 137–150. Tübingen: Narr, 1990.

Lamprecht, Sterling L. "The Fable of the Bees." *The Journal of Philosophy* 23, 21 (1926): 561–579.

Landreth, Harry. "The Economic Thought of Bernard Mandeville." *History of Political Economy* 7, 2 (1975): 193–208.

Lecler, J. "'Liberalisme economique et libre pensée au XVIIIe siècle: Mandeville et *La Fable des abeilles.*" *Etudes* 230 (1937): 624–645.

Leibacher-Ouvrard, Lise. *Libertinage et utopies sous le règne de Louis XIV.* Geneva: Droz, 1989.

Letwin, William. *The Origins of Scientific Economics.* London: Methuen, 1963.

Levi, Anthony, SJ. *French Moralists: The Theory of the Passions, 1585–1649.* Oxford: Clarendon Press, 1964.

Lindebloom, G.A. *Herman Boerhave.* London: Methuen, 1968.

Lindgren, Ralph. *The Social Philosophy of Adam Smith.* The Hague: Nijhoff, 1973.

Lipking, Lawrence. *The Ordering of the Arts in Eighteenth-Century England.* Princeton University Press, 1970.

Long, Douglas. "Adam Smith's 'Two Cities'." *Studies in Political Thought* 1, 1 (1992): 43–60.

Lovejoy, Arthur O. *Reflections on Human Nature.* Baltimore: John Hopkins University Press, 1961.

Lucretius. *De Rerum Novarum.* Translated by W.E. Leonard. New York: Dutton, 1957.

McCulloch, J.R. (ed.), *Early English Tracts of Commerce*. Cambridge Economic History Society, 1952.

Macintosh, J.J. "Robert Boyle on Epicurean Atheism." In *Atoms, Pneuma and Tranquility. Epicurean and Stoic Themes in European Thought*. Edited by Margaret J. Osler, pp. 197–219. Cambridge University Press, 1991.

MacIntyre, Alasdair. *After Virtue*. Notre Dame University Press, 1981.

McKee, Francis. "The Earlier Works of Bernard Mandeville, 1685–1715." Ph D thesis, Glasgow University, 1991.

McKendrick, Neil, Brewer, John and Plumb, J.H., editors. *The Birth of a Consumer Society*. London, Hutchinson, 1983.

McKenzie, Alan T. "'The Countenance You Show Me': Reading the Passions of the Eighteenth Century." *The Georgia Review* 32 (1978): 758–778.

McTaggart, M.J. "Mandeville: Cynic or Fool?" *Philosophical Quarterly*. 16 (1966): 221–233.

Magendie, Maurice. *La Politesse mondaine et les théories de l'honnêteté en France au XVIIe siècle, de 1600 a 1660*. (1925) Geneva: Slatkine Reprints, 1970.

Manier, Edward. *The Young Darwin and His Cultural Circle*. Dordrecht and Boston: Reidel, 1978.

Manuel, Frank. *The Enlightenment Confronts the Gods*. New York: Atheneum, 1967.

Marburg, Clara. *Sir William Temple, a Seventeenth-Century Libertine*. New Haven: Yale University Press, 1932.

Marshall, Gordon. *In Search of the Spirit of Capitalism: An Essay on Max Weber's Protestant Ethic Thesis*. New York: Columbia University Press, 1982.

Marx, Karl. *Capital*. Moscow: Foreign Languages Publishing House, n.d.

Masters, Roger D. *The Political Philosophy of Rousseau*. Princeton University Press, 1968.

Mauzi, Robert. *L'Idée du bonheur dans la littérature et la pensée française au XVIIIe siècle*. Geneva: Slatkine Reprint, 1979.

Maxwell, J.C. "Ethics and politics in Mandeville." *Philosophy* 26 (1951): 242–252.

Mayo, T.F. *Epicurus in England (1650–1725)*. Dallas: Southwest Press, 1934.

Meek, Ronald L. *Social Science and the Ignoble Savage*. Cambridge University Press, 1976.

Meek, Ronald L. and Skinner, Andrew S. "The Development of Adam Smith's Ideas on the Division of Labour." *Economic Journal* 85 (1973): 1096–1116.

Merrick, Jeffrey. "Royal Bees: The Gender Politics of the Bee in Early Modern Europe." In *Studies in Eighteenth-Century Culture* Edited by J.W. Yolton and Leslie Ellen Brown, 18 (1988): 7–38.

Merton, Robert. "The Unanticipated Consequences of Purposive Social Action." *American Sociological Review* 1 (1936): 894–904.

Mitchell, Harvey. "'The Mysterious Veil of Self-Delusion' in Adam Smith's *Theory of Moral Sentiments*." *Eighteenth-Century Studies* 20 (1987):

405–421.

Monro, Hector. *The Ambivalence of Bernard Mandeville*. Oxford: Clarendon Press, 1975.

Mooney, Michael. *Vico in the Tradition of Rhetoric*. Princeton University Press, 1985.

Moore, J. R. "Mandeville and Defoe." In *Mandeville Studies*. Edited by Irwin Primer, pp. 119–125. The Hague: Nijhoff, 1975.

Moore, James. "Hume's Theory of Justice and Property." *Political Studies* 24 (1976): 103–119.

"The Social Background of Hume's Science of Human Nature." In *McGill Hume Studies*. Edited by David Fate Norton, Nicholas Cipaldi and Wade L. Robinson, pp. 23–41. San Diego: Austin Hill, 1976.

Morel, Jean. "Recherches sur les sources du *Discours sur l'Inégalité*." *Annales de la Société Jean-Jacques Rousseau* 5 (1909): 163–164.

Morize, André. *L'Apologie du luxe an XVIIIe siècle et 'Le Mondaine' de Voltaire*. Geneva: Slatkine Reprint, 1970.

Mosner, Ernest Campbell. *The Life of David Hume*. 2nd edition. Oxford: Clarendon Press, 1980.

Mulier, E.O.G. Haitsma. *The Myth of Venice and Dutch Republican Thought in the Seventeenth Century*. Assen: Van Gorcum, 1980.

Norton, David Fate. *David Hume: Common-Sense Moralist, Skeptical Metaphysician*. Princeton University Press, 1982.

"Hume and the Foundations-Problem: Cross-Border Influences." Paper presented at the Cross-Cultural Enlightenment Conference, University of Victoria. April 1993.

Onken, August. "Das Adam Smith-Problem." *Zeitschrift für Socialwissenschaft* 1 (1898): 25–33, 101–108, and 276–287.

Osler, Margaret J. "Fortune, Fate and Divination: Gassendi's Volantarist Theology and the Baptism of Epicureanism." In *Atoms, Pneuma and Tranquility: Epicurean and Stoic Themes in European Thought*. Edited by Margaret J. Osler, pp. 155–174. Cambridge University Press, 1991.

"Providence and Divine Will in Gassendi's View of Scientific Knowledge." *Journal of the History of Ideas* 44 (1983): 549–560.

Parsons, Talcott. "'Capitalism' in Recent German Literature: Sombart and Weber." *The Journal of Political Economy* 36 (1928): 641–661.

Patterson, Annabel. "Fables of Power." In the *Politics of Discourse*. Edited by Kevin Sharpe and Steven N. Zwicker, pp. 271–296. Berkeley: University of California Press, 1987.

Paulson, Ronald. "Life as Journey and as Theater: Two Eighteenth-Century Narrative Structures." *New Literary History* 8, 1 (1976): 43–58.

Hogarth: His Life, Art and Times. 2 volumes. New Haven: Yale University Press, 1972.

Pedicord, Harry W. "The Changing Audience." In *The London Theatre World, 1660–1800*. Edited by Robert D. Hume, pp. 229–246. Carbondale, Illinois: Southern Illinois University Press, 1980.

Penelhum, Terence. *Butler.* London: Routledge, 1985.

Peters, E.A. "Cervantes in England." *Bulletin of Hispanic Studies* 24 (1947): 226–238.

Pitkin, Hanna Fenichel. *Fortune is a Woman: Gender and Politics in the Thought of Niccolo Machiavelli.* Berkeley: University of California Press, 1984.

Pocock, J.G.A. *The Ancient Constitution and the Feudal Law: English Historical Thought in the Seventeenth Century.* Cambridge University Press, 1957.

"Early Modern Capitalism: The Augustan Perception." In *Feudalism, Capitalism and Beyond.* Edited by Eugene Kamenka and R.S. Neale, pp. 62–83. Canberra: Australian National University Press, 1975.

The Machiavellian Moment: Florentine Political Thought and the Atlantic Republican Tradition. Princeton University Press, 1975.

"Virtue and Commerce in the Eighteenth Century." *Journal of Interdisciplinary History* 3 (1972): 119–134.

Virtue, Commerce and History. Cambridge University Press, 1985.

Popkin, Richard. *The History of Scepticism From Erasmus to Spinoza.* Berkeley: University of California Press, 1979.

"Isaac de Pinto's Criticism of Mandeville and Hume on Luxury." *Studies on Voltaire and the Eighteenth-Century* 154 (1976): 1705–1714.

"Samuel Sorbière's Translation of Sextus Empiricus." *Journal of the History of Ideas* 14, 4 (1953): 617–621.

Price, Martin. *To the Palace of Wisdom: Studies in Order and Energy from Dryden to Blake.* Garden City, New York: Doubleday, 1964.

Primer, Irwin. "Bernard Mandeville." In *The Dictionary of Literary Biography.* Detroit: Gale Research Company, 1991.

"A Bibliographical Note on Bernard Mandeville's *Free Thoughts.*" *Notes and Queries* 214 (1969): 187–188.

"Mandeville and Shaftesbury: Some Facts and Problems." In *Mandeville Studies.* Edited by Irwin Primer, pp. 126–141. The Hague: Nijhoff, 1975.

Pullen, Charles. "Lord Chesterfield and Eighteenth-Century Appearance and Reality." *Studies in English Literature, 1500–1800* 8 (1968): 501–515.

Ramsay, Andrew Michael, Chevalier de. *Essai sur le gouvernement civil.* Paris, 1720.

Raphael, D.D. "The Impartial Spectator." In *Essays on Adam Smith,* edited by A.S. Skinner and Thomas Wilson, pp. 83–89. Oxford: Clarendon Press, 1975.

Rashid, Salim. "Mandeville's *Fable*: Laissez-Faire or Libertinism?" *Eighteenth-Century Studies* 18, 3 (1985): 313–330.

Raven, James. *Judging New Wealth. Popular Publishing and Responses to Commerce in England, 1750–1800.* Oxford: Clarendon Press, 1992.

Rawson, Claude. "Gentlemen and Dancing-Masters." In *Henry Fielding and the Augustan Ideal Under Stress,* pp. 3–34. London: Routledge, 1972.

Reed, Walter L. *An Exemplary History of the Novel.* Chicago: University of Chicago Press, 1981.

Rétat, Pierre. *Le Dictionnaire de Bayle et la lutte philosphique au XVIIIe siècle.* Paris: Société D'Edition "Les Belles Lettres," 1971.

Richter, Melvin. *The Political Theory of Montesquieu.* Cambridge University Press, 1977.

Robinson, Joan. *Economic Philosophy.* Chicago: Aldine, 1963.

Rogerson, Brewster. "The Art of Painting the Passions." *Journal of the History of Ideas,* 14, 1 (1953): 68–94.

Rosenberg, Aubrey. *Tyssot de Patot and His Work, 1655–1738.* The Hague: Nijhoff, 1972.

Rosenberg, Nathan. "Mandeville and Laissez-Faire." *Journal of the History of Ideas* 24 (1963): 183–196.

Rosenfeld, Leonora Cohen. *From Beast-Machine to Man-Machine.* Oxford University Press, 1941.

Ross, Ellen. "Mandeville, Melon and Voltaire: The Origins of the Luxury Controversy in France." *Studies on Voltaire and the Eighteenth Century* 155 (1976): 1897–1912.

Ross, Stephanie. "Painting the Passions: Charles Le Brun's Conference sur L'Expression." *Journal of the History of Ideas* 45, 1 (1984): 25–47.

Rossi, Paulo. *The Dark Abyss of Time. The History of the Earth and the History of Nations from Hooke to Vico.* Translated by Lydia D. Cochrane. Chicago University Press, 1984.

Rothkrug, Lionel. *Opposition to Louis XIV: The Political and Social Origins of the French Enlightenment.* Princeton University Press, 1965.

Rousseau, G.S. "Mandeville and Europe: Medicine and Philosophy." In *Mandeville Studies.* Edited by Irwin Primer, pp. 11–21. The Hague: Nijhoff, 1975.

Runte, Roseanne. "From La Fontaine to Porchat: The Bee in the French Fable." In *Studies in Eighteenth-Century Culture* 18. Edited by J.W. Yolton and Leslie Ellen Brown, pp. 79–90.

Sackmann, Paul. *Bernard de Mandeville und die Bienenfabel-Controverse.* Leipzig: Mohr, 1897.

Sarasohn, L.T. "The Ethical and Political Philosophy of Pierre Gassendi." *Journal of the History of Philosophy* 20 (1982): 239–261.

Schatz, Albert. "Bernard Mandeville: Contribution a l'étude des origines du liberalisme économique." *Vierteljahrschrift fur Social- und Wirtschaftsgeschichte* 1 (1903): 434–480.

Scheurleer, T.L. and Posthumus Meyes, G.H.M. *Leiden University in the Seventeenth Century: An Exchange of Learning.* Leiden: Brill, 1975.

Schneider, L. "Mandeville as Forerunner of Modern Sociology." *Journal of the History of the Behavioural Sciences,* 6 (1970): 219–30.

Schreyer, Rudiger. "Condillac, Mandeville and the Origin of Language." *Historigraphica Linguistica* 1, 2 (1978): 15–43.

Scribiano, Emanuala Maria. *Natura umana e società competitiva: studio sul Mandeville.* Milan: Feltrinelli, 1980.

"La Presenza di Bayle nell'opera di Bernard Mandeville." *Giorale Critico della Filosophia Italiana* 60 (1981): 186–220.

Sekora, John. *Luxury: The Concept in Western Thought, Eden to Smollett.* Baltimore: Johns Hopkins University Press, 1977.

Simmel, Georg. *Philosophie des Geldes.* Leipzig: Dunker & Humblot, 1900.

The Philosophy of Money. 2nd edition. Translated by Tom Bottomore and David Frisby. London: Routledge, 1990.

Skinner, Andrew. "The Development of Adam Smith's Ideas on the Division of Labour." *Economic Journal* 83 (1973): 1094–1116.

Smart, Alastair. "Dramatic Gesture and Expression in the Age of Hogarth and Reynolds." *Apollo* 82 (1965): 90–97.

Sombart, Werner. *Der Moderne Capitalismus.* Leipzig: Dunker and Humblot, 1902.

Sowell, Thomas. "Adam Smith in Theory and Practice." In *Adam Smith and Modern Political Economy.* Edited by Gerald D. O'Driscoll, Jr., pp. 3–18. Ames, Iowa: Iowa State University Press, 1979.

Speck, W.A. "Bernard Mandeville and the Middlesex Grand Jury." *Eighteenth-Century Studies* 11 (1978): 362–374.

"Conflict in Society." In *Britain After the Glorious Revolution*, pp. 135–154. London: Macmillan, 1969.

"Mandeville and the Eutopia Seated in the Brain." In *Mandeville Studies.* Edited by Irwin Primer. The Hague: Nijhoff, 1975, pp. 66–79.

The Spectator. Edited by Donald Bond. 5 volumes. Oxford University Press, 1965.

Spengler, Joseph J. "Smith Versus Hobbes: Economy Versus Polity." In *Adam Smith and The Wealth of Nations.* Edited by F.R. Glahe, pp. 33–60. Boulder: Colorado Associated University Press, 1978.

Spiller, R.G. *"Concerning Natural Experimental Philosophie": Meric Casaubon and the Royal Society.* The Hague: Nijhoff, 1980.

Spink, J.S. *French Free Thought from Gassendi to Voltaire.* London: Athlone Press, 1960.

Sprott, S.E. *The English Debate on Suicide: From Donne to Hume.* La Salle, Illinois: Open Court Press, 1961.

Starobinski, Jean. *Jean-Jacques Rousseau: la transparence et l'obstacle.* Paris: Gallimard, 1971.

Stephen, Sir Leslie. *History of English Thought in the Eighteenth Century.* New York: Harcourt, Brace & World, 1962. 2 volumes.

"Mandeville's 'Fable of the Bees'." In *Essays on Free-Thinking and Plain Speaking*, pp. 243–278. London: Smith, Elder, 1907.

Tabor, Eva. *Skepticism, Society and the Eighteenth-Century Novel.* New York: St. Martin's Press, 1987.

Tawney, R.H. *Religion and the Rise of Capitalism.* (1926) New York: Harcourt, Brace, 1954.

Thijssen-Schoute, C. Louise. "La Cartesianism aux Pays-Bas." In *Descartes et le cartesianisme hollandais.* Edited by E.J. Dijksterhuis, *et al.*, pp. 183–260. Paris: PUF, 1950.

Thirsk, Joan. *Economic Policy and Projects.* Oxford: Clarendon Press, 1978.

Thompson, E.P. "Patrician Society, Plebeian Culture." *Journal of Social*

History 7, 4 (1977): 382–405.

Troeltsch, Ernst. *Die Bedeutung des Protestantismus für die Entstehung der Modernen Welt*. Berlin: Oldenberg, 1906.

Trousson, Raymond. *Voyages aux pays de nulle part*. Editions de l'Université de Bruxelles, 1979.

Tuck, Richard. *Natural Rights Theories*. Cambridge University Press, 1979.

Van Kley, Dale. "Pierre Nicole, Jansenism and the Morality of Enlightened Self-Interest." In *Anticipations of the Enlightenment*. Edited by Alan C. Kors and Paul Korshin, pp. 69–85. Philadelphia: University of Pennsylvania Press, 1987.

Van Tijn, T. "Pieter De La Court: Zijn lever en zijn economische denkbeelden." *Tijdschrift Voor Geschiedenis* 64 (1956): 304–370.

Vaughan, Frederick. *The Tradition of Political Hedonism*. New York: Fordham University Press, 1982.

Vichert, Gordon S. "Bernard Mandeville's *The Virgin Unmask'd*." In *Mandeville Studies*. Edited by Irwin Primer, pp. 1–10. The Hague: Nijhoff, 1975.

"The Theory of Conspicuous Consumption in the Eighteenth Century." In *The Varied Pattern: Studies in the Eighteenth Century*. Edited by Peter Hughes and David Williams, pp. 253–267. University of Toronto Press, 1971.

Viner, Jacob. *Religious Thought and Economic Society*. Edited by Jacques Melitz and Donald Winch. Durham: Duke University Press, 1978.

The Role of Providence in the Social Order. Princeton University Press, 1972.

"Satire and Economics in the Augustan Age of Satire." In *The Augustan Milieu: Essays Presented to Louis A. Landa*. Edited by H.K. Miller, G. Rothstein and G.S. Rousseau, pp. 77–101. Oxford: Clarendon Press, 1970.

Studies in the Theory of International Trade. New York: Harper and Row, 1937.

Wade, Ira O. *The Clandestine Organization and Diffusion of Philosophic Ideas in France from 1700 to 1750*. Princeton University Press, 1938.

The Intellectual Origins of the French Enlightenment. Princeton University Press, 1971.

Voltaire and Madame de Châtelet. Princeton University Press, 1941.

Watt, Ian. *The Rise of the Novel*. London: Perigrine Books, 1963.

Weber, Max. "Die Protestantische Ethik und der 'Geist' des Kapitalismus." *Archiv für Sozialwissenschaft und Sozialpolitik* 20 (1905): 1–54.

Wellbery, David E. *Lessing's "Laocoon": Semiotics and Aesthetics in the Age of Reason*. Cambridge University Press, 1984.

Wells, G. A. "Condillac, Rousseau and Herder on the Origin of Language." *Studies on Voltaire and the Eighteenth Century* 230 (1985): 233–246.

Wiles, Richard C. "The Theory of Labour in Later English Mercantilism." *Economic History Review* 2nd series, 30, 1 (1968): 113–126.

Wilson, Charles. "The Other Face of Mercantilism." In *Revisions in Mercantilism*. Edited by D.C. Coleman, pp. 118–139. London: Methuen, 1969.

Wilson, Thomas. "Sympathy and Self-Interest." In *The Market and the State*. Edited by Thomas Wilson and Andrew Skinner, pp. 73–99. Oxford University Press, 1976.

Winch, Donald. "Adam Smith: Scottish Moral Philosopher as Political Economist." *Historical Journal* 35, 1 (1992): 91–113.

Adam Smith's Politics: An Essay in Historiographic Revisionism. Cambridge University Press, 1978.

Wood, Neal. "The Value of Asocial Sociability: Contributions of Machiavelli, Sidney and Montesquieu." In *Machiavelli and the Nature of Political Thought*. Edited by Martin Fleisher, pp. 282–307. New York: Atheneum, 1972.

Wood, Paul. "The Natural History of Man in the Scottish Enlightenment." *History of Science* 28 (1989): 89–123.

Worthen, William. *The Idea of the Actor*. Princeton University Press, 1984.

Wright, John P. *The Sceptical Realism of David Hume*. Manchester University Press, 1983.

Yolton, John W. *Locke and French Materialism*. Oxford: Clarendon Press, 1991.

Thinking Matter: Materialism in Eighteenth-Century Britain. Minneapolis: University of Minnesota Press, 1983.

Zeyss, Richard. *Adam Smith und der Eigennutz*. Tübingen: Laupp, 1889.

Index

IDEAS IN CONTEXT

Edited by Quentin Skinner (general editor), Lorraine Daston, Wolf Lepenies, Richard Rorty and J.B. Schneewind

Titles marked with an asterisk are also available in paperback